BUTLER COUNTY, OHIO
LAND RECORDS
VOLUME 1: 1803-1817

Shirley Keller Mikesell

HERITAGE BOOKS
2008

HERITAGE BOOKS
AN IMPRINT OF HERITAGE BOOKS, INC.

Books, CDs, and more—Worldwide

For our listing of thousands of titles see our website at
www.HeritageBooks.com

Published 2008 by
HERITAGE BOOKS, INC.
Publishing Division
100 Railroad Ave. #104
Westminster, Maryland 21157

Copyright © 1997 Shirley Keller Mikesell

Other books by the author:

Early Settlers of Indiana's Gore, 1803-1820
Early Settlers of Montgomery County, Ohio: Genealogical Abstracts from Land Records, Tax Lists, and Biographical Sketches
Early Settlers of Montgomery County, Ohio: Genealogical Abstracts from Common Pleas Court Records Civil and Probate
Early Settlers of Montgomery County, Ohio: Genealogical Abstracts from Marriage and Divorce Records 1803 - 1827, Early Deeds Recorded Late, Election Abstracts, Obituary of an Early Settler
Butler County, Ohio, Land Records, Volume 2: 1816 - 1823 and Miami University Land Leases 1810 - 1823

All rights reserved. No part of this book may be reproduced or transmitted in any form or by any means, electronic or mechanical, including photocopying, recording or by any information storage and retrieval system without written permission from the author, except for the inclusion of brief quotations in a review.

International Standard Book Numbers
Paperbound: 978-0-0-7884-0666-9
Clothbound: 978-0-7884-7016-5

TABLE OF CONTENTS

Introduction VII

A Brief History of Butler County.... 1
    with maps

Book A 4
Book B 53
Book C 104
Book D 149
Book E 204

Appendix 252
The Symmes Miami Purchase, Forfeiture
    and Volunteer Settlers explained

Index 253

INTRODUCTION TO BUTLER COUNTY LAND RECORDS

The original intent was to abstract Butler County land records from the time of statehood in 1803 until the census of 1820 -- in one volume. The project quickly grew to an unwieldy size. It seemed a better plan to divide the material into two parts, to make each book of a managable size.

Identification of a person's residence was included if it was outside Butler County. When a Butler Countian was named as living within a certain township, that information was noted; this may have been the clerk's means of distinguishing between two men of the same name. Citing only a county of residence indicates that county was in Ohio; i.e. "of Warren County". Cincinnati, the seat of Hamilton County to the south, and Dayton, the seat of Montgomery County on the north, are simply named in the text, not given their full labels in the interest of saving space.

Justices of the Peace are identified only the first time found to avoid redundancy. Some of these gentlemen held office for many years and so are not indexed every time. The same is true for some of the largest landowners. If an entry seemed to have significance, that page index is underlined.

Names may be spelled in a variety of ways within the same deed. This is not a typing error, but an attempt to be faithful to the original ledgers.

```
****** Abbreviations used in the text ******

adj........adjoining the land of
admtr......administrator of estate
appt.......appointed
atty.......attorney
Co.........county
decd.......deceased
JP.........Justice of the Peace
NW Ter'y...Northwest Territory
rec........recorded
S-T-R......section - township - range
Ter'y......Territory
twp........township
witn.......witness
(x)........signature mark
plus standard genealogical abbreviations
     such as dau, s/n/law, etc.
```

BUTLER COUNTY LAND RECORDS: A BRIEF HISTORY

Butler County was formed in 1803 when Ohio was granted statehood. Prior to this event, the land was part of Hamilton County of the Northwest Territory.

Two surveys define Butler County. Land east of the Great Miami River lays within the Miami Purchase, bought in 1788 by John Cleves Symmes and sold privately. Contrary to almost all other surveys, the townships rank from west to east, while ranges run south to north. (The Between the Miamis Survey, contiguous to Symmes' purchase on the north, followed the same pattern to avoid confusion.)

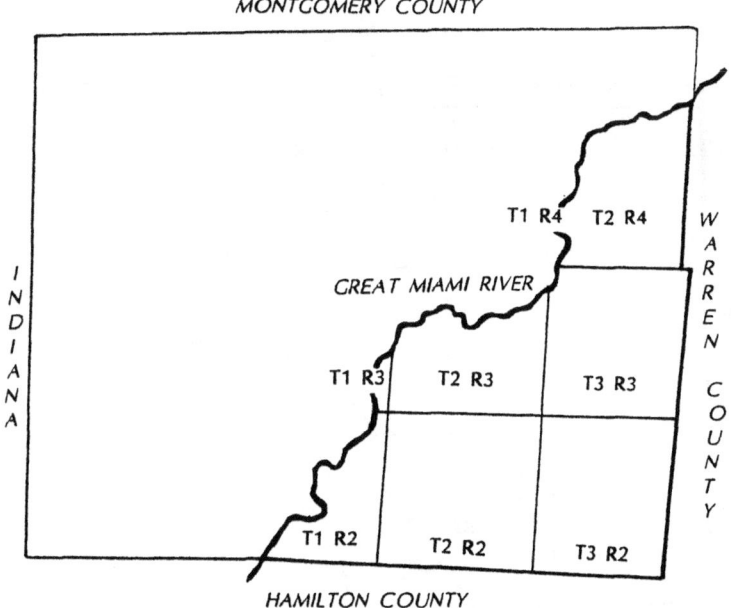

SYMMES' MIAMI PURCHASE OF 1788
AS CONTAINED IN EARLY BUTLER COUNTY

BUTLER COUNTY LAND RECORDS: A BRIEF HISTORY

Western Butler County lays within the Miami River Survey. This area, frequently referred to as Congressional lands, was sold through the Cincinnati Land Office by the Federal Government commencing in 1800. It was measured in the more common west to east Range, south to north Township.

Butler County was slightly larger in 1803 than now. In 1808, the southern border was straightened; Hamilton County gained a mile of land. Preble County, formed in 1808 to the north, incorporated Butler County's top tier of sections along the new border. The final adjustment came in 1815 when Warren County annexed the first and second sectional townships of the fifth range, Butler's north-east corner.

MONTGOMERY COUNTY

T6 R2	T6 R1	T4 R3	T3 R4	T2 R5
T5 R1	T5 R2	T3 R3	T2 R4	T1 R5
T4 R1	T4 R2	T2 R3	T1 R4	
T3 R1	T3 R2	T1 R3		

INDIANA

GREAT MIAMI RIVER

WARREN COUNTY

HAMILTON COUNTY

THE CONGRESSIONAL LANDS OF 1800
AS CONTAINED IN EARLY BUTLER COUNTY

2

BUTLER COUNTY LAND RECORDS: A BRIEF HISTORY

Butler's original five townships were Liberty, Fairfield, Lemon, St. Clair and Ross. Wayne and Millford were formed in 1805 from St. Clair. Two years later, St. Clair yielded land again to Reily Township. In 1810, Madison arose from Lemon. The following year, Morgan was carved from Ross, Oxford from Millford and Hanover from portions of Reily and St. Clair. The last township, Union, separated from Liberty in 1823.

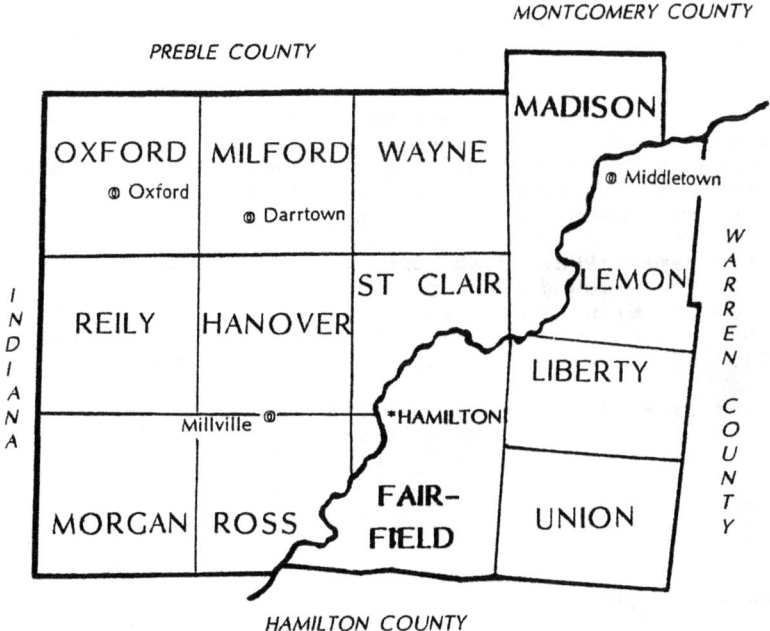

BUTLER COUNTY TOWNSHIPS

WITH SOME EARLY COMMUNITIES

BUTLER COUNTY LAND RECORDS: BOOK A

Book A has been retyped which makes it much easier to use. Unfortunately, either the typist was not proficient or the original was very difficult to read. Numerous small errors appear: dates such as 1888 in the text of a deed dated 1808, etc. More significant is that names vary: Sarah becomes Samuel, etc. These copying errors are repeated as given.

Deed dated 1803. BENJAMIN LINE & REBECKAH his wife to ISRAEL BALL of Hamilton Co. S 5, T 2, R 3. BENJAMIN died 1798; deed obtained from Capt. MAHLON FORD of US Army. Signed BENJAMIN LINE (seal), REBECKAH (x) LINE. Witn: JAMES HEATON, JOHN VINNEDGE. JP WILLIAM McCLELLAND. rec 25 Aug, 1803. p 1

Deed dated 1803. JONATHAN DAYTON of NJ to SAMUEL STITES of Hamilton Co. S 10, T 2, R 3. Signed ISRAEL LUDLOW for Jonathan Dayton. Witn: none. JP JACOB LEWIS. rec 1808. p 2

Deed dated 1803. JOHN HARVEY & ELIZABETH his wife of Liberty Twp to JOSEPH POTTER of same. S 1, T 2, R 3. Bound by land of JOHN HARVEY, JOSEPH PEAK, PETER MURPHY & WILLIAM LEGG. Signed JOHN HARVEY, ELIZABETH HARVEY Witn: WILLIAM PATTON, WILLIAM HARVEY. JP WILLIAM SYMMES. rec 1803. pp 2, 3

Deed dated 1803. JOHN LODER to JOSEPH POTTER. S 1, T 2, R 3. Bound by land of Col. SPENCER, WILLIAM LEGG JR, WILLIAM LEGG SR, JOHN CLEVES SYMMES. Signed JOHN LODER. Witn: JOHN CLEVES SYMMES, WILLIAM LEGG SR. $65 mortgage payment credit. rec 1803. pp 3, 4

Deed dated 1795. JOHN CLEVES SYMMES & SUSAN his wife of Hamilton Co, NW Ter'y to CHARLES BRUCE of Hamilton. S 6, T 1, R 2. LUTHER RITCHEL represented said 200 acres for past 7 years. Signed JOHN CLEVES SYMMES, SUSAN SYMMES. Witn: ISAAC MILLS, ISAAC S. SWEARINGEN, FRANCIS DUNLAVY. JP WILLIAM McCLURE. rec 1803. p 4

page 5 blank

Mortgage dated 1803. JOSEPH POTTER of Liberty Twp. to SAMUEL POTTER of same. S 1, T 2, R 3. Signed JOSEPH POTTER. Witn: WILLIAM SYMMES, JOHN REILY. rec 1803. p 6

Quitclaim dated 1803. ABRAHAM GARRISON JR & MARY his wife of Springfield Twp, Hamilton Co to ABRAHAM GARRISON SR of Colerain Twp, Hamilton Co. Forfeit land in S 21, T 2, R 2 deeded to A. Garrison JR by

BUTLER COUNTY LAND RECORDS: BOOK A

JOHN CLEVES SYMMES in 1798. Signed ABRAHAM GARRISON JR, MARY GARRISON. Witn: JNO. TORRENCE, JP JOHN GREER. rec 1803. p 7

Deed dated 1803. ABRAHAM GARRISON & RACHEL his wife of Colrain Twp, Hamilton Co, to JOHN DIXON of Fairfield Twp. S 21, T 2, R 2. Signed ABRAHAM GARRISON, RACHEL GARRISON. Witn: as above. rec 1803. p 7

Deed dated 1795. JONATHAN PHILLIPS & ELIZABETH his wife of Maidenhead, NJ to RALPH W. HUNT of same. S 13, T 3, R 3. Signed JONA. PHILLIPS, ELIZA PHILLIPS. Witn: JOHN PHILLIPS, JANE HOUSTON. rec 1803. p 8

Deed dated 1803. OLIVER SPENCER of Hamilton Co to JOSEPH CRANE of same. S 31, T 3, R 3. Signed OLIVER SPENCER. Witn: JOHN WALLACE, EDW. MEEKS. rec 1804. p9

Deed dated 1804. JOEL WILLIAMS & PHEBE his wife to WILLIAM BIGHAM of Lancaster Co, PA. S 33, T 2, R 3. Deed conveyed to BIGHAM & " a ROBERT IRWIN" in 1797. Signed JOEL WILLIAMS, PHEBE WILLIAMS. Witn: JP WILLIAM MITCHELL, REUBEN DOWTY. rec 1804. p 10

Deed dated 1803. JONATHAN DAYTON of NJ to MELYN BAKER. (MALYN in text.) S 33, T 3, R 3. Signed ISRAEL LUDLOW for Jonathan Dayton. Witn: JP LUKE FOSTER, R. PATTERSON. rec 1804. p 11

Deed dated 1804. JOHN LUDLOW & SUSAN his wife of Hamilton Co to PETER VORHES of KY. S 14, T 3, R 3. Balance of section deeded to DAVID WILLIAMSON & HENRY VANDIKE. Signed JOHN LUDLOW, SUSAN LUDLOW. Witn: ANDREW HILANDS, MARY HILANDS. rec 1804. p 12

Deed dated 1803. JONATHAN DAYTON of NJ to JOHN McEOWEN. S 22, T 2, R 3. Bound by PATRICK MOORE's land. Signed ISRAEL LUDLOW for Jonathan Dayton. Witn: JAMES HEATON, MAX fo LUDLOW. rec 1804. p 13

Deed dated 1804. JOHN ROBINSON of Deerfield Twp, Warren Co to JAMES KANNADY. S 18 "in Lemon Twp". Signed JOHN ROBINSON. Witn: JOHN BEATY, WILLIAM ROBINSON. rec 1804. p 14

Deed dated 1804. JOHN ROBINSON (above) to JOHN BEATY. S 18 "in Lemon Twp". Signed JOHN ROBINSON. Witn: WILLIAM ROBINSON, JAMES KENNEDY. rec 1804. pp 14, 15

Deed dated 1804. JOHN ROBINSON (above) to WILLIAM ROBINSON. S 18 "in Lemon Twp". Signed JOHN ROBINSON, JAMES BEATY, JAMES KENNEDY. rec 1804. p 15

BUTLER COUNTY LAND RECORDS: BOOK A

Deed dated 1804. ANDW. CHRISTY & ELIZABETH his wife to HENRY HOUSE of Warren Co. S 4, T 2, R 3. Signed ANDW. CHRISTY, ELIZABETH (x) CHRISTY. Witn: ISAAC WILES, JOHN NELSON. rec 1804. p 16

Deed dated 1799. JOHN BUCHANAN & REBECKAH his wife of Hamilton Co, NW Ter'y, to ABLE STOUTT. Hamilton outlot 20. Signed JNO. BUCHANAN, REBECKAH BUCHANAN. Witn: JOHN GORDON, WILLIAM McCLELLAN. rec 1804. pp 16, 17

Deed dated 1803. ABLE STOUTT to ISAAC WILLES. Hamilton outlot 20. "together with DOSHE, my wife". Signed ABEL STOUTT, THEODOCIA STOUTT. Witn: ISAAC STANLEY, JACOB LEWIS. rec 1804. pp 17, 18

Deed dated 1802. ANDREW CHRISTY & ELIZABETH his wife of Hamilton Co to ISAAC WILES. Hamilton lot 201. Signed ANDREW CHRISTY, ELIZABETH (x) CHRISTY. Witn: JOHN NELSON, HENRY HOUSE. rec 1804. pp 18, 19

Deed dated 1804. BENJAMIN ENYART to DAVID ARMSTON. S 9, T 2, R 3. Signed BENJAMIN ENYART. Witn: DAVID ENYART, JOHN LINE. rec 1804. p 19

Deed dated 1804. JOHN HUSTON & MARGARET his wife to SAMUEL MILLER. S 23, T 2, R 2. Bound by DAVID CUMINGS. Signed JOHN HUSTON, MARGARET (x) HUSTON. Witn: JOHN REILY, JOHN SUTHERLAND. rec 1804. pp 19, 20

pp 21, 22 bound upside down, page order reversed

Deed dated 1803. JAMES SMITH, sheriff of Hamilton Co, NW Ter'y, to DANIEL COOPER of same. Judgement obtained by Cooper against JOHN CLEVES SYMMES. Sheriff seized land in S 7 & 15, T 1, R 1 & S 9, T 1, R 2 Sold at auction in 1802 to Cooper. Signed JAMES SMITH, Sheriff. witn: none. rec 1804. p 22

Plat dated 1804. Town of Rossville. Signed by proprietors JOHN SUTHERLAND, HENRY BROWN, JACK BURNET, JAMES SMITH, WILLIAM RUFFIN. rec 1804. p 21

Deed dated 1803. WILLIAM LEGG SR & CASANDRA his wife to JOHN LODER. S 1, T 2, R 3. Signed WILLIAM LEGG SR, CASANDRA (x) LEGG. Witn: JOHN CLEVES SYMMES, JOSEPH POTTER, JOSEPH PEAK, WILLIAM VIRGIN. rec 1804. p 23

Deed dated 1804. JOHN GORDON to JOHN SUTHERLAND & HENRY BROWN. Hamilton lots 119, 120. Signed JOHN GORDON. Witn: JACOB LEWIS, WILLIAM SCOTT. rec 1804. p 24

BUTLER COUNTY LAND RECORDS: BOOK A

Deed dated 1800.   JOHN BROWN & MARGRET his wife of Hamilton Co to JOHN SUTHERLAND of same. Hamilton lot 103.   Signed JNO. BROWN, MARGRET (x) BROWN. Witn: WILLIAM RUFFIN, DAN CONNER. JP JOSEPH PRINCE of Hamilton Co. rec 1804. p 25

Deed dated 1804.   HENRY VANDIKE & POLLY his wife of Mercer Co, KY to PETER VORHES of same. S 14, T not given, R 3. Signed HENRY VAN DIKE, POLLY (x) VAN DIKE. Witn: none. rec 1804. p 26

Deed dated 1804.   CHARLES WEST to JOHN PHELPS of Washington Co. S 20, T 3, R 3. Signed CHARLES WEST. Witn: IRA HUNT, LUCY DAVIS, THOMAS HUNT. JP ISC. S. SWEARINGEN of Liberty Twp. rec 1804. p 27

Deed dated 1795. ISRAEL LUDLOW to BENJAMIN FRITZ RANDOLF. JOHN CLEVES SYMMES purchased land in the third or military range except sections 8, 11, 16, 26 & 29 (reserved by Congress). In 1794, the land was sold to JONATHAN DAYTON. He then sold S 2 & 3, T 1, R 3 to LUDLOW in 1795, who partitioned the land into Hamilton town lots. Lots 173, 174, 175, 176 sold in this transaction. Signed ISRAEL LUDLOW. Witn: TOMPSON CLARK, WILLIAM HERBERT. rec 1804. p 28

Deed dated 1795. ISRAEL LUDLOW to BENJAMIN FRITZ RANDOLF. Hamilton lots 22, 23, 26, 27. Signed and witness as above. rec 1804. p 29

Deed dated 1804. ISRAEL LUDLOW to SARAH FITZ RANDOLPH. Hamilton lots 166. Signed and witness as above. rec 1804. p 30 (Clerk's margin note: SAMUEL FITZ RANDOLPH)

Deed dated 1795. ISRAEL LUDLOW to ANDREW CHRISTY. Hamilton lot 201. Signed ISRAEL LUDLOW. Witn: BENJAMIN DAVIS, BENJAMIN F. RANDOLPH. Assignment of interest in said lot to ISAAC WILES, signed JOHN CLAP, dated 1802. Witn: JOHN PANTON, JOHN GREER. rec 1804. p 31

Deed dated 1795. ISRAEL LUDLOW to BENJAMIN DAVIS. Hamilton lot 162. Signed ISRAEL LUDLOW. Witn: BENJAMIN F. RANDOLPH, ANDREW CHRISTY. Assignment of title to ISAAC STANDLEY, signed BENJAMIN DAVIS, dated 1798. Witn: JOHN GORDON, JNO. BUCHANAN. rec 1804. p 32

Deed dated 1804. NANCY DAVIS, admtr of BENJAMIN DAVIS in Hamilton Co, NW Ter'y to ISAAC STANLEY.

BUTLER COUNTY LAND RECORDS: BOOK A

Hamilton lot 162. Purchased by Stanley before Davis' death. Signed NANCY DAVIS. Witn: JOHN REILY, JAMES HEATON. rec 1804. pp 33, 34

Deed dated 1804. MATTHEW HUESTON & CATHERINE his wife to JOHN SUTHERLAND. Hamilton lot 37. Signed M. HUESTON, CATHERINE HUESTON. Witn: DAVID SLOAN, JP CELADON SYMMES. rec 1804. p 35

Deed dated 1803. JAMES SMITH, sheriff of Hamilton Co, NW Ter'y to JOHN WATSON of same. WILLIAM LAMME obtained judgement against JOHN CLEVES SYMMES in 1801. Sheriff seized S 1, T 1, R 2, sold at auction to Watson. Signed JAMES SMITH, Sheriff. Witn: none. rec 1804. p 36

Deed dated 1801. ISRAEL LUDLOW & CHARLOTTE his wife to PHILIP GORDON of Hamilton Co. Hamilton lot 139. Signed ISRAEL LUDLOW, CHARLOTTE CHAMBERS LUDLOW. Witn: C. KILLGORE. rec 1804. p 37

Deed dated 1803. MOSES BEACH to NICHOLAS PARSEL. S 30, T 3, R 3. Signed MOSES BEACH. Witn: JAMES HEATON, UZAL BEACH. rec 1804. p 38

Deed dated 1803. WILLIAM NIXON & PHANNY his wife of Gorges Twp, Fayette Co, PA to ALLAN NIXON of Hamilton Co, NW TER'Y. S 20, T3, R 2 conveyed to Nixon in 1800. Said WILLIAM NIXON JR as heir conveyed deed to ALLAN NIXON. Signed WILLIAM NIXON, PHANNY (x) NIXON. Witn: THOS. WYNN, JOHN CLARK. rec 1804. p 39

Deed dated 1799. ISRAEL LUDLOW & CHARLOTTE his wife to JOHN HAMILTON JR of Hamilton Co. Hamilton lot 9. Signed ISRAEL LUDLOW, CHARLOTTE CHAMBERS LUDLOW. Witn: ELIZA DILL, JOHN MERCER. Assignment of title to FREDERICK FISHER dated 1799, signed JOHN HAMILTON SR for HAMILTON JR. Witn: JOHN TORRENCE, D. C. ORCUTT, JACOB LEWIS. rec 1804. p 40

page 41 blank

Deed dated 1804. JOHN HAMILTON JR to FREDERICK FISHER. Hamilton lot 9. Signed JOHN HAMILTON JR. Witn: JOHN REILY, JOHN HAMILTON SR. rec 1804. p 42

Mortgage dated 1804. FREDERICK FISHER to JOHN HAMILTON JR. Lot 9 and loghouse held as security. Signed F. FISHER. Witn as above. rec 1804. pp 42, 43

Deed dated 1804. DAVID HENDRICKS & ROSANNAH his wife

BUTLER COUNTY LAND RECORDS: BOOK A

to GEORGE SNYDER. Hamilton lot 213. Signed DAVID HENDRICKS, ROSANNAH (x) HENDRICKS. Witn: JACOB LEWIS, JOHN WINGATE. rec 1804. p 43

Deed dated 1804. JOHN McCORMACK & CATHERINE his wife to EDWARD HARLAN. Hamilton lot 235. Signed J. McCORMICK, CATHERINE (x) McCORMICK. Witn: JOHN REILY, JACOB LEWIS. rec 1804. p 44

Deed dated 1804. JOHN McCORMACK & CATHERINE his wife to GEORGE HARLAN. Hamilton lot 225. Signed JOHN McCORMICK, CATHERINE (x) McCORMICK. Witn: JOHN REILY, JACOB LEWIS. rec 1804. p 45

Deed dated 1804. BENJAMIN ENYART & JOANNA his wife to MICHAEL AWL. S 12, T 3, R 3. Signed BENJAMIN ENYART, JOANNA (x) ENYART. Witn: JAMES HEATON, MARY HEATON. rec 1804. p 46

Deed dated 1804. CHRISTOPHER DIXON to JOSEPH HENRY. S 31, T 2, R 4. Signed CHRISTOPHER (x) DIXON. Witn: WM. MCCLURE, ALEX (x) FLEMING. rec 1804. pp 47, 48

Deed dated 1799. JOHN CLEVES SYMMES & SUSAN his wife of Hamilton Co, NW Ter'y to WILLIAM LEGG. S 1, T 2, R 3. Signed JOHN CLEVES SYMMES (unsigned by wife) Witn: THOMAS VIRGIN, BENJAMIN (x) BISHOP. rec 1804. p 49

Deed dated 1801. RALPH W. HUNT & MARY his wife of Hamilton Co, NW Ter'y to JACOB POWERS. S 13, T 3, R 3. Balance of section conveyed to WILLIAM PHILLIPS. Signed RALPH W. HUNT, MARY HUNT. Witn: HUGH HOGAN, MARY POWERS (Mary lined out; DAV. printed above). rec 1804. p 50

Deed dated 1800. EPHRAIM MARTIN & CATHERINE his wife to BENJAMIN INYARD*. S 12 T 3 R 3. Signed EPH. MARTIN, CATHERINE MARTIN. Witn: SAMUEL JANE, CATHERINE KINNAN. rec 1804. p 51 *BENJ ENYART?

Quitclaim dated 1804. DANIEL HOLE & MARY his wife of Warren Co to SAMUEL STUART. S 9, T 3, R 3. Signed DANIEL HOLE, MARY (x) HOLE. Witn: ICHABOD B. HALSEY, MALHEAS CORWIN. JP MATTHEAS CROWIN. rec 1804. p 52

Quitclaim dated 1801. JAMES SUTTON to ARCH STEELE. S 29, T not given, R 4. Signed JAMES SUTTON. Witn: JOHN PATTERSON. Assigned in 1804 by ARCH STEELE to JOSEPH LUMMIS. rec 1804. p 53

Partition dated 1804. Land owned by JAMES MARTIN, MATTHEW RICHARDSON, JESSE SIMPSON & JAMES SIMPSON,

BUTLER COUNTY LAND RECORDS: BOOK A

all of Butler Co, divided into three equal portions. S 23, T 5, R 2. Signed JAMES MARTIN, MATTHEW RICHARDSON, JESSE SIMSON, JAMES SIMSON. Witn: JP MATH WINTON. rec 1804. pp 53, 54, 55

page 56 blank

Mortgage dated 1804. MARTHA DAVIS to WILLIAM MARKS & MOSES CRUME of Nelson Co, KY. Land in S 34, T 3, R 3 to be paid off by 1808. Signed WILLIAM (x) MARKS, MOSES CRUME. Witness: JOHN REILY, JOHN GREER. rec 1804. p 57

Deed dated 1795. JONATHAN DAYTON to AMOS VALLENTINE of Hamilton Co. S 10, T 3, R 3. Signed JONA. DAYTON. Witn: BENJAMIN WILLIAMSON, W. DAYTON, JOHN SMITH. JP MATTHEW NIMMO. rec 1804. p 58

Partition dated 1801. Land owned by AMOS VALLENTINE above divided between Vallentine and SAMUEL SHANNON.* Judgement obtained by ISRAEL LUDLOW & WILLIAM McCLELLAN. rec 1804. p 59 *margin note stated S. SHERMAN to Vallentine, reverse of deed order, different name

Deed dated 1804. JAMES DUNN to JOHN DUNN. S 14, T 3, R 2. Signed JAMES DUNN. Witn: JOHN REILY, WM. SMITH. rec 1804. p 59

Deed dated 1802. JOHN RUNYON JR & MARGARET his wife of Piscataway, NJ to JACOB LEWIS & DEBORAH his wife of Hamilton Co and KY. S 24, T 2, R 2. Entire section of land previously conveyed to RICHARD RUNYON, ANNA RUNYON, DANIEL RUNYON, JOHN RUNYON, ISRAEL RUNYON, ELIAS RUNYON, PETER RUNYON & JANE RUNYON as heirs of ELIAS RUNYON, decd. Signed JOHN RUNYON, MARGARET RUNYON. Witn: JP SAMUEL RANDOLPH, UHUR PYATT. rec 1804. p 60

Mortgage dated 1804. MOSES VAIL to ARCHIBALD STARK. S 4, T 2, R 2. Payment due 1806. Signed ARCHIBALD STARK. Witn: HENRY WEAVER, EZRA FREEMAN. rec 1804. p 61

page 62 blank

Deed dated 1803. SIMEON BROADWELL of Morris Twp, Morris Co, NJ to JAMES CLARK of Fairfield, Hamilton Co. S 36, T 2, R 2. Land previously conveyed from John Cleves Symmes to JONATHAN AGDON to DAVID BROADWELL to SIMEON. Signed SIMEON BROADWELL. Witn: SYLVESTER D. RUSSEL, WILLIAM BROADWELL. rec 1804. p 63

BUTLER COUNTY LAND RECORDS: BOOK A

Deed dated 1797. ISRAEL LUDLOW to ABIGAIL BROWN of Hamilton. Hamilton lots 82, 93. Signed ISRAEL LUDLOW, CHARLOTTE CHAMBERS LUDLOW. Witn: SINEUS PIERSON, THO. GIBSON. JP THEO. GIBSON. rec 1804. p 64

Deed dated 1804. SIMEON BROADWELL of Morris Twp, Morris Co, NJ to JACKSON AYERS of Hanover Twp, Morris Co NJ. S 36, T 2, R 2. Signed SIMEON BROADWELL. Witn: STEPN. J. AGDEN, CHARLES RUSSELL. rec 1804. p 65

page 66 blank

Deed dated 1801. ISAAC REED to GEORGE SOUTHARD & ABRAHAM SOUTHARD. S 13, T 2, R 4. Signed ISAAC REED. Witn: WILLIAM PATTON, DAVID PATTON. rec 1804. p 67

Mortgage dated 1802. JACOB BELL to DAVID PATTON & ISAAC REED. S 13, T 2, R 4. Final payment due 1806. Signed DAVID PATTON, ISAAC REED. Witn: ANDW. CHEW, ABRAHAM SOUTHARD, THOMAS BERY. rec 1804. p 68

Mortgage dated 1803. WILLIAM PATTON to ISAAC REED. S 30, T 2, R 4. Based on $2 per acre @ 6% interest. Signed ISAAC REED. Witn: GEORGE F. TENNERY, THOMAS GRAY. rec 1804. p 69

Deed dated 1804. DAVID COX & NANCY his wife of Liberty Twp to JOHN VANNICE & ISAAC PAXTON. S 15, T 3, R 2. Signed DAVID COX, no wife's signature. Witn: JOHN W. BROWNE, MARY ANNE BROWNE. JP JAMES EWING. rec 1804. p 70

Quitclaim dated 1804. JAMES SUTTON to DAVID & JAMES ENOCH. S 29, T 2, R 4. Signed JAMES SUTTON. Witn: DANIEL GRIFFIN, EZRA F. FREEMAN, JAMES BARNETT. JP JOHN RITCHEL. rec 1804. p 71

Deed dated 1803. JOHN CLEVES SYMMES to JOHN COX JR. S 15, T 3, R 2. MICHAEL AYRES' claim to land rejected by JCS. Signed JOHN CLEVES SYMMES. Witn: HANNAH WILLIS, JOHN COX. rec 1804. p 72

Deed dated 1804. JOHN COX & ANNE his wife of Warren Co to ABEL McFARLAND of Washington Co, PA. S 15, T 3, R 2. Signed JOHN (x) COX, ANNE (x) COX. Witn: DANIEL SUTTON, JP IGNATIUS BROWN. rec 1804. p 73

Quitclaim dated 1804. EVAN BANE to ALLEN CULLUM. S 12, T 2, R 2. Land now lived upon by Cullum and JOSEPH HALL. Signed EVAN BANES. Witn: THOMAS GOODWIN, JOHN PEARSON. rec 1804. p 74

BUTLER COUNTY LAND RECORDS: BOOK A

Quitclaim dated 1804. JOHN SMITH to DAVID GRIFFIS. S 32 T 3, R 3. Land seized in judgement obtained by ROBERT MAXWELL against John Cleves Symmes. Sheriff's sale to Smith. Signed JOHN SMITH. Witn: JOSEPH DELAPLAINE, WILLIAM WILSON. rec 1805. p 75

Deed dated 1804. DANIEL CONNER & SUSAN his wife of Cincinnati to JOHN SUTHERLAND & HENRY BROWN. Hamilton lot 19. Signed DANIEL CONNER, SUSAN CONNER. Witn: SAMUEL LYONS, HENRY WEAVER. rec 1805. p 76

Deed dated 1804. ALBIN SHAW & EUNICE his wife of Hamilton Co to GEORGE FRUIT. S 34, T 3, R 2. Signed ALBIN SHAW, EUNICE SHAW. Witn: JP JUDAH WILLEY, HARTMAN VANTREES. rec 1805. p 77

Deed dated 1804. ALBIN SHAW & EUNICE his wife of Hamilton Co to JACOB HIDAY. "land as appears in Hamilton Co Bk E #2, p 720." Bound by land of JEREMIAH BUTTERFIELD, DAVID WADE. Signed ALBIN SHAW, EUNICE SHAW. Witn: ROBERT (x) BAILY, JOHN (x) HINGERFORD. rec 1805. p 78

Deed dated 1802. JAMES SMITH, Sheriff of Hamilton Co seized land after JOHN McGREW obtained judgement against John Cleves Symmes. Land sold at auction: S 31, T 3, R 2 sold to JONATHAN SEELY; S 7, T 3, R 3 sold to WILLIAM McMILLEN; S 17, T 5, R 1 sold to CHARLES AVERY. Signed JAMES SMITH, Sheriff. Witn: none. rec 1805. p 79

page 80 blank

Deed dated 1803. BENJAMIN McPIATT of Boone Co, KY to JAMES JOHNSTON. S 9, T 1, R 2. Signed BENJ. McPIATT. Witn: JP JAMES LOWES, JAMES A. LOWES. rec 1805. p 81

Deed dated 1804. USA to EDMUND RICHARDSON & JOHN RICHARDSON of Warran Co. S 29, T 3, R 2. rec 1805. p 82

Deed dated 1803. CORNELIUS QUICK to RALPH PHILLIPS of Hunterdon Co, NJ. S 6 T 2, R 2. Signed CORNELIUS (x) QUICK. Witn: JAS. DUNN, RALPH W. HUNT. rec 1805. p 82

Deed dated 1804. CORNELIUS RIKER SEDAM & ELIZA his wife of Hamilton Co to THOMAS McCULLOUGH. S 1, T 1, R 3. Signed CORN. R. SEDAM, ELIZA SEDAM. Witn: JOSEPH PEAUGH, JOHN MAHONY. JP WILLIAM SEMOND. rec 1805. p 83

BUTLER COUNTY LAND RECORDS: BOOK A

Deed dated 1804. CORNELIUS RIKER SEDAM & ELIZA his wife of Hamilton Co to WILLIAM McCLELLAN & JOHN SUTHERLAND. S 1, T 1, R 3. Signed CORN. R. SEDAM, ELIZA SEDAM. Witn: as previous entry. rec 1805. p 84

page 85 lined out; information repeated on page 87

Deed dated 1804. CORNELIUS RIKER SEDAM & ELIZA his wife of Hamilton Co to JAMES HAMILTON. S 1, T 1, R 3. Signed CORN. R. SEDAM, ELIZA SEDAM. Witn: as previous entry. rec 1805. p 86

Deed dated 1804. CORNELIUS RIKER SEDAM & ELIZA his wife of Hamilton Co to ISAAC WILES. S 1, T 1, R 3. Signed CORN. R. SEDAM, ELIZA SEDAM. Witn: as previous entry. rec 1805. p 87

Deed dated 1804. CORNELIUS RIKER SEDAM & ELIZA his wife of Hamilton Co to ISAAC STANLEY. S 1, T 1, R 3. Signed CORN. R. SEDAM, ELIZA SEDAM. Witn: as previous entry. rec 1805. p 88

Deed dated 1804. CORNELIUS RIKER SEDAM & ELIZA his wife of Hamilton Co to NANCY DAVIS of Hamilton. S 1, T 1, R 3. Signed and witn as above. rec 1805. p 89

Deed dated 1805. NANCY DAVIS to ISAAC STANLEY. S 1 T 1, R 3. Signed NANCY DAVIS. Witn: BENJAMIN DAVIS JOHN GREER, JOHN REILY. rec 1805. p 90

Deed dated 1804. CORNELIUS RIKER SEDAM & ELIZA his wife of Hamilton Co to JOHN WINGATE. S 1, T 1, R 3. Signed CORN. R. SEDAM, ELIZA SEDAM. Witn: JOHN MAHONY JOSEPH PEAUGH. rec 1805. p 91

Deed dated 1804. USA to ELIAS BAUDINOT of Philadelphia. S 14, 20 & 21, T -, R -. rec 1805. p 92

Deed dated 1803. DAVID BROADWELL of Hanover Twp, Morris Co, NJ to SIMEON BROADWELL. S 36, T 2, R 2. Signed DAVID BROADWELL. Witn: SYLVESTER D. RUSSELL, R. TUCKER. rec 1805. pp 92, 93

Deed dated 1804. HAITHORN HOOD & ELENOR his wife of Fairfield Twp to JOSEPH POTTER of Liberty Twp. S 15, T 2, R 2. Signed HATHHAN (x) HOOD, ELENOR (x) HOOD. Witn: TOBIAS TALBOT, JP JOHN TALBOT. rec 1805. p 94

Deed dated 1802. HATHHAN HOOD & ELENOR his wife to TOBIAS TALBOT. S 15, T 2, R 2. (See next entry.) Previously owned by JOHN GASTON. Signed HEATHHAM HOOD,

BUTLER COUNTY LAND RECORDS: BOOK A

ELINOR HOOD. Witn: JOHN GREER, NANCY DAVIS. rec 1805. p 95

Deed dated 1802. JOHN GASTON & MARY his wife to HEATHHORN HOOD. S 15, T 2, R 2. Signed JOHN GASTON, MARY GASTON. Witn: JOHN GREER, MATTHEW McDOWELL. rec 1805. p 95

Deed dated 1805. BENJAMIN FITZ RANDOLPH & EASTHER his wife to JOSEPH FITZ RANDOLPH. S 15, T 2, R 3. Signed BENJAMIN FITZ RANDOLPH, EASTHER (x) FITZ RANDOLPH. Witn: WILLIAM SYMMES, SARAH F. RANDOLPH. rec 1805. p 96

Deed dated 1804. SAMUEL ENYART & ANNA his wife to ROBERT ROSEBROUGH. S 24, T 2, R 2. Signed SAMUEL ENYART, ANNA ENYART. Witn: JACOB LEWIS, DRAKE RANDOLPH. rec 1805. p 97

Deed dated 1787. JOHN CLEVES SYMMES to heirs of MICHAEL HAUN, decd: SARA, JOSEPH, SALME, SAMUEL, MICHAEL, POLLY, JOHN & BETSY HAUN. S 27, T 2, R 2. Signed JOHN CLEVES SYMMES. Witn: PETER WILSON, WM. H. HARRISON, ROB'T McCLURE. rec 1805. p 98

Deed dated 1805. ISAAC MATSON & JOANAH his wife to DANIEL GOBLE. S 23, T 3, R 3. Signed ISAAC MATSON, JOANAH (x) MATSON. Witn: STEPHEN WOOD, JOSEPH SEAL. rec 1805. p 99

Deed dated 1805. JONATHAN DAYTON of NJ to JAMES LYON. S 20, T 2, R 3. Signed JOHN REILY for JONATHAN DAYTON. Witn: WILLIAM CORRY, STEPHEN REEDER. rec 1805. p 100

Deed dated 1805. SAMUEL HARPER of Liberty Twp to PETER DeMOSS of St. Clair Twp. S 17, T 3, R 2. Signed SAMUEL (x) HARPER. Witn: JOHN REILY, WILLIAM CORRY, HENRY THOMPSON. rec 1805. p 101

Deed dated 1805. JAMES LYON & JOHN LYON to ELIAS WALLEN. S 21, T 2, R 3. Signed JAMES LYON (only). Witn: WILLIAM CORRY, JOHN REILY. rec 1805. p 102

Deed dated 1805. JOSEPH POTTER & ELENER his wife to PHILLIP DROLLINGER. S 1, T 2, R 3. Bound by land of JOHN HERVEY, JACOB PEAK, PETER MURPHY, WILLIAM LEGG. Signed JOSEPH POTTER, ELENER POTTER. Witn: ARCHIBALD STARK, WILLIAM SYMMES. rec 1805. p 103

Deed dated 1804. EDWARD MEEKS & DOROTHEA his wife to ELLIS JOHN. S 14, T 3, R 2. Bound by land of

BUTLER COUNTY LAND RECORDS: BOOK A

DANIEL SKINNER, JAMES IRWIN. Signed EDW. MEEKS,
DOROTHEA MEEKS. Witn: IGNATIUS ROSS, JP ICHABOD
BENTON MILLER. rec 1805. p 104

Deed dated 1804. ELLIS JOHN & MARGARET his wife to
MICHAEL HILDEBRAND. S 14, T 3, R 2. Signed ELLIS
JOHN, MARGARET JOHN. Witn: JP ADRIAN HEGEMAN JR,
JONATHAN HUTCHENSON. rec 1805. p 105

Mortgage dated 1804. MICHAEL HILDEBRAND to ELLIS
JOHN. Final payment by 1807. Signed MICHAEL
HILDEBRAND. Witn: as above. rec 1805. p 106

Deed dated 1795. ISRAEL LUDLOW to ANDREW CHRISTY.
Hamilton lots 189, 190. Signed ISRAEL LUDLOW. Witn:
BENJAMIN DAVIS, BENJAMIN F. RANDOLPH. Title assigned
by Christy to SOLOMON LYONS, dated 1798. Signed
ANDREW CHRISTY. Witn: none. SOLOMON LINE assigned
rights to JAMES LYON, dated 1805. Signed SOLOMON
LINE. Witn: EZEKIEL BALL. rec 1805. p 107

Deed dated 1805. ANDREW CHRISTY & ELIZABETH his wife
to JAMES LYON. Hamilton lots 189, 190. Signed
ANDREW CHRISTY, ELIZABETH (x) CHRISTY. Witn: JACOB
LEWIS, SAMUEL ENYART. rec 1805. p 108

Deed dated 1803. JAMES SMITH, Sheriff of Hamilton Co
to CHARLES AVERY, JONATHAN SEELY & WILLIAM McMILLAN.
S 25, T 3, R 4. JOHN McCLAIN, admtr of estate of
ALLEN McCLAIN, obtained judgement against John Cleves
Symmes in 1801. Land seized, sold at auction to
three named above. Signed JAMES SMITH, Sheriff.
Witn: none. rec 1805. p 109

Deed dated 1795. ISRAEL LUDLOW to JOHN LUDLOW. S 2
& 3, T 1, R 3. Signed ISRAEL LUDLOW. Witn. W.C.
SCHENCK, JOHN HENRY. rec 1805. p 110

Deed dated 1788. ISRAEL LUDLOW to STEPHEN LUDLOW.
Hamilton lots 192, 193, 204, 205. Signed & witness
as above. rec 1805. p 111

Power of attorney dated 1804. FREDERICK FISHER of
Detroit, Indiana Ter'y, granted POA to JOHN GUNN of
Fort Hamilton and WILLIAM DUFF of Attawa Town, Indi-
ana Ter'y to sell land, collect debts. Signed F.
FISHER. Witn: MATT. ERNEST, ALEX DUFF. rec 1805. p112

Quitclaim dated 1805. DARIUS C. ORCUTT to ANDREW
CHRISTY. Hamilton lot 198. Signed D.C. ORCUTT.
Witn: A. ST.CLAIR JR, JAMES SMITH. HENRY WEAVER, JP.
rec 1805. p 113

BUTLER COUNTY LAND RECORDS: BOOK A

Deed dated 1796. HUGH DEMPSTER & LETY his wife to WILLIAM KELLY. Hamilton lot 149. Title transferred to Kelly, but lot # included in deed held by BERIAH McGUFFIN. Signed HUGH DEMPSTER, LETY (x) DEMPSTER. Witn: BERIAH MAGOFFIN, DANIEL DUGAN. Statement of satisfaction by Kelly, dated 1798. Wtn: JOHN BUCK-HANIN, MOSES KEDEY, JAMES FISHER. Undated statement by B. Mafoffin: deed for lot 149 is property of Dempster. Wtn: MICHAEL SLOAN, JOHN HORLAND. Statement of satisfaction by Kelly dated 1798. Wtn: MOSES KELLEY, JAMES FISHER. rec 1805. p 114

Deed dated 1805. HENRY WATTS & CATHERINE his wife to FREDERICK FISHER. Hamilton lots 187, 188. Signed HENRY WATTS, CATHERINE (x) WATTS. Wtn: ISAAC WILES, JACOB LEWIS. rec 1805. pp 114, 115

Deed dated 1805. JOHN FISHER, admr for JAMES FISHER, to FRANCIS WELLS. Hamilton lot 210. Signed JOHN FISHER. Witn: EZEKIEL WALKER, JACOB LEWIS. rec 1805. pp 115, 116

Deed dated 1805. JOHN GASTON & MARY, his wife, to WILLIAM MURRAY of Dauphin Co, PA. Hamilton lot 145. Signed JOHN GASTON, MARY GASTON. Witn: CELADON SYMMES. rec 1805. p 116

Deed dated 1804. USA to ISAAC GELDERSLEEVE, heir of JOHN GELDERSLEEVE. S 14, 23, T 2, R 3. rec 1805.p117

Mortgage dated 1804. ISAAC GELDERSLEEVE, ISAAC VAN NUYS, admtr of JOHN GELDERSLEEVE, CORNELIUS VAN NUYS & ISAAC PAXTON to ALEXANDER WILSON. S 14 & 23, T 2, R 3. Signed I. GILDERSLEEVE, ISSAC VAN NUYS, CORNELIUS VAN NUYS, ISAAC PAXTON. Witn: JOHN MAHARD, ANNA MAHARD. JP ALEXANDER WILSON. rec 1805. p 117

Deed dated 1805. ISAAC VAN NUYS, admr for ISAAC GIL-DERSLEEVE, to ALEXANDER WILSON. S 14 & 23, T 2, R 3. Signed ISAAC VAN NUYS. Witn: JOHN WINGATE, WILLIAM NOBLE. rec 1805. p 118

Receipt dated 1795. ISRAEL LUDLOW to MICHAEL McNAMIE. Payment for Hamilton lots 18, 151. Signed ISRAEL LUDLOW. Part paymt rec'vd from Mr. McCULLOUGH. MICHAEL McNAMIE assigned lot 18 rights to AZAREAS THORN. Signed MICHAEL McNAMIE. Witn: J.W. LLOYD. Order to make deed for lot 151 to JOHN BRASHER signed MICHAEL McNAMIE. Witn: ISRAEL LUDLOW. rec 1805. p 119

Request dated 1802. JOHN BRASHER requested deed for

BUTLER COUNTY LAND RECORDS: BOOK A

Hamilton lot 151 be made to JOHN SMITH. Signed JOHN BRASHER. Witn: ISRAEL LUDLOW. rec 1805. p 120

Assignment dated 1802. JOHN SMITH assigned rights to lot 151 to J. LEWIS. Signed JOHN SMITH. Witn: JAMES HAMILTON. rec 1805. p 120

Quitclaim dated 1791. Dr. CLARKSON FREEMAN to ISAAC FREEMAN, both sons of ABRAHAM FREEMAN. Warrants 295 & 296 of the Symmes Purchase. Signed CLARKSON FREEMAN. Witn: ELIAS CAMPBEL, JOHN WILHELM. rec 1805. p 120

page 121/122 bound out of order

Deed dated 1803. JOSEPH HOLLOWAY to JOHN MAXWELL. S 3, T 1, R 2. Signed JOSEPH HOLLOWAY. Witn: DAV. BEATY, JOHN R. BEATY. rec 1805. p 123

Deed dated 1804. CORNELIUS RIKER SEDAM & ELIZA his wife to THOMAS GRAY. S 1, T 1, R 3. Signed CORN. R. SEDAM, ELIZA SEDAM. Witn: JOSEPH PEAUGH, JOHN MAHONY JP WILLIAM SEMOND. rec 1805. pp 123, 124

Deed dated 1804. CORNELIUS RIKER SEDAM & ELIZA his wife to MATTHEW HUSTON. S 1, T 1, R 3. Signed and witn as above. rec 1805. pp 124, 125

Deed dated 1805. FREDERICK FISHER to WILLIAM HERBERT Hamilton lots 187, 188. Signed JOHN GUNN for Fisher. Witn: JOSHUA DELPLANE, THOS. McCULLOUGH, JOHN REILY. rec 1805. pp 125, 126

Deed dated 1803. ELIAS BOUDINOT of Philadelphia to CHARLES STEWART. S 13, T 2, R 4. Signed ELIAS BOUDINOT by ABJAH HUNT, att'y, and CORN. R. SEDAM, att'y for E. BUDINT. Witn: WM. STANLEY, DAVID HUNT. rec 1805. p 126

Deed dated 1804. CORNELIUS RIKER SEDAM & ELIZA his wife to WILLIAM HERBERT. S 1, T 1, R 3. Signed CORN. R. SEDAM, ELIZA SEDAM. Witn: JOSEPH PEAUGH, JOHN MAHONY. rec 1805. p 121

Deed dated 1804. DANIEL C. COOPER of Montgomery Co to JOHN MAXWELL. S 9, T 1, R 2. Signed DANIEL C. COOPER. Witn: JOHN REILY, JACOB LEWIS. rec 1805. p122

Deed dated 1805. SAMUEL STITES & MARTHA his wife to JOHN SMALLEY. S 10, T 2, R 3. Signed SAMUEL STITES, MARTHA STITES. Witn: JOHN PARSEL, JONATHAN SMALLEY,

BUTLER COUNTY LAND RECORDS: BOOK A

HENRY VAIL. rec 1805. p 127

Deed dated 1805. JONATHAN DAYTON to PETER SHEAFOR. S 30, T 3, R 3. Signed JONA. DAYTON. Witn: GEORGE SOUTHARD, WILLIAM SHEAFOR. rec 1805. p 128

Deed dated 1805. JONATHAN DAYTON to THOMAS POWERS. S 7, T 2, R 3. Signed JONA. DAYTON. Witn: PETER SHEAFOR, ABRAHAM HUFF. rec 1805. p 129

Deed dated 1805. JONATHAN DAYTON to SOLOMON LINE. S 14, T 2, R 3. Signed JONA. DAYTON. Witn: PETER SHEAFOR, JOHN REILY. rec 1805. pp 129, 130

Deed dated 1805. JONATHAN DAYTON to AMOS VALLANTINE. S 10, T 3, R 3. Signed JONA. DAYTON. Witn: JOSEPH DELAPLAINE, JOHN MAHARD. rec 1805. p 130

Deed dated 1805. HUGH CRAIG to JOSEPH STEWART. S 9, T 3, R 3. Signed HUGH CRAIG. Witn: ISAAC S. SWEARINGEN, JAMES STEWART. rec 1805. p 131

Deed dated 1805. JONATHAN DAYTON to JOHN SMALLEY. S 10, T 2, R 3. Signed JONA. DAYTON. Witn: SOLOMON LINE, JOHN REILY. rec 1805. p 132

Deed dated 1805. JONATHAN DAYTON to SAMUEL KENNEDY. S 21, T 2, R 3. Signed JONA. DAYTON by JOHN REILY. Witn: JOHN WINGATE, WILLIAM CORRY. rec 1805. p 133

Deed dated 1804. BENJAMIN ENYART to LEVI MOORE. S 9, T 2, R 3. Signed BENJAMIN ENYART. Witn: JAMES CROOKS, ISAIAH BALL, JAMES HEATON. rec 1805. p 134

Mortgage dated 1805. JOHN WELCH to JOHN SMOCK. No S-T-R; "currently home of John Welch". Bound by JOHN SAMPLE's land. Payment due 1807. Signed JOHN WELCH. Witn: HENRY WEAVER, CHARLES MASTERSON. rec 1805. p135

Partition dated 1805. JONATHAN DAYTON to JOSEPH FITZ RANDOLPH. S 14, T 2, R 3. Signed JONA. DAYTON. Witn: SOLOMON LINE, JOHN REILY. rec 1805. pp 135, 136

Partition dated 1805. JOSEPH FITZ RANDOLPH to JONATHAN DAYTON. S 14, T 2, R 3. Signed JOSEPH FITZ RANDOLPH. Witn: above. JP WM. MITCHELL. rec 1805. p 137

Deed dated 1805. JOHN CLEVES SYMMES to STACY POTTS of Harrisburg, PA. S 30 & 36, T 3, R 2. Signed JOHN CLEVES SYMMES. Witn: JOHN W. BROWNE, CHARLOTTE BROWNE rec 1805. p 138

Heartfelt thanks to my husband...
Without his research assistance,
this project would never have been completed

BUTLER COUNTY LAND RECORDS: BOOK A

Deed dated 1805. JONATHAN DAYTON to ZOPHAR BALL. S 21, T 2, R 3. Bound by land of JAMES LYON, PATRICK MOORE, SAMUEL KENNEDY. Signed JONA. DAYTON by JOHN REILY. Witn: WILLIAM CORRY, JAMES HASLET. rec 1805. p 139

Deed dated 1804. JOHN DOTY to STEPHANAS CLARK. S 18, T 2, R 2. Signed JOHN DOTY. Witn: DANIEL DOTY, ZINA DOTY. rec 1805. p 140

Deed dated 1794. JOHN CLEVES SYMMES to JONATHAN DAYTON. Gave title to entire third range, excepting previous sales, no S, T. Signed JOHN CLEVES SYMMES. Witn: J.N. CUMMINGS, ISRAEL HEDDEN. rec 1805. p 141

Deed dated 1796. JOHN CLEVES SYMMES to JONATHAN DAYTON. S 23, T 2, R 3. Signed JOHN CLEVES SYMMES. Witn: SAM. MEEKER, W.P. MEEKER. rec 1805. p 142

Deed dated 1805. JOSEPH POWERS to JONATHAN DAYTON. S 3, T 1, R 2. Bound by JOHN BALDWIN's land. Signed JOSEPH POWERS. Witn: GEORGE DRUMMOND. rec 1805. p 143

Deed dated 1805. GEORGE DRUMMOND to JONATHAN DAYTON. S 3, T 1, R 2. Bound by land of JOSEPH POWERS, JOHN BALDWIN, DAVID BEATY. Signed GEORGE DRUMMOND. Witn: JOHN MAHARD, ENOS TERRY. rec 1805. p 144

Deed dated 1805. MICHAEL AULD & SARAH his wife to JAMES STEWART. S 12, T 3, R 3. Signed MICHAEL AULD, SARAH AULD. Witn: JOHN BEATY, WM. GOULEY. rec 1805. p 145

Deed dated 1804. MOSES EASTON & ELIZABETH his wife to ARON BAKER. S 17, T 3, R 3. Signed MOSES EASTON, ELIZABETH EASTON. Witn: W. McCLURE, JOSEPH HENRY. rec 1805. p 146

Deed dated 1805. SAMUEL KENNEDY to JONATHAN DAYTON. S 21, T 2, R 3. Signed SAM. KENNEDY. Witn: JOHN WINGATE, WILLIAM CORRY. rec 1805. p 147

Deed dated 1805. ZOPHAR BALL to JONATHAN DAYTON. S 21, T 2, R 3. Signed ZOPHAR BALL. Witn: JOHN REILY, WILLIAM CORRY, JAMES HASLET. rec 1805. pp 147, 148

Deed dated 1803. RALPH PHILLIPS of Hunterdon Co, NJ to CORNELIUS QUICK. S 6, T 2, R 2. Signed RALPH PHILLIPS. Witn: JAS. DUNN, RALPH W. HUNT. rec 1805. p 148

Deed dated 1805. CORNELIUS QUICK & HANNAH his wife

BUTLER COUNTY LAND RECORDS: BOOK A

to ASBEL WALLER. S 6, T 2, R 2. Signed CORNELIUS (x) QUICK, HANNAH (x) QUICK. Witn: JOHN McCAINE, JACOB LEWIS. rec 1805. p 149

Deed dated 1805. WILLIAM LEGG & CASSANDRA his wife to ASHBEL WALLER. S 1, T 2, R 3. Signed WILLIAM LEGG, CASSANDRA (x) LEGG. Witn: LUCY DAVIS, JACOB LEWIS. rec 1805. p 150

Deed dated 1805. CHARLOTTE CHAMBERS LUDLOW, JAMES FINLAY, JOHN LUDLOW & SINEAS PIERSON, admrs of ISRAEL LUDLOW, to MATTHEW HUSTON. Hamilton lot 113. Signed CHARLOTTE CHAMBERS LUDLOW, JAMES FINDLAY, JOHN LUDLOW & SINEAS PIERSON. Witn: JOS. CONN SR, JAMES EWING. rec 1805. p 151

Deed dated 1805. CHARLOTTE CHAMBERS LUDLOW, JAMES FINLAY, JOHN LUDLOW & SINEAS PIERSON, admrs of ISRAEL LUDLOW, to JAMES CRAVEN. Hamilton lot 195. Signed CHARLOTTE CHAMBERS LUDLOW, JAMES FINDLAY, JOHN LUDLOW & SINEAS PIERSON. Witn: above. rec 1805. p 152

Deed dated 1805. CHARLOTTE CHAMBERS LUDLOW & JAMES FINDLAY to MICHAEL McNAMIE. Hamilton lots 18, 151. Purchase made prior to death of Israel Ludlow. Signed CHARLOTTE CHAMBERS LUDLOW, JAMES FINDLAY. Witn: above. rec 1805. pp 153, 154

Deed dated 1805. CHARLOTTE CHAMBERS LUDLOW & JAMES FINDLAY to EPHARAIM KIBBEY. Hamilton lot 2. Purchase made prior to death of Israel Ludlow. Signed CHARLOTTE CHAMBERS LUDLOW, JAMES FINDLAY. Witn: above. rec 1805. pp 155, 156

Deed dated 1805. CHARLOTTE CHAMBERS LUDLOW, JAMES FINLAY, JOHN LUDLOW & SINEAS PIERSON, admrs of ISRAEL LUDLOW, to CELADON SYMMES. Hamilton lot 70. Signed CHARLOTTE CHAMBERS LUDLOW, JAMES FINDLAY, JOHN LUDLOW & SINEAS PIERSON. Witn: above. rec 1805. p 157

Deed dated 1805. CHARLOTTE CHAMBERS LUDLOW, JAMES FINLAY, JOHN LUDLOW & SINEAS PIERSON, admrs of ISRAEL LUDLOW, to THOMAS McCULLOUGH. S 2, T 1, R 3. Signed CHARLOTTE CHAMBERS LUDLOW, JAMES FINDLAY, JOHN LUDLOW & SINEAS PIERSON. Witn: above. rec 1805. p 159

Deed dated 1805. CONSTANCE McMILLAN & WILLIAM CORRY exrs for WILLIAM McMILLAN, JACOB BURNET & JAMES SMITH to DAVID CONGER. S 12, T 2, R 2. Signed CONSTANCE McMILLAN, WILLIAM CORRY, JAC. BURNET, JAMES SMITH. Witn: JOHN MAHARD, ETH'N STONE. rec 1805. p 160

BUTLER COUNTY LAND RECORDS: BOOK A

Deed dated 1800. JOHN CLEVES SYMMES to JAMES McCLELLAND of KY. S 32, T 3, R 3. Signed JOHN CLEVES SYMMES. Witn: JAMES SILVER, BETTY SILVER. rec 1805. p 161

Deed dated 1805. WILLIAM McKINSTRY & CATHERINE his wife to PETER LINTNER. S 30, T 2, R 2. Signed WILLIAM (x) McKINSTRY, CATHERINE (x) McKINSTRY. Witn: JOHN REILY, JAMES McCLELLAND. rec 1805. p 162

Mortgage dated 1805. WILLIAM McKINSTRY to PETER LINTNER. S 30, T 2, R 2. Final payment due from Lintner in 1808. Signed PETER LINTNER. Witn: JOHN REILY, JAMES McCLELLAND. rec 1805. p 163

page 164 blank

Deed dated 1805. CHARLOTTE CHAMBERS LUDLOW, JAMES FINLAY, JOHN LUDLOW & SINEAS PIERSON, admrs of ISRAEL LUDLOW, to JAMES HAMILTON. Hamilton lot 86. Signed CHARLOTTE CHAMBERS LUDLOW, JAMES FINDLAY, JOHN LUDLOW & SINEAS PIERSON. Witn: JOS. CONN SR, JAMES EWING. rec 1805. p 165

Deed dated 1805. JACOB LEWIS & DEBORAH his wife to SAMUEL ENYART. Hamilton lot 151. Signed JACOB LEWIS, DEBORAH LEWIS. Witn: WILLIAM SYMMES, JOSEPH F. RANDOLPH. rec 1805. p 166

Deed dated 1795. ISRAEL LUDLOW to ANDREW CHRISTY. Hamilton lot 185. Signed ISRAEL LUDLOW. Witn: BENJAMIN DAVIS, BENJAMIN FITZ RANDOLPH. rec 1805. pp 166, 167

Deed dated 1805. ANDREW CHRISTY & ELIZABETH his wife to JACOB LEWIS. Hamilton lot 185. Signed ANDW. CHRISTY, ELIZABETH (x) CHRISTY. Witn: WILLIAM SYMMES SAMUEL ENYART. rec 1805. p 168

Deed dated 1805. CHARLOTTE CHAMBERS LUDLOW, JAMES FINLAY, JOHN LUDLOW & SINEAS PIERSON, admrs of ISRAEL LUDLOW, to SAMUEL ENYART. Hamilton lot 89. Signed CHARLOTTE CHAMBERS LUDLOW, JAMES FINDLAY, JOHN LUDLOW & SINEAS PIERSON. Witn: JOS. CONN SR, JAMES EWING. rec 1805. pp 168, 169

Deed dated 1805. CHARLOTTE CHAMBERS LUDLOW, JAMES FINLAY, JOHN LUDLOW & SINEAS PIERSON, admrs of ISRAEL LUDLOW, to SAMUEL ENYART. Hamilton lot 152. Signed CHARLOTTE CHAMBERS LUDLOW, JAMES FINDLAY, JOHN LUDLOW & SINEAS PIERSON. Witn: above   rec 1805. pp 169, 170

BUTLER COUNTY LAND RECORDS: BOOK A

Mortgage dated 1805. WILLIAM WALLACE to ELUAH LONG-FELLOW. S 8, T 2, R 3. Payment due 1808. Signed WILLIAM WALLACE. Witn: JOHN REILY, WILLIAM COOLEY, THOMAS LOGAN. rec 1805. p 170

Deed dated 1787. JOHN CLEVES SYMMES to JOHN CAIN. S 36, T 2, R 2. JONATHAN AGDEN forfeited land: lack of settlement or improvement. Signed JOHN CLEVES SYMMES. Witn: ELIHEE ENAS, RICHARD CAIN. rec 1805. p 171

Deed dated 1805. JONATHAN DAYTON to TIMOTHY WOODRUFF S 21, T 2, R 3. Bound by land of JOANH* ENYART, ZOPHER BALL, SAMUEL KENNEDY. Signed JONATHAN DAYTON by JOHN REILY. Witn: WILLIAM CORRY, JOHN SMOCK. rec 1805. p 172 *JONAH -- JOANNAH?

Deed dated 1805. MAHLON FORD of NJ to JOHN SMALLEY. S 3, T -, R 3. Bound by land of DAVID URMSTON, ANDREW CHRISTY. Signed MAHLON FORD by OLIVER SPENCER, atty. Witn: EDW. MEEK, JOHN L. GANO. rec 1805. p 173

Deed dated 1805. JOHN NOBLE CUMMINS of Essex Co, NJ to JOHN MORRIS. S 17, T 2, R 2. Signed JOHN NOBLE CUMMINS by WILLIAM C. SCHENK, his atty. Witn: URIGHAN OEOLL, JOHN BERT. JP JACOB REEDER. rec 1805. p 174

Deed dated 1799. JOHN CLEVES SYMMES to JOHN HERVEY. S 1, T 3, R 3. Signed JOHN CLEVES SYMMES. Witn: JP JAMES SILVER, HENRY G. COCHRAN. rec 1805. p 175

Deed dated 1805. SAMUEL ENYART & ANNA his wife to MICHAEL LAFERTY. Hamilton lots 151, 152. Signed SAMUEL ENYART, ANNA ENYART. Witn: JNO. TORRENCE, JACOB LEWIS. rec 1805. pp 175, 176

Deed dated 1805. PHILIP DROLLINGER to JOSEPH POTTER. S 1, T 2, R 3. Bound by land of JOHN NERVEY (HERVEY) JOSEPH PEAK, PETER MURPHY, WILLIAM LEGG. Signed PHILIP DROLLINGER. Witn: WILLIAM SYMMES, ARCHEBALD STARK. rec 1805. pp 176, 177

Deed dated 1805. JONATHAN DAYTON to AMOS VALLENTINE. S 30, T 3, R 3. Bound by land of MOSES BEACH, PETER SHEAFOR. Signed JONA. DAYTON. Witn: ENOS CUTLER, JOHN MAHARD. rec 1805. p 177

Deed dated 1804. AMOS VALLENTINE & RHODY his wife to PETER WILLIAMSON, late of PA. S 10, T 3, R 3. Signed AMOS VALLANTINE, RHODY (x) VALLANTINE. Witn: ISC. S. SWEARINGEN, JOHN (x) MURPHY. rec 1805. p 178

BUTLER COUNTY LAND RECORDS: BOOK A

Deed dated 1805.   MOSES VAIL & MARY his wife to JOHN McCRAKEN. S 4, T 2, R 2. Signed MOSES VAIL, MARY VAIL. Witn: WILLIAM SYMMES, CELADON SYMMES. rec 1805. p 179

Deed dated 1805. NICHOLAS PARSEL & CATHERINE his wife to DANIEL BOYD. S 30, T 3, R 3. Signed NICHOLAS PARSEL, CATHERINE (x) PARSEL. Witn: SALLY STEELE, PATSY McCLURE. rec 1805. p 180

Deed dated 1805. JOHN VANCE to AMOS TRAVIS. S 35, T 3, R 2. Signed JOHN VANCE. Witn: WILLIAM HARVEY, ISAAC SHIELDS. rec 1805. p 181

Deed dated 1804. MAHLON FORD of Morris Co, NJ to JUSTUS JONES. S 22, T 3, R 3. Signed MAHLON FORD by OLIVER SPENCER, atty. Witn: JOHN ARMSTRONG, O. M. SPENCER. rec 1805. p 182

Deed dated 1803. RENUE RUNYON of PISCATAWAY, Middlesex Co, NJ and ANNE his wife to JOHN AYRES of PA. S 18, T 3, R 2. Signed REUNE RUNYON, ANNE RUNYON. Witn: SAMUEL RANDOLPH, S. F. RANDOLPH. rec 1805. p 183

Deed dated 1805. The heirs of MICHAEL HAHN to JOSEPH HAHN. S 27, T 2, R 2. Not signing but named as heirs in text were JOHN HAHN and ELIZABETH HAHN, possibly minors. Signed MARTIN WAGNER, SARAH (x) WAGNER late Hahn, JOSEPH POWERS, SALOME (x) POWERS late Hahn, POLLY (x) HAHN, SAMUEL HAHN, MICHAEL HAHN. Witn: CELADON SYMMES, PHEBE SYMMES. rec 1805. p 184

Deed dated 1805. DANIEL BOYD & ANNA his wife to RHODA VALENTINE. S 30, T 3, R 3. Signed DANIEL BOYD, ANNA BOYD. Witn: I.S. SWEARINGEN, BARBARA SWEARINGEN. rec 1805. p 185

Deed dated 1804. CALEB SWAN of Washington DC to SARAH WALKER, wife of JAMES WALKER, late of Cincinnati. Given as gift; James to have no control. S 15, T 2, R 2. Signed C. SWAN. Witn: ROBERT W. PEACOCK, W. KITTY, NATHL. FRYE JR. rec 1804. p 186

Mortgage dated 1805. MATTHEW VANDUYNE to RALPH PHILLIPS of NJ. S 6, T ?, R ?. Payment due 1808. Signed MATTHEW VANDUYN. Witn: JOHN PARADISE JR, JP CALEB SHREVE. rec 1805. p 187

Deed dated 1788. ISRAEL LUDLOW & CHARLOTTE his wife to PHEBE GRIFFEN. Hamilton lot 197. Signed ISRAEL LUDLOW, CHARLOTTE CHAMBERS LUDLOW. Witn: SINEAS PIERSON, JP THO. GIBSON. GRIFFEN assigned rights and

BUTLER COUNTY LAND RECORDS: BOOK A

title to deed to JOHN BUCHANON, dated 1797. Signed PHEBEY GRIFFIN._ Witn: JOHN GORDON & DAVID ENOCH. BUCHANON assigned rights and title to DAVID ENOCH, dated 1799. Signed JNO. BUCHANNON. Witn: MILES WHITMORE. ENOCH assigned rights and title to PHEBY GRIFFIN, dated 1804. Signed DAVID ENOCH. Witn: ISAAC ENOCH. rec 1805. pp 188, 189

Deed dated 1805. PHEBE GRIFFIN to JOHN SUTHERLAND & HENRY BROWN. Hamilton lot 197. Signed PHEBY GRIFFIN. Witn: TIMOTHY GREEN, WILLIAM CORRY. rec 1805. p 190

Deed dated 1805. CHARLOTTE CHAMBERS LUDLOW, JOHN FINDLAY, JOHN LUDLOW & SINEAS PIERSON to SAMUEL DICK. Hamilton lot 102. Signed CHARLOTTE CHAMBERS LUDLOW, JOHN FINDLAY, JOHN LUDLOW, SINEAS PIERSON. Witn: JOS. CONN SR, JAMES EWING. rec 1805. p 191

Deed dated 1805. SAMUEL CULBERTSON of Malden, Upper Canada to SAMUEL C. VANCE of Lawrenceburg, Indiana Ter'y. Hamilton lots 33, 122. Signed SAM. CULBERTSON. Witn: SOLOMON LIBLEY, WILLIAM FORSETH. rec 1805. p 193

Deed dated 1805. CELADON SYMMES & PHEBE his wife to MATTHEW HUESTON. S 34, T 2, R 2. Signed CELADON SYMMES, PHEBE SYMMES. Witn: POLLY DUVALL, JACOB LEWIS. rec 1805. p 193

Deed dated 1805. BENJAMIN ENYART & JOANNA his wife to JOHN McCRAKEN. S 12, T 3, R 3. Signed BENJAMIN ENYART, JOANNA (x) ENYART. Witn: JAMES HEATON, MARY HEATON. rec 1805. p 194

Deed dated 1805. JOHN McCRAKEN & MARTHA his wife to JAMES STEWART. S 12, T 3, R 3. Signed JOHN McCRAKEN MARTHA McCRAKEN. Witn: W. McCLURE, MARTHA McCLURE. rec 1805. p 195

Deed dated 1805. WILLIAM I. PHILLIPS of NJ to JACOB POWERS. S 13, T 3, R 3. Signed WILLIAM I. PHILLIPS. Witn: ISC.S. SWEARINGEN, JOHN LINN. rec 1805. p 196

Deed dated 1805. CHARLOTTE CHAMBERS LUDLOW, JOHN FINDLAY, JOHN LUDLOW & SINEAS PIERSON to JAMES SMITH, SAMUEL DICK & WILLIAM McCLELLAN. S 2 & 3, T 1, R 3. Signed CHARLOTTE CHAMBERS LUDLOW, JOHN FINDLAY, JOHN LUDLOW, SINEAS PIERSON. Witn: JOS. CONN SR, JAMES EWING. rec 1805. p 197

Mortgage dated 1804. GEORGE FRUIT to SARAH SHAW, KNOLES SHAW, JOHN SHAW & SALLA SHAW. Land in S 34, T

BUTLER COUNTY LAND RECORDS: BOOK A

3, R 2 conveyed by ALBAN SHAW as collateral; payment to be made 1806. Signed GEORGE FRUIT. Witn: HARTMAN VANTREES, JP JUDAH WILLEY. rec 1805. pp 198, 199

Deed dated 1805. THOMAS HUNT JR, THOMAS HUNT SR, CHARLES WEST & DURAN WHITTLESEY to ARTHUR ELLIOT. S 20, T 3, R 3. Signed THOMAS HUNT JR, THOMAS HUNT SR, CHARLES WEST, DURAN WHITTLESEY. Witn: JOHN PHELPS, TREC. HUNT. rec 1805. p 200

Deed dated 1805. THOMAS HUNT JR, THOMAS HUNT SR, CHARLES WEST & DURAN WHITTLESEY to ELEAZAR HUNT & HENRY WEST. S 20, T 3, R 3. Signed THOMAS HUNT JR, THOMAS HUNT SR, CHARLES WEST, DURAN WHITTLESEY. Witn: IRA HUNT, ARTHUR ELLIOT. rec 1805. pp 200, 201

Deed dated 1804. RICHARD KEENE & NANCY his wife to WALTER TUCKER. S 18, T 3, R 2. Signed RICHARD KEENE NANCY KEENE. Witn: AMOS GREGG, BARBARA SWEARINGEN. rec 1806. p 201

Deed dated 1806. WALTER TUCKER & NANCY his wife to JOHN CARSON. S 18, T 3, R 2. Signed WALTER (x) TUCKER, NANCY (x) TUCKER. Witn: JOHN REILY, WILLIAM CORRY. rec 1806. p 202

Deed dated 1805. JONATHAN DAYTON to GEORGE DRUMMOND. S 3, T 1, R 2. Bound by land of JOSEPH POWERS, JOHN BALDWIN, DAVID BEATTY. Signed JONA. DAYTON. Witn: JOHN MAHARD, ENOS TERRY. rec 1806. p 203

Deed dated 1805. EDWARD MEEKS & DOROTHEA his wife to JOHN JAMESON. S 23, T 3, R 2. Signed EDW. MEEKS, DOROTHEA MEEKS. Witn: EDWARD LARKIN, JP MOSES KITCHEL JP JOHN ARMSTRONG. rec 1806. p 204

Mortgage dated 1805. DAVID CONGER to CONSTANCE McMILLAN, WILLIAM CORRY, JACOB BURNET & JAMES SMITH, admrs of WILLIAM McMILLAN. S 12, T 2, R 2. Payment due 1806. Signed DAVID CONGER. Witn: AARON GOFORTH. rec 1806. p 205

Deed dated 1806. MATTHEW McDOWELL to WILLIAM McKEAN. S 29, T 3, R 3. Signed MATTHEW McDOWELL. Witn: WILLIAM MINGS, JOHN HAMILTON. rec 1806. p 206

Deed dated 1805. CHARLOTTE CHAMBERS LUDLOW, JOHN FINDLAY, JOHN LUDLOW & SINEAS PIERSON to ISAAC WILES. Lot 28 adjoining Hamilton. Signed CHARLOTTE CHAMBERS LUDLOW, JOHN FINDLAY, JOHN LUDLOW, SINEAS PIERSON. Witn: JOS. CONN SR, JAMES EWING. rec 1806. p 207

BUTLER COUNTY LAND RECORDS: BOOK A

Deed dated 1805. HENRY WATTS & CATHERINE his wife to ISAAC WILES. Hamilton lot 186. Signed HENRY WATTS, CATHERINE (x) WATTS. Witn: JOHN GUNN, JACOB LEWIS. rec 1806. p 208

Deed dated 1806. MAHLON FORD to WILLIAM HAYS SR. S 3, T 2, R 3. Signed OLIVER SPENCER, agent for MAHLON FORD. Witn: A.M. SPENCER, JOHN ARMSTRONG. rec 1806. p 208

Deed dated 1787. JOHN CLEVES SYMMES to JOSEPH McMAKING. S 4, T 2, R 2. Land forfeited by JOHN N. CUMMINS for non-improvement. Signed JOHN CLEVES SYMMES. Witn: GARRET VANNERT, SILAS HOWELL. rec 1806. p 209

Deed dated 1805. WILLIAM HARVEY & ISABELLA his wife to JOSEPH McMAKEN. S 34, T 3, R 2. Signed WILLIAM HARVEY, ISABELLA HARVEY. Witn: WILLIAM SYMMES, ISAAC VANDUYN. rec 1806. p 210

Deed dated 1806. JOSHUA DELPLANE to JAMES DELPLANE. S 25, T 4, R 2. Signed JOSHUA DELPLANE. Witn: WILLIAM CORRY, JOHN REILY. rec 1806. p 211

Deed dated 1804. WILLIAM HARVEY & ISABELLA his wife to JOHN VANCE. S 35, T 3, R 2, purchased from UZAL BEATS, bought from ALLEN COLLUM, the original settler. Signed WILLIAM HARVEY, ISABELLA HARVEY. Witn: WILLIAM SYMMES, JOSEPH McMAKEN. rec 1806. p 212

Deed dated 1805. FERDINAND BROKAW & TINEY his wife to JOHN VANCE. S 4, T 2, R 2. Signed FERDINAND BROKAW, TINEY (x) BROKAW. Witn: HENRY VANDIKE, SIMON DEARSOT. rec 1806. p 213

Deed dated 1806. CELADON SYMMES & PHEBE his wife to JOHN CLEVES SYMMES JR. Hamilton lot 180. Signed CELADON SYMMES, PHEBE SYMMES. Witn: THOMAS MORRIS, POLLY DUVALL. rec 1806. p 216

Deed dated 1805. JUSTIS JONES & SARAH his wife of Champaign Co to JOHN BAKER. S 22, T 3, R 3. Signed JUSTUS JONES, SARAH (x) JONES. Witn: JOHN RUNYON, JOHN WARD. rec 1806. p 217

Deed dated 1805. JAMES HAMILTON to EPHARAIM CATTERLIN. S 1, T 1, R 3. Signed JAMES HAMILTON. Witn: THOMAS HUNTER, PHILIP ROUND. rec 1806. p 218

Deposition dated 1806. ISAAC MATSON swore that JOHN CLEVES SYMMES left deed in his possession to replace

BUTLER COUNTY LAND RECORDS: BOOK A

lost deed made by Symmes and his wife Susan. Signed ISAAC MATSON. Witn: JP W. McCLURE. rec 1806. p 218

Mortgage dated 1806. GEORGE SNIDER to JAMES WITHEROWN. Hamilton lot 213. Payment due 1807. Signed GEORGE SNIDER. Witn: JOHN REILY, WILLIAM CORRY. rec 1806. p 219

Deed dated 1805. CHARLOTTE CHAMBERS LUDLOW & JAMES FINDLAY, admrs of ISRAEL LUDLOW, to DARIUS C. ORCUTT. Hamilton lot 198; finalize sale begun by Ludlow in 1804. Signed CHARLOTTE CHAMBERS LUDLOW, JAMES FINDLAY. Witn: JOS. CONN SR, JAMES EWING. rec 1806. p 220

Deed dated 1805. CHARLOTTE CHAMBERS LUDLOW & JAMES FINDLAY to MICHAEL McNAMIE. Hamilton lots 18, 151; finalize sale begun by Ludlow in 1795. Signed CHARLOTTE CHAMBERS LUDLOW, JAMES FINDLAY. Witn: JOS. CONN SR, JAMES EWING. rec 1806. pp 221, 222

Deed dated 1805. CHARLOTTE CHAMBERS LUDLOW & JAMES FINDLAY to HENRY WATTS. Hamilton lots 186, 187, 188; finalize sale begun by Ludlow in 1795. Signed CHARLOTTE CHAMBERS LUDLOW, JAMES FINDLAY. Witn: JOS. CONN SR, JAMES EWING. rec 1806. p 223

Deed dated 1806. JONATHAN DAYTON to PATRICK MOORE. S 22, T 2, R 3. Bound by JOHN McEOWEN's land. Signed JONA. DAYTON by JOHN REILY, his atty in fact. Witn: JAMES LANIER, ISAAC STANLEY. rec 1806. p 224

Deed dated 1805. CHARLOTTE CHAMBERS LUDLOW & JAMES FINDLAY to JOHN TORRENCE. Hamilton lots 123, 160 & outlots; finalize sale by Ludlow in 1795. Signed and witn as above. rec 1806. pp 225, 226

Deed dated 1804. JOHN BRADY to ADAM DICKEY & SAMUEL DICKEY. Land purchased by JAMES BRADY, dec'd, from CALVIN MORREL, contract dated 12/24/1795. No S, T, R 4. Signed JOHN BRADY. Witn: JOE BURNET, JACOB KAUTZ. rec 1806. p 227

Deed dated 1805. JONATHAN DAYTON to THOMAS COHOON. S 36, T 3, R 3. Bound by land of MOSES BEACH, ABRAHAM FREEMAN. Signed JONA. DAYTON. Witn: WM. STANLEY, DANIEL ROE. rec 1806. pp 227, 228

Deed dated 1805. JOHN HARDEN & CATRIN his wife to ROBERT SIGARSON. S 25, T 3, R 3. Bound by JOHN HOLDEN. Signed JOHN(x) HARDEN, CATRIN (x) HARDEN. Witn: JOS. IRWIN, THOS. HUNT. rec 1806. p 229

BUTLER COUNTY LAND RECORDS: BOOK A

Deed dated 1806.   JOHN COLWELL to THOMAS McINTIRE.   S 27, T 3, R 2.   Signed JOHN COLWELL.   Witn: ISC. S. SWEARINGEN, JAMES McINTIRE.   rec 1806.   p 230

Deed dated 1806.   JOHN HARDEN & CATRIN his wife to JOHN HOLDEN.   S 25, T 3, R 3.   Signed JOHN(x) HARDEN, CATRIN (x) HARDEN.   Witn: JOHN GOLDTRAP, JACOB HARDING.   rec 1806.   p 230

Deed dated 1806.   JOHN HARDEN & CATRIN his wife to JOSEPH MALOLLY.   S 25, T 3, R 3.   Signed JOHN (x) HARDEN, CATRIN (x) HARDEN.   Witn: JOHN GOLDTRAP, JACOB HARDING.   rec 1806.   p 231

Deed dated 1805.   CHARLOTTE CHAMBERS LUDLOW,   JAMES FINDLAY, JOHN LUDLOW & SINEAS PIERSON, admrs of ISRAEL LUDLOW, to JOHN SUTHERLAND.   Hamilton lot 114. Signed CHARLOTTE CHAMBERS LUDLOW, JAMES FINDLAY, JOHN LUDLOW, SINEAS PIERSON.   Witn: JOS.   CONN SR, JAMES EWING.   rec 1806.   p 232

Deed dated 1805.   JOAB CORNSTOCK* & EUNICE his wife to heirs of ASA HARVEY: ASA HARVEY, CHRISTOPHER HARVEY, RICHARD MACK & BETTY his wife; CHARLES CONE & JANE his wife; JOHN RAMSEY JR & LUCY his wife; SAMUEL HUSTON & ELIZABETH his wife all of Hamilton Co, and JABEZ WARNER JR & SARAH, his wife of East Haddam, Middlesex Co, CT.   S28, T 3, R 2.   Signed JOAB CORNSTOCK, EUNICE CORNSTOCK.   Witn: JOHN ANDREWS, RUTH C. CORNSTOCK.   rec 1806.   p 233   * probably misinterpretation by typist. Should be JOAB COMSTOCK, etc.

Deed dated 1806. JOHN BEATY to JOHN R. BEATY.   S 18, T -, R -.   Signed JOHN BEATY.   Witn: JOHN MORROW, ROBERT (x) McINTIRE.   rec 1806.   p 234

Deed dated 1795.   ISRAEL LUDLOW to CORNELIUS VAN NUYS Hamilton lot 215.   Signed ISRAEL LUDLOW.   Witn: ISSAC VAN NUYS, CORNELIUS A. VAN ARSDALEN. JP JAMES SLAUGHTER.   rec 1806.   p 235

Deed dated 1795.   ISRAEL LUDLOW to CORNELIUS VAN NUYS Hamilton lot 214.   Signed ISRAEL LUDLOW.   Witn: ISSAC VAN NUYS, CORNELIUS A. VAN ARSDALEN. JP JAMES SLAUGHTER.   rec 1806.   pp 236, 237

Deed dated 1802.   JAMES MARSHALL & FANNY his wife to GODFREY WAGGONER.   S 20, T 2, R 2.   Signed JAMES MARSHALL, FANNY MARSHALL.   Witn: JOHN GREER.   rec 1806. p 237

BUTLER COUNTY LAND RECORDS: BOOK A

Deed dated 1806. ADRIAN HEGEMAN & ELIZABETH his wife to DANIEL AVERY. S 28, T 3, R 2. Belonged formerly to JACOB BURNET, deeded to WILLIAM WOOD as assignee of DANIEL GRIFFING. Seized and sold by sheriff to DANIEL CONNER, resold to A.H. Signed ADRIAN HEGEMAN, ELIZABETH HEGEMAN. Witn: ISC. S. SWEARINGEN. rec 1806. p 238

Deed dated 1806. THOMAS McINTIRE & MARGARET his wife to JOHN COLWELL. S 27, T 3, R 2. Signed THOMAS McINTIRE, MARGARET (x) McINTIRE. Witn: ISC. S. SWEARINGEN, JAMES McINTIRE. rec 1806. p 239

Deed dated 1806. ISAAC STANLEY to GEORGE McCORMACK. Hamilton lot 138. Signed ISAAC STANLEY. Witn: JACOB LEWIS, WILLIAM McCLELLAN. rec 1806. pp 239, 240

Deed dated 1805. JONATHAN DAYTON to JOSEPH POWERS. S 3, T 1, R 2. Bound by JOHN BALDWIN's land. Signed JONA. DAYTON. Witn: JONAH BUFFINGTON, GEORGE DRUMMOND rec 1806. p 240

Deed dated 1806. JOHN INGRAM of Clark Co, Indiana Ter'y. to AARON RICHARDSON. S 17, T 3, R 3. Signed JOHN INGRAM. Witn: JOHN REILY, JAMES HEATON. rec 1806. p 241

Deed dated 1806. ISAAC MATSON & JOANNA his wife to JAMES MAPES. S 23, T 3, R 3. Bound by DANIEL GOBLES' land. Signed ISAAC MATSON, JOANN (x) MATSON. Witn: ISC. S. SWEARINGER, DANIEL GOBLES. rec 1806. p 242

Deed dated 1801. JONATHAN DAYTON to Col. JOHN CONWAY of Middlesex, NJ. S 19, T 2, R ? Signed JONA. DAYTON. Witn: RICH. COX, SUSAN W. DALTON. rec 1806. p 243

Deed dated 1805. THOMAS BROWN of NY & JOSEPH BARROW of NY, exrs of JOHN CORNWAY, to JAMES PATON. S 19, T 2, R 3. Extract from CONWAY's will: funds to be divided between his daus JANE BROWN, CATHERINE SLECK. Signed THOMAS BROWN, JOSEPH BARROW. Witn: DAVID PATON ICHABOD POTTER. rec 1806. pp 244, 245

Deed dated 1805. JAMES PATON to JOSEPH BLOOMFIELD. S 19, T 2, R 3. Signed JAMES PATON. Witn: CHARLOTTE TAYLOR, THOMAS PATON. rec 1806. p 246

Assignment dated 1806. CHARLES AVERY to JOSEPH BLOOMFIELD. Annexed deed from JOHN R. MILLS, collector for Hamilton Co. No S-T-R. Signed C. AVERY. Witn: ANNA AVERY, ISAAC HUMPHREYS. rec 1806. p 247

BUTLER COUNTY LAND RECORDS: BOOK A

Deed dated 1806. THOMAS McCULLOUGH & ELIZABETH his wife to WILLIAM MURRY. S 2, T 1, R 3. Signed THOS. McCULLOUGH, ELIZABETH McCULLOUGH. Witn: J. REILY, ISAAC STANLEY. rec 1806. pp 247, 248

Deed dated 1806. THOMAS McCULLOUGH & ELIZABETH his wife to SAMUEL BEELOR of KY. Hamilton lot 83. Signed THOS. McCULLOUGH, ELIZABETH McCULLOUGH. Witn: ISAAC STANLEY, J. WHITE. rec 1806. pp 248, 249

Deed dated 1806. THOMAS McCULLOUGH & ELIZABETH his wife to CELADON SYMMES. S 2, T 1, R 3. Signed THOS. McCULLOUGH, ELIZABETH McCULLOUGH. Witn: J. REILY, ISAAC STANLEY. rec 1806. p 249

Assignment date 1806. JAMES SMITH, WILLIAM McCLELLAN & MARY his wife to JOHN SUTHERLAND & HENRY BROWN. S 2 & 3, T 1, R 3. SAMUEL DICK a joint tenant with SMITH & McCLELLAN. Signed JAMES SMITH, WILLIAM McCLELLAN, MARY McCLELLAN. Witn: WILLIAM CORRY, HENRY WEAVER. rec 1806. p 250

Deed dated 1806. WILLIAM McCLELLAN & MARY his wife to HENRY BROWN. S 1, T 1, R 3. Signed WILLIAM Mc-CLELLAN, MARY McCLELLAN. Witn: WILLIAM CORRY, HENRY WEAVER. rec 1806. p 251

Mortgage dated 1805. TIMOTHY WOODRUFF to JONATHAN DAYTON. S 21, T 2, R 3. Signed TIMOTHY WOODRUFF. Witn: JOHN REILY, WILLIAM CORRY. rec 1806. p 252

Deed dated 1806. GEORGE SNIDER & SUSANNAH his wife to LAWRENCE KAWANAUGH*. Hamilton lot 213. Signed GEORGE SNIDER, SUSANNAH (x) SNIDER. Witn: ISAAC STANLEY, HENRY HITE. rec 1806. p 253. * misinterpretation by typist. Should be LAWRENCE CAVENAUGH.

Deed dated 1799. JOHN CLEVES SYMMES to GEORGE BYRES. S 17, T 2, R 2. Previous assignees: "GEORGE BYRES, surviving widow of PHILIP BIRES", ABRAHAM WATSON, THOMAS McADAMS, WILLIAM PATTEN, WILLAM VANARSDOLE, FERDIANAD BROKAW, DAVID GRUMMON. Signed JOHN CLEVES SYMMES. Witn: SARAH PRINCE, JAMES MAGILL. rec 1806. p 254

page 256 is duplicated by page 257.

Deed dated 1805. JEREMIAH BUTTERFIELD & POLLY his wife to JACOB HIDAY. S 34, T 3, R 2. Signed JEREMIAH BUTTERFIELD, POLLY BUTTERFIELD. Witn: JOSEPH BOLTON, JUDAH WILLEY. rec 1806. p 257

BUTLER COUNTY LAND RECORDS: BOOK A

Deed dated 1806. Admtrs of Israel Ludlow to ISAAC STANLEY. Hamilton lot 181. Signed CHARLOTTE CHAMBERS LUDLOW, JAMES FINDLAY, JOHN LUDLOW, SINEUS PIERSON. Witn: N.C. FINDLAY, JOHN MAHARD. rec 1806. p 258

Deed dated 1806. Admtrs of Israel Ludlow to ISAAC STANLEY. Hamilton lot 138. Signed CHARLOTTE CHAMBERS LUDLOW, JAMES FINDLAY, JOHN LUDLOW, SINEUS PIERSON. Witn: N.C. FINDLAY, JOHN MAHARD. rec 1806. p 259

Deed dated 1806. Admtrs of Israel Ludlow to ISAAC WILES. Hamilton lot 75. Signed CHARLOTTE CHAMBERS LUDLOW, JAMES FINDLAY, JOHN LUDLOW, SINEUS PIERSON. Witn: N.C. FINDLAY, JOHN MAHARD. rec 1806. pp 259, 260

Deed dated 1806. Admtrs of Israel Ludlow to ISAAC WILES. Hamilton lot 106. Signed CHARLOTTE CHAMBERS LUDLOW, JAMES FINDLAY, JOHN LUDLOW, SINEUS PIERSON. Witn: N.C. FINDLAY, JOHN MAHARD. rec 1806. pp 260, 261

Deed dated 1806. Admtrs of Israel Ludlow to ISAAC WILES. Hamilton lot 164. Signed CHARLOTTE CHAMBERS LUDLOW, JAMES FINDLAY, JOHN LUDLOW, SINEUS PIERSON. Witn: N.C. FINDLAY, JOHN MAHARD. rec 1806. p 261

Deed dated 1806. Admtrs of Israel Ludlow to ELEANOR MOORE. Hamilton lot 161. Signed CHARLOTTE CHAMBERS LUDLOW, JAMES FINDLAY, JOHN LUDLOW, SINEUS PIERSON. Witn: N.C. FINDLAY, JOHN MAHARD. rec 1806. p 262

Deed dated 1806. Admtrs of Israel Ludlow to ELEANOR MOORE. Hamilton lot 112. Signed CHARLOTTE CHAMBERS LUDLOW, JAMES FINDLAY, JOHN LUDLOW, SINEUS PIERSON. Witn: N.C. FINDLAY, JOHN MAHARD. rec 1806. p 263

Deed dated 1806. GEORGE BUYERS & NANCY his wife to JAMES JAMES. S 17, T 2, R 2. Signed GEORGE (x) BUYERS, NANCY (x) BUYERS. Witn: JAMES WALKER, PAUL MICHAEL. rec 1806. p 264

Mortgage dated 1806. JAMES JAMES of Center Co, PA to GEORGE BUYERS. Final paymt above due 1808. Signed JAMES JAMES. Witn: JAMES WALKER. rec 1806. p 265

Deed dated 1806. Auditors apptd by court to WILLIAM CORRY and JOHN REILY. 3 acres containing original Ft. Hamilton, seized in settlement obtained by PEYTON SHORT of KY against Brig. Gen. JAMES WILKINSON. Signed DAVID BEATY, CHARLES BRUN, JOHN WINGATE. Witn: JAS. SMITH, JNO. TORRENCE. rec 1806. p 266

BUTLER COUNTY LAND RECORDS: BOOK A

Deed dated 1806. Admtrs of ISRAEL LUDLOW to ABRAHAM GARRISON. Hamilton lot 12. Signed CHARLOTTE CHAMBERS LUDLOW, JAMES FINDLAY, JOHN LUDLOW, SINEAS PIERSON. Witn: N.C. FINDLAY, JOHN MAHARD. rec 1806. p 267

Deed dated 1806. Admtrs of ISRAEL LUDLOW to ABRAHAM GARRISON. Hamilton lot 171 Signed CHARLOTTE CHAMBERS LUDLOW, JAMES FINDLAY, JOHN LUDLOW, SINEAS PIERSON. Witn: N.C. FINDLAY, JOHN MAHARD. rec 1806. p 268

Deed dated 1806. Admtrs of ISRAEL LUDLOW to ABRAHAM GARRISON. Hamilton lot 137. Signed CHARLOTTE CHAMBERS LUDLOW, JAMES FINDLAY, JOHN LUDLOW, SINEAS PIERSON. Witn: N.C. FINDLAY, JOHN MAHARD. rec 1806. p 269

Deed dated 1806. Admtrs of ISRAEL LUDLOW to ABRAHAM GARRISON. Hamilton outlot 12. Signed CHARLOTTE CHAMBERS LUDLOW, JAMES FINDLAY, JOHN LUDLOW, SINEAS PIERSON. Witn: N.C. FINDLAY, JOHN MAHARD. rec 1806. p 270

Deed dated 1806. Admtrs of ISRAEL LUDLOW to AARON KING. Hamilton lot 72. Signed CHARLOTTE CHAMBERS LUDLOW, JAMES FINDLAY, JOHN LUDLOW, SINEAS PIERSON. Witn: N.C. FINDLAY, JOHN MAHARD. rec 1806. p 271

Deed dated 1806. AARON KING to JOHN REILY. Hamilton lot 72. Signed AARON (x) KING. Witn: WILLIAM CORRY, CELADON SYMMES. rec 1806. p 272

Deed dated 1806. ABRAHAM GARRISON & RACHEL his wife to HUMPHREY NICHOLS. Hamilton lot 71. Signed ABRAHAM GARRISON, RACHEL (x) GARRISON. Witn: JACOB LEWIS JOSEPH HUNTER. rec 1806. p 273

Deed dated 1806. JOHN CHAMBERLIN & NANCY his wife to GEORGE LOY. S 32, T 2, R 5. Signed JOHN CHAMBERLIN, NANCY CHAMBERLIN. Witn: JACOB LOY, JOSEPH CATROW. rec 1806. p 274

Deed dated 1806. JOHN CHAMBERLIN & NANCY his wife to JACOB LOY. S 32, T 2, R 5. Signed JOHN CHAMBERLIN, NANCY CHAMBERLIN. Witn: JOSEPH CATROW, HENRY WEAVER. rec 1806. p 275

Deed dated 1806. JOHN CHAMBERLIN & NANCY his wife to JOSEPH CATROW. S 32, T 2, R 5. Signed JOHN CHAMBERLIN, NANCY CHAMBERLIN. Witn: JACOB LOY, HENRY WEAVER. rec 1806. p 276

Mortgage dated 1806. JOSEPH CATROW & POLLY his wife to JOHN CHAMBERLIN. Paymt due on above by 1807.

BUTLER COUNTY LAND RECORDS: BOOK A

Signed JOSEPH CATROW, POLLY (x) CATROW. Witn: JACOB LOY, HENRY WEAVER. rec 1806. pp 276, 277

Deed dated 1806. JOHN CAMPBELL & NANCY his wife to WILLIAM SMITH BRIGGS. S 33, T 3, R 2. Signed JOHN CAMPBELL, NANCY CAMPBELL. Witn: NATHAN GRIFFITH, JUDAH WILLEY. rec 1806. p 277

Mortgage dated 1806. WILLIAM SMITH BRIGGS to JOHN CAMPBELL. Final paymt on above due 1807. Signed WM. SMITH BRIGGS. Witn: ISRAEL WILLEY, JUDAH WILLEY. rec 1806. p 278

Deed dated 1806. SOLOMON LINE & SALOME his wife to DENNIS BALL. S 14, T 2, R 3. Signed SOLOMON LINE, SALOME (x) LINE. Witn: JONATHAN LINE, JOHN LINE. JP EZEKIEL BALL. rec 1806. p 279

Deed dated 1805. BENJAMIN LINE & REBECKAH his wife to SOLOMON LINE & BENJAMIN ENYART, trustees of Baptist Church. S 15, T 2, R 3. Signed BENJAMIN LINE, REBECKAH (x) LINE. Witn: HENRY LINE, SARAH (x) LINE. rec 1806. p 280

Deed dated 1805. MATTHEW VANDINE to ISAAC VANDINE. S 6 T 2, R 2. Signed MATTHEW VANDUYN. Witn: ELIZABETH (x) FREEMAN, MARY (x) SEWARD. rec 1806. p 282

Deed dated 1804. JONATHAN DAYTON & SUSAN his wife to ROBERT WHITEHILL JR of Waynesburgh, Greene Co, PA. Land north of Hamilton, R 3; bound by Miami River on 2 sides, land of JOHN McCOWEN, SOLOMON LINES. Signed JONATHAN DAYTON, SUSAN DAYTON. Witn: ELIAS I. DAYTON, FRANCIS B. AGDEN. rec 1806. p 283

Deed dated 1806. JOHN L. GANO & MARY his wife to JAMES IRWIN. S 14, T 3, R 2. Signed JOHN L. GANO, MARY GANO. Witn: JAMES EWING, JOHN McCLEAN. rec 1806. p 284

Deed dated 1804. ALEXANDER McWHORTER, JOHN CHETWOOD & ELIAS BOUDINOT, trustees for the estate of HANNAH KINNEY, wife of Col. ABRAHAM KINNEY as set up by the will of WILLIAM BURNET of New Ark, NJ, to ELIAS CRANE of New Ark, NJ. S 21, T 2, R 2. Signed ALEX MAWHORTER, JOHN CHETWOOD, ELIAS BOUDINOT. Witness: ANN ABELVIE, JOHN BALLARD. rec 1806. pp 285, 286

Agreement dated 1799. CORNELIUS R. SEDAM and JESSE HUNT, agent for ABIJAH HUNT, to WILLIAM McCLURE. To convey land on Dick's Creek now inhabited by -- FLEMING upon paymt of $3000. Signed CORN. R. SEDAM,

BUTLER COUNTY LAND RECORDS: BOOK A

JS. HUNT for A. HUNT, WM. McCLURE JR. Witn: CHAS. KILLGORE, THOMPSON WACHOP. rec 1806. p 287

Deed dated 1805. SIMEON BROADWELL of Morris, Morris Co, NJ to WILLIAM BROADWELL of same. S 36, T 2, R 2, except land conveyed to JACKSON AYERS and JAMES CLARK Signed SIMEON BROADWELL. Witn: ABM. CANFIELD JR, WILLIAM MITCHEL, JOHN DOUGHTY, JP JOHN McCARTER. rec 1806. pp 287, 288

Deed dated 1805. WILLIAM BROADWELL to DAVID GARRISON* of Hanover, Morris Co, NJ. S 36, T 2, R 2. Signed WILLIAM BROADWELL. Witn. WM. BEACH, ABM. CANTERFIELD JR. rec 1806. p 289 *clerk's margin note: to DAVID GARRIGUS

Deed dated 1801. ALLEN CULLUM & POLLY his wife to JOSEPH HALL. S 12, T 2, R 2. Signed ALLEN (x) CULLUM, POLLY (x) CULLUM. Witn: JOHN CLEVES SYMMES, JOHN BROWN. rec 1806. p 290

Deed dated 1806. JONATHAN DAYTON to DAVID GARRIGUS. S 37, T 2, R 3. Signed JONATHAN DAYTON by JOHN REILY atty. Witn: PATRICK MOORE, JAMES CLARK. rec 1806. p 291

Deed dated 1806. WILLIAM HENRY HARRISON, Govn'r, Indiana Ter'y & ANNA his wife to CATHARINE STOCKTON of NJ, widow of PHILLIP STOCKTON, & ELIAS BOUDINOT, exctr of Stockton's estate. S 33, T 3, R 2; previously owned by ISAAC TUTHILL REVES. Signed WILLIAM HENRY HARRISON, ANNA HARRISON. Witn: HENRY HOUSE, CHAS. LABASHE. JP THO. I. DAVIS. rec 1806. p 292

Quitclaim dated 1803. WILLIAM BETTS to CATHARINE STOCKTON & ELIAS BOUDINOT as above. S 9, T 3, R 2. Signed WM. BETTS. Witn: JOEL WILLIAMS, JOSEPH BLACK. rec 1806. p 293

page 294 blank

Deed dated 1803. JOHN CLEVES SYMMES to CATHARINE STOCKTON & ELIAS BOUDINOT. S 9, T 3, R 2. Signed JOHN CLEVES SYMMES. Witn: JOS. CONN, C. AVERY. JP MICHAEL JONES. rec 1806. p 295

Deed dated 1805. RALPH PHILLIPS of Hunterdon Co, NJ to MARTIN VAN DUYN. S 6, T 2, R 2. Signed RALPH PHILLIPS. Witn: RALPH W. HUNT, WILLIAM WILLIAMS. rec 1806. p 296

BUTLER COUNTY LAND RECORDS: BOOK A

Deed dated 1795. ISRAEL LUDLOW to REBECKAH FITZ RANDOLPH. Hamilton lot 165. Signed ISRAEL LUDLOW. Witn: TOMPSON CLARK, WILLIAM HERBERT. rec 1806. p 297

Deed dated 1806. MATTHEW HUESTON & CATHERINE his wife to SAMUEL LYON. S 1, T 1, R 3. Signed M. HUESTON, CATHERINE HUESTON. Witn: CELADON SYMMES, THOMAS HUNTER. rec 1806. p 298

Deed dated 1806. JACKSON AYERS & ELIZABETH his wife to DAVID GARRIGUS. S 36, T 2, R 2. Signed JACKSON AYERS, ELIZABETH AYERS. Witn: JOHN REILY, ISAAC STANLEY, MOSES JOHNSON. rec 1806. p 299

Deed dated 1806. Admtrs of ISRAEL LUDLOW to THOMAS FLEMING. S 14, T 2, R 2. Bound by JOHN WILKINSON's land. Signed CHARLOTTE CHAMBERS LUDLOW, JAMES FINDLAY, JOHN LUDLOW, SINEAS PIERSON. Witn: N.C. FINDLAY, JOHN MAHARD. rec 1806. p 300

page 301 x'd out, duplicated on page 303

Deed dated 1805. MAHLON FORD of Morris Co, NJ to SAMUEL ENYART. S 3, T ?, R 2. Signed OLIVER SPENCER agent for Ford. Witn: O. M. SPENCER, ANNA SPENCER. rec 1806. p 302

Deed dated 1806. EPHRAIM KIBBEY & PHEBE his wife to JOSEPH SMITH. Hamilton lot 199. Signed EPHRAIM KIBBEY, PHEBE KIBBEY. Witn: ANDREW LYTLE, CALVIN SAYRE. rec 1806. p 302

Partition. EDMUND RICHARDSON to JOHN RICHARDSON. S 20, T 3, R 2. Signed EDMUND RICHARDSON. Witn: ISAAC STANLEY, WILLIAM SMITH. rec 1806. p 303.

Partition. JOHN RICHARDSON to EDMUND RICHARDSON. S 20, T 3, R 2. Signed JOHN RICHARDSON. Witn: ISAAC STANLEY, WILLIAM SMITH. rec 1806. p 304

Deed dated 1806. Admtrs of ISRAEL LUDLOW to WILLIAM PATTON. Hamilton lot 202. Signed and. witn as above. rec 1806. pp 304, 305

Deed dated 1806. Admtrs of ISRAEL LUDLOW to WILLIAM PATTON. Hamilton lot 203. Signed and witn as above. rec 1806. p 305

Deed dated 1806. EVAN BANES & LINA his wife to JOHN BLUE. S 12, T 2, R 2. Signed EVAN BANES, LINA (x) BANES. Witness: ENOS WILLIAMS, JAMES ARMSTRONG,

BUTLER COUNTY LAND RECORDS: BOOK A

JONAS SEAMAN, FRANCES DUNLAVY, ANW. CHENOWETH. rec 1806. p 306

Deed dated 1806. ISAAC WILES & ELIZABETH his wife to WILLIAM ROBY. Hamilton lot 164. Signed ISAAC WILES, ELIZABETH (x) WILES. Witn: ISAAC STANLEY, JOHN GRANT. rec 1806. p 307

Mortgage dated 1806. JOHN VAN NISE to ISAAC COON, GEORGE SUTTON, JEREMIAH SUTTON, DAVID SUTTON, ROSE-ANNAH SUTTON and JOHN SUTTON. Payment in order to convey deed to S 15, T 3, R 2. Signed JOHN VAN NISE. Witn: SAMUEL AYERS, DAVID AYERS. rec 1806. p 308

page 309 blank

Deed dated 1806. WILLIAM LEGG JR & SUSANNAH his wife to ASHBEL WALLER.   S 6, T 2, R 2. Signed WILLIAM LEGG, SUSANNAH (x) LEGG. Witn: JP WILLIAM HAYS, ANDW. CHRISTY. rec 1806. p 310

Deed dated 1806. GEORGE NIXON & MARY ANNA his wife of George Twp, Fayette Co, PA to ALLEN NIXON. S 20, T 3, R 2. Land previously owned by WILLIAM NIXON, father of George and Allen. Signed GEO. NIXON, MARY ANNA NIXON. Witn: MOSES NIXON, RICHARD WEAVER. rec 1806. p 311

Deed dated 1806. ISRAEL COON & SARAH his wife, GEORGE SUTTON, JEREMIAH SUTTON & REBECKAH his wife, DAVID SUTTON & MARY his wife, ROSEANNAH SUTTON & JOHN SUTTON to JOHN VAN NISE. S 15, T 3, R 2. Signed ISRAEL COON, SARAH COON, ELIJAH SMITH as atty for JEREMIAH & REBECKAH SUTTON, DAVID SUTTON, MARY SUTTON, ROSEANNAH SUTTON, JOHN SUTTON. Witn: DAVID AYERS, SAMUEL AYERS. rec 1806. pp 312, 313

Deed dated 1806. MAHLON FORD to DAVID URMSTON. S 3, T 2, R 3. Signed OLIVER SPENCER, agent for Ford. Witn: A.M. SPENCER, JOHN ARMSTRONG. rec 1806. p 313

Deed dated 1806. JOHN FINNEY & ELIZABETH his wife to WILLIAM LEGG JR. S 6, T 2, R 2. Signed JOHN FINNEY, ELIZABETH (x) FINNEY. Witn: WILLIAM SYMMES, JOSEPH POTTER. rec 1806. p 314

Deed dated 1806. PETER VORHEES & LAMME his wife to DAVID WILLIAMSON. S 14, T 3, R 3. Bound by land of JOHN BEATY, PETER VORHEES. Signed PETER VORHEES, LAMME VORHEES. Witn: DANL NELSON, THOMAS HILL. rec 1806. p 315

BUTLER COUNTY LAND RECORDS: BOOK A

Deed dated 1806. OLIVER SPENCER & ANNE his wife to JAMES REED. S 31, T 3, R 3. Signed OLIVER SPENCER, ANNE SPENCER. Witn: JP CHARLES SWEARINGEN. rec 1806. p 316

Deed dated 1806. JONATHAN DAYTON to DAVID URMSTON. S 13, T 2, R 3. Signed JONATHAN DAYTON by JOHN REILY, his atty. Witn: JOSEPH F. RANDOLPH, JAMES REED. rec 1806. p 317.

Deed dated 1806. WILLIAM PATTON & JANE his wife to JAMES HEATON. Hamilton lots 202, 203. Signed WILLIAM PATTON, JANE PATTON. Witn: SAM. McCULLAGH, THOMAS WOOLVERTON. JP JOHN VENNEDGE. rec 1806. p 319

Deed dated 1806. JOHN LUDLOW & SUSAN his wife to SAMUEL LYON. Hamilton lot 54. Signed JOHN LUDLOW, SUSAN LUDLOW. Witn: SALLY LYON, MARY LUDLOW. JP ENAS HUSON. rec 1806. p 319

Deed dated 1806. JONAH ENYART & ELIZABETH his wife to DAVID BURNET. S 21, T 2, R 3. Bound by land of WILLIAM PATTON, TIMOTHY WOODRUFF. Signed JONA ENYART ELIZABETH (x) ENYART. Witn: JOHN REILY, FRANCIS McMILLAN. rec 1806. p 320

Deed dated 1806. Dr. EVAN BANES to RICHARD L. THOMAS. S 12, T 2, R 2; S 36, T 5, R 1; S 6, T 4, R 1; except lands conveyed to -- JONES and RICHARD BENHAM. Signed EVAN BANES. Witn: BENJAMIN RICE, LEWIS RUE. JP SILAS HURIN. rec 1806. p 321

Deed dated 1806. ANDREW CHRISTY & ELIZABETH his wife to ISAAC WILES. Hamilton lot 198. Signed ANDW. CHRISTY, ELIZABETH (x) CHRISTY. Witn: JAMES HAYS, WILLIAM HAYS. rec 1806. p 322

Deed date 1799. JONATHAN DAYTON to JOHN REEVE, assignee of WILLIAM CLARK of Burlington Co, NJ. S 19, T 3, R 3. Signed JONA. DAYTON. Witn: RUB. COX, ELIAS I. DAYTON. rec 1806. p 323

Deed dated 1805. CHARLOTTE CHAMBERS LUDLOW & JAMES FINDLAY to SAMUEL McCONNELL. Hamilton lot 36. Signed CHARLOTTE CHAMBERS LUDLOW, JAMES FINDLAY. Witn: JOS. CONN SR. JAMES EWING. rec 1806. p 324

page 325 blank

Deposition dated 1791. JOSEPH McMAHIN applied for S 4, T 2, R 2, property of Col. JNO. N. CUMMINS, based on forfeiture by non-settlement. Unsigned by

BUTLER COUNTY LAND RECORDS: BOOK A

applicant. JOHN CLEVES SYMMES, Registrar of Miami Land Office. JP JAMES EWING. rec 1806. p 326

Deposition dated 1791. GEORGE CULLUM JR applied for land 2 34, T 3, R 2, property of MAHLON FORD, based on forfeiture by non-settlement. Signed and witness as above. rec 1806. p 326

Deed dated 1806. JOHN WINGATE & MARY his wife to WILLIAM RIDDLES. Hamilton lot 149. Signed JOHN WINGATE, MARY WINGATE. Witn: ROBT. ROSEBROUGH, JOHN REILY. rec 1806. p 327

Mortgage dated 1806. JOHN WINGATE & THOMAS DILLON to ROBERT ROSEBROUGH. S 24, T 2, R 2. Paymt due 1808. Signed JOHN WINGATE, THOS. DILLON. Witn: JOHN REILY, WM. RIDDELS. rec 1806. p 325

Deed dated 1806. JOHN BUCHANAN & REBEH. his wife to JOHN WINGATE. Hamilton lot 149. Signed JOHN BUCHANAN, REBEH. BUCHANAN. Witn: AR. ST.CLAIR JR, WILLIAM CORRY. rec 1806. p 330

Deed dated 1806. ROBERT ROSEBROUGH & MARY his wife to THOMAS DILLON. S 24, T 2, R 2. Signed ROBERT ROSEBROUGH, MARY (x) ROSEBROUGH. Witn: JOHN REILY, WM. RIDDELS. rec 1806. p 330

Deed dated 1806. JONATHAN DAYTON to JOHN HARDIN. S 25, T 3, R 3. Signed JONA. DAYTON. Witn: EDWARD WHITE, AARON DAYTON. JP JAMES LYON. JP ZEBULON FOSTER. rec 1806. p 331

Deed dated 1795. ISRAEL LUDLOW to Capt. DARIUS C. ORCUTT. Hamilton lot 16. Signed ISRAEL LUDLOW. Witn: THOS. McCULLOUGH, JOHN GREER. JP D.C. ORCUTT. rec 1806. p 332

Deed dated 1806. DARIUS CURTISS ORCUTT to SAMUEL McCONNELL. Hamilton outlot 16. Signed D.C. ORCUTT. Witn: JOHN ORBISON, JACOB LINE, ISAAC STANLEY. rec 1806. p 333

Deed dated 1806. WILLIAM SMITH & ELIZABETH his wife to WILLIAM HALL, late of Center Co. PA. S 32, T 2, R 2. Signed WILLIAM SMITH, ELIZABETH SMITH. Witn: JP JAS. DUNN, WILLIAM MITCHEL. rec 1806. p 334

Deed dated 1806. WILLIAM SYMMES & REBECKAH his wife to PHILLIP DROLLINGER. S 9, T 2, R 2. Signed WILLIAM SYMMES, REBECKAH SYMMES. Witn: ISC. S. SWEARINGEN, THOMAS (x) McGRAW. rec 1806. p 335

BUTLER COUNTY LAND RECORDS: BOOK A

Deed dated 1806. Admtrs of ISRAEL LUDLOW to SAMUEL C. VANIE. Hamilton outlot 9. Signed CHARLOTTE CHAMBERS LUDLOW, JAMES FINDLAY, JOHN LUDLOW, SINEAS PIERSON. Witn: N.C. FINDLAY, JOHN MAHARD. rec 1806. p 336

Deed dated 1806. SAMUEL STITES & MARTHA his wife to JOSEPH DELAPLANE. S 12, T 3, R 3. Bound by land of JOHN LOWRY, -- STUART. Signed SAMUEL STITES, MARTHA STITES. Witn: JOSEPH FOUTS, JAMES FOWLER. rec 1806. p 337

Deed dated 1806. JOSEPH DELAPLANE & JANE ANN his wife to MATTHEW G. WALLACE. S 12, T 3, R 3. Signed JOSEPH DELAPLANE, JANE ANN DELAPLANE. Witn: HANNAH WILLIS, JAMES EWING. rec 1806. pp 337, 338

Deed dated 1806. KNOLES SHAW & SOPHIA his wife to FRANCIS WHITINGER. S 33, T 3, R 2. Signed KNOLES SHAW, SOPHIA (x) SHAW. Witn: JUDAH WILLEY, JNO. BRASHER. rec 1806. pp 338, 339

Deed dated 1806. SAMUEL LYON & MARGARET his wife to LUDLOW PIERSON. Hamilton lot 54. Signed SAMUEL LYON MARGARET (x) LYON. Witn: SALLY LYON, EPHRAIM LUMMINS. rec 1806. p 339

Deed dated 1806. SAMUEL LYON & MARGARET his wife to LUDLOW PIERSON. S1, T 1, R 3. Signed SAMUEL LYON, MARGARET (x) LYON. Witn: STEPHEN LUDLOW, EPHARIAM LUMMIS. rec 1806. p 340

Deed dated 1806. GEORGE DRUMMOND & RONANNA his wife to CORNELIUS HALL. S 3, T 1, R 2. Bound by land of JOSEPH POWERS, DANIEL PIERSON, JOSHUA ROWLAND. Signed GEORGE DRUMMOND, RONANNA DRUMMOND. Witn: WM. McCLELLAN, WILLIAM CORRY. rec 1807. p 341

Mortgage date 1806. JOSHUA ROWLAND to CORNELIUS HALL. S 3, T 1, R 2. Paymt due 1807. Bound by land of DAVID BEATY, DAVID BRANT, PETER WILCOCKS & DANIEL PIERSON. Signed JOSHUA ROWLAND. Witn: JOHN REILY, GEORGE DRUMMOND, WM. McCLELLAN. rec 1807. p 342

Deed dated 1803. WILLIAM LUDLOW & ELIZABETH his wife to SAMUEL TAPPEN. S 20, T 2, R 2. Signed WILLIAM LUDLOW, ELIZABETH LUDLOW. Witn: BENJAMIN PRICE, JOHN (x) HAND. rec 1807. p 343

Deed dated 1798. JOHN CLEVES SYMMES to DAVID POWERS, assignee of SETH BATES. S 20, T 2, R 2. Forfeited

BUTLER COUNTY LAND RECORDS: BOOK A

by THOMAS KING. Signed JOHN CLEVES SYMMES. Witn: JAMES BENNETT, JAMES (x) MARSHALL, PAUL PETRO. rec 1807. p 344

Deed dated 1806. Admrs of ISRAEL LUDLOW to DARIUS C. ORCUTT. Hamilton lot 122. Signed CHARLOTTE CHAMBERS LUDLOW, JAMES FINDLAY, JOHN LUDLOW, SINEAS PIERSON. Witn: N.C. FINDLAY, JOHN MAHARD. rec 1807. pp 344,345

Mortgage dated 1806. MATHEW B. WALLACE to ABRAHAM GARRISON. S 31, T 2, R 2. Paymt due 1807. Signed M. G. WALLACE. Witn: JOHN REILY, JACOB LEWIS. rec 1807. pp 345, 346

Deed dated 1798. JOHN CLEVES SYMMES to MARY HAYLE, wife of PHILIP HAYLE & late widow of MICHAEL HAWN. S 27, T 2, R 2. Forfeited by WILLIAM FINDAL of NJ. Signed JOHN CLEVES SYMMES. Witn: PETER WILSON, WM. H. HARRISON, ROBT. McCLURE, AARON CADWELL. rec 1807. p 347

Quitclaim dated 1806. ASA HERVEY, CHRISTOPHER HARVEY, CHARLES CONE & JANE his wife, RICHARD MACK & BETTY his wife, JOHN RAMSEY JR & LUCY his wife, JABEZ WARNER JR & ELIZABETH his wife of CT, and SAMUEL HUSTON & ELIZABETH his wife to JAOB CORNSTOCK*. S 9, T ?, R ?; S 28, T 3, R 2 and S 5, T 2, R 2. Signed ASA HERVEY, CHRISTOPHER HARVEY, CHARLES CONE, JANE CONE, RICHARD MACK, BETTY MACK, JOHN RAMSEY JR, LUCY RAMSEY, SAMUEL HUSTON, ELIZABETH HUSTON and JUDAH WILLEY, atty for JABEZ & SARAH WARNER. Witn: M. PARKISON, JAMES STEEL, JOHN CAMPBELL, STEPHEN CAMPBELL. JP JAMES MOORE. rec 1807. pp 348, 349 *JOAB COMSTOCK

Deed dated 1807. JOSEPH PARKS & JANE his wife to JAMES RUSSEL. S 10, T 2, R 4. Signed JOSEPH PARKS, JANE PARKS. Witn: EZEKIAL BALL, HANNAH BALL. rec 1807. p 350

Quitclaim dated 1806. Heirs of ASA HARVEY to CHARLES CONE & JANE his wife. S 4, T ?, R ?; S 29, T 3, R 2. Signed ASA HERVEY, CHRISTOPHER HARVEY, RICHARD MACK, BETTY MACK, JOHN RAMSEY JR, LUCY RAMSEY, SAMUEL HUSTON, ELIZABETH HUSTON and JUDAH WILLEY, atty for JABEZ & SARAH WARNER. Witn: M. PARKISON, JAMES STEEL, JOHN CAMPBELL, STEPHEN CAMPBELL. rec 1807. p 351

Deed dated 1804. BENJAMIN ENYART to RUFUS ENYART. S 9, T 2, R 3. Bound by land of DAVID ARMSTONS. Signed BENJAMIN ENYART. Witn: JOHN LINE, SAMUEL ENYART. rec 1807. p 352

BUTLER COUNTY LAND RECORDS: BOOK A

Deed dated 1807. BENJAMIN ENYART & JOANNA his wife to RUFUS ENYART. S 9, T 2, R 3. Bound by land of DAVID ARMSTONS. Signed BENJAMIN ENYART, JONNA (x) ENYART. Witn: PATRICK MOORE, JOHN VINNEDGE. rec 1807. p 353

Deed dated 1807. GEORGE HARLAN, tax collector of Fairfield Twp, to JAMES HEATON. Hamilton lot 9. Signed GEO. HARLAN, Collector. Witn: ISAAC STANLEY. DANIEL (x) HILL. rec 1807. p 354

Deed dated 1805. ELLIS JOHN & MARGARET his wife to BENJAMIN DECKER of KY. S 14, T 3, R 2. Signed ELLIS JOHN, MARGARET JOHN. Witn: JOSEPH GRAHAM, CATRIN (x) LOWRY. rec 1807. p 355

Deed dated 1807. GEORGE ADAMS & SARAH his wife to CHARLES BRUCE. S 6, T 1, R 2. Bound by JAMES SEWARD's land. Signed GEO. ADAMS, SARAH (x) ADAMS. Witn: JOHN AYERS, JOHN REILY. JP JOHN McCALL. rec 1807. pp 355, 356

Mortgage dated 1807. CHARLES BRUCE to GEORGE ADAMS. S 6, T 1, R 2. Paymt due 1810. Signed CHARLES BRUCE. Witn: JOHN AYERS, JOHN REILY. rec 1807. pp 356, 357

Deed dated 1807. JOSEPH POWERS & SALOME his wife to CORNELIUS HALL. S 3, T 1, R 2; bound by DANIEL PIERSON's land. Signed JOSEPH POWERS, SALOME (x) POWERS. Witn: JOHN REILY, WILLIAM CORRY. rec 1807. pp 357, 358

Deed dated 1805. JOHN HARVEY & ELIZABETH his wife to JOHN AYERS. S 1, T 2, R 3. Signed JOHN HARVEY, ELIZ- ABETH (x) HARVEY. Witn: SAM HEIGHWAY, SAMUEL SEWARD, JP WILLIAM HAYS, JANE (x) HAYS. rec 1807. p 358

Deed dated 1807. RUBEN CARTER & CATHERINE his wife to JOHN AYRS. S 10, T 2, R 2. Signed REUBEN CARTER, CATHERINE (x) CARTER. Witn: HUMPHRY NICHOLS, MOSES CRANE. rec 1807. p 359

Deed dated 1806. CORNELIUS R. SEDAM & ELIZA his wife to WILLIAM MURRY. S 1, T 1, R 3. Signed CORN. R. SEDAM, ELIZA SEDAM. Witn: GEO. CARPENTER, BELINDA BRADFORD, JP WILLIAM T. CULLORN. rec 1807. p 360

Deed dated 1807. AUDITORS appted by Court to THOMAS McCULLOUGH. Hamilton lot 28 seized in judgement obtained by JOHN HAMILTON against JOSEPH W. LOYD,

BUTLER COUNTY LAND RECORDS: BOOK A

sold at auction. Signed ISAAC STANLEY, JNO. TORRENCE
ISAAC WILES. Witn: CHAS. BRUCE, JOSEPH F. RANDOLPH.
rec 1807. p 361

Deed dated 1807. ROBERT DUNN & LYDIA his wife to
CORNELIUS HALL. S 2, T 1, R 2. Signed ROBERT DUNN,
LYDIA (x) DUNN. Witn: JOHN DUNN, JAMES ELLIOT, JP
JAMES DUNN. rec 1807. p 362

Deed dated 1807. STEPHEN VAIL to AARON VAIL & RANDAL
VALE. S 21, T 2, R 4 "for natural love and affection". Bound by ANDREW CLAWSON's land. Signed
STEPHEN VAIL. Witn: HENRY VAIL, HENRY WEAVER. rec
1807. p 363

Deed dated 1807. GEORGE HARLAN, tax collector of
Fairfield Twp, to WILLIAM MURRY. Hamilton lot 214.
Signed GEO. HARLAN, Collector. Witn: ISAAC STANLEY,
ISAAC WILES. rec 1807. p 364

Deed dated 1806. AMOS VALLENTINE & RODA his wife to
PETER WILLIAMSON. S 10, T 3, R 3. Signed AMOS
VALLENTINE, RODA (x) VALLENTINE. Witn: ISC. S.
SWEARINGEN, GEORGE WILLIAMSON. rec 1807. p 365

Deed dated 1807. JOSEPH ELY & CATHARINE his wife to
MOSES VAIL. No S-T-R, only description. Signed
JOSEPH ELY, CATHARINE ELY. Witn: EPHRAIM SIMPSON, JP
AARON REEDER.. rec 1807. p 366

Deed dated 1807. WILLIAM McCLELLAND, Sheriff Butler
Co, to ISAAC SWEARINGEN. S 18, T 3, R 2. Court
ordered partition of land of PATRICK GRAHAM, decd, by
THOMAS HILL, DANIEL NELSON & JOHN BEATY. Unable to
satisfy heirs JOSEPH, LEVI, MARY, AARON & SARAH
GRAHAM; the land was ordered sold and proceeds
divided. Signed WILLIAM McCLELLAND. Witn: JOHN
REILY. rec 1807. p 367

Quitclaim dated 1796. GEORGE COLLUM JR to USUAL
BATES. S 34, T 3, R 2. Signed GEORGE (x) COLLUM.
Witn: DAVID EDGAR, MARY EDGAR, JP WILLIAM CULLOM. rec
1807. p 368

Deed dated 1806. WILLIAM PETERS (late major USA) to
WILLIAM STANLEY of Cincinnati. S 15, T 2, R 2. Signed
WILLIAM PETERS. Witn: P.T. SCHENCK, JONATHAN TAYLOR
JOHN N.C. SCHENCK, GRIFFIN YEATMAN. rec 1807. pp
368, 369

Deed dated 1807. MICHAEL LAFFERTY to HUGH MOORE.
Hamilton lots 151, 152. Signed MICHAEL LAFFERTY.

BUTLER COUNTY LAND RECORDS: BOOK A

Witn:JOHN REILY, JOHN VINNEDGE. rec 1807. p 369.

Deed dated 1795. JONATHAN DAYTON to JESSE BALDWIN of New Ark, NJ. All land within 3d range excluding S 8, 11, 16, 26 & 29 in every twp. Signed JONA. DAYTON. Witn: ELIAS I. DAYTON, NATHAN WOODRUFF. rec 1807.p370

Mortgage dated 1807. FREDERICK BLUE to JOSHUA DAVIS. S 7, T 2, R 3. Final paymt due 1808. Signed FREDERICK BLUE. Witn: JOSEPH WORTH, FRAZEE BISHOP. rec 1807. p 371

Deed dated 1806. CELADON SYMMES & PHEBE his wife to JOSHUA DAVIS. Hamilton lot 178. Signed CELADON SYMMES, PHEBE SYMMES. Witn: JOHN REILY, WILLIAM McCLELLAN. rec 1807. p 372

Deed dated 1807. GEORGE HARLAN, Collector of Fairfield Twp, to DAVID BEATY. Hamilton lot 47. Signed GEO. HARLAN, Collector. Witn: HENRY HITE, DAVID SMITH. rec 1807. p 373

Deed dated 1807. ABRAHAM GARRISON & RACHEL his wife to ISAAC STANLEY. Hamilton lot 137. Signed ABRAHAM GARRISON, RACHEL (x) GARRISON. Witn: DAVID SLOAN, CELADON SYMMES. rec 1807. p 374

Deed dated 1807. EPHRAIM CATTERLIN & SALLEY his wife to JOHN SUTHERLAND & HENRY BROWN. S 1, T 1, R 3. Signed EPHRAIM CATTERLIN, SALLEY CATTERLIN. Witn: ISAAC STANLEY, JOHN REILY. rec 1807. pp 374, 375

Deed dated 1807. DAVID GRIFFIS & POLLY his wife to JAMES & WILLIAM MURRAY. S 32, T 3, R 3. Signed DAVID GRIFFIS, POLLY GRIFFIS. Witn: ISC. S. SWEARINGEN, ROBERT LONG. rec 1807. pp 375, 376

Deed dated 1807. WILLIAM STANLEY & SALLEY his wife to JOHN REILY. Hamilton lot 73. Signed WILLIAM STANLEY, SALLEY STANLEY. Witn: LEWIS HOWELL, JOHN MAHARD rec 1807. p 377

Deed dated 1807. ZEBULON PIKE of Dearborn Co, IN Ter'y to JOHN TORRENCE. Hamilton lots 147, 148. Signed ZEBULON PIKE. Witn: THOMAS ALSTON, JOHN REILY. rec 1807. p 378

Deed dated 1806. ASA HARVEY of Crosby to JONATHAN CILLEY of Colerain Twp, Hamilton Co. 1/4 of a mill in S 4, T 2, R -. Share of partition to ASA HARVEY & CHRISTOPHER HARVEY, heirs of ASA HARVEY, dec'd.

BUTLER COUNTY LAND RECORDS: BOOK A

Signed ASA HARVEY. Witn: RICH. SINCLER, JOSEPH CILLEY. rec 1807. p 379

Mortgage dated 1806. JONATHAN DAYTON to DAVID URMSTON. S 13, T 2, R 3. Final paymt to Dayton in 1807. Signed DAVID URMSTON. Witn: JOSEPH F. RANDOLPH, JAMES REID. rec 1807. p 380.

Deed dated 1806. THOMAS POWERS & MARY his wife to JONATHAN DAVIS. Signed THOMAS POWERS, MARY POWERS. Witn: JOSEPH JINKINSON, HANNAH BALL. rec 1807. p 381

Deed dated 1807. JOSHUA DAVIS & JEREMIAH his wife to FRADRICK BLUE. S 7, T 2, R 3. Signed JOSHUA DAVIS, JEMIMA (x) DAVIS. Witn: JOSEPH WORTH, FRAZEE BISHOP. rec 1807. p 382

Deed dated 1807. GEORGE HARLAN, collector, to ISAAC STANLEY. Hamilton lot 161. Signed GEO. HARLAN, Collector. Witn: ABEL BALL, HENDERSON HARVEY. rec 1807. pp 382, 383

Deed dated 1807. GEORGE HARLAN, collector, to ISAAC STANLEY. Hamilton lot 2. Signed GEO. HARLAN, Collector. Witn: ABEL BALL, HENDERSON HARVEY. rec 1807. p 383

Deed dated 1807. GEORGE HARLAN, collector, to ISAAC STANLEY. Hamilton lot 3. Signed GEO. HARLAN, Collector. Witn: ABEL BALL, HENDERSON HARVEY. rec 1807. p 384

Deed dated 1807. GEORGE HARLAN, collector, to ISAAC STANLEY. Hamilton lot 146. Signed GEO. HARLAN. Witn: ABEL BALL, HENDERSON HARVEY. rec 1807. p 385

Deed dated 1807. GEORGE HARLAN, collector, to ISAAC STANLEY. Hamilton lot 134. Signed GEO. HARLAN, Collector. Witn: ABEL BALL, HENDERSON HARVEY. rec 1807. p 386

Deed dated 1807. GEORGE HARLAN, collector, to ISAAC WILES. Hamilton lot 51. Signed GEO. HARLAN, Collector. Witn: none. rec 1807. p 387

Deed dated 1807. LUDLOW PIERSON & ELENOR his wife to JOSEPH HOUGH. S 1, T 1, R 3. signed LUDLOW PIERSON, ELENOR PIERSON. Witn: JAMES GRIFFITH, ISAAC STANLEY. rec 1807. p 388.

Deed dated 1806. GEORGE DRUMMOND & ROSANNA his wife to JOSHUA ROWLAND. S 3, T 1, R 2. Bound by land of

BUTLER COUNTY LAND RECORDS: BOOK A

DAVID BEATY, DAVID BRANT, PETER WILCOCK, DAVID PIERSON. Signed GEORGE DRUMMOND, ROSANNA DRUMMOND. Witn: WM. McCLELLAN, WILLIAM CORRY. rec 1807. p 389

Deed dated 1807. AMOS VALLENTINE & RODY his wife to children LEVI VALLENTINE & HANNAH VALLENTINE. S 30, T 3, R 3. Signed AMOS VALLENTINE. (no wife's sign) Witn: ISC. S. SWEARINGEN, THOMAS HUNT. rec 1807. p390

Deed dated 1807. ALBIN SHAW & EUNICE his wife to FRANCES WHITEINGER. S 30, T 3, R 2. Bound by land of JAOB CORNSTOCK*, heirs of ASA HARVEY decd, KNOLES SHAW. Signed ALBIN SHAW, EUNICE SHAW. Witn: JOHN MANSFIELD, JUDAY WILLEY. rec 1807. p 391 *COMSTOCK

Deed dated 1806. ABRAHAM GARRISON & RACHEL his wife to Rev. MATTHEW G. WALLACE of Cincinnati. S 31, T 2, R 2. Signed ABRAHAM GARRISON, RACHEL (x) GARRISON. Witn: JOHN REILY, JACOB LEWIS. rec 1807. p 392

Deed dated 1806. JOHN JOHNSON & ABIGAIL his wife of New Ark, NJ to STEPHEN CRANE of same. S 31, T 3, R 3. Signed JOHN JOHNSON, ABIGAIL JOHNSON. Witn: UZAL JOHNSON, ELIAS ASBORN. rec 1807. p 393

Deed dated 1807. ELIAS CRANE & PHEBE his wife to MOSES CRANE. S 20, T 2, R 2. Signed ELIAS (x) CRANE, PHEBE (x) CRANE. Witn: WM. SYMMES, GODFREY WAGNER. rec 1807. p 394

Deed dated 1807. Admntrs of ISRAEL LUDLOW to JOSEPH NELSON. S 14, T 2, R 2. Signed CHARLOTTE CHAMBERS LUDLOW, JAMES FINDLAY. Witn: CATHARINE McFARLAND, N.C. FINDLAY. rec 1807. p 395

Deed dated 1807. JOSEPH NELSON & MARY his wife to JOHN CLAP. S 14, T 2, R 2. Signed JOHN NELSON, MARY (x) NELSON. Witn: ENOS HURON, JAMES McDONALD. rec 1807. p 396

Deed dated 1807. CHARLES CONE & JANE his wife to GRACE CONE. S 28, T 3, R 2. Signed CHARLES CONE, JANE CONE. Witn: JUDAH WILLEY, EZRA SPENCER. rec 1807. p 397

Deed dated 1807. USA to THOMAS COOCH. S 32, T 5, R 2. rec 1807. p 398

Deed dated 1806. WILLIAM ROBEY & SARAH his wife to MICHAEL LAFFERTY. Hamilton lot 164. Signed WILLIAM (x) ROBEY, SARAH (x) ROBEY. Witn: WM. HAYS, JAMES HAYS. rec 1807. p 399

BUTLER COUNTY LAND RECORDS: BOOK A

Deed dated 1807. MICHAEL LAFFERTY to HUGH MOORE of Cincinnati. Hamilton lot 164. Signed MICHAEL LAFFERTY. Witn: CELADON SYMMES, ISAAC HENDERSON. rec 1807. p 400

Plat map dated 1806. Town of JEFFERSON. S 32, T 3, R 3. Signed JOHN PATTERSON. Witn: CELADON SYMMES. rec 1807. p 401

Deed dated 1807. JOHN CARSON & MARY his wife of Warren Co to NEHEMIAH CHARLES. S 18, T 3, R 2. Signed JOHN CARSON, MARY CARSON. Witn: ISC. S. SWEARINGEN, MARY (x) CARSON. rec 1807. p 402

Deed dated 1806. Admtrs of ISRAEL LUDLOW to JOSEPH HOUGH. Hamilton lot 84. Signed CHARLOTTE CHAMBERS LUDLOW, JAMES FINDLAY, JOHN LUDLOW, SINEAS PIERSON. Witn: JOHN DICKEY, JOHN MAHARD. rec 1807. p 403

Deed dated 1806. Admtrs of ISRAEL LUDLOW to JOSEPH HOUGH. S 2, T 1, R 3. Signed and witn as above. rec 1807. p 404

page 405 blank

Deed dated 1807. JAMES McCLELLAN to DANIEL McCLELLAN S 15, T 2, R 4. Signed JAMES McCLELLAN. Witn: THOS C. WADE, JAMES BARNET. rec 1807. p 406

Deed dated 1807. JAMES McCLELLAN to JAMES McCLELLAN JR & BENJAMIN McCLELLAN. S 15, T 2, R 4. Signed JAMES McCLELLAN. Witn: ISAAC ROBINS, JAMES SUTTON JR. rec 1807. p 407

Deed dated 1807. OLIVER SPENCER & ANN his wife to ISAAC STANLEY & ISAAC WILES. S 31, T 3, R 3. Signed OLIVER SPENCER, ANN SPENCER. Witn: CHARLES SWEARINGEN, CATY SWEARINGEN. rec 1807. pp 407, 408

Mortgage dated 1807. LEVI GORE to ISAAC WILES. Hamilton lot 51. Paymt due 1810. Signed LEVI GORE. Witn: ISAAC STANLEY, BENJ. RANDLE. rec 1807. p 409

Deed dated 1795. WILLIAM MUIR to JOSEPH KENEDY. S 30, T 2, R 2. Signed WILLIAM MUIR. Witn: I. DARNELLE, DAVID CUMMINGS, RICHARD McCRANE. JP AARON CADWELL. rec 1807. p 410

Deed dated 1807. JOSEPH KENNEDY of Campbell Co, KY to ELIHU WOODRUFF. S 30, T 2, R 2. Signed JOSEPH KENNEDY. Witn: JAMES HEATON, SAMUEL DARKIES. rec 1807. p 411

BUTLER COUNTY LAND RECORDS: BOOK A

Mortgage dated 1807. ELIHU WOODRUFF to JOSEPH KENNEDY. S 30, T 2, R 2. Paymt due 1809. Signed ELIHU WOODRUFF. Witn: JAMES HEATON, SAMUEL DARKIES. rec 1807. p 412

Deed dated 1805. ARTHUR VANDERVEER & ALLCHEY his wife of Warren Co to TUNIS VANDERVEER. All of S 27 & 28, T 2, R 5. Bound by land of WILLIAM BARKALOW, WILLIAM FRANCIS. Signed ARTHUR VANDERVEER, ALLCHEY VANDERVEER. Witn: WILLIAM FRANCIS, JOHN FRANCIS, JP JACOB REEDER. rec 1807. p 413

Deed dated 1805. ARTHUR VANDERVEER & ALLCHEY his wife to TUNIS VANDERVEER. S 26, T 2, R 5. Bound by land of JOHN FRANCIS, WILLIAM FRANCIS. Signed and witn as above. rec 1807. p 414

Deed dated 1807. TUNIS VANDERVEER & MARGARET his wife to HENDRICK LANE of Warren Co. S 34, 27, 26 T 2, R 5. Signed TUNIS VANDERVEER, MARGARET VANDERVEER. Witn: W.C. SCHENCK, JOHN C. DEATH. rec 1807. pp 415, 416

Deed dated 1807. TUNIS VANDERVEER & MARGARET his wife to JOHN FRANCIS of Warren Co. S 28, T 2, R 5. Bound by DANIEL DUBOIS' land. Signed and witn as above. rec 1807. p 416

Deed dated 1807. TUNIS VANDERVEER & MARGARET his wife to BENJAMIN DUBOIS of Warren Co. S 28, T 2, R 5. Signed and witn as above. rec 1807. p 417

Deed dated 1807. TUNIS VANDERVEER & MARGARET his wife to DANIEL DUBOIS of Warren Co. S 28, T 2, R 5. Signed and witn as above. rec 1807. p 418

Deed dated 1805. FREDERICK FISHER to WILLIAM DILLON. Hamilton lots 187, 188. Signed F. FISHER. Witn: JOSHUA DELAPLANE, JOHN REILY. rec 1807. p 419

Deed dated 1807. USA to JOHN McEOWEN. S 7, T 3, R 3. rec 1807. p 420

Deed dated 1807. USA to ARTHUR ST. CLAIR JR. S 16, 21, 27 & 28, T 2, R 3. rec 1807. p 420

Deed dated 1804. DAVID GIBSON & AGNESS GIBSON, admtrs of estate of JOHN DAVIS, to ELIHU WOOD. S 13, T 1, R 2. Land bought from BRICE VIRGIN in 1798. AGNESS identified as wife of JOHN. Signed DAVID GIBSON, AGNESS (x) DAVIS. Witn: CHARLES CONE, STEPHEN CAMPBELL. rec 1807. p 421

BUTLER COUNTY LAND RECORDS: BOOK A

Deed dated 1804.   JONATHAN CILLY & DORCAS his wife of Hamilton Co to ELIHU WOOD. S 13, T 1, R 2. Signed JONA. CILLEY, DORCAS CILLEY. Witn: JOSIAH MAGOON, JUDAH WILLEY. rec 1807. p 422

page 423 blank

Deed dated 1806. Admtrs of ISRAEL LUDLOW to TIMOTHY WOODRUFF. Hamilton lot 223. Signed CHARLOTTE CHAMBERS LUDLOW, JAMES FINDLAY, JOHN LUDLOW, SINEAS PIERSON. Witn: JOHN DICKEY, JOHN MAHARD. rec 1807. p 424

Deed dated 1807.   ASA PEEK & SARAH his wife to PAUL HUSTON. S 31, T 2, R 2. Signed ASA PEEK, SARAH (x) PEEK. Witn: WM. GRAY, ROBERT FOWLER. rec 1807. p 425

Deed dated 1807.   SAMUEL SMITH & MARTHA his wife to MARSH WILLIAMS. S 4, T 5, R 2. Signed SAMUEL SMITH, MARTHA (x) SMITH. Witn: JAMES HEATON, JOHN TOLER. rec 1807.   p 426

Deed dated 1803.   HAITHORN HOOD & ELENOR his wife to STEPHEN VAIL JR of Hamilton Co.   S 15, T 2, R 2. Signed HAITHORN (x) HOOD, ELENOR (x) HOOD. Witn: ROBT. WARWICK, WILLIAM SYMMES. rec 1807. p 427

Deed dated 1803.   STEPHAN VAIL JR & ELIZABETH his wife of Cincinnati to NATHANIEL WOODRUFF of Hamilton Co. S 15, T 2, R 2. Signed STEPHEN VAIL, ELIZABETH (x) VAIL. Witn: JAMES EWING, HENRY (x) VAIL. rec 1807. p 428

Deed dated 1805. NATHANIEL WOODRUFF & PHEBE his wife to STEPHEN VAN SCOYOC of Hamilton Co. S 15, T 2, R 2. Signed NATHANIEL (x) WOODRUFF, PHEBE (x) WOODRUFF. Witn: LUKE FOSTER, PHEBE FOSTER. rec 1807. pp 428,429

Deed dated 1807.   ELIHU WOODRUFF & MARGARET his wife to ABEL CARY. S 13, T , R 2. Signed ELIHU WOODRUFF, MARGARET WOODRUFF. Witn: JAMES HEATON, ISAAC STANLEY. rec 1807.   p 429

Deed dated 1795.   ISRAEL LUDLOW & CHARLOTTE his wife to MARTHA BARTON. Hamilton lot 39. Signed ISRAEL LUDLOW, CHARLOTTE CHAMBERS LUDLOW. Witn: G. COOD, NATH. WALLAC. JP THEO. GIBSON. rec 1807. p 430.

Deed dated 1807.   ARCHIBALD MAHAN & ELIZABETH his wife to Dr. DAVID SLOAN. Hamilton lot 39. Signed ARCHIBALD MAHAN, ELIZABETH (x) MAHAN. Witn: JOHN WINGATE, GEO. HARLAN.   rec 1807. p 431, corrected in error to 432.

BUTLER COUNTY LAND RECORDS: BOOK A

Deed dated 1807. LEVI GORE & REBECCAH his wife to LUDLOW PIERSON. Hamilton lot 199. Signed LEVI GORE, REBECCAH (x) GORE. Witn: ISAAC STANLEY, BENJAMIN RANDEL, NICHOLAS DAVS. rec 1807. p 432

Mortgage date 1807. LAWRENCE CAVENAUGH to LUDLOW PIERSON. Hamilton lot 54; paymt due 1810. Signed L. CAVENAUGH. Witn: ISAAC STANLEY, BENJAMIN DAVIS. rec 1807. p 433

Deed dated 1807. ISAAC S. SWEARINGEN & BARBARA his wife to REUBEN REEDER. S WR, T E, R 2. Signed ISC. S. SWEARINGEN, BARBARA SWEARINGEN. Witn: GEORGE REEDER, WILLIAM HARPER. rec 1807. p 434

Deed dated 1807. USA to NATHAN STUBBS, assignee of JACOB SALADAY. S 35, T 4, R 3. rec 1807. p 435

Deed dated 1807. SAMUEL DICKEY & CATHERINE his wife to ALAN SIMSON. S 7, T 2, R 4. Bound by land of ANDREW WAGNER. Signed SAMUEL DICKEY, CATHERINE DICKEY. Witn: LEONARD WEAVER, HENRY WEAVER. rec 1807. p 436

Deed dated 1807. SAMUEL DICKEY & CATHERINE his wife to ANNA MARTIN. S 7, T 2, R 4. Bound by land of ALAN SIMSON. Signed and witn as above. rec 1807. p 437

Deed dated 1807. SAMUEL DICKEY & CATHERINE his wife to ANDREW WAGNER. S 7, T 2, R 4. Signed and witn as above. rec 1807. p 438

Repeat of USA to STUBBS x'd out. p 439

Deed dated 1807. SAMUEL DICKEY & CATHERINE his wife to ANDREW WAGNER. S 7, T 2, R 4. Signed SAMUEL DICKEY, CATHERINE DICKEY. Witn: LEONARD WEAVER, HENRY WEAVER. rec 1807. p 441

Mortgage dated 1807. ELIHU WOODRUFF to JOSEPH KENNEDY of KY. S 30, T 2, R 2; paymt due 1808. Signed ELIHU WOODRUFF. Witn: JAMES HEATON, SAMUEL DARKIES. rec 1807. p 441

Deed dated 1807. JOHN REILY to JAMES REED. Hamilton lots 72, 73. Signed JOHN REILY. Witn: JOHN HALL, JAS. McBRIDE. rec 1807. p 442

Quitclaim dated 1807. Heirs of ASA HARVEY to KNOLES SHAW. ASA HARVEY's portion of S 33, T 3, R 2 & S 5, T 2, R 2 bought jointly with JOHN SHAW dec'd, KNOLES SHAW, ALBIN SHAW, NOAH WILLEY & JEREMIAH BUTTERFIELD;

BUTLER COUNTY LAND RECORDS: BOOK A

purchase made 1801. Signed ASA HARVEY, CHRISTOPHER HARVEY, RICHARD MACK, BETTY MACK, CHARLES CONE, JANE CONE, JOHN RAMSEY, LUCY RAMSEY, SAM'L HUSTON, ELIZABETH HUSTON, JUDAH WILLEY as atty for JABEZ WARNER JR & SARAH WARNER of CT. Witn: JOHN JONES, RUFUS CONE, ISRAEL WILLEY, WILLIAM (x) PICKENS, GRACE (x) CONE, JP THOMAS LARISON. rec 1808. pp 443, 444

page 445 blank

Deed dated 1807. KNOLES SHAW & SOPHIA his wife to SAMUEL SMITH. No S-T-R; Bound by land of ASA HARVEY, Mr. DOMIAH. Signed KNOLES SHAW, SOPHIA (x) SHAW. Witn: JUDAH WILLEY, ISAAC STANLEY. rec 1808. p 446

Deed dated 1807. AUDITORS appted by court to BARNABUS McCAREN. JOHN HAMILTON obtained judgement against JOSEPH W. LOYD; sheriff seized Hamilton lot 24. Signed ISAAC STANLEY, JOHN TORRENCE & ISAAC WILES. Witn: CHS. BRUCE, JOSEPH F. RANDOLPH. rec 1808. p 447

page 448 blank

Deed dated 1807. AUDITORS appted by court to WILLIAM CORRY. JOHN HAMILTON obtained judgement against JOSEPH W. LOYD; sheriff seized Hamilton lot 87. Signed and witn as above. rec 1808. p 449

page 450 blank

Deed dated 1806. SAMUEL DICK to JOHN REILY. Hamilton lot 102. Signed SAMUEL DICK. Witn: WILLIAM CORRY, WM. McCLELLAN. rec 1808. p 451

Mortgage dated 1808. ARTHUR ELLIOT to THOMAS HILL. S 13, T 3, R 3. Paymt due 1812. Signed ARTHUR ELLIOT. Witn: ISC. S. SWEARINGEN, ARTHUR W. ELLIOT. rec 1808. p 452

Deed dated 1808. JOSEPH ELY & CATHARINE his wife to WILLIAM WOODWARD. S 5, T 1, R 5. Signed JOSEPH ELY, CATHARINE ELY. Witn: MOSES BADGLEY, HENRY WEAVER. rec 1808. p 453

Deed dated 1808. JOSEPH ELY & CATHARINE his wife to RHEUBEN WOODWARD. S 5, T 1, R 5. Signed and witn as above. rec 1808. p 454

Deed dated 1808. JOSEPH ELY & CATHARINE his wife to JOHN McKEAN. S 5 & 8, T 1, R 5. Signed as above. Witn: ZEBULON BARKALOW, HENRY WEAVER. rec 1808. p 455

BUTLER COUNTY LAND RECORDS: BOOK A

Deed dated 1808. JOSEPH ELY & CATHARINE his wife to GEORGE LOY. S 5, T 1, R 5. Signed JOSEPH ELY, CATHARINE ELY. Witn: MOSES BADGLEY, HENRY WEAVER. rec 1808. p 456

Deed dated 1808. THOMAS HILL & SARAH his wife to ARTHUR ELLIOT. S 13, T 3, R 3. Signed THOMAS HILL. SARAH HILL. Witn: ARTHUR W. ELLIOT, ISC. S. SWEARINGEN. rec 1808. p 457

Deed dated 1807. JONATHAN DAYTON to JOHN SMALLEY. S 10, T 2, R 3. Signed JONA. DAYTON. Witn: JOSEPH DELAPLANE, JAMES EWING. rec 1808. p 458

Deed dated 1808. EDMUND RICHARD of Warren Co to SAMUEL KENNEDY & JANE, his wife, late RICHARDSON, dau of EDMUND. S 20, T 3, R 2. Signed EDMUND RICHARDSON. Witn: JOHN SUTHERLAND, JOHN REILY. rec 1808. p 459

Deed dated 1806. JOHN CHAMBERLIN & NANCY his wife to NATHANIEL EVERINGEN. S 32, T 2, R 5. Bound by land of GEORGE LOY, JAMES TAPSCOTT. Signed JOHN CHAMBERLAIN, NANCY CHAMBERLAIN. Witn: HENRY WEAVER, SUSAN WEAVER. rec 1808. p 460

Deed dated 1806. Admtrs of ISRAEL LUDLOW to JOHN REILY. Hamilton lot 99. Signed CHARLOTTE CHAMBERS LUDLOW, JAMES FINDLAY, JOHN LUDLOW, SINEAS PIERSON. Witn: N.C. FINDLAY, JOHN MAHARD. rec 1808. p 461

Deed dated 1806. Admtrs of ISRAEL LUDLOW to JOHN REILY. Hamilton lot 100. Signed and witn as above. rec 1808. p 462

Deed dated 1806. Admtrs of ISRAEL LUDLOW to JOHN REILY. Hamilton lot 101. Signed and witn as above. rec 1808. p 463

Deed dated 1807. WILLIAM McCLELLAN, Sheriff to JOHN SUTHERLAND & HENRY BROWN. SAMUEL DILLON obtained judgement against JAMES HAMILTON. Seized S 1, T 1, R 3. Signed WILLIAM McCLELLAN. Witn: JAMES SCOTT, JOHN REILY. rec 1808. p 464

page 465 blank

Deed dated 1806. Admtrs of ISRAEL LUDLOW to JOHN TORRENCE. Hamilton lot 124. Signed CHARLOTTE CHAMBERS LUDLOW, JAMES FINDLAY, JOHN LUDLOW, SINEAS PIERSON. Witn: HENRY WEAVER, SUSAN WEAVER. rec 1808. p 467

BUTLER COUNTY LAND RECORDS: BOOK A

Deed dated 1806. Admtrs of ISRAEL LUDLOW to JOHN TORRENCE. Hamilton lot 125. Signed and witn as previous entry. rec 1808. p 467

End of BOOK A; Begin BOOK B

Deed dated 1808. Admtrs of ISRAEL LUDLOW to JOHN TORRENCE. Hamilton lot 126. Signed and witn as above. rec 1808. p 1

Deed dated 1805. WILLIAM SYMMES & REBECKAH his wife to ARCHIBALD STARK. S 9, T 2, R 2. Signed WILLIAM SYMMES, REBECKAH SYMMES. Witn: SAM'L HYNDMAN, WILLIAM WALLACE. rec 1808. pp 1, 2

Deed dated 1808. JAMES HEATON & MARY his wife of Hamilton to DANIEL MILLIKIN of same. Hamilton town lots 202, 203. Signed JAMES HEATON, MARY HEATON. Witn: ISAAC STANLEY, ISAAC WILES. rec 1808. pp 2, 3

Mortgage dated 1807. JOHN McGARA to WILLIAM SQUIER. Security: half interest in Vail's Mills, a gristmill and sawmill on Big Miami River near Middletown. Debt to be paid by 1811. Signed JOHN McGARA. Witn: JP EZEKIEL BALL, WM. GRANT JR. rec 1808. pp 3, 4

Bond dated 1808. JAMES HAMILTON to JOHN HAMILTON JR. James to convey deed for S 4, T 2, R 3 when USA issues patent. Signed JAMES HAMILTON. Witn: M. WINTON. rec 1808. pp 4, 5

Deed dated 1807. **MICHAEL** LAFFERTY of Hamilton to HUGH MOORE of Cincinnati. Hamilton town lots 151, 152. Signed **MICHEL** LAFFERTY. Witn: JOHN REILY, PATRICK MOORE. rec 1808. pp 5, 6

Mortgage dated 1807. DAVID GARRIGUS to JAMES WATSON. Land in S 15, T 1, R 2. Signed DAVID GARRIGUS. Witn: WM. WALLACE, WM. McCLELLAN. rec 1808. pp 6, 7

Lease dated 1804. BENJAMIN ENYART to JOHN LINE. S 9, T 2, R 3. Signed BENJAMIN ENYART. Witn: SAMUEL ENYART, RUFUS ENYART. rec 1808. pp 7, 8

Deed dated 1804. BENJAMIN ENYART to JOHN LINE. Land above to be held by Line. In the event of his death, to be held by Line's wife SARAH, the dau of Enyart, and her children. Signed BENJAMIN ENYART. Witn: DAVID ENYART, DAVID ARMSTON. rec 1808. pp 8, 9

Mortgage dated 1808. PHILIP McGONIGAL of Hamilton to HUGH MOORE & MICHAEL LAFFERTY. Hamilton town lots

BUTLER COUNTY LAND RECORDS: BOOK B

151, 152. Debt to be paid by 1809. Signed PHILIP McGONIGAL. Witn: PALLUS P. STUART, JAMES McBRIDE. rec 1808. pp 9, 10

Deed dated 1807. USA to JOHN SUTHERLAND & HENRY BROWN. S 31 & 32, T 2, R 3 and S 36, T 4, R 2. rec 1808. p 10

Deed dated 1807. USA to JOHN YOUNG of Hamilton. S 10, T 5, R 2. rec 1808. pp 10, 11

Deed dated 1807. BENJAMIN ENYART to DAVID ENYART. S 9, T 2, R 3. Signed BENJAMIN ENYART. Witn: CORNELIUS DOTY, JP JOHN VINNEDGE. rec 1808. pp 11, 12

Deed dated 1807. USA to LEARING MARSH of Hamilton Co. S 29, T 2, R 5. rec 1808. p 12

Deed dated 1808. LEARING MARSH & MARY his wife to JOHN MARSH. S 29, T 2, R 5. Signed LEARING MARSH, MARY (x) MARSH. Witn: DANIEL DUBOIS, JP HENRY WEAVER. rec 1808. pp 12, 13

Deed dated 1808. LEARING MARSH & MARY his wife to DANIEL DUBOIS. S 29, T 2, R 5. Signed as above. Witn: TIMOTHY MARSH, HENRY WEAVER. rec 1808. pp 13, 14

Deed dated 1808. LUDLOW PIERSON & ELENDOR his wife of Hamilton to JOHN HARVEY. Hamilton town lot 199. Signed LUDLOW PIERSON, ELENDOR (x) PIERSON. Witn: HENRY HESLY, JOHN VINNEDGE. rec 1808. pp 14, 15

Deed dated 1808. AZARIAS THORN of Hamilton to STEPHEN SCUDDER of same. Half of lot 9, Hamilton town. Signed AZARIAS THORN. Witn: JAMES HEATON, THEODOCIA THORN. rec 1808. pp 15, 16

Deed dated 1807. BENJAMIN ENYART to SAMUEL ENYART. S 9, T 2, R 3. Signed BENJAMIN ENYART. Witn: DAVID ENYART, JOHN BREES. rec 1808. pp 16, 17

Deed dated 1807. DAVID GARRIGUS & ABIGAIL his wife to WILLIAM FRAZER. S 7, T 2, R 3. Signed DAVID GARRIGUS, ABIGAIL (x) GARRIGUS. Witn: JAMES HEATON, JOHN HALL, ISAAC STANLEY. rec 1808. pp 17, 18

Bill of sale dated 1808. ALEXANDER WILLIAMS to JOHN QUICK. Livestock, farm crops and implements, household goods. Signed ALEXANDER (x) WILLIAMS. Witn: JOHN CHAPMAN, RACHEL (x) CHAPMAN. rec 1808. p 18

BUTLER COUNTY LAND RECORDS: BOOK B

Deed dated 1807. ELIAS CRANE & PHEBE his wife to UZAL EDWARDS. S 21, T 2, R 2. Signed ELIAS (x) CRANE, PHEBE (x) CRANE. Witn: WM. SYMMES, GODFREY WAGNER. JP JOSEPH HUNTER, Fairfield Twp. rec 1808. pp 18, 19

Deed dated 1808. WILLIAM COOLEY & NANCY his wife to REYNARD RYNEARSON. S 33, T 5, R 2. Signed WILLIAM COOLEY, NANCY (x) COOLEY. Witn: JOHN SUTHERLAND, JOHN BAXTER. rec 1808. pp 19, 20

Deed dated 1808. WILLIAM COOLEY & NANCY his wife to ROBERT MOORE of Hamilton Co. S 33, T 5, R 2. Signed WILLIAM COOLEY, NANCY (x) COOLEY. Witn: JOHN SUTHERLAND, JOHN BAXTER. rec 1808. pp 20, 21

Deed dated 1807. WILLIAM HERBERT of Hamilton to ISAAC STANLEY of same. Conveyed Hamilton town lots 125, 126 in payment of debt. Signed WILLIAM HERBERT. Witn: TIMOTHY GREEN, JOHN VINNEDGE. rec 1808. p 21

Deed dated 1807. USA to JOHN SUTHERLAND & HENRY BROWN. S 2, T 4, R 2. rec 1808. p 22

Deed dated 1807. JOHN MATSON JR & MARY his wife of Cincinnati to EDWARD COEN of Ross Twp. S 31, T 3, R 2. Bound by DAVID FRANCIS's land. Signed JOHN MATSON, MARY MATSON. Witn: JOHN MAHARD, ANN MAHARD. rec 1808. pp 22, 23

Mortgage dated 1808. WILLIAM HERBERT of Hamilton to ISAAC STANLEY. Hamilton town lots 187, 188. Signed WILLIAM HERBERT. Witn: JAMES McBRIDE, JOHN ORBISON. rec 1808. pp 23, 24

Deed dated 1804. CORNELIUS R. SEDAM & ELIZA his wife of Hamilton Co to JOHN TORRENCE of Hamilton. Lot 2 in S 1, T 1, R 3. Signed CORNS. R. SEDAM, ELIZA SEDAM. Witn: JOSEPH PRAUGH, JOHN MAHONEY. JP WILLIAM LEMOND. rec 1808. pp 24, 25

Mortgage dated 1808. DANIEL WOODRUFF to JOHN SMITH of Cincinnati. S 32, T 3, R 3. Bound by JAMES McCLELLAND. Debt to be paid by 1813. Signed DANIEL WOODRUFF. Witn: DAVID WADE. rec 1808. pp 25, 26

Deed dated 1807. MAHLON FORD & SOPHIA his wife of Morris Twp, Morris Co, NJ to JOSHUA DAVIS, Piscataway Twp, Middlesex Co, NJ. S 22, T 3, R 3. Signed MAHLON FORD, SOPHIA B. FORD. Witn: CATH. DOUGHERTY, JNO. DOUGHERTY. rec 1808. pp 26, 27

BUTLER COUNTY LAND RECORDS: BOOK B

Deed dated 1808. ISAAC STANLEY & NAKEY his wife and ISAAC WILES & ELIZABETH his wife to BENJAMIN RANDEL. S 31, T 3, R 3. Signed ISAAC STANLEY, ISAAC WILES, NAKEY (x) STANLEY, ELIZABETH (x) WILES. Witn: THOS. McCULLOUGH, WILLIAM BROWN. rec 1808. pp 27, 28

Deed dated 1808. JOSHUA DAVIS of Middlesex Co, NJ to VINCENT DAVIS, his son. S 22, T 3, R 3. Bound by JOHN BAKER. Signed JOSHUA DAVIS. Witn: WILLIAM WEBSTER, JONATHAN SPINNING. rec 1808. pp 28, 29

Deed dated 1808. JOHN GROVES to THOMAS WALKER. S 3, T 5, R 2. Bound by DAVID BEATY, DAVID BRANT, PETER WILCOCKS, DANIEL PEIRSON. Signed JOHN (x) GROVES. Witn: JOHN REILY, JAS. McBRIDE. rec 1808. pp 29, 30

Mortgage dated 1808. JAMES REID of Wayne Twp to ORMSBY & STANLEY of Cincinnati. S 31, T 3, R 3. Signed JAMES REID. Witn: LEWIS HOWELL, W.S. HATCH. rec 1808. pp 30, 31

pages 31/32 and 33/34 bound in reverse order

Deed dated 1808. HUGH MOORE & MARY his wife and MICHAEL LAFERTY to PHILIP McGONIGAL. Hamilton town lots 151, 152. Signed HUGH MOORE, MICH'L LAFERTY, MARY MOORE. Witn: JAMES McBRIDE, JOHN McGONIGLE. rec 1808. pp 31, 32

Deed dated 1807. AMOS VALLENTINE & RHODY, his wife to PETER WILLIAMSON. S 10, T 3, R 3. Signed AMOS VALLANTINE, RODY (x) VALLANTINE. Witn: ISC. S. SWEARINGEN, GEORGE WILLIAMSON. rec 1808. pp 32, 33

Deed dated 1808. HEZEKIAH BROADBERRY & AGNESS his wife to JAMES CLARK. S 35, T 2, R 2. Signed HEZEKIAH BROADBURY, AGNESS BROADBURY. Witn: ISAAC STANLEY, NELLY DUVALL. rec 1808. pp 33, 34

Deed dated 1808. ABEL CARY & EUNICE his wife to JOHN MORRIS. S 13, T 1, R 2. Signed ABEL CARY, EUNICE CARY. Witn: DANIEL MILLIKIN, JOHN HEATON. rec 1808. pp 34, 35

Deed dated 1808. JOHN MORRIS & ELIZABETH his wife to ELIHU WOODRUFF. S 17, T 2, R 2. Signed JOHN MORRIS, ELIZABETH (x) MORRIS. Witn: as above. rec 1808. p 35

Deed dated 1808. ELIHU WOODRUFF & MARGARET his wife to JOHN MORRIS. S 13, T 1, R 2. Signed ELIHU WOODRUFF, MARGRET WOODRUFF. Witness: JEREMIAH DUVALL,

BUTLER COUNTY LAND RECORDS: BOOK B

JAMES HEATON. rec 1808. pp 35, 36

Deed dated 1808. WILLIAM HALL & ANNA his wife to CORNELIUS HALL. Conveyance from JAMES HENRY of NJ to WILLIAM HALL of Centre Co, PA in 1808, recorded Hamilton Co Bk E, p 237 for S32, T 2, R 2. Half of parcel held in trust for Cornelius Hall; trust now discharged and title conveyed. Signed WILLIAM HALL, ANNA HALL. Witn: CELADON SYMMES, JOHN HALL. rec 1808. pp 36, 37

Quitclaim dated 1808. Heirs of JOHN SHAW to JOSEPH COX. S 20, T 3, R 2. Land purchased 1802, recorded Hamilton Co Bk E, p 592. Signed KNOLES SHAW, REUBEN ROAD (and his wife) HULDAH ROAD, ALBIN SHAW, JOHN SHAW, SALLA SHAW. Witn: JUDAH WILLEY, SAMUEL DILLON. rec 1808. pp 37, 38

Partition dated 1808. MATTHEW RICHARDSON & ANN his wife, JESSE SIMPSON & ANN his wife and JAMES SIMPSON to JAMES MARTIN. Tenants in common on S 23, T 5, R 2; land now divided. Signed MATTHEW RICHARDSON, JESSE SIMPSON, JAMES SIMPSON, ANN RICHARDSON, ANN SIMPSON. Witn: JP R. LYTLE, JAMES SCOTT. rec 1808. pp 40, 41

page 41/42 bound upside down

Partition dated 1808. JAMES MARTIN & ANN his wife, MATTHEW RICHARDSON & ANN his wife to JESSE SIMPSON & JAMES SIMPSON. land as above. Signed JAMES MARTIN, MATTHEW RICHARDSON, ANN MARTIN, ANN RICHARDSON. Witn: as above. rec 1808. pp 41, 42

Deed dated 1807. THOMAS HUNT SEIGNER & DURAN WHITTLE-SEY of Liberty Twp and THOMAS HUNT GUNIER & CHARLES WEST of Turtle Creek Twp, Warren Co to HORATIO SHARP of Liberty Twp. S 20, T 3, R 3. Signed THOMAS HUNT, DURAN WHITTLESEY, THOMAS HUNT JR, CHARLES WEST. Witn: ISC. S. SWEARINGEN, JOHN HARDEN, SILAS HURIN, E. HATHAWAY. rec 1808. pp 42, 43

Deed dated 1808. JAMES MAPES & NELLEY his wife to GABRIEL HENSLEY. S 23, T 3, R 3. Bound by DANIEL GOBEL. Signed JAMES MAPES, NELLEY (x) MAPES. Witn: JP WILLIAM MITCHELL, STEPHEN ARMSTRONG, ESTHER (x) MITCHELL. rec 1808. pp 43, 44

Deed dated 1808. JOSHUA DAVIS of Middlesex Co, NJ to OLIVER KELLEY. S 22, T 3, R 3. Bound by JOHN BAKER's

BUTLER COUNTY LAND RECORDS: BOOK B

land. Signed JOSHUA DAVIS. Witn: WILLIAM WEBSTER, JONATHAN SPINNING. rec 1808. p 44

Deed dated 1808. BENJAMIN RANDLE & ALLA his wife to JERVICE HUFFAM of St. Clairs Twp. S 31, T 3, R 3. Signed BENJAMIN RANDEL, ALLA RANDEL. Witness: JP JAMES MILLS, JAMES WHITE. rec 1808. pp 44, 45

Deed dated 1804. USA to JACOB MILLER. S 25, T 4, R 1. rec 1808. pp 45, 46

Deed dated 1808. JACOB MILLER to WILLIAM MITCHELL. S 25, T 4, R 1. Signed JACOB MILLER. Witn: JOHN REILY, ISAAC STANLEY. rec 1808. pp 46, 47

Deed dated 1808. SAMUEL TAPPEN of Warren Co to DAVID POWERS. S 20, T 2, R 2. Signed SAMUEL TAPPEN. Witn: JONATHAN CRANE, ISAAC HUNT. rec 1808. p 47

Deed dated 1807. EDWARD COEN & MARGARET his wife of Ross Twp to JAMES COEN of same. S 31, T 3, R 2. Signed EDWARD COEN, MARGARET (x) COEN. Witn: JP MAXWELL PARKISON, MAHALA PARKINSON, JAMES SHIELDS. rec 1808. pp 47, 48

Deed dated 1808. WILLIAM BALDWIN & MARY his wife to MARK HARRIS. S 18, T 2, R 4. Signed WILLIAM BALDWIN MARY BALDWIN. Witn: JACOB KEMP, HENRY WEAVER. rec 1808. pp 48, 49

Deed dated 1807. NATHANIEL BELL & MARY his wife of Wayne Twp to DANIEL PAGE of same. S 1, T 3, R 3. Signed NATHANIEL BELL, MARY (x) BELL. Witn: MATTHEW (x) MASHBURN, JP NATHAN STUBBS. rec 1808. pp 49, 50

Deed dated 1808. OBEDIAH SCHENCK & ABIGAIL his wife to JOHN CASSIDY & PATRICK CASSIDY. Lot 3 in S 10, T 1, R 2. "partitioned as portion of ABIGAIL FREEMAN by Butler Co Court of Common Pleas". Obediah "intermarried with" Abigail. Signed OBEDIAH SCHENCK, ABBEY SCHENCK. Witn: WILLIAM SCHENCK, EZRA F. FREEMAN. rec 1808. pp 50, 51

Deed dated 1808. JOEL WILLIAMS & PHEBE his wife of Cincinnati to DANIEL BROUIS. S 3, T 2, R 3E. Signed JOEL WILLIAMS, PHEBE WILLIAMS. Witn: ROBT. SMITH, JOHN MAHARD. rec 1808. pp 51, 52

Deed dated 1808. WILLIAM BALDWIN & MARY his wife of Lemon Twp to EDWARD GEE of same. S 18, T 2, R 4.

BUTLER COUNTY LAND RECORDS: BOOK B

Signed WILLIAM BALDWIN, MARY BALDWIN. Witn: JOHN SAMUEL MAN, HENRY WEAVER. rec 1808. pp 52, 53

Deed dated 1808. EDWARD GEE of Lemon Twp to JOB GEE of same. S 18, T 2, R 4. Signed EDWARD (x) GEE. Witn: as above. rec 1808. p 53

Deed dated 1807. SAMUEL BONNEL of Springfield Twp, Hamilton Co to LEWIS BONNEL of same. S 7, T 3, R 3. Signed SAM'L BONNEL. Witn: JAMES COLWELL, ROBERT CARSON. JP THOMAS HIGGINS of Hamilton Co: "appeared before me SAMUEL BONNEL & ELIZABETH his wife." rec 1808. pp 53, 54

Deed dated 1808. HUMPHREY NICHOLES & ISABELLA his wife to WILLIAM NICHOLES. S 2, T 2, R 3. Signed HUMPHREY NICHOLS, ISABELLA (x) NICHOLS. Witn: ISC. S. SWEARINGEN, SALLY (x) NICHOLS. rec 1808. pp 54, 55

Deed dated 1808. HUMPHREY NICHOLES & ISABELLA his wife to WILLIAM NICHOLES. Hamilton town lots 12, 71. Signed HUMPHREY NICHOLS, ISABELLA (x) NICHOLS. Witn: as above. rec 1808. pp 55, 56

Deed dated 1808. JOHN VAUGHN & RUTH CROSBY VAUGHN his wife of Ross Twp to JAMES NICHOLS of same. S 25, T 3, R 1E. Signed JOHN VAUGHN, RUTH CROSBY VAUGHN. Witn: JP MAXWELL PARKISON, JAMES SHIELDS. rec 1808. pp 56, 57

Deed dated 1808. JOHN HARDEN & CATRIN his wife to ANDREW WAYT. S 25, T 3, R 3. Bound by JOSEPH MALOLLY. Signed JOHN (x) HARDEN, CATRIN (x) HARDEN. Witn: ISC. S. SWEARINGEN, JOSEPH MULLALLOY. rec 1808. p 57

Deed dated 1808. ARCHIBALD STARK & NELLY his wife to JOHN SINNARD. S 9, T 2, R 2. Signed ARCHIBALD STARK, NALLY STARK. Witn: JOSEPH POTTER, WILLIAM SINNARD. rec 1808. pp 57, 58

Deed dated 1803. JAMES THOMSON & ANN his wife to THOMAS GALISPY. S 21 & 15, R 3, R 2. Signed JAMES (x) THOMSON, ANN (x) THOMSON. Witn: TMS. CAMPBELL, THOMAS MULLEN. rec 1808. pp 58, 59

Bill of sale dated 1808. FRANCIS WHITEINGER to HENRY WHITEINGER. "all my property, real and personal, lands and tenements, cattle and furniture", etc. No S-T-R. Signed FRANCIS WHITINGER. Witn: EMANUEL VANTREES, DAVID McCANCE. rec 1808. p 59

BUTLER COUNTY LAND RECORDS: BOOK B

Deed dated 1808. PHILIP McGONNEGAL & CATHERINE his wife of Hamilton to HUGH MOORE of Cincinnati. Hamilton town lots 51, 52. Mortgage held by Moore. Signed PHILIP (x) McGONNEGAL, CATHERINE (x) McGONNEGAL. Witn: ELIAS GLOVER. rec 1808. pp 59, 60

Bill of sale dated 1808. PHILIP McGONNEGAL to HUGH MOORE. Interest in 20 acres of corn on land rented from JOHN SMITH, livestock, household goods, guns and other personal property. Signed PHIL COGAL. Witn: as previous entry. rec 1808. p 60

Deed dated 1808. WILLIAM SYMMES & REBEKAH his wife to DANIEL SYMMES of Cincinnati. S 9, T 3, R 2. Signed WM. SYMMES, REBEKAH SYMMES. Witn: JOHN BROWN, ETH'N A. BROWN. rec 1808. pp 60, 61

Deed dated 1807. ZACHEUS GOLDSMITH & MARY his wife of Southhold, Suffolk Co, NY to DAVID SLOAN of Fairfield Twp. No S-T-R; in Fairfield Twp. Bound by land of CELADON SYMMES, WILLIAM WELLS, WILLIAM OSBORN & -- HUNT. Signed ZACHEUS GOLDSMITH, POLLY GOLDSMITH. Witn: THOMAS L. LESTER, STEPHEN CRANE. rec 1808. p 61

Deed dated 1808. DAVID GARRIGUS & ABIGAIL his wife to WILLIAM DAVID. S 7, T 2, R 3. Signed DAVID GARRIGUS, ABIGAIL (x) GARRIGUS. Witn: JAMES HEATON, JACKSON AYERS. rec 1808. pp 61, 62

Deed dated 1808. ABRAHAM FREEMAN to DR. CLARKSON FREEMAN of Lancaster, Lancaster Co, PA. S 35, T 3, R 3. Bound by land of HENRY FREEMAN, DAVID GREGORY. Signed ABM. FREEMAN. Witn: JP WM. HAYS, JONATHAN PARKER. rec 1808. p 62

Deed dated 1808. ABRAHAM FREEMAN to ABRAHAM FITZ FREEMAN JR. S -, T 3, R 3. Bound by land of DAVID & SAMUEL GREGORY, ABRAHAM FREEMAN, OBADIAH SCHENCK. Conveyance based on condition that AFF JR give quitclaim and release to AF (admr of estate of ISAAC FREEMAN) the $100 to which AFF JR was heir. Signed ABM. FREEMAN. Witn: as above. rec 1808. pp 62, 63

Deed dated 1808. ABRAHAM FREEMAN to JOHN FITZ FREEMAN. S 35, T 3, R 3, except "land already deeded to CLARKSON FREEMAN, ABRAHAM FITZ FREEMAN JR & HENRY FITZ FREEMAN." Conditions as above. Signed and witn as above. rec 1808. pp 63, 64

Deed dated 1808. JOHN SMITH & ELIZABETH his wife of Cincinnati to GEORGE LEE of same. S 32, T 3, R 3.

BUTLER COUNTY LAND RECORDS: BOOK B

Bound by DAVID GRIFFIS' land. Signed JOHN SMITH, ELIZABETH SMITH. Witn: THOMAS H. SILL, JOHN MAHARD. rec 1808. p 64

Deed dated 1808. JOHN LUCAS & JEMIMA his wife to ALEXANDER WEIR. S 11 7 12, T 2, R 4. Signed JOHN LUCAS, JEMIMA (x) LUCAS. Witn: WILLIAM SCHENCK, SUSANNA LUCAS. JP THOS. C. WADE. rec 1808. pp 64, 65

Power of Attorney dated 1808. CLARKSON FREEMAN of PA named JOHN CASSADY as attorney to recover personal property and money due from ABRAHAM FREEMAN. Signed CLARKSON FREEMAN. Witn: DAVID GRIFFIS, JOHN FITZ FREEMAN. rec 1808. pp 65, 66

Deed dated 1808. ABRAHAM FREEMAN to Dr. CLARKSON FREEMAN of PA. Listing of livestock, personal property, household goods, farm produce to be conveyed on condition that CF pay $896 by 1810. Signed ABRAHAM FREEMAN. Witn: as above. rec 1808. p 66

Deed dated 1807. JOHN LUCAS & JEMIMA his wife to GEORGE SMOCK of Summerset Co, NJ. Money paid by JOHN WELCH on behalf of Smock. S 12, T 2, R 4. Bound by JAMES LEE. Signed JOHN LUCAS, JEMIMA LUCAS. Witn: JOHN WELCH, SUSANAH LUCAS. rec 1808. pp 66, 67

Deed dated 1805. JOHN DOTY of Fairfield Twp to SAMUEL CLARK of same. S 18, T 2, R 2. Bound by land of DANIEL DOTY, GEORGE BYERS, STEPHANAS CLARK. Signed JOHN DOTY. Witn: GEORGE SNIDER, JACOB LEWIS. rec 1808. pp 67, 68

Deed dated 1808. THOMAS ESPY & ELIZABETH his wife of Warren Co to JOHN SUTHERLAND. Hamilton lot 38. Signed THOMAS ESPY, ELIZABETH (x) ESPY. Witn: JOHN REILY, JAMES McBRIDE. rec 1808. p 68

Deed dated 1808. JOEL WILLIAMS & PHEBE his wife of Cincinnati to DANIEL BROSHIES. S 3, T 3, R 2. Signed JOEL WILLIAMS, PHEBE WILLIAMS. Witn: JOHN MAHARD, WM. OLIVER. rec 1808. pp 68, 69

Mortgage dated 1807. EZRA F. FREEMAN to JOSEPH CARPENTER. S 4, T 1, R 2. "land where JAMES BLACKBURN now resides". Signed EZRA F. FREEMAN, JOSEPH CARPENTER. Witn: SAMUEL JANES, JAS. SMITH. rec 1808. pp 70, 71

Deed dated 1808. JOHN CLEVES SYMMES to JOHN H. PIAT, assignee of STEPHEN LUDLOW, assignee of JOHN STRATTON

BUTLER COUNTY LAND RECORDS: BOOK B

the first settler. S 9, T 1, R 2. PIAT in residence 7 years, complied with terms and entitled to deed. Signed JOHN CLEVES SYMMES. Wtn: OBADIAH STEVENS, GEORGE LARISON. rec 1808. pp 71, 72

Statement dated 1808. MARTHA SMITH appeared as grantor agreeable to sale. Signed JOAB COMSTOCK, JP. Margin note: S. SMITH to M. WILLIAMS. rec 1808. p 72

Deed dated 1808. DAVID GARRIGUS & ABIGAIL his wife to JOHN MAXWELL. S 15, T 1, R 2. Signed DAVID GARRIGUS, ABIGAIL (x) GARRIGUS. Witn: ISAAC STANLEY, JAMES CLARK. rec 1808. pp 72, 73

Deed dated 1808. HENRY F. FREEMAN to CLARKSON FREEMAN of PA. S 35, T 3, R 3. Signed WILLIAM HENRY FREEMAN. Witn: AARON BOWMAN, BENJAMIN DAVIS. rec 1808. pp 73, 74

Deed dated 1808. BROWN WILSON of St. Clairs Twp to ANN WILSON. S 29, T 3, R 3. Signed BROWN WILSON. Witn: JAMES (x) POLLY, JOHN BURNS. rec 1808. p 74

Deed dated 1808. JOHN SMITH & ELIZABETH his wife of Cincinnati to JOEL WOODRUFF of Lebanon, Warren Co. S 2, T 2, R 3. Signed JOHN SMITH, ELIZABETH SMITH. Witn: LEWIS D. SMITH, JOHN MAHARD. rec 1808. pp 74,75

Mortgage dated 1808. SAMUEL JOHNSON of Ross Twp to MAXIWELL PARKISON & MAHALA his wife of the same. S 6, T 4, R 1. Signed SAMUEL JOHNSON. Witn: JOHN RICHMOND, REUBEN DOTY. rec 1808. pp 75, 76

Deed dated 1808. WILLIAM McCLELLAN, Sheriff of Butler Co to JAMES McBRIDE. GEORGE FITHIAN obtained judgement against AARON SCUDER. Seized Rossville lot 9, sold at auction. Signed WM. McCLELLAN. Witn: ISAAC STANLEY, ARCHIBALD TALBOTT. rec 1808. pp 76, 77

Deed dated 1808. JOHN YOUNG to ROBERT YOUNG. S 10, T 5, R 2. Signed JOHN YOUNG. Witn: JP ROBERT OGLE, ALEXANDER YOUNG. rec 1808. pp 77, 78

Quitclaim dated 1808. MARGARET COEN of Ross Twp, on behalf of her minor children JANE & EDWARD COEN JR to EDWARD COEN on behalf of same, his grandchildren. JAMES COEN, late husband of MGT, left will dated 5-27-1808 giving S 31, T 3, R 2 to chdrn. Mortgage held by EDWARD; to be given up if Margaret relinquishes title in favor of chdrn. Margaret to have residence unless remarries. Signed MARGARET COEN.

BUTLER COUNTY LAND RECORDS: BOOK B

Witn: MAHALA PARKINSON, MAXWELL PARKISON. rec 1809. pp 78, 79

Lien dated 1809. PATRICK SHIELDS to DANIEL SHIELDS. Livestock, household chattels, notes due from JOHN HARPER, BENJAMIN WARD, JAMES THROCKMORTON, JOSEPH BURGE, OBADIAH SCHENCK & WM. HARVEY. Signed PATRICK SHIELDS. JP SQUIER LITTELL. rec 1809. p 79

Bond dated 1807. HENRY CRUSE & JACOB LINGLE to JAMES AYRES. To convey good deed to 10 acre plot, no S-T-R. Signed HENRY CRUSE (german script), JACOB LINGALL. Witn: JAMES HEATON, THOS. McCULLOUGH. Assignment to THOMAS McCULLOUGH in 1808. Signed JAMES AYRES. Witn: JOHN LODER, REZIN VIRGIN. rec 1809. pp 79, 80

Deed dated 1808. AMOS VOLUNTINE of Warren Co to WILLIAM ROBINSON of same. S 10, T 3, R 3. Bound by PETER WILLIAMSON's land. Signed AMOS VALLANTINE. Witn: ISC. S. SWEARINGEN, P. WILLIAMSON. rec 1809. p 80

Deed dated 1798. JOHN CLEVES SYMMES of Hamilton Co, NW Ter'y to JOHN WALKER of same. S 5, T 1, R 2. Bound by JOSEPH WALKER's land. Land recpt presented by JOHN WALKER or WILLIAM LEMOND. Signed JOHN CLEVES SYMMES. Witn: BETSEY THOMPSON, JOSEPH POTTER. JP GEORGE CULLOM, Hamilton Co. rec 1809. pp 80, 81

Deed dated 1809. JAMES CUMMINGS & SARAH his wife to SAMUEL ALEXANDER. S 30, T 2, R 2. Signed JAMES CUMMINS, SARAH (x) CUMMINS. Witn: ISAAC STANLEY, JULIA CUMMINS. rec 1809. pp 81, 82

Statement dated 1809. THOMAS HUNT JR & CHARLES WEST conveyed title. ISAAC STANLEY, JP. Margin note: T. HUNT and others to H. SHARP. rec 1809. p 82

Deed dated 1808. DAVID BURNET of Hamilton Co, OH to ROBERT HILL of Dearborn Co "of state aforesaid". S 21, T 2, R 3. Bound by land of WILLIAM PATTON, TIMOTHY WOODRUFF. Signed DAVID BURNET. Witn: ENOS HURIN, JESSE HILL. rec 1809. pp 82, 83

Deed dated 1803. MOSES BEACH to DANIEL WOODRUFF. S 30, T 3, R 3. Signed MOSES BEACH. Witn: JAMES HEATON, NICHOLAS PARCELL. rec 1809. pp 83, 84

Deed dated 1808. JOHN HERVY & ELIZABETH his wife of Lemon Twp to WILLIAM PATTON. Hamilton lot 199. Signed JOHN HARVEY, ELIZABETH (x) HARVEY. Witn: ADAM DICKEY, GEORGE M. MAKEN. rec 1809. pp 84, 85

BUTLER COUNTY LAND RECORDS: BOOK B

Deed dated 1808.   ZOPHAR BALL to ISAIAH BALL & DENNIS BALL. S 21, T 2, R 3. Bound by land of JAMES LYON. PATRICK MOORE, SAMUEL KENNEDY, TIMOTHY WOODRUFF. Signed ZOPHAR BALL. Witn: JAMES McBRIDE, JOHN REILY. rec 1809. p 85

Deed dated 1807. USA to HENRY RHEA of PA. S 20, 30 & 29, T 2, R 3. rec 1809. pp 85, 86

Deed dated 1809. JOHN CLEVES SYMMES to DAVID CUMMINS of Fairfield Twp. S 17, T 2, R 2. Signed JOHN CLEVES SYMMES. Witn: ROBERT STEEL, BINA DOTY. JP JAMES SMITH. rec 1809. pp 86, 87

Deed dated 1809. EZRA FITZ FREEMAN to DAVID BEATY. S 4, T 1, R 2. Signed EZRA FITZ FREEMAN. Witn: CELADON SYMMES, DAVID BEATY JR. rec 1809. p 87

Deed dated 1808. MATTHEW WINTON & ELIZABETH his wife to ADAM RICKEY. S 32, T 3, R 3. Signed MATH. WINTON ELIZA. WINTON. Witn: CHARLES SWEARINGEN, JOHN WINTON. rec 1809. pp 87, 88

Deed dated 1809. GEORGE DEYBREAD & SUSANA his wife of Rosstown to BRYSON BLACKBURN of same. S 27, T 3, R 1. Signed GEORGE DEYBREAD (german script), SUSANA (x) DEYBREAD. Witn: MOSES (x) WRAILKEL, JOSEPH DEY- BREAD. rec 1809. pp 88, 89

Deed dated 1808. JACOB BURNET & REBECCA his wife and extrs of WILLIAM McMILLAN to MARTIN BAUM. S 12, T 3, R 2. BURNET & McMILLAN sold land to WILLIAM WILSON who assigned land to BAUM. McMillan's will directed exrs to convey title. Signed JAC. BURNET, REBECCA BURNET, CONSTANCE McMILLAN, WILLIAM CORREY. Witn: SAM'L PERRY, JOHN MAHARD. rec 1809. pp 89, 90

Deed dated 1808. MARTIN BAUM & ANN his wife of Cin- cinnati to JACOB BURNET of same. S 12, T 3, R 2. Signed MARTIN BAUM, ANN BAUM. Witn: N. LONGWORTH, JOHN MAHARD. rec 1809. pp 90, 91

Deed dated 1808. WILLIAM ROBINSON of Warren Co to AMOS VALENTINE of same. S 18, T 3, R 3. Signed WIL- LIAM ROBINSON. Witn: ISC. S. SWEARINGEN, P. WILLIAM- SON. rec 1809. pp 91, 92

Deed dated 1808. WILLIAM SYMMES & REBECKAH his wife to DANIEL SYMMES of Hamilton Co. S 9, T 2, R 2. Bound by PHILIP DROLLENGER's land. Signed WM. SYMMES

BUTLER COUNTY LAND RECORDS: BOOK B

REBECKAH SYMMES. Witn: ETH'N A. BROWN, BARTHO. FLEMING. JP STEPHEN WOOD. rec 1809. pp 92, 93

Bill of sale dated 1809. JAMES FREEL to "my son" CHARLES FREEL. Livestock, etc. Mentions account due JACOB MORES. Signed JAMES FREEL. Witn: BENONEY (x) FREEL, ESTER (x) FREEL. rec 1809. p 93

Deed dated 1809. OLIVER SPENCER & ANNA his wife of Hamilton Co to THOMAS WEST of same. (WEST JR in text) S 30, 31, T 3, R 3. Bound by land of JOHN LODER, ANDREW CHRISTY, -- WOODRUFF, BA. BAKER. Signed OLIVER SPENCER, ANNA SPENCER. Witn: STEPHEN H. BROWN, WILLIAM FLORER. rec 1809. pp 93, 94

Deed dated 1809. OLIVER SPENCER & ANNA his wife of Hamilton Co to LEWIS BAYLEY of same. S 31, T 3, R 3. Signed OLIVER SPENCER, ANNA SPENCER. Witn: WM. PERRY, WARHAM STACY. rec 1809. pp 94, 95

Deed dated 1809. JOHN CLEVES SYMMES to BRICE VIRGIN of Liberty Twp. S 2, T 2, R 3. Deed to replace one issued 1801. Deposition of deed loss dated 1809, signed BRICE VIRGIN. Witn: JP JAMES EWING. Bound by Mr. CONKLING's land, bought of JOEL WOODRUFF. Signed JOHN CLEVES SYMMES. Witn: JP WILLIAM HAYS, GUILFORD BURNS. rec 1809. pp 95, 96

Deed dated 1794. JOHN CLEVES SYMMES to JONATHAN OGDEN of Morris Co, NJ. S 36, T 2, R 2. Signed JOHN C. SYMMES. Witness: FREDERICK KING, JOSEPH JOHNSON. rec 1809. pp 96, 97

Deed dated 1808. DR. DAVID SLOAN & RACHEL his wife to HANNAH HUNTER "relict of JOSEPH HUNTER". S 28, T 2, R 2 purchased in Joseph's lifetime. Signed DAVID SLOAN, RACHEL SLOAN. Witn: CELADON SYMMES, PHEBE SYMMES. rec 1809. pp 97, 98

Deed dated 1809. JOSEPH JENKINSON & SARAH his wife of Hamilton Co to JOHN SUTHERLAND. Hamilton lot 86. Signed JOSEPH JENKINSON, SARAH JENKINSON. Witn: JOHN JENKINSON, BENJAMIN WARD. rec 1809. p 99

Deed dated 1804. JOHN N. CUMMING of NJ by his atty WILLIAM C. SCHENCK to CATHARINE CARTER. S 10, T 2, R 2. Signed JOHN NOBLE CUMMING by WILLIAM C. SCHENCK, atty. Witn: CHARLES KILLGORE, JOHN A. McDONALD. rec 1809. pp 99, 100

BUTLER COUNTY LAND RECORDS: BOOK B

Deed dated 1807. ALEXANDER CHAMBERS & MARY his wife to JACOB SNYDER. S 18, T 2, R 4. Signed ALEXANDER (x) CHAMBERS, MARY (x) CHAMBERS. Witn: LEONARD WEAVER, HENRY WEAVER. rec 1809. pp 100, 101

Mortgage dated 1807. ISAAC S. SWEARINGEN to AARON GRAHAM & SARAH GRAHAM. S 18, T 3, R 2. Signed ISAAC S. SWEARINGEN. Witn: JOHN REILY, HENRY WEAVER. rec 1809. pp 101, 102

Deed dated 1808. GEORGE LEE of Cincinnati to JOHN SMITH of same. S 32, T 3, R 3. Bound by DAVID GRIFFE'S land. Signed GEORGE LEE. Witn: THOMAS H. SILL, JOHN MAHARD. rec 1809. pp 102, 103

Deed dated 1809. JOHN V. S. DAVIS to JOHN SMITH of Hamilton Co. S 32, T 3, R 3. Bound by land of DANIEL WOODRUFF, WILLIAM and ARTHUR LEGG, GEORGE LEE, DANIEL GRIFFITH, JAMES McCLELLAND. Signed JOHN V.S. DAVIS. Witn: ARTHUR LEGG, THOMAS H. SILL. rec 1809. pp 103, 104

Mortgage dated 1809. ARTHUR LEGG to JOHN SMITH of Hamilton Co. S 2, T 2, R 3. Signed ARTHUR LEGG. Witn: A.D. SMITH, THOMAS H. SILL. rec 1809. pp 104, 105

Deposition dated 1809. JAMES DUNN witnessed 1803 deed made by JAMES SEWARD of Fairfield Twp to his son CALEB SEWARD; also witnessed by REUBEN ROOD & JOHN CAMPBLE. DUNN, questioned by JOSEPH HOHN, testified he did not hear Seward say transfer was "on account of a demand against him" nor that the deed was to be "given up whenever call upon." Signed JAS. DUNN. Witn: HENRY WEAVER, CELADON SYMMES. rec 1809. p 105

Deposition dated 1809. REUBEN ROOD testified he saw J. SEWARD sign the deed. Signed REUBEN ROOD. Witn: above. rec 1809. p 105

Deed dated 1808. JOEL WOODRUFF & POLLY his wife of Lebanon, Warren Co, to JOSIAH CONKLING. S 2, T 2, R 3. Signed JOEL WOODRUFF, POLLY (x) WOODRUFF. Witn: ENOS WILLIAMS, EDWARD WOODRUFF. rec 1809. pp 105, 106

Deed dated 1808. GEORGE CULLOM SR & <u>MARGARET</u> his wife of Hamilton Co to EDWARD CULLOM. S 36, T 3, R 2. Signed GEORGE CULLOM, <u>MARGRET</u> CULLOM. Witn: none. rec 1809. pp 106, 107

Deed dated 1809. JOHN CLEVES SYMMES to JAMES <u>AYRES</u> of Liberty Twp. In 1788, Symmes issued land warrant

BUTLER COUNTY LAND RECORDS: BOOK B

233 to RUNE RUNYAN of NJ. later transferred to JOHN AYERS, father of James, deed dated 1803. S18, T 3, R 2. New deed to clarify conveyance. Signed JOHN CLEVES SYMMES. Witn: KITTY WOOD, STEPHEN WOOD. rec 1809. pp 107, 108

Quitclaim dated 1800. JOHN M. McDONALD & REBECCA McDONALD to SAM'L EWING & MARGARET his wife. all of Hamilton Co, NW Ter'y. In 1796, J.C. SYMMES issued deed to heirs of JOHN McDONALD. S 33, T 2, R 2. Signed JOHN McDONALD, REBECCA McDONALD. Witn: JAMES McGILL, WILLIAM MITCHELL. rec 1809. p 108

Deed dated 1809. MATTHEW HUESTON & CATHERINE his wife to NATHAN HORNER. S 11, T 5, R 1. Signed M. HUESTON, CATHERINE HUESTON. Witn: H.B. HAWTHORN and JP JAMES MILLS. rec 1809. pp 108, 109

Deed dated 1809. MATTHEW HUESTON & CATHERINE his wife to JAMES ADAMS. S 11, T 5, R 1. Signed M. HUESTON, CATHERINE HUESTON. Witn: H.B. HAWTHORN and JP JAMES MILLS. rec 1809. pp 109, 110

Notice dated 1809. ABRAHAM FREEMAN & EZRA FREEMAN notified: Court of Common Pleas to hear JAMES SMITH and others at house of EMMA TORRENCE in Hamilton at request of JAMES BLACKBURN. Re land purchase in S 4, T 1, R 2 by Blackburn. Signed JAS. DUNN, HENRY WEAVER, CELADON SYMMES, associate justices, Butler Co. rec 1809. p 110

Deposition dated 1809. HUGH B. HAWTHORN testified he saw BLACKBURN serve notice on ABRAM FREEMAN. Blackburn questioned AF: concerning land conveyed from EZRA to ABRAHAM, did ABRAHAM ever have a deed? Ans: yes & recorded it at Cincinnati. Question: do you have the original? Ans: "I expect I have if EZRA has not taken it away as he is often plundering among my papers." Signed H. B. HAWTHORN. Witn: JAS. DUNN, CELADON SYMMES. rec 1809. pp 110, 111

Deposition dated 1809. JAMES SMITH testified during his term as sheriff, EZRA FREEMAN had suits filed against him by JOHN BROWN in 1799 and THOMAS COCHRAN in 1800. Smith seized S 4, T 1, R 2. Before sale to be held, ABRAHAM, father of EZRA, showed Smith a deed transferring land to Abraham. who had settled judgements against Ezra. Abraham mentioned debts he paid for his son "in Jersey" and here. Later suit against EZRA filed by JOEL WILLIAMS, settled by

BUTLER COUNTY LAND RECORDS: BOOK B

father. Signed JAMES SMITH. Witn: JAMES DUNN. CELADON SYMMES. rec 1809. p 112.

Deposition dated 1809. ANDERSON SPENCER testifed he was at farm of ABRAHAM FREEMAN when JAMES BLACKBURN questioned AF concerning land Blackburn bought, later claimed by EZRA FREEMAN as his. AF said Blackburn had paid in full; the land was AF's to sell; that Blackburn should "advertise him (Ezra) in the newspapers as a rascal". Signed ANDERSON SPENCER. Witn: above. rec 1809. p 112

Deed dated 1809. MAXWELL PARKISON & MAHALA his wife of Ross Twp to JOHN PARKISON of same. John a partner in original purchase of S 24, T 3, R 1. Signed MAXWELL PARKISON, MAHALA PARKISON. Wtn: JAMES ARMSTRONG #2 -- (german script). JP GEORGE HEMINGER, Ross Twp. rec 1809. pp 112, 113

Deed dated 1809. MAXWELL PARKISON & MAHALA his wife of Ross Twp to JAMES PARKISON of same. James a partner in original purchase of S 24, T 3, R 1. Signed MAXWELL PARKISON, MAHALA PARKISON. Wtn: JAMES ARMSTRONG, #2 -- (german script). rec 1809. pp 113, 114

Bond dated 1808. THOMAS McCULLOUGH to JAMES SYERS. McCullough to convey title to 10 acres (no S-T-R) as soon as he obtains deed from CRUSE & LINGLE. Signed THOS. McCULLOUGH. Witn: JAMES HEATON, JOHN HEATON. rec 1809. p 115

Deed dated 1809. OLIVER SPENCER & ANNE his wife of Hamilton Co to ISAAC TURNER of same. S 31, T 3, R 3. Bound by land of W. STACY, THOMAS WEST JR. Signed OLIVER SPENCER, ANNE SPENCER. Witn: JP WM. PERRY. rec 1809. pp 115, 116

Deed dated 1809. OLIVER SPENCER & ANNE his wife of Hamilton Co to WAREHAM STACY of same. S 31, T 3, R 3. Signed OLIVER SPENCER, ANNE SPENCER. Witn: WM. PERRY, WARHAM STACY. rec 1809. pp 116, 117

Deed dated 1809. WILLIAM HAYS SR to DANIEL WOODMANSEE of PA. S 3, T 2, R 3. Signed WILLIAM HAYS. Witn: ANN MAHARD, JOHN MAHARD. rec 1809. p 117

Deed dated 1807. LUDLOW PIERSON & ELENOR his wife to LAWRENCE CAVENAUGH. Hamilton lot 54. Signed LUDLOW PIERSON, ELENDOR PIERSON. Witn: ISAAC STANLEY. BENJAMIN DAVIS. rec 1809. pp 117, 118

BUTLER COUNTY LAND RECORDS: BOOK B

Mortgage dated 1809. JOHN HALL to LAWRENCE CAVENAUGH. Hamilton lot 54. Signed JOHN HALL. Witn: WM. MURRAY CHARLES SWEARINGEN. rec 1809. pp 118, 119

Deed dated 1808. GEORGE HEMINGER & MARY his wife to MICHAEL SHOOK. S 34, T 3, R 1. Signed GEORGE HEMINGER, MARY (x) HEMINGER. Witn: LOTT ABRAHAM, JOSEPH DEYBREAD. rec 1809. pp 119, 120

Mortgage dated 1808. JOHN C. WINANS of Lebanon, Warren Co to JOHN VANNUYS & ISAAC PAXTON of same. S 15. T 3, R 2. Signed JOHN C. WINANS. Witn: JOHN McLEAN. rec 1809. pp 120, 121

Deed dated 1808. ELIEZER WEST & HENRY WEST to GEORGE ROBY. S 20, T 3, R 3. Signed ELIEZER WEST, HENRY WEST. Witn: ISC. S. SWEARINGEN, THOS. HUNT. rec 1809. p 121

Deed dated 1809. JOAB COMSTOCK & EUNICE his wife of Crosby Twp, Hamilton Co to WILLIAM ANTHONY of Ross Twp. S 28, T 3, R 2. Title bond given to Anthony by Comstock in 1804. Signed JOAB COMSTOCK, EUNICE COMSTOCK. Witness: JP JUDAH WILLEY, THANKFUL COMSTOCK. rec 1809. pp 121, 122

Deed dated 1809. WILLIAM McCLELLAN & MARY his wife to JOHN SUTHERLAND & HENRY BROWN. S 25, T 4, R 2. Signed WM. McCLELLAN, MARY McCLELLAN. Witn: JP JAMES MILLS, JOHN BAXTER. rec 1809. p 123

Deed dated 1809. USA to EDWARD BEBB of Hamilton Co. S 27, T 3, R 1. rec 1809. pp 123, 124

Deed dated 1809. JOHN WINGATE, Sheriff of Butler Co to DAVID BEATY. Judgement obtained by CORNELIUS HALL against JOSHUA ROWLAND; seized S 3, T 1, R 2. Sold to Beaty. Bound by land of BEATY, DAVID BRANT. PETER WILCOCKS, DANIEL PARSONS. Signed JOHN WINGATE, Sheriff. Witn: none. rec 1809. pp 124, 125

Deed dated 1809. DAVID BURNET & PHEBE his wife of Hamilton Co to WILLIAM PATTON. S 21, T 2, R 3. Bound by TIMOTHY WOODRUFF, PATTON's land bought of JONAH ENYART, & land formerly owned by JAMES LYON. Signed DAVID BURNET, PHEBE (x) BURNET. Witn: THOMAS HUNTER, ISAAC STANLEY. rec 1809. pp 125, 126

Mortgage dated 1809. THOMAS SIMMONS to ROBERT TAYLOR JR. S 36, T 5, R 2. Paymt due 1811. Signed THOMAS (x) SIMMONS. Witn: JAMES McBRIDE, JOHN REILY. rec

BUTLER COUNTY LAND RECORDS: BOOK B

1809. pp 126, 127

Deed dated 1809. JOHN SUTHERLAND to SOLOMIN LINE. Hamilton lot 38. Signed JOHN SUTHERLAND. Witn: H. B. HAWTHORN, DAVID CONNER. rec 1809. pp 127, 128

Deed dated 1809. JOHN SUTHERLAND to THOMAS BLAIR. Hamilton lot 86. Signed JOHN SUTHERLAND. Witn: ROBERT GILKEY, JOHN BAXTER. rec 1809. pp 128, 129

Deed dated 1809. JOHN WINGATE, Sheriff, to WILLIAM PATTON & PHILIP GORDON. Patton obtained judgement against JONAH ENYART. Seized S 13, T 4, R 2. GORDON also obtained judgement for damages caused by delay in executing prior judg'mt. Auction to Patton & Gordon. Signed JOHN WINGATE. Witn: NOAH WADE, WM. HARLAND. JP JAMES MILLS. rec 1809. pp 129, 130, 131

Deed dated 1809. THOMAS HUNT SR, THOMAS HUNT JR & DURAN WHITTLESEY to JOHN PHELPS. S 20, T 3, R 3. Signed THOS. HUNT, THOS. HUNT JR, DURAN WHITTLESEY. Witn: ISC. S. SWEARINGEN, JONATHAN SPINNING. rec 1809. pp 131, 132

Deed dated 1809. SAMUEL AYRES & ANNA his wife to ALBERT BONTA. Rossvlle lot 100. Signed SAMUEL AYRES, ANNA AYRES. Witn: JAMES WHITE, JAMES MILLS. rec 1809. pp 132, 133

Deed dated 1804. JAMES ADAMS & POLLY his wife to JOHN SUTHERLAND. Hamilton lots 7, 252. Signed JAMES (x) ADAMS, POLLEY (x) ADAMS. Witn: JACOB LULLEN, CELADON SYMMES. rec 1809. pp 133, 134

Deed dated 1802. JAMES HENRY of Somerset Co, NJ to BENJA. M. PIATT of Boone Co, KY. S 9, T 1, R 2. Signed JAMES HENRY. Witn: CHARLES OGDEN, JOHN PIATT. rec 1809. pp 134, 135

Deed dated 1809. ALBERT BANTA to JOHN MURPHY. S 31, T 3, R 4. Signed ALBERT BANTA. Witn: JAMES MILLS, JAMES WHITE. rec 1809. pp 135, 136

Deed dated 1809. SAMUEL AYRES & ANNA his wife to JOSEPH HOUGH & THOMAS BLAIR. Rossville lots 82, 89. Signed SAM'L AYRES, ANNA AYRES. Witn: ISAAC STANLEY. ELEANOR DUVALL. rec 1809. pp 136, 137

Deed dated 1809. OLIVER SPENCER & ANNA his wife of Hamilton Co to JOHN LODER. S 31, T 3, R 3. Signed

BUTLER COUNTY LAND RECORDS: BOOK B

OLIVER SPENCER, ANNA SPENCER. Witn: STEPHEN H. BROWN & WILLIAM FLOREN. JP WILLIAM PERRY. rec 1809. p 137

Deposition dated 1809. ISAAC SEWARD swore SAMUEL SEWARD executed a deed for S 5, T 2, R 2 to JOHN FREEMAN. Deed was produced. Signed ISAAC (x) SEWARD. Witn: JAS. DUNN, HENRY WEAVER. rec 1809. pp 137, 138

Deed dated 1809. SAMUEL PAINE & MARY his wife of Wayne Twp to JOHN PAGE of same. S 9, T 3, R 3. Witn: EPHRAIM SMITH, NATHAN STUBBS. Signed SAMUEL PAINE, MARY (x) PAINE. rec 1809. pp 138.

Deed dated 1809. AMOS VOLUNTINE of Warren Co to ISAAC WOOD of same. S 18, T 3, R 3. Signed AMOS VALLENTINE. Witn: EBENEZER HATHAWAY, JP ENOS WILLIAMS. rec 1809. p 139

Deed dated 1809. ISAAC MATSON & JOANNA his wife of Hamilton Co to EBENEZER WILSON. S 23, T 3, R 3. Bound by land of DANIEL GOBLE, JAMES MAPES. Signed ISAAC MATSON, JOANNA MATSON. Witn: ISAAC STANLEY, JAMES McBRIDE. rec 1809. pp 139, 140

Deed dated 1808. JOHN YOUNG to ALEXANDER YOUNG. S 10, T 5, R 2. Signed JOHN YOUNG. Witn: ROBERT OGLE, ROBERT YOUNG. rec 1809. pp 140, 141

Deed dated 1809. GEORGE HARLAN, Collector of Fairfield Twp to ISAAC WILES. Seized Hamilton lot 200 for unpaid tax. Signed GEO. HARLAN. Witn: JAMES MILLS, JAMES HEATON. rec 1809. pp 141, 142.

Deed dated 1809. JOHN SUTHERLAND & HENRY BROWN to JACOB LEWIS. Rossville outlot 5. Signed JOHN SUTHERLAND, HENRY BROWN. Witn: WM. BOMBERGER JR, WM. PHARES JR. rec 1809. pp 142, 143

Deed dated 1809. JOSIAH WILSON & MARY his wife to JOHN HALL. S 13, T -, R 2. Bound by land of WILLIAM WHITE, BENJAMIN LONG. Signed JOSIAH WILSON, MARY WILSON. Witn: DAVID GARRIGUS, ISAAC STANLEY. rec 1809. pp 143, 144

Deed dated 1809. ALEXANDER WILSON to JOHN WILSON, his son. S 14 & 23, T 2, R 3. Signed ALEXANDER WILSON. Witn: JAMES McBRIDE, JAMES MILLS. rec 1809. pp 144, 145

Deed dated 1809. MARSH WILLIAMS & NANCY his wife to

BUTLER COUNTY LAND RECORDS: BOOK B

JOHN MARSH of Essex Co, NJ. S 4, T 5, R 2. Signed MARSH WILLIAMS, NANCY WILLIAMS. Witn: ABEL TERRIELL, JOHN T. MARSH. rec 1809. pp 145, 146

Mortgage dated 1809. JOHN BARTON to JACOB POWERS. S 13, T 3, R 3. Payment due 1810. Signed JOHN BARTON. Witn: ADAM LINN, ADAM LINN JR. rec 1809. pp 146, 147

Mortgage dated 1809. ADAM LINN to JACOB POWERS. S 13, T 3, R 3. Signed ADAM LINN. Witn: JOHN LINN, JACOB POWERS SR, ISC. S. SWEARINGEN. rec 1809. p 147

Deed dated 1809. GEORGE ISAMENZER & MARY his wife to GEORGE SHOOK of Hamilton Co. S 34, T 3, R 1. Signed GEORGE HEMINGER, MARY (x) HEMINGER. Witn: EMANUEL VANTREES, JOHN BENEFEIL, DAVID McCANES. rec 1809. pp 147, 148

Deed dated 1809. REUBEN CARTER & CATHARINE his wife to ALEXANDER D. HAMILTON of Hamilton Co. S 10, T 2, R 2. Signed REUBEN CARTER, CATHARINE (x) CARTER. Witn: JAMES McBRIDE, WM. TRUM. CRISSEY. rec 1809. pp 148, 149

Deed dated 1809. JOSEPH ELY & CATHARINE his wife to ABRAM STREET. S 8, T 1, R 5. Signed JOSEPH ELY, CATHERINE ELY. Witn: JOHN McKEAN, HENRY WEAVER. rec 1809. pp 149, 150

Deed dated 1809. JOHN SMITH & ELIZABETH his wife to LEVI WALLER. S 2, T 2, R 3. Signed JOHN SMITH, ELIZABETH SMITH. Witn: MOSES MASSTERS, THOMAS H. SILL. JP DA. McCORMICK. rec 1809. pp 151, 152

Deed dated 1809. SAMUEL DAVIS & SUSAN his wife of Wayne Twp to ANTHONY BURNS SR. S 18, T 3. R 3. Bound by land of PATRICK LOGAN, SAMUEL KIRKPATRICK, JOSEPH EVANS. Signed SAM'L DAVIS, SUSAN DAVIS. Witn: JP CHARLES SWEARINGEN, DAVID DUFFIELD. rec 1809. pp 152, 153

Deed dated 1809. WILLIAM DILLON of Hamilton to JOHN WINGATE. Hamilton lots 187, 188. Signed WILLIAM DILLON. Witn: THOS. BLAIR, ISAAC STANLEY. rec 1809. pp 153, 154

Deed dated 1809. JOHN WINGATE & EMMA his wife to RALPH W. HUNT of Warren Co. Hamilton lots 187, 188. Signed JOHN WINGATE, AMMA WINGATE. Witn: NOAH WADE, JAMES MILLS. rec 1809. pp 154, 155

BUTLER COUNTY LAND RECORDS: BOOK B

Deed dated 1809. HENRY HOUSE & ANN his wife to PIERSON SAYRE, late of PA. S 4, T 2, R 3. Signed HENRY HOUSS, ANN HOUSS. Witn: JP WILLIAM HAYS. JACOB RUSH, ELIAS SAYRE. rec 1809. pp 155, 156

Deed dated 1809. JOHN CLEVES SYMMES to DAVID GARRIGUS of Fairfield Twp. S 36, T 2, R 2. Signed JOHN CLEVES SYMMES. Witn: JACKSON AYRES, JAMES CLARK. rec 1809. pp 156, 157

Deed dated 1809. JOHN CLEVES SYMMES to JACKSON AYRES of Fairfield Twp. S 36, T 2, R 2. Signed JOHN CLEVES SYMMES. Witn: DAVID GARRIGUS, JAMES CLARK. rec 1809. pp 157, 158

Deed dated 1809. JOHN CLEVES SYMMES to JAMES CLARK of Fairfield Twp. S 36, T 2, R 2. Witn: JACKSON AYRES, DAVID GARRIGUS. rec 1809. pp 159, 160

Deed dated 1809. THOMAS BLAIR & MARGARET his wife to JAMES CLARK. S 25, T 4, R 2. Signed THOS. BLAIR, MARGARET BLAIR. Witn: ISAAC STANLEY, H.B. HAWTHORN. rec 1809. p 160

Deed dated 1809. JOHN WINGATE, Sheriff of Butler Co, to JAMES FERGUSON. Judgement obtained by Ferguson against JOSHUA DAVIS. Seized S 22, T 3, R 3; sold at auction. Signed JOHN WINGATE. Witn: DANIEL MILLIKIN, JAMES McBRIDE. rec 1809. pp 161, 162

Deed dated 1809. JAMES CUMMINS & SARAH his wie to ROBERT FLEMING of Frederick Co, MD. S 30, T 2, R 2. Signed JAMES CUMMINS, SARAH (x) CUMMINS. Witn: NOAH WADE, JAMES McBRIDE. rec 1809. pp 162, 163

Deed dated 1809. PETER LINTNER & MARY his wife to ROBERT FLEMING as above. S 30, T 2, R 2. Signed PETER LINTNER, MARY (x) LINTNER. Witn: as above. rec 1809. pp 163, 164

Deed dated 1809. ALLEN CULLUM & POLLY his wife to ROBERT FLEMING as above. S 12, T 2, R 2. Signed ALLEN CULLUM, POLLY CULLUM. Witn: as above. rec 1809. pp 164, 165

Deed dated 1809. THOMAS JOHNSON to STEPHEN GILL. S28, T 3, R 2. Signed THOMAS JOHNS. Witn: GEORGE McMAKEN, ISC. S. SWEARINGEN. rec 1809. p 165

Deed dated 1808. JAMES LYON & NANCY his wife of Fairfield Twp to WILLIAM PATTON of same. S 21, T 2, R 3.

BUTLER COUNTY LAND RECORDS: BOOK B

Bound by PATRICK MOORE's land. Signed JAMES LYON, NANCY (x) LYON CESS(?). Witn: TIMOTHY WOODRUFF, JAMES LEESON. rec 1809. pp 166, 167

Deed dated 1809. JOSEPH ELY & CATHARINE his wife to WILLIAM WOODWARD. S 5, T 1, R 5. Bound by GEORGE LOY's land. Signed JOSEPH ELY, CATHARINE ELY. Witn: JOHN McKEAN, HENRY WEAVER. rec 1809. pp 167, 168

Deed dated 1809. AARON BAKER & HANNAH his wife of Dayton Twp, Montgomery Co to GEORGE ROBY of Lemon Twp. S 17, T 3, R 3. Bound by land of AARON RICHARDSON, JOSEPH PATTERSON. Signed AARON BAKER, HANNAH BAKER. Witn: WM. M. SMITH, ROBERT A. SMITH. rec 1809. pp 168, 169

Deed dated 1809. GEORGE ROBY to ELEAZER WEST. S 20, T 3, R 3. Signed GEORGE ROBY. Witn: THOMAS HUNT, ISAAC STANLEY. rec 1809. pp 169, 170

Deed dated 1809. PHILIP DROLLINGER & HANNAH his wife to JOHN MERRIL of same. S 1, T 2, R 3. Signed PHILIP DROLLINGER, HANNAH (x) DROLLINGER. Witn: WM. SYMMES, ISC. S. SWEARINGEN. rec 1809. pp 170, 171

Deed dated 1809. JOHN WINGATE, Sheriff, to ROBERT SMITH of Shelby Co, KY. JOHN CLEVES SYMMES recovrd debt against JAMES McCLELLAND. Seized S 32, T 3, R 3; sold to Smith. Signed JOHN WINGATE, Sheriff. Witn: H.B. HAWTHORN, JAMES MILLS. rec 1809. pp 171, 172, 173

Deed dated 1807. JOSEPH JENKINSON to HUGH WILSON. Hamilton lot 86. Signed JOSEPH JENKINSON. Witn: ALEX'R FOWLER, JOHN McCLUTCHE. rec 1809. pp 173, 174

Deed dated 1809. SAM'L FERGUSON & ELIZABETH his wife to THOMAS FERGUSON. S 1, T 2, R 3. Signed SAMUEL (x) FERGUSON, ELIZABETH (x) FERGUSON. Witn: JOHN BLUE, HENRY WEAVER. rec 1809. pp 174, 175

Deed dated 1809. ALEXANDER WILSON to ALEXANDER WILSON JR, his son. S 14 & 23, T 2, R 3. Bound by land conveyed to JOHN WILSON, son of Alexander (Sr). Signed ALEXANDER WILSON. Witn: JAMES SMITH, JAMES MILLS. rec 1810. pp 175, 176

Deed dated 1809. GEORGE HARLAN, Collector of Fairfield Twp, to ISAAC STANLEY. Hamilton lot 2. Signed GEO. HARLAN, Collector. Witn: M. HUESTON, THOS. McCULLOUGH. rec 1810. pp 176, 177

BUTLER COUNTY LAND RECORDS: BOOK B

Mortgage dated 1809. ALEXANDER WILSON of St. Clair Twp to ALEXANDER WILSON JR of same. (order reversed?) Money owed by Wilson Jr to father. S 14 & 23, T 2, R 3. Payment due by 1814. Signed ALEXANDER WILSON. Witn JAMES MILLS, JAMES SMITH. rec 1810. pp 177, 178

Deed dated 1809. JOHN SUTHERLAND & HENRY BROWN to ISAAC BEAUCHAMP of KY. Rossville lot 91. Signed JOHN SUTHERLAND, HENRY BROWN. Witn: WM. BOMBERGER JR, WM. PHARES JR. rec 1810. pp 179, 180

Deed dated 1807. GEORGE HARLAN, collector of Fairfield Twp to ANDERSON SPENCER. Hamilton lot 49. Signed GEO. HARLAN. Witn: H.B. HAWTHRON, JAMES MILLS rec 1810. pp 180, 181

Deed dated 1809. GEORGE HARLAN, collector of Fairfield Twp to ANDERSON SPENCER. Hamilton lot 50. Signed and witn as above. rec 1810. pp 181, 182

Deed dated 1809. JOHN RICHARDSON & JANE his wife of Ross Twp to JOHN BROWN SEIGNIOR (meant SR) of same. S 29, T 3, R 2. Signed JOHN RICHARDSON, JEAIN RICHARDSON. Witn: PATRICK O. NEIL, ROBERT DUNWOODY. rec 1810. pp 182, 183

Deed dated 1809. WILLIAM THOMAS & MARGARET his wife to EDMUND LISTON. S 1, T 2, R 3. Signed WILLIAM THOMAS, MARGARET (x) THOMAS. Witn: SAMUEL (x) FERGUSON, HENRY WEAVER. rec 1810. pp 183, 184

Deed dated 1809. EDMUND LISTON & ELIZABETH his wife to THOMAS SWIFTH. S 1, T 2, R 3. Signed EDMUND LISTON, ELIZABETH (x) LISTON. Witn: WILLIAM THOMAS, HENRY WEAVER. rec 1810. pp 184, 185

Deed dated 1809. JOSIAH CONKLING & ELSE his wife to SKILLMAN ALGER. S 2, T 2, R 3. Signed JOSIAH CONKLING, ELSE (x) CONKLING. Witn: JOHN McGRIFFIN, DANIEL CRUME. rec 1810. pp 185, 186

Deed dated 1810. JAMES WITHROW & SARAH his wife to ROBERT ERVIN. S 32, T 3, R3. Signed JAMES WITHROW, SARAH WITHROW. Witn: JOHN McGRIFFITH, DANIEL CRUME. rec 1810. pp 186, 187

Deed dated 1810. JOHN WINGATE & EMMA WINGATE, late EMMA TORRENCE, admr of JOHN TORRENCE, to JOHN SUTHERLAND & HENRY BROWN. Hamilton lots 147, 148. Signed JOHN WINGATE, AMMA WINGATE. Witn: NOAH WADE, JAMES MILLS. rec 1810. pp 187, 188

BUTLER COUNTY LAND RECORDS: BOOK B

Deed dated 1809. JOHN SUTHERLAND & HENRY BROWN to THOMAS HILL. Rossville lot 81. Signed JOHN SUTHERLAND, HENRY BROWN. Witn: WM. BOMBERGER JR, WM. PHARES JR. rec 1810. p 188

Deed dated 1806. JOHN BALDWIN & ELIZABETH his wife of Hamilton Co to DANIEL PARSON. S 3, T 1, R 2. Signed JOHN BALDWIN, ELIZABETH (x) BALDWIN. Witn: HENRY VANDIKE, JOHN BRECOUNT. rec 1810. pp 188, 189

Mortgage dated 1810. OLIVER STEVENS to AZARIAS THORN. Hamilton lots 7, 17, 18, 19. Signed OLIVER STEVENS. Witn: NOAH WADE, ISAAC STANLEY. rec 1810. pp 189, 190

Deed dated 1809. WILLIAM ANTHONY & FANNE his wife of Ross Twp to JOHN BROWN. S 28, T 3, R 2. Bound by land of JOHN RICHARDSON, JOAB COMSTOCK. Signed WILLIAM ANTHONY, FANNEY (x) ANTHONY. Witn: JOAB COMSTOCK, MAXWELL PARKISON. rec 1810. pp 190, 191

Deed dated 1809. WILLIAM PATTON & JANE his wife to JOHN SMILIE. S 13, T 4, R 2. Signed WILLIAM PATTON, JANE PATTON. Witn: TIMOTHY WOODRUFF SEN, ISAAC STANLEY. rec 1810. pp 191, 192

Deed dated 1810. SAMUEL ENYART & ANNA his wife to JAMES CUMMINS. S 3, T 2, R 3. Signed SAMUEL ENYART, ANNA ENYART. Witn: JOSEPH SUTTON, HENRY WEAVER. rec 1810. pp 192, 193

Deed dated 1810. SAMUEL ENYART & ANNA his wife to ROBERT FLEMING. S 24, T 2, R 2. Signed SAMUEL ENYART ANNA ENYART. Witn: NOAH WADE, JOHN SUTHERLAND. rec 1810. pp 193

Deed dated 1809. JOHN REILY of Hamilton to JOHN HALL & ISAAC MOSS. Hamilton lots 72, 73. Signed JOHN REILY. Witn: JAMES McBRIDE, W. CORRY. rec 1810. pp 193, 194

Deed dated 1809. LAWRENCE CAVENAUGH & ANN his wife of Hamilton to JOHN HALL. Hamilton lot 54. Signed L. CAVENAUGH, ANN CAVENAUGH. Witn: WM. MURRAY, CHARLES SWEARINGEN. rec 1810. pp 194, 195

Deed dated 1799. JOHN CLEVES SYMMES to ISAAC SWEARINGEN, assignee of NICHOLAS MALSON the first settler. S 24, T 3, R 2. GABRIEL ALLEN purchased land; did not meet settlement terms. Swearingen now on land the required seven years. Signed JOHN CLEVES SYMMES. Witn: REUBEN ROOD, DANIEL (x) VAN S-. rec 1810. p 195

BUTLER COUNTY LAND RECORDS: BOOK B

Deed dated 1809. ISAAC S. SWEARINGEN & BARBARA his wife to JOHN V. SWEARINGEN. S 18, T 3. R 2. Signed ISC. S. SWEARINGEN, BARBARY (x) SWEARINGEN. Witn: MICHAEL AYERS, JOHN CLEVES SYMMES. rec 1810. p 196

Deed dated 1809. JOHN SUTHERLAND & HENRY BROWN to JOHN REILY. Rossville lot 59. Signed JOHN SUTHERLAND, HENRY BROWN. Witn: WM. BOMBERGER JR, WM. PHARES JR. rec 1810. pp 196, 197

Deed dated 1809. HENRY BROWN to JOHN REILY. Hamilton lot 24, 27, 34, 37. Signed HENRY BROWN. Witn: WM. BOMBERGER JR, WM. PHARES JR. rec 1810. p 197

Deed dated 1810. JOHN WINGATE & EMMA WINGATE admtr of JOHN TORRENCE to THOMAS BLAIR. Hamilton lot 24. Signed JOHN WINGATE, AMMA WINGATE. Wtn: NOAH WADE, JAMES MILLS. rec 1810. pp 197, 198

Deed dated 1810. JOHN SUTHERLAND & HENRY BROWN to THOMAS BLAIR. Rossville lot 88. Signed JOHN SUTHERLAND, HENRY BROWN. Witn: JAMES STEELE, JAMES BECK. rec 1810. pp 198, 199

Deed dated 1810. JOHN SUTHERLAND & HENRY BROWN to JOSEPH HOUGH & THOMAS BLAIR. Rossville lot 83. Signed JOHN SUTHERLAND, HENRY BROWN. Witn: JAMES STEELE, JAMES BECK. rec 1810. p 199

Deed dated 1809. JOHN VAN NUYS & ELIZABETH his wife to WILLIAM MURRAY. Hamilton lot 214. Signed JOHN VANNICE, ELIZABETH VANNICE. Witness: JAMES MILLS, SAML. T. COUNCELL. rec 1810. p 200

Deed dated 1809. JOHN SUTHERLAND & HENRY BROWN to WILLIAM MURRAY. Rossville lots 1, 8. Signed JOHN SUTHERLAND, HENRY BROWN. Witn: WM. BOMBERGER JR, WM. PHARES JR. rec 1810. pp 200, 201

Deed dated 1800. ARTHUR VANDERVEER & ALLCHEY his wife of Warren Co to WILLIAM FRANCIS. S 27, T 2, R 5. Signed ARTHUR VANDERVEER, ALLCHEY VANDERVEER. Witn JACOB REEDER, JOHN FRANCIS. rec 1810. pp 201, 202

Deed dated 1808. WILLIAM BARKALOW & MARY his wife to JOHN COX. S 33, T 2, R 5. Bound by JAMES TAPSCOTT's land. Signed WILLIAM P. BARKALOW, MARY BARKALOW. Witn: ROBERT SHAW, HENRY WEAVER. rec 1810. p 202

Deed dated 1810. JOHN REILY & NANCY his wife to THOMAS BLAIR. Rossville lot 29. Signed JOHN REILY,

BUTLER COUNTY LAND RECORDS: BOOK B

NANCY REILY. Witn: WM. McCLELLAN, JAMES McBRIDE. rec 1810. p 203

Mortgage dated 1809. DAVID ENOCH & ZADOCK SEXTON to JONATHAN JONES. Personal property, including two stills. To be paid July, 1810. Signed DAVID ENOCH, ZADOCK SEXTON. Witn: ELIZABETH BALL, MATTHEW NICOL, ROBERT BROWN. rec 1810. pp 203, 204

Deed dated 1810. JOHN WINGATE & <u>EMMA</u> WINGATE, late EMMA TORRENCE, admr of JOHN TORRENCE, to AZZURE REED MILLS. Rossville lot 4. Signed JOHN WINGATE, <u>AMMY</u> WINGATE. Witn: NOAH WADE, J. CARPENTER. rec 1810. pp 204, 205

Deed dated 1809. JOHN SUTHERLAND & HENRY BROWN to JAMES MILLS. Rossville lot 4. Signed JOHN SUTHER- LAND, HENRY BROWN. Witn: WM. BOMBERGER JR, WM. PHARES JR. rec 1810. pp 205, 206

Deed dated 1809. ABRAHAM DEMOTT & HANNAH his wife of Preble Co to ADAM DEEM. S 6, T 2, R 4. Signed ABRAHAM DEMOTT, HANNAH DEMOTT. Witn: none. rec 1810. p 206

Deed dated 1819. JOHN SUTHERLAND & HENRY BROWN to JOHN REILY. S 31 & 32, T 2, R 3, being outlot 29, town of Rossville. Signed JOHN SUTHERLAND, HENRY BROWN. Witn: JAMES STEELE, JAMES BECK. rec 1810. pp 206, 207

Deed dated 1809. JOHN SCHENCK to MICHAEL PIERCE. S 1, T 2, R 3. Signed JOHN SCHENCK. Witn: WILLIAM THOMAS, HENRY WEAVER. rec 1810. pp 207, 208

Deed dated 1810. JOHN REILY & NANCY his wife to JOHN SUTHERLAND. Rossville lots 24, 27, 34, 37. Signed JOHN REILY, NANCY REILY. Witn: WM. McCLELLAN, JAMES McBRIDE. rec 1810. pp 208, 209

Deed dated 1810. GEORGE DEYBREAD & SUSANA his wife of Ross Twp to ELIZABETH STILES of same. S 3, T 3, R 1 Signed GEORGE (x) DEYBREAD, SUSANA (x) DEYBREAD. Witn DAVID McCANCE, THOMAS MATTHEWS. rec 1810. pp 209, 210

Mortgage dated 1809. JOHN PATTERSON to JOSEPH EVANS. S 32, T 3, R 3. Signed JOHN PATTERSON. Witn: WM. CORRY, JAMES McBRIDE. rec 1810. p 210

Deed dated 1809. EBENEZER PADDOCK SR & <u>KEZIA</u> his wife to EBENEZER PADDOCK JR. S 36, T 3, R 3. Signed

BUTLER COUNTY LAND RECORDS: BOOK B

EBENEZER PADDOCK, KEZIAH (x) PADDOCK. Witn: SAML (x) FERGUSON, HENRY WEAVER. rec 1810. pp 210, 211

Deed dated 1809. WILLIAM THOMAS & MARGARET his wife to SAMUEL FERGUSON. S 1, T 2, R 3. Signed WILLIAM THOMAS, MARGARET (x) THOMAS. Witn: EDMOND LISTON, HENRY WEAVER. rec 1810. pp 211, 212

Deed dated 1809. SAMUEL FERGUSON & ELIZABETH his wife to ATHEL FERGUSON. S 1, T 2, R 3. Signed SAMUEL (x) FERGUSON, ELIZABETH (x) FERGUSON. Witn: HENRY WEAVER, JOHN BLUE. rec 1810. pp 212, 213

Deed dated 1809. EDMOND LISTON & ELIZABETH his wife to WILLIAM PADACK. S 1, T 2, R 3. Signed EDMOND LISTON, ELIZABETH (x) LISTON. Witn: WILLIAM THOMAS, HENRY WEAVER. rec 1810. p 213

Deed dated 1810. WILLIAM McCLELLAN & MARY his wife to JOB DeCAMP. S 25, T 4, R 2. Signed WM. McCLELLAN, MARY McCLELLAN. Witn: JAMES MILLS, JP JAMES SMITH. rec 1810. pp 213, 214

Deed dated 1809. DANIEL PERRY & RHODA his wife to LUTHER TILLSON. S 3, T 5, R 2. Signed DANIEL PERRY, ROHDY (x) PERRY. Witn: MARSH WILLIAMS, DAVID WILLIAMS. rec 1810. pp 214, 215

Mortgage dated 1810. LAWRENCE CAVENAUGH of Fairfield Twp to JOHN HALL of same. Paymt due 1812. S 23, T 4, R 2. Signed L. CAVENAUGH. Witn: WM. MURRAY, DELLY MURRAY. rec 1810. pp 215, 216

Mortgage dated 1810. LAWRENCE CAVENAUGH to ISAAC MORSE. S 24, T 3, R 2. Signed L. CAVENAUGH. Witn: JAMES HEATON, JOHN HALL. rec 1810. p 216

Plat dated 1810. Town of Lamberton. Proprietor WILLIAM BARKALOW. Witn: ISAAC STANLEY. rec 1810. p 217

Deed dated 1809. NICHOLAS JONES & LYDIA his wife to THOMAS FLEMING. S 14, T 2, R 2 except land sold to JOSEPH COLBY & JOSEPH COLBY JR. Signed NICHOLAS (x) JONES, LYDIA (x) JONES. Witn: JP M. HUESTON, ABRAHAM PIATT. rec 1810. pp 217, 218

Deed dated 1810. JACOB BURNET & REBECCA his wife of Cincinnati to JOHN BECKET of Liberty Twp. S 28, T 3, R 2. Signed JACOB BURNET, REBECCA BURNET. Witn: THOMAS H. SILL, JAMES EWING. rec 1810. p 218

BUTLER COUNTY LAND RECORDS: BOOK B

Deed dated 1810. JOHN SUTHERLAND & HENRY BROWN to JAMES ROSS. Rossville lot 90. Signed JOHN SUTHERLAND, HENRY BROWN. Witn: JAMES STEELE, JAMES BECK. rec 1810. p 219

Mortgage dated 1809. WARHAM STACY to OLIVER SPENCER. S -, T 3, R 3. Signed WARHAM STACY. Witn: JP WM. PERRY, WM. STUMP. rec 1810. pp 219, 220

Mortgage dated 1809. LEWIS BAYLEY of Hamilton Co to OLIVER SPENCER. S 31, T 3, R 3. Signed LEWIS BAYLEY Witn as above. rec 1810. p 220

Mortgage dated 1809. ISAAC TURNER of Hamilton Co to OLIVER SPENCER. S 31, T 3, R 3. Signed ISAAC TURNER Witn as above. rec 1810. pp 220, 221

Deed dated 1810. THOMAS WEST JR & POLLY his wife of Hamilton Co to JOSEPH MULLALLY. S 31, T 3, R 3. Signed THOMAS WEST JR, POLLY WEST. Witn: JAMES MIRANDA, WM. PERRY. rec 1810. p 221

Deed dated 1810. **ABRAM** DEMOTT & HANNAH his wife of Preble Co to WILLIAM BALDWIN. S 6, T 2, R 4. Signed **ABRAHAM** DEMOTT, HANNAH DEMOTT. Witn: EDWARD BALDWIN, JOHN QUINN. rec 1810. pp 221, 222

Deed dated 1809. JACOB MILLER to JOHN HARPER. S 25, T R, R 1. Signed JACOB MILLER and JOHN HARPER. Witn: JAMES GATES, WM. MITCHELL. rec 1810. p 222

Deed dated 1810. PETER CATROW & CHRISTIANNAH his wife of Lemon Twp to MICHAEL TEMPLE of same. S 25, T 3, R 4. Signed PETER (x) CATROW, CHRISTIANNAH (x) CATROW. Witn: #1 (german script), HENRY WEAVER. rec 1810. pp 222, 223

Deed dated 1799. JOHN CLEVES SYMMES of NW Ter'y to ELIAS BOUDINOT of Rose Hill in PA. S 13 & 25, T 1, R 4. Signed JOHN CLEVES SYMMES. Witn: JAMES PRITCHARD JOHN WINGATE. rec 1810. pp 223, 224

Quitclaim dated 1810. Heirs of ENOCH MATSON to THOMAS MATSON & his wife ELIZABETH. S 23, T 3, R 3 conveyed in 1804 to ENOCH by his father JOHN MATSON, now dec'd. Heirs listed: JAMES MATSON and his wife LAVINA, JOHN MATSON & his wife MARY, ISAAC MATSON & his wife JOANNA, ANN COX, MARY HUBBARD and ELIZABETH TAYLOR. Signed JAMES MATSON, LAVINA MATSON, JOHN MATSON, MARY MATSON, ISAAC MATSON, JOANNA MATSON. Witn: JAMES SILVER, DAVID DUFF. rec 1810. p 224

BUTLER COUNTY LAND RECORDS: BOOK B

Deed dated 1809.   JOHN VANNICE & ELIZABETH his wife and ISAAC PAXTON & MAGDALENE his wife to JOHN C. WINANS of Warren Co.   S 15, T 3, R 2.   Signed JOHN VANNICE, ELIZABETH (x) VANNICE, ISAAC PAXTON, MAGDALENE (x) PAXTON.   Witn: JOHN WINGATE, ROBERT TAYLOR, JAMES MILLS, WILL. BRODERICK.   rec 1810.   pp 224, 225

Deed dated 1803.   ELIAS BOUDINOT of Philadelphia to CHARLES STEWART.   S 3, T 2, R 4.   Signed ELIAS BOUDINOT by ABIJAH HUNT his atty, CORNL. R. SEDAM atty for E. BUDINT, ELIAS BOUDINET by JAC. BURNET, his agent.   Witn: WM. STANLEY, DANIEL HUNT, JOHN REILY, JAMES McBRIDE.   rec 1810.   pp 225, 226

Deed dated 1810.   JOSEPH MULLALLY & ELIZABETH his wife to ALLEN CULLUM.   S 25, T 3, R 3.   Signed JOSEPH MULLALAY, ELIZABETH (x) MULLALLY.   Witn: LEVI WALLER SOLMON WALLER.   rec 1810.   pp 226, 227

Power of Attorney dated 1809.   GEORGE KUNS SR of Allegheny Twp, Hunterdon Co, PA apptd "my well beloved son" JACOB KUNS of Jefferson Twp, Montgomery Co as atty to convey S 29, T 4, R 2.   Signed GEORGE KUNS (german script).   Witn: DAVID STEWART, JOHN STEWART. rec 1810.   p 227

Deed dated 1810.   GEORGE KUNS as above by JACOB KUNS his atty to JOSEPH GRIPE.   S 29, T 4, R 2.   Signed GEORGE KUNS SR by JACOB KUNS (in german).   Witn: DANIEL MARTIN, ISAAC G. BURNET.   rec 1810.   pp 227, 228

Deed dated 1806.   ISAAC OGG & POLLY his wife to JOEL WILLIAMS.   No S-T-R.   Land purchased from KNOLES SHAW in 1804, rec Hamilton Co Bk F #1, p 103.   Bound by DAVID WADE's land, WILLIAM's land bought from JACOB HIDAY.   Signed ISAAC (x) OGG, POLLY (x) OGG.   Witn: JUDAH WILLEY, ALEXR. KIRKPATRICK.   rec 1810. p 228

Deed dated 1810.   GEORGE HARLAN, collector of Fairfield Twp to GEORGE SOUDER of same.   Hamilton lot 211 Signed GEORGE HARLAN.   Witn: DAN'L MILLIKIN, CHARLES SWEARINGEN.   rec 1810.   pp 228, 229

Deed dated 1810.   ISAAC STANLEY to GEORGE SNIDER. Hamilton lot 146.   Signed ISAAC STANLEY.   Witn: JOHN REILY, JAMES MILLS.   rec 1810.   pp 229, 230

Deed dated 1806.   Admtrs of ISRAEL LUDLOW to EDWARD HARLAN.   Hamilton lot 230.   Signed CHARLOTTE CHAMBERS LUDLOW, JOHN FINDLAY, JOHN LUDLOW, SINEAS PIERSON. Witn: N.C.   FINDLAY, JOHN MAHARD.   rec 1810.   p 230

BUTLER COUNTY LAND RECORDS: BOOK B

Deed dated 1810. JOHN SUTHERLAND & HENRY BROWN of Hamilton to JAMES McCLAMROCH of same. Rossville lots 11 & 71. Signed JOHN SUTHERLAND, HENRY BROWN. Witn: JAMES STEELE, JAMES BECK. rec 1810. p 231

Deed dated 1810. JOHN LUCAS & JAMIMA his wife to PHINEAS McCRAY. S 1, T 2, R 4. Signed JOHN LUCAS, JAMIMA (x) LUCAS. Witn: ELIZABETH (x) McCRAY, HENRY WEAVER. rec 1810. pp 231, 232

Deed dated 1807. GEORGE HARLAN, Tax Collector of Fairfield Twp, to BARNEY McCARRON. Hamilton lot 24. Signed GEO. HARLAN, Collector. Witn: WM. WILSON, M. HUESTON. rec 1810. p 232

Deed dated 1807. GEORGE HARLAN, Collector of Fairfield Twp, to BARNEY McCARRON. Hamilton lot 21. Signed and witness as above. rec 1810. pp 232, 233

Deed dated 1807. GEORGE HARLAN, Collector of Fairfield Twp, to BARNEY McCARRON. Hamilton lot 24. Signed and witness as above. rec 1810. p 233

Plat dated 1810. Town of Oxford in S 22, 23, 26 & 27 T 5, R 1. JAMES HEATON, surveyor. Established for the creation of Miami University by school trustees. WILLIAM LUDLOW, Pres. pro tem. JAMES McBRIDE, Sec'y pro tem. rec 1810. pp 234, 235, 236

Deed dated 1807. USA to ENOCH EVERINGHAM. S 13, T 4, R 1. rec 1810. p 236

Deed dated 1808. ENOCH EVERINGHAM to JOSEPH KITCHELL S 13, T 4, R 1. Signed ENOCH EVERINGHAM. Witn: ROBT. BRECKENRIDGE, JOHN SHANKE. rec 1810. p 237

Deed dated 1797. WILLIAM LUDLOW of Springfield Twp, Hamilton Co, NW Ter'y to JOHN EANYARD of Cincinnati Twp. (ENYARD & ENYART in text). S 20, T 2, R 2. Signed WILLIAM LUDLOW. Witn: HENRY (x) COLLINS, JOHN LITTON. rec 1810. pp 237, 238

Deed dated 1810. JOHN CLEVES SYMMES to WILLIAM ENYERT of Fairfield. Balance of S5, T 2, R 2 after deducting land sold to DANIEL MARSH of NJ. Signed JOHN CLEVES SYMMES. Witn: JOHN N. PACK, JOHN RICHARDSON. rec 1810. p 238

Deed dated 1809. PETER MURPHEY & ELEANOR his wife to HUMPHREY NICKLES. S 2, T 2, R 3. Signed PETER (x) MURPHEY, ELEANOR (x) MURPHEY. Witn: JOHN (x) MURPHY,

BUTLER COUNTY LAND RECORDS: BOOK B

ISC. S. SWEARINGEN. rec 1810. p 239

Deed dated 1809. ALEXANDER HAMILTON & MARY his wife of Hamilton Co to WILLIAM BUTLER of same. S 10, T 2, R 2. Signed A. HAMILTON, MARY HAMILTON. Witn: WM. FRM. CRISSEY, ASHBEL WALLER. rec 1810. pp 239, 240

Deed dated 1810. BARNABAS McCARREN & POLLY his wife to LUDLOW PIERSON. Hamilton lot 24. Signed BARNABUS McCARRAN, MARY McCARAN. Witn: JONATHAN PIERSON, JOHN REILY. rec 1810. pp 240, 241

Deed dated 1809. JOHN SUTHERLAND & HENRY BROWN to JACOB BURNET of Cincinnati. Rossville lots 2, 12, 31, 48, 60 & 69. Signed JOHN SUTHERLAND, HENRY BROWN. Witn: WM. BOMBERGER JR, WM. PHARES JR. rec 1810. p241

Deed dated 1809. JOHN SUTHERLAND & HENRY BROWN to JACOB BURNET of Cincinnati. Rossville lots 6, 25. Signed and witness as above. rec 1810. pp 242, 243

Deed dated 1809. JOHN SUTHERLAND & HENRY BROWN to MICHAEL DELAROCH. Rossville lots 1, 2, 9, 10, 21. Signed and witn as above. rec 1810. p 243

Deed dated 1809. JOHN SUTHERLAND & HENRY BROWN to MICHAEL DELAROCH of Rossville. Rossville lots 4, 14. Signed and witness as above. rec 1810. pp 243, 244

Deed dated 1809. JOHN SUTHERLAND & HENRY BROWN to THOMAS McCULLOUGH. Rossville lot 3. Signed and witness as above. rec 1810. pp 244, 245

Deed dated 1810. THOMAS McCULLOUGH & ELIZABETH his wife to MICHAEL DELORAS of Rossville. Rossville lot 3. Signed THOS. McCULLOUGH, BETSY McCULLOUGH. Witn: JAMES WHITE, TIMOTHY GREEN. rec 1810. p 245

Deed dated 1809. BENJAMIN ENYART & MARY his wife to GERSHAM MOORE. S 12, T 2, R 3. Signed BEJAMIN ENYART, MARY (x) ENYART. Witn: PAUL SAUNDERS, JOHN VINNEDGE. rec 1801. pp 245, 246.

Deed dated 1809. BENJAMIN ENYART & MARY his wife to LEWIS MOORE. S 12, T 2, R 3. Signed and witness as above. rec 1801. pp 246, 247.

Deed dated 1809. Major SAMUEL READING by his agent JOHN R. MILLS to DAVID ENYART. Lot 1 in S 7, T 3, R 3. Signed SAMUEL READING by JRM, agent. Witn: JP THOS. HIGGINS, JOHN V. HIGGINS. rec 1810. p 247

BUTLER COUNTY LAND RECORDS: BOOK B

Deed dated 1810. WILLIAM BARKALOW & MARY his wife to ZEBULON BARKALOW. S 33, T 2, R 5. Signed WM. P. BARKALOW, MARY BARKALOW. Witn: WILLIAM F. BARKALOW, HENRY WEAVER. rec 1810. pp 247, 248

Deed dated 1810. EDWARD MEEKS & DOROTHEA his wife to WILLIAM ELLIOTT. S 23, T 3, R 2. Bound by land of - JAMESON, DANIEL CALDWELL, THOMAS JOHN & ETHAN ALLAN JOHN. Signed EDW. MEEKS, DOROTHEA G. MEEKS. Witn: JOHN LIANAN, JP WM. PERRY. rec 1810. pp 248, 249

Deed dated 1810. JONATHAN DAYTON to JOSHUA ELLIOTT. S 23, T 3, R 3. Signed JONATHAN DAYTON by JOHN REILY atty. Witn: NICHOLAS CURTIS, ISAAC STANLEY. rec 1810. pp 249, 250

Deed dated 1810. EDWARD HARLAN & SARAH his wife to ISAAC STANLEY. Hamilton lot 235. Signed EDWARD HARLAN, SARAH (x) HARLAN. Witn: JAMES MILLS, WILLIAM HERBERT. rec 1810. pp 250, 251

Deed dated 1810. WILLIAM **WALLAS** of Sandusky to JOHN SUTHERLAND & HENRY BROWN. Hamilton lot 121. Signed WILLIAM **WALKER**. Witn: DANIEL BAKER, A. BRUTH. rec 1810. p 251

Deed dated 1810. JOHN SUTHERLAND & HENRY BROWN to JAMES MILLS. Rossvill lot 9. Signed JOHN SUTHERLAND HENRY BROWN. Witn: JAMES STEELE, JAMES BECK. rec 1810. pp 251, 252

Deed dated 1810. CHARLES CATROW & CATHARINE his wife to GEORGE STUMP. S 25, T 3, R 4. Signed CHARLES (x) CATROW, CATHARINE (x) CATROW. Witn: BROOK BUXTON, HENRY WEAVER. rec 1810. pp 252, 253

Deed dated 1810. CHARLES CATROW & CATHARINE his wife to JOHN LOY. S 25, T 3, R 4. Signed CHARLES (x) CATROW, CATHARINE (x) CATROW. Witn: GEORGE STUMP (german script, HENRY WEAVER. rec 1810. pp 253, 254

Deed dated 1809. **BENJAMIN** ENYART & MARY his wife to PAUL SAUNDERS. S 12, T 2, R 3. Signed **B'JAMIN** ENYART, MARY (x) ENYART. Witn: LEWIS MOORE, JOHN VINNEDGE. rec 1801. pp 254, 255

Deed dated 1810. JACOB POWERS & NANCY his wife to JAMES FINNEY. S 13, T 3, R 3. Signed JACOB POWERS, NANCY (x) POWERS. Witn: P. WILLIAMSON, SAMUEL STEWART. rec 1810. p 255

BUTLER COUNTY LAND RECORDS: BOOK B

Deed dated 1809.   JOHAN SMITH & ELIZABETH his wife to
WILLIAM LEG.   S 2, T 2, R 3.   Signed JOHN SMITH,
ELIZABETH SMITH.   Witn: P. T. SCHENCK, THOS. H. SILL.
rec 1810.   pp 255, 256

Deed dated 1809.   JOHN SUTHERLAND & HENRY BROWN to
ELIZABETH SYMMES, WILLIAM SYMMES, PHEBE SYMMES the
younger, ESTHER SYMMES & TIMOTHY SYMMES, sons and
daus, heirs of WILLIAM SYMMES. Rossville lots 45,
64, 95 & 96, outlot 34 purchased in Wm's lifetime.
Signed JOHN SUTHERLAND, HENRY BROWN. Witn: WM.
BOMBERGER JR, WM. PHARES JR.   rec 1810.   pp 256, 257

Deed dated 1810. Heirs (sons & daus) of JOHN SCOTT
to WILLIAM ROBISON. S 25, T 5, R 2. Signed JAMES
SCOTT, JAMES YOUNG (& his wife) JANE YOUNG, DAVID
SCOTT, ROBERT SCOTT, JOHN E. SCOTT, RICHARD SCOTT,
MARY SCOTT, JANE SCOTT. Witn: MATTW. G. WALLACE, JP
MATTH. RICHARDSON. rec 1810.   p 257

Deed dated 1810.   THOMAS PRICE & SELAH his wife to
DANIEL WILSON of Green Co. S 19, T 5, R 2. Signed
THOMAS PRICE, SELAH (x) PRICE. Witn: MATTHEW
RICHARDSON, BETSY SIMSON.   rec 1810.   p 258

Quitclaim dated 1810. ISAAC MATSON & _JOANNAH_ his
wife, heirs of ENOCH MATSON, to ELIZABETH TAYLOR.
S 23, T 3, R 3. Signed ISAAC MATSON, _JOANNA_ MATSON.
Witn: JP JAMES SILVER, DAVID DUFF. rec 1810.   pp
258, 259

Deed dated 1808. STEPHEN CRANE & MARY his wife to
DAVID WILLIAMSON.   S 15, T 3, R 3 in Liberty Twp.
Signed STEPHEN CRANE, MARY (x) CRANE.   Witness: P.
WILLIAMSON, ROBERT McINTIRE. rec 1810.   pp 259, 260

Deed dated 1810. CELADON SYMMES & PHEBE his wife to
THOMAS BLAIR. Hamilton lot 70. Signed CELADON
SYMMES, PHEBE SYMMES. Witn: H.B. HAWTHORN, BENJAMIN
DAVIS.   rec 1810.   pp 260, 261

Deed dated 1810.   JOHN TAYLOR & _ESTHER_ his wife of
Rossville to JOHN SUTHERLAND. Rossville lots 23, 28,
33, 38. Signed JOHN TAYLOR, _HETEY_ TAYLOR. Witn:
ISAAC STANLEY, G. DICK.   rec 1810.   pp 261, 262

Deed dated 1810. TIMOTHY WOODRUFF & PHEBE his wife
to JOHN SUTHERLAND & HENRY BROWN. Hamilton lot 223.
Signed TIMOTHY WOODRUFF, PHEBE WOODRUFF. Witn: HENRY
WEAVER, LEWIS MOORE.   rec 1810.   p 262

BUTLER COUNTY LAND RECORDS: BOOK B

Deed dated 1810. GERSHAM MOORE & ANNEY his wife to DANIEL HEATON. S 12, T 2, R 3. Signed GERSHAM MOORE ANNEY (x) MOORE. Witn: HENRY WEAVER, LEWIS MOORE. rec 1810. p 263

Deed dated 1810. EZRA F. FREEMAN to YORK, "a free black man commonly known as YORK FREEMAN". S 4, T 1, R 2. Bound by land of THOMAS MURDOCK, JOHN WALKER. Signed EZRA F. FREEMAN. Witn: GEORGE KIRKPATRICK, SALLY CASSIDY, MICHAEL HAGAMAN. rec 1810. pp 263, 264

Mortgage dated 1810. JOHN G. WINANS of Lebanon, Warren Co, to JOHN VANNUYS & ISAAC PAXTON. S 15, T 3, R 2. Signed JOHN G. WINANS. Witn: ADAM NUTT, ABRM. YEAZLE. rec 1810. pp 264, 265

Deed dated 1810. JOHN SUTHERLAND & HENRY BROWN to ROBERT IRWIN. Rossville lot 61. Signed JOHN SUTHERLAND, HENRY BROWN. Witn: JAMES STEELE, JAMES BECK. rec 1810. pp 265, 266

Deed dated 1810. JACOB BURNET & REBECCA his wife of Cincinnati to JOHN CALDWELL of Liberty Twp. S 8, T 3, R 2. Bound by JOHN BECKET's land. Signed JAC. BURNET, REBECCA BURNET. Witn: THOS. H. SILL, JAMES EWING. rec 1810. pp 266, 267

Deed dated 1810. JACOB BURNET & REBECCA his wife to DANIEL AVERY. S 28, T 3, R 2. Signed as above. Witn: JOHN MAHARD, JOHN CALDWELL. rec 1810. pp 267, 268

Deed dated 1810. BENJAMIN ENYART & MARY his wife to DAVID ENYART. S 12, T 3, R 3. Signed BENJAMIN ENYART MARY (x) ENYART. Witn: JOHN AYRES, ZACARIAH SUTTON. rec 1810. pp 268, 269

Deed dated 1808. THOMAS JOHNSTON & MARTHA his wife and STEPHEN GILL & JEAN his wife to JOHN JOHNSON. S 28, T 3, R 2. Signed THOMAS JOHNSON, MARTHA JOHNSON, STEPHEN GILL, JAIN GILL. Witn: HENRY (x) MILLER, ISC. S. SWEARINGEN. rec 1810. pp 269, 270

Deed dated 1810. THOMAS JOHNSON SR of Liberty Twp to JOHN JOHNSON of same. S 28, T 3, R 2. Signed THOMAS JOHNSON. Witn: JAMES HEATON, THOMAS JOHNSON JR. rec 1810. p 270

Deed dated 1810. THOMAS JOHNSON SR of Liberty Twp to THOMAS JOHNSON JR, JAMES JOHNSON & SAMUEL JOHNSON. S 28, T 3, R 2. Signed THOMAS JOHNSON SR. Witn: JAMES HEATON, JOHN JOHNSON. rec 1810. p 271

BUTLER COUNTY LAND RECORDS: BOOK B

Deed dated 1810. MICHAEL PEARCE & PHEBE his wife of "Mattison Twp" to ANDREW HAMILTON of same. S 6, R 4 of "said Twp". Bound by land of THOMAS SWIFT, ISAAC MARTIN, RUSSEL POTTER, JACOB MILLER. Signed MICHAEL PEARCE, PHEBE PEARCE. Witn: STEPHEN GARD, RACHEL GARD. rec 1810. pp 271, 272

Deed dated 1810. JOSIAH WILSON & MARY his wife to BENJAMIN LONG. S 13, T 3, R 2. Signed JOSIAH WILSON, MARY WILSON. Witn: ISAAC STANLEY, SAMUEL BROWN. rec 1810. pp 272, 273

Deed dated 1810. ABRAHAM DEMOTT & HANNAH his wife of Preble Co to LAWRENCE MONTFORT of Warren Co. S 6, T 2, R 4. Signed A. DEMOT. HANNAH DEMOTT. Witn: JAMES PANTIER, JOSEPH WILLIAMS. rec 1810. pp 273, 274

Deed dated 1810. JOSEPH PEAK & RUTH his wife to WILLIAM ELLIOTT. S 1, T 2, R 3. Bound by land of PETER MURPHEY, JOHN HERVEY. Signed JOSEPH PEAK, RUTH PEAK. Witn: ELIAZER WEST, WILLIAM HUNT. JP JOHN AYRES. rec 1810. pp 274, 275

Deed dated 1810. DAVID GARRIGUS & ABIGAIL his wife to JOHN MAXWELL. S 15, T 1, R 2. Signed DAVID GARRIGUS, ABIGAIL GARRIGUS. Witn: JACOB GARRIGUS, MARY GARRIGUS. rec 1810. pp 275, 276

Deed dated 1809. USA to WILLIAM McKAIN. S 27, T 5, R 2. rec 1810. pp 276, 277

Deed dated 1810. ADAM DEEM & GENCY his wife to WILLIAM BALDWIN. Bound by ALLEN SIMPSON's land. S 6, T 2, R 4. Signed ADAM DEEM, GENCY DEEM. Witn: RICHARD BROWN, NATHAN STUBBS. rec 1810. pp 277, 278

Deed dated 1809. REES PRICE & SARAH his wife to WILLIAM SCOTT. Hamilton lot 178 & outlot 21. Signed REES PRICE, SARAH PRICE. Witn: ELIAS I. DAYTON, FIELDING LOWRY. rec 1810. pp 278, 279

Deed dated 1810. AMOS VALLENTINE of Warren Co to DAVID MULFORD. S 30, T 3, R 3. Signed AMOS VALLENTINE. Witn: ENOS WILLIAMS, RD. CUNNINGHAM. rec 1810. pp 279, 280

Deed dated 1810. ISAAC WILES & ELIZABETH his wife to JOHN HALL, house carpenter. Hamilton lot 186. Signed ISAAC WILES, ELIZABETH (x) WILES. Witn: ISAAC STANLEY, SAML. ASTON. rec 1810. pp 280, 281

BUTLER COUNTY LAND RECORDS: BOOK B

Deed dated 1810. JAMES REED, house joiner, to JOHN HALL. Hamilton lots 72, 73. Signed JAMES REED. Witn: WILLIAM MURRAY, JOEL HANCOCK. rec 1810. pp 281, 282

Deed dated 1810. ISAAC MOSS to JOHN HALL. Hamilton lots 72, 73. Signed ISAAC MOSS. Witn: WILLIAM MURRAY, JOEL HANCOCK. rec 1810. pp 282, 283

Deed dated 1810. JOHN HALL to DAVID K. ESTE. Hamilton lots 72, 73. Signed JOHN HALL. Witn: JOHN IRWIN. ISAAC STANLEY. rec 1810. p 283

Deed dated 1810. WILLIAM HARLAN & HANNAH his wife to DAVID K. ESTE. Rossville lot 78. Signed WM. HARLAND HANNAH (x) HARLAND. Witn: ISAAC STANLEY, JOHN HALL. rec 1810. pp 284

Deed dated 1810. WILLIAM DILLON to ISAAC WILES. Hamilton lot 195. Signed WILLIAM DILLON. Witn: NOAH WADE, WM. MURRAY. rec 1810. pp 284, 285

Deed dated 1798. JOHN GORDON of Hamilton Co, NW Ter'y, to ANDREW McGARVEY of same. Hamilton lot 177 in S 2, T 1, R 3. Signed JOHN GORDON. Witn: THOS. McCULLOUGH, BENJAMIN DAVIS. rec 1810. pp 285, 286

Deed dated 1809. JOHN SMITH & ELIZABETH his wife of Hamilton Co to JOHN V. L. DAVIS. S 32, T 3, R 3. Bound by land of DANIEL WOODRUFF, WILLIAM & ARTHUR LEGG, GEORGE LEE, DANIEL GRIFFITH, JAMES McCLELLAND. Signed JOHN SMITH, ELIZABETH SMITH. Witn: THOS. H. SILL, ARTHUR LEGG. rec 1810. pp 286, 287

Deed dated 1801. JOHN CLEVES SYMMES & SUSAN his wife of NW Ter'y to sons & daus, heirs of GABRIEL ALLEN of NJ: ELIZABETH ALLEN, RICHARD F. ALLAN, PHEBE ALLAN, SAMUEL ALLAN & RACHEL ALLAN. S 24, T 3, R 2. Signed JOHN CLEVES SYMMES, SUSAN SYMMES. Witn: WILLIAM RUFFIN, W. WHISTLER. rec 1810. pp 287, 288

Deed dated 1810. WILLIAM McCLELLAN, Sheriff of Butler Co, to SALEM POCOCK. Judgement obtained by THOMAS HUNT against ELEAZAR WEST. S 20, T 3, R 3 seized, sold to Pocock. Signed WILLIAM McCLELLAN. Witn: JAMES McBRIDE, JOHN WHITWORTH. rec 1810. pp 288, 289, 290

Deed dated 1810. THOMAS SWIFTH & REBECCA his wife to AARON HOUGHHAM SR. S 1, T 2, R 3. Signed THOMAS SWIFT SR, REBECCA SWIFT. Witn: HENRY WEAVER, AARON HOUGHHAM JR. rec 1810. pp 290, 291

BUTLER COUNTY LAND RECORDS: BOOK B

Mortgage dated 1810. AARON HOUGHHAM SR to AARON HOUGHHAM JR. S 1, T 2, R 3. Signed AARON HOUGHHAM (no SR, JR). Witn: HENRY WEAVER, THOMAS SWIFT. rec 1810. pp 291, 292

Deed dated 1810. EZRA F. FREEMAN to ROBERT FLEMING. S 4, T 1, R 2. Signed EZRA F. FREEMAN. Wtn: NOAH WADE, JOHN AYERS. rec 1810. p 292

Agreement dated 1810. EZRA F. FREEMAN to THOMAS MURDOCK. Notes against JOSIAH BROWNSON of Trumble Co held by Murdock; Atty JOHN L. EDWARDS to collect. Freeman to convey S 4, T 2, R 1 to Murdock when money recvd. Signed EZRA F. FREEMAN. Witn: ASAHEL MURDOCK, JOHN CASSIDY. rec 1810. pp 292, 293

Deed dated 1807. PETER MURPHEY & ELENOR his wife to HUMPHREY NICHOLES. S 2, T 2, R 3. Signed PETER (x) MURPHEY, ELENOR (x) MURPHEY. Witn: JOHN MURPHEY, ISC. S. SWEARINGEN. rec 1810. pp 293, 294

Deed dated 1810. DANIEL PAGE to JOSEPH KELLY. S 1, T 3, R 3. Bound by NATHANIEL BELL's land. Signed DANIEL PAGE. Witn: GEORGE KELLY, JP NATHAN STUBBS. rec 1810. p 294

Power of Atty dated 1809. DAVID EDWARDS named as atty for heirs of JOHN GILDERSLEEVE: SILAS GILDER-SLEEVE of Orange Co, NY; HANNAH BREESE wife of JOHN & sister of JG; ASA GILDERSLEEVE, PATIENCE CHURCHEL wife of LEMUEL & sister of JG, all of Tioga Co, NY; SUSANNA BREESE wife of AZARIAH and sister of JG of Somerset Co, NJ; DAVID EDWARDS only child of RACHEL EDWARDS, dec, sister of JG of Somerset Co, NJ; EZEKIEL DAY, SARAH DAY, PHEBE DAY, LOT DAY & SEPH-RONIA DAY of Morris Co, NJ, children of MARY DAY sister of JG. Signed JOHN BREESE, HANNAH BREESE, ASA GILDERSLEEVE, LEMUEL CHURCHILL, PATIENCE CHURCHILL, SALLY DAY, SILAS GILDERSLEEVE, AZARIAH BREES, SUSANNA (x) BREES, EZEKIEL DAY, ELIZABETH DAY, PHEBE DAY, LOT DAY. Witn: CALEB BAKER, SARAH BAKER, SAM'L SEELY, ZOPHER FINCH, JAMES FINCH JR, JOHN BREES, HUGH McEOWEN, JONAT'N OGDEN, LERING W. EDWARDS, JOHN AYERS. rec 1810. pp 295, 296

Deed dated 1809. MATTHEW WINTON & ELIZABETH his wife to JAMES MILLS & WILLIAM McCLAIN. S 5, T 2, R 3. Signed MATTW. WINTON, ELIZA WINTON. Witn: THOS. McCULLOUGH, JOHN HANCOCK, CHARLES SWEARINGEN. rec 1810. p 297

BUTLER COUNTY LAND RECORDS: BOOK B

Deed dated 1810. JAMES MILLS & SARAH his wife and WILLIAM McCLAIN & ISABELL his wife to ROBERT IRWIN. S 5, T 2, R 3. Signed JAMES MILLS, WILLIAM McCLEAN, SARAH MILLS, ISABELL McCLEAN. Witn: JAMES SMITH, SAML ASTEN. rec 1810. pp 297, 298

Quitclaim dated 1810. ADAM LEE & CATHARINE his wife, PHEBE SMITH, JOHN SUNDERLAND & SALLY his wife, ISAAC PAXTON & LANEY his wife, JOHN VANNUYS & ISAAC VANNUYS to DAVID EDWARDS, atty for heirs of JOHN GILDERSLEEVE S 14 & 23, T 2, R 3. Patent made to ISAAC GILDER-SLEEVE, decd son & heir of JOHN. Women all identified as having the maiden name VANNUYS. Signed CATHARINE (x) LEE, PHEBE (x) SMITH, SARAH (x) SUNDERLAND, ISAAC PAXTON, LANEY (x) PAXTON, ISAAC VANNUYS, JOHN VANNUYS. Witn: CALEB WILLIAMS, JAMES SMITH, HENRY WALLACE, JP DANIEL REEDER. rec 1810. pp 298, 299

Deed dated 1810. HUMPHREY NICKLES & ISABELLA his wife to SAMUEL ENYART. S 2, T 2, R 3. Signed HUMPHREY NICKLES, ISABELLA (x) NICKLES. Witn: SAML BAYLES, JOHN VINNEDGE. rec 1810. p 300

Deed dated 1810. JAMES FINNY & SARAH his wife to PHILIP MUTCHNER. S 13, T 3, R 3. Signed JAMES FINNEY, SARAH FINNEY. Witn: P. WILLIAMSON, JOHN BARTON. rec 1810. pp 300, 301

Deed dated 1810. JAMES FERGUSON & JANE his wife of Cincinnati to PHILIP MUTCHNER. S 22, T 3, R 3. Signed JAMES FERGUSON, JANE FERGUSON. Witn: ALIJAH F. FERGUSON, JOHN MAHARD. rec 1810. pp 301, 302

Mortgage dated 1810. JOHN & WILLIAM PEARSON to JAMES FERGUSON above. S 22, T 3, R 3. Payt due 1811. Signed JOHN PIERSON, WILLIAM PIERSON. Witn: NATHL REEDER, JP ETHAN STONE. rec 1810. pp 302, 303

Mortgage dated 1810. JAMES FINNEY to JACOB POWERS. S 13, T 3, R 3 in Liberty Twp. Signed JAMES FINNEY. Witn: JOHN LINN, ADAM LINN, JP P. WILLIAMSON. rec 1810. pp 303, 304

Deed dated 1810. JOHN HALL, carpenter to JONATHAN PIERSON, taylor. Hamilton lot 54. Signed JOHN HALL. Witn: JAMES MILLS, LUDLOW PIERSON. rec 1810. p 304

Deed dated 1810. JOHN HALL to JONATHAN PIERSON. Hamilton lot 73. Signed JOHN HALL. Witn: JAMES MILLS, LUDLOW PIERSON. rec 1810. p 304, 305

BUTLER COUNTY LAND RECORDS: BOOK B

Deed dated 1810. KING DEARMOND & HANNAH his wife of Ross Twp to JOHN HALSTEAD (see below) of same. S 26, T 3, R 1. Dearmond, assignee of JOHN N. MILES, given patent in 1808. Signed KING DEARMOND, HANNAH (x) DEARMOND. Witn: JAMES PARKISON, M. PARKISON. rec 1810. pp 305, 306

Deed dated 1810. MAURICE JONES & NANCY his wife of Ross Twp to JOHN HOLSTEAD (see above). S 30, T 3, R 2. Signed MAURICE JONES, NANCY (x) JONES. Witn: M. PARKISON, JAMES MARSHALL. rec 1810. pp 306, 307

Deed dated 1810. THOMAS BLAIR & PEGGY his wife to ANDERSON SPENCER. Hamilton lot 70. Signed THOS. BLAIR, PEGGY BLAIR. Witn: DAN MILLIKIN, H.B. HAW-THORN, JOS. HOUGH. rec 1810. p 308

Deed dated 1810. DAVID DUFFIELD & REBECKAH his wife to WILLIS WHITSON. S 17, T 3, R 3. Signed DAVID DUFFIELD, REBECAH DUFFIELD. Witn: JOHN (x) HOFFMAN. rec 1810. pp 308, 309

Deed dated 1808. WILLIAM BALDWIN & MARY his wife to STOPHEL REED. S 18, T 2, R 4. Signed WILLIAM BALD-WIN, MARY BALDWIN. Witn: JOHN SAMUEL MAN, HENRY WEAVER. rec 1810. p 310

Deed dated 1807. ALEXANDER CHAMBERS & MARY his wife of Lemon Twp to CHRISTOPHER REED of same. S 18, T 2, R 4. Bound by JACOB SNIDER's land. Signed ALEXANDER (x) CHAMBERS, MARY (x) CHAMBERS. Witn: SAML CHAM-BERS, HENRY WEAVER. rec 1810. p 311

Deed dated 1810. EDMOND LISTON & ELIZABETH his wife to DANIEL COLLVER. S 1, T 2, R 3. Bound by land of THOMAS SWIFTH, JOHN SCHENCK. Signed EDMOND LISTON, ELIZABETH (x) LISTON. Witn: JAMES MATTIX, HENRY WEAVER. rec 1810. pp 311, 312

Deed dated 1810. JESSE HUNT & ELIZABETH his wife of Cincinnati and ABIJAH HUNT of Natchez, Miss'pi Ter'y to JOSEPH GASTON. S 27, T 2, R 2. Signed JESSE HUNT, ABIJAH HUNT by JH as atty, ELIZA. HUNT. Witn: JOHN W. BROWN, GRIFFIN YEATMAN. rec 1810. pp 312, 313

Deed dated 1810. RICHARD S. THOMAS & FRANCES his wife of Warren Co to PEYTON SHORT SYMMES of Cincinnati. S 22, T 2, R 2. Signed RICHARD S. THOMAS, FRANCES THOMAS. Witn: WILLIAM (x) FREEMAN, JOHN W. BROWN. rec 1810. pp 314, 315

BUTLER COUNTY LAND RECORDS: BOOK B

Deed dated 1805. JOHN CHAMBERLAIN & NANCY his wife to JAMES TAPSCOTT. S 32, T 2, R 5. Signed JOHN CHAMBERLAIN, NANCY CHAMBERLAIN. Witn: W. C. SCHENCK, MARTIN (x) McCREA. rec 1810. pp 315, 316

Deed dated 1808. WILLIAM BARKALOW & MARY his wife of Lemon Twp to JAMES TAPSCOTT. S 34, T 2, R 5. Bound by land of JOHN COSC. Signed WILLIAM P. BARKALOW, MARY BARKALOW. Witn: ROBERT SHAW, HENRY WEAVER. rec 1810. p 316

Deed dated 1810. JOHN WINGATE & WILLIAM DILLON to ISAAC WILES. S 24, T 2, R 2. Signed JOHN WINGATE, WILLIAM DILLON, AMMA WINGATE. Witn: NOAH WADE, JAMES MILLS. rec 1810. p 317

Mortgage dated 1810. GARRETT VAN NOSDOLL to CULBERT-SON PARK of Cincinnati. S 4, T 3, R 2. Signed GARRETT VAN ARSDALLEN. Witn: SAML PETERSON, JOHN MAHARD. rec 1810. pp 317, 318

Deed dated 1810. JOHN CLEVES SYMMES to JOHN VANNICE of St. Clair Twp. S 15, T 3, R 2. Signed JOHN CLEVES SYMMES. Witn: THOMAS RANDOLPH, ISAAC DUNN. rec 1810. pp 318, 319

Deed dated 1810. Heirs of JOHN GILDERSLEEVE to JOHN VANNUYS. S 14 & 23, T 2, R 3. Signed SILAS GILDER-SLEEVE, JOHN BREES, HANNAH BREES, ASA GILDERSLEEVE, LEMUEL CHURCHEL, PATIENCE CHURCHEL, AZARIAH BREES, SUSANNA BREES, EZEKIEL DAY, SARAH DAY, ELISEBETH DAY, PHEBE DAY, LOTH DAY, SEPHRONIAH DAY, by DAVID EDWARDS atty, and DAVID EDWARDS (for himself). Witn: JAMES HEATON, DAN MILLIKIN. rec 1810. pp 319, 320, 321

Deed dated 1809. JOHN WINGATE, Sheriff of Butler Co, to HENRY WASON. Judgement obtained against JOSEPH CILLY & BENJAMIN CILLY, admTrs of JONATHAN CILLY, by Wason. Seized S 34, T 3, R 2, sold at auction. Signed JOHN WINGATE, Sheriff. Witn: ISAAC STANLEY, WILLIAM HAYS. rec 1810. pp 321, 322, 323

Deed dated 1810. HENRY WASON & SARAH his wife to JAMES JOICE of Hamilton Co. S 34 or 35, T 3, R 2. Bound by land formerly owned by JACOB HIDAY, now property of JOEL WILLIAMS. Signed HENRY WASON, SARAH (x) WASON. Witn: WILLIAM WALLACE, WILLIAM EVANS, JP ROBT SMITH. rec 1810. p 323

Mortgage dated 1809. ALEXANDER SIMPSON to SAMUEL SMITH of Hamilton Co. Bound by land of ALBIN SHAW,

BUTLER COUNTY LAND RECORDS: BOOK B

JOSEPH BOLTIN. No S-T-R given. Paymt due 1810. Signed ALEXANDER (x) SIMPSON. Witn: AARON POWERS, JAMES COMSTOCK. rec 1811. p 324

Deed dated 1810. SAMUEL C. VANCE of LAWRENCEBURGH, Indiana Ter'y & MARY his wife to JOHN SUTHERLAND & HENRY BROWN. Hamilton lot 122. Signed SAM. C. VANCE MARY M. VANCE. Witn: none. rec 1811. pp 324, 325

Deed dated 1811. SAMUEL McCONNELL of Vincennes, Indiana Ter'y to JOHN SUTHERLAND & HENRY BROWN. Hamilton outlot 16. Signed SAMUEL McCONNELL. Witn: JOHN WHITWORTH, H.B. HAWTHORN. rec 1811. pp 325, 326

Deed dated 1811. ANDERSON SPENCER & MARY his wife to JACOB RICKARD. Hamilton lot 70. Signed ANDERSON SPENCER, MARY (x) SPENCER. Witn: ABRAM COLWELL, JAMES MARTIN. rec 1811. pp 326, 327

Deed dated 1810. JONATHAN PIERSON to JOHN WARD. Hamilton lot 54. Signed JONATHAN PIERSON. Witn: ABRAM COLWELL, SAMUEL DARKIES. rec 1811. p 327

Deed dated 1811. JOHN CLAPP & CHARLOTTE his wife to JACOB HOUSE of Hamilton Co. S 14, T 2, R 2. Signed JOHN CLOPP, CHARLOOT (x) CLAP. Witn: M. HUESTON, ROBERT GRAY. rec 1811. pp 327, 328

Deed dated 1811. SAMUEL BEELER JR & MARGARET his wife to SAMUEL BEELER SR. S 25, T 5, R 1. Bound by JOEL COLLINS' land. Signed SAML BEELER JR, MARGARET (x) BEELER. Witn: MATTH. RICHARDSON, HENRY WATTS. rec 1811. pp 328, 329

Mortgage dated 1807. DAVID SLOAN to ZACHEUS GOLDSMITH of Southold, Suffolk Co, NY. Land in Fairfield Twp bound by land of CELADON SYMMES, WILLIAM WELLS, WILLIAM OSBORN, MR. HUNT. Notes bearing seals of SLOAN and STEPHEN CRANE payable in 2 years. Signed DAVID SLOAN. Witn: THOMAS S. LESTER, STEPHEN CRANE. rec 1811. pp 329, 330

Deed dated 1811. AARON RICHARDSON of Warren Co to ELIAS ROBY. S 17, T 3, R 3. Signed ARON (x) RICHARDSON. Witn: DAVID FUDGE, GEO. KESLING, ANDREW SURFACE. rec 1811. pp 330, 331

Deed dated 1810. SAMUEL McCLARY & MARY his wife to JAMES YOUNG. S A4, T 5, R 2. Signed SAMUEL McCLARY, MARY McCLARY. Witn: MATTHEW RICHARDSON, BETSEY SIMSON. rec 1811. pp 331, 332

BUTLER COUNTY LAND RECORDS: BOOK B

Deed dated 1800. DAVID CUMMINGS of Hamilton Co, NW Ter'y to RICHARD CAIN of same. S 30, T 2, R 2. Signed DAVID CUMMINGS. Witn: D.C. ORCUTT, JOHN GREER. rec 1811. p 332

Deed dated 1811. THOMAS BLAIR & PEGGY his wife to PEREGRINE ARNDORF. Rossville lots 82, 83, 88, 89. Signed THOS. BLAIR, PEGGY BLAIR. Witn: ISAAC STANLEY, JOSEPH HOUGH. rec 1811. pp 332, 333

Deed dated 1811. SAMUEL BEELOR JR & MARY his wife to JAMES BEELOR. S 25, T 5, R 1. Signed SAML BEELER JR MARY (x) BEELER. Witn: MATTH. RICHARDSON, HENRY WATTS. rec 1811. pp 333, 334

Mortgage dated 1811. ANDREW SMITH of Milford Twp to DAVID WALKER of Hamilton Co. Notes held on S 36, T 5, R 2. Signed ANDREW SMITH. Witn: GILBERT MARSHAL, MATH. RICHARDSON. rec 1811. pp 334, 335

Deed dated 1810. JOHN DEBOLT & RACHEL his wife to JOSEPH WEBB. S 11, T 3, R 3. Signed JOH DEBOLT, RACHEL (x) DEBOLT. Witn: LAZARUS LANGSTON, NATHAN STUBBS JP. rec 1811. pp 335, 336

Deed dated 1811. MATTHEW WINTON & ELIZABETH his wife to JAMES WITHROW. S 32, T 3, R 3. Signed MATTW. WINTON, ELIZABETH WINTON. Witn: BENJAMIN DANFORD, CHARLES SWEARINGEN. rec 1811. pp 336, 337

Deed dated 1811. JAMES WITHROW & SARAH his wife to ALEXANDER WILSON. S 32, T 3, R 3. Bound by JOHN PATTERSON's land. Signed JAMES WITHEROE, SARAH (x) WITHROW. Witn: JAMES BRYAN, JOHN SWEARINGEN. rec 1811. p 337

Deed dated 1811. JOHN HORMEL of Warren Co to SAMUEL MATTIX. S 30, T 2, R 4. Wife mentioned in text, no name or signature. Signed JOHN HORMEL. Witn: ENOS WILLIAMS. rec 1811. p 338

Deed dated 1810. DANIEL HEATON to EBENEZER HEATON JR of Warren Co. S 12, T 2, R 3. Signed DANIEL HEATON. Witn: ABRAHAM VAN SICKLE, HENRY WEAVER. rec 1811. pp 338, 339

Quitclaim dated 1811. Heirs of RUDOLPH FLEENOR to STEPHEN SLIPHER & ELIZABETH his wife, late FLEENOR. S 13 & 24, T 2, R 3. All parties named as son, dau or s/n/law of RUDOLPH. Signed GEORGE FLEENOR, DANIEL FLEENOR, JACOB SLIPHER (german script) (& his wife)

BUTLER COUNTY LAND RECORDS: BOOK B

SUSANNAH (x) SLIPHER, GEORGE KERSHNER (& his wife) MARGARET (x) KERSHNER, MARY (x) FLEENOR. Witn: JAMES SMITH, JACOB BAUM, DAVID FLEENOR. rec 1811. pp 339, 340

Deed dated 340, 341. DAVID GARRIGUS & ABIGAIL his wife to WILLIAM DAVID. S 7, T 2, R 3. Signed DAVID GARRIGUS, ABIGAIL GARRIGUS. Witn: JAMES HEATON, DANIEL CLARK. rec 1811. pp 340, 341

Deed dated 1811. JOHN HORMEL & ELENOR his wife of Warren Co to AARON SOUTHARD. S 30, T 2, R 4. Signed JOHN HORMEL, ELENOR (x) HORMEL. Witn: ENOS WILLIAMS, JACOB MORRIS. rec 1811. pp 341, 342

Mortgage dated 1811. SAMUEL MATTIX & ELENOR his wife to JOHN HORMEL as above. S 30, T 2, R 4. Signed SAMUEL MATTIX, ELENOR (x) MATTIX. Witn: ENOS WILLIAMS. rec 1811. pp 342, 343

Deed dated 1810. JONATHAN PIERSON & MATILDA his wife to JOHN HALL. S 18, T 1, R 4. Signed JONATHAN PIERSON, MATILDA PIERSON. Witn: JAMES MILLS, LUDLOW PIERSON. rec 1811. pp 343, 344

Deed dated 1810. LUDLOW PIERSON, cabinet maker, & ELENOR his wife to JOHN HALL. S 18, 19, 20, 16, 17, T 1, R 4. Signed LUDLOW PIERSON, ELENOR (x) PIERSON. Witn: JAMES MILLS, JOSEPH HOUGH. rec 1811. pp 344, 345

Deed dated 1810. JOHN GARRISON & SUSANNAH his wife of Wayne Twp to SILAS GARRISON. S 10, T , R 3. Bound by land of S. DAVIS, D. DUFFLES, SAML GARRISON, AARON GARRISON. Signed JOHN GARRISON, SUSANNAH (x) GARRISON. Witn: SAMUEL GARRISON, AARON GARRISON. rec 1811. pp 345, 346

Deed dated 1810. THOMAS BLAIR, merchant, & PEGGY his wife to JAMES MILLS. Rossville outlot 29. Signed THOS. BLAIR, PEGGY BLAIR. Witn: ISAAC STANLEY, JOSEPH BALDWIN. rec 1811. pp 346, 347

Deed dated 1811. JAMES MILLS & SARAH his wife of Rossville to JAMES ROSS of same. Rossville outlot 29. Signed JAMES MILLS, SARAH MILLS. Witn: WM. McCLELLAN, ISAAC STANLEY. rec 1811. pp 347, 348

Deed dated 1811. DAVID GARRIGUS & ABIGAIL his wife to DANIEL CLARK. S 36, T 2, R 2. Signed DAVID GARRIGUS, ABIGAIL GARRIGUS. Witn: JAMES HEATON, ISRAEL WOODRUFF. rec 1811. p 348

BUTLER COUNTY LAND RECORDS: BOOK B

Deed dated 1811. SAMUEL BEELER JR & MARY his wife to JOEL COLLINS. S 25, T 5, R 1. Signed SAML BEELER JR MARY (x) BEELER. Witn: MATTH. RICHARDSON, HENRY WATTS. rec 1811. pp 348, 349

Deed dated 1811. SAMUEL BEELER JR & MARY his wife to ELEAZAR HOAG. S 25, T 5, R 1. Signed and witness as above. rec 1811. pp 348, 349

Deed dated 1809. JOHN SUTHERLAND & HENRY BROWN to SAMUEL SCOTT of KY. Rossville lot 42. Signed JOHN SUTHERLAND, HENRY BROWN. Witn: WM. BOMBERGER JR, WM PHARES JR. rec 1811. p 351

Deed dated 1810. MALYN BAKER of Mad River, Champaign Co to WILLIAM STANLEY of Cincinnati. S 33, T 3, R 3. Signed MALYN BAKER. Witn: W.L. HATCH, GRIFFIN YEATMAN. rec 1811. pp 351, 352

Deed dated 1811. JAMES FINDLAY & JANE his wife of Cincinnati to JOHN COON. S 7, T 1, R 5. Signed JAMES FINDLAY, JANE FINDLAY. Witn: JOSEPH McMURRAY, GRIFFIN YEATMAN. rec 1811. pp 352, 353

Deed dated 1811. THOMAS HUNT JR & SARAH his wife and CHARLES WEST & MARY his wife, all of Turtle Creek Twp, Warren Co and DURAN WHITTLESEY & RUTH his wife of Liberty Twp to THOMAS HUNT SR of Liberty Twp. S 20, T 3, R 3. Bound by land of JOHN PHELPS, PETER VORHEES, HORATIO SHARP, JOSHUA ELLIOTT. Signed THOS. HUNT JR, SARAH HUNT, CHARLES WEST, MOLLY WEST, DURAN WHITTLESEY, RUTH WHITTLESEY. Witn: P. WILLIAMSON, JAMES ALLEN. rec 1811. pp 353, 354

Deed dated 1807. THOMAS HUNT SR, THOMAS HUNT JR, and CHARLES WEST to DURAN WHITTLESEY. S 20, T 3, R 3. Signed THOMAS HUNT, THOMAS HUNT JR, CHARLES WEST. Witn: ISC. S. SWEARINGEN, JOHN HARDEN, JP SILAS HURIN E. HATHAWAY. JP's note names ANNA HUNT, wife of Thos Sr, SARAH HUNT, MOLLY WEST (as above) relinq. right of dower. rec 1811. pp 354, 355

Mortgage dated 1811. THOMAS HUNT SR to OLIVER SPENCER of Hamilton Co. S 20, T 3, R 3. Signed THOMAS HUNT. Witn: DURAN WHITTLESEY, GRIFFIN YEATMAN. rec 1811. pp 355, 356

Mortgage dated 1811. DURAN WHITTLESEY to OLIVER M. SPENCER of Hamilton Co. S 20, T 3, R 3. Signed DURAN WHITTLESEY. Witn: THOS. HUNT, GRIFFIN YEATMAN rec 1811. p 356

BUTLER COUNTY LAND RECORDS: BOOK B

Deed dated 1811. DAVID GARRIGUS & ABIGAIL his wife to DANIEL CLARK. Affection for s/n/law and "for maintenance of my daughter EUNICE CLARK, wife of him". S 36, T 2, R 2. Signed DAVID GARRIGUS, ABIGAIL GARRIGUS. Witn: JAMES HEATON, ISRAEL WOODRUFF. rec 1811. p 357

Deed dated 1811. JOHN NOBLE CUMMINS of Essex Co, NJ by WILLIAM C. SCHENCK, atty, to JOSEPH F. RANDOLPH. S 17, T 2, R 2. Signed W.C. SCHENCK for JNC. Witn: BENJAMIN F. RANDOLPH, P.T. SCHENCK. rec 1811. pp 357, 358

Deed dated 1811. JOHN GARRISON & SUSANNA his wife to MOSES CRUME. S 19, T 3, R 3. Signed JOHN GARRISON, SUSANNA (x) GARRISON. Witn: BETSEY SIMSON, MATTH. RICHARDSON. rec 1811. pp 358, 359

Deed dated 1803. ROBERT McCLELAN of KY to JAMES WILKINS of McKeesport, PA. S 32, T 2, R 3. Signed ROBT McCLELLAN. Witn: JOHN REILY, JAC. BURNET. rec 1811. pp 359, 360

Deed dated 1811. JAMES WILKINS & LYDIA his wife of Belmont Co to WILLIAM MURRAY. S 32, T 2, R 3. Signed JAMES WILKINS, LYDIA WILKINS. Witn: SOLOMON WARDELL, STERLING JOHNSTON. rec 1811. pp 360. 361

Deed dated 1810. THOMAS COOCH & HANNAH his wife to JOHN IRWIN. S 29, T 5, R 2. Signed THOS. COOCH, HANNAH COOCH. Witn: THOS. SANKEY, WILLIAM PRICE. rec 1811. pp 361, 362

Deed dated 1810. SAMUEL BEELER & MARY his wife to Trustees of Methodist Church: DAVID LEA, JOHN MELOAN, GEORGE HOWARD, JOHN HICKMAN & MORTON IRWIN. S 25, T 1, R 5. Signed SAML BEELER JR, MARY (x) BEELER. Witn: MATTH. RICHARDSON, J.F. ROYSDON. rec 1811. p 362, 363

Deed dated 1809. THOMAS DILLON to JOHN WINGATE. S 24, T W, R 2. Signed THOMAS DILLON. Witn: NOAH WADE, D. WADE. rec 1811. pp 363, 364

Deed dated 1808. JOHN SMITH & ELIZABETH his wife of Cincinnati to DANIEL WOODRUFF. S 32, T 3, R 3.Signed JOHN SMITH by JAC. BURNET, his agent, ELIZABETH SMITH. Witn: DAVID WADE. rec 1811. pp 364, 365

Quitclaim dated 1811. DAVID FLEENOR & SUSANNAH his wife to GEORGE FLEENER, DANIEL FLEENOR, MARY M. FLEENER, GEORGE KERSHNER & MARGARET his wife,

BUTLER COUNTY LAND RECORDS: BOOK B

STEPHEN SLIPHER & ELIZABETH his wife, JACOB SLIPHER & SUSANNAH his wife. S 13, T 2, R 3. Signed DAVID FLEENER, SUSANNAH (x) FLEENER. Witn: JAMES SMITH. rec 1811. pp 365, 366, 367

Quitclaim dated 1811. Heirs of RUDOLPH FLEENER to DANIEL FLEENER. S 13, T 2, R 3. Signed GEORGE FLEENER, SUSANNAH (x) SLIPHER, ELIZABETH (x) SLIPHER, JACOB SLIPHER (german script), STEPHEN (x) SLIPHER, GEORGE KERSHNER, MARGARET (x) KERSHNER, MARY M. (x) FLEENER. Witn: JAMES SMITH, JACOB BAUM, DAVID FLEENER. rec 1811. pp 365, 366, 367

Deed dated 1809. JOHN WINGATE to WILLIAM DILLON. S 24, T 2, R 2. Signed JOHN WINGATE. Witn: THOS. BLAIR, ISAAC STANLEY. rec 1811. p 367

Deed dated 1810. JOHN SMITH & ELIZABETH his wife of Hamilton Co to SHADRACH HARRISON. S 2, T 2, R 3. Signed JOHN SMITH, ELIZABETH SMITH. Witn: W.H. POOL, OWEN LEGG. rec 1811. pp 367, 368

Deed dated 1810. JACKSON AYERS to DANIEL SYMMES of Cincinnati. S 36, T 2, R 2. Bound by land conveyed to JAMES CLARK by SIMEON BROADWELL. Signed JACKSON AYERS. Witn: JNO. ANDREW, PEYTON S. SYMMES. rec 1811. pp 368, 369

Deed dated 1811. LEVI JENNINGS & ELIZABETH his wife of Montgomery Co to JOHN CLARK. S 32, T 2, R 4. Signed LEVI JENNINGS, ELIZABETH JENNINGS. Witn: JOHN H. CRAWFORD, DANL HERMAN. rec 1811. pp 369, 370

Deed dated 1810. JOHN SINNARD & PEGGY his wife to JOHN VANCE. S 9, T 2, R 2. Signed JOHN SINNARD, PEGGY (x) SINNARD. Witn: MICHAEL SYERS, JOSEPH (x) THOMPSON. rec 1811. pp 370, 371

Deed dated 1810. MATTHEW WINTON & ELIZABETH his wife to JAMES WITHROW. S 32, T 3, R 3. Signed MATTH. WINTON, ELIZA. WINTON. Witn: JOHN McGUFFIN, DANL CRUME. rec 1811. pp 371, 372

Quitclaim dated 1811. Heirs of RUDOLPH FLEENER to JACOB SLIPHER & SUSANNAH his wife, late FLEENER. S 13 & 24, T 2, R 3. Signed GEORGE FLEENER, DANIEL FLEENER, STEPHEN SLIPHER, ELIZABETH (x) SLIPHER, GEORGE KERSHNER, MARGARET (x) KERSHNER, MARY M. FLEENER. Witn: JAMES SMITH, DAVID FLEENER. rec 1811. pp 372, 373

BUTLER COUNTY LAND RECORDS: BOOK B

Deed dated 1811. JOHN WINGATE & EMMA WINGATE, late TORRENCE, admrs of estate of JOHN TORRENCE, to WILLIAM RIDDLE. Hamilton outlot 15. Signed JOHN WINGATE, AMMA WINGATE. Witn: ABRAM COLWELL, JAMES MILLS. rec 1811. pp 373, 374

Deed dated 1811. JOHN VAN NICE & ELIZABETH his wife to WILLIAM THOMPSON. S 15, T 3, R 2. Signed JOHN VANNICE, ELIZABETH VANNICE. Witn: JAMES SMITH, WILL. BRODERICK. rec 1811. p 374

Deed dated 1811. JOHN CLEVES SYMMES to JOHN N. PACK of Fairfield Twp. S 14, T 2, R 2. Signed JOHN CLEVES SYMMES. Witn: WM. ENYART, EZRA DARBY. rec 1811. pp 374, 375

Deed dated 1811. JOHN CLEVES SYMMES to JOHN ENYART of Fairfield Twp. S 14, T 2, R 2. Signed JOHN CLEVES SYMMES. Witn: BRYSON MARKLAND, JOHN HART. rec 1811. pp 375, 376

Deed dated 1811. USA to ABRAHAM HARTZELL, assignee of JOHN DRAKE & JOHN BAKER. S 25, T 3, R 3. rec 1811 p 376

Mortgage dated 1810. JOHN HALL to JOSEPH HOUGH. S 16, 17, 18, 19, 20, T 1, R 4. Paymt due 1814. Signed JOHN HALL. Witn: JAMES MILLS, LUDLOW PIERSON. rec 1811. p 377

Deed dated 1811. ROBERT FLEMING to EZRA FITZ FREEMAN S 4, T 1, R 2. Signed ROBERT FLEMMING. Witn: THOMAS FLEMMING, NOAH WADE. rec 1811. pp 377, 378

Deed dated 1811. JAMES WITHROW & SARAH his wife to JOSEPH BALDWIN. S 28, T 3, R 3. Signed JAMES WITHROW, SARAH (x) WITHROW. Witn: BENONY GOBLE, JOHN SWEARINGEN. rec 1811. pp 379, 380

Deed dated 1810. MATTHEW WINTON & ELIZABETH his wife, to AARON GRIFFING of Bourbon Co, KY. S 32, T 3, R 3. Signed MATTH. WINTON, ELIZA. WINTON. Witn: JOSEPH BALDWIN, CHARLES SWEARINGEN. rec 1811. pp 380, 381

Deed dated 1811. JONATHAN DAYTON & SUSAN his wife of NJ to DAVID MULFORD. S 36, T 3, R 3. Signed JONA. DAYTON, SUSAN DAYTON. Witn: ELIAS I. DAYTON. rec 1811. pp 381, 382

BUTLER COUNTY LAND RECORDS: BOOK B

Deed dated 1811. BENJAMIN D. DAVIS, Collector of Fairfield Twp to JAMES JOHNSON of same. S 9, T 1, R 2. Signed BENJAMIN D. DAVIS. Witn: JAMES HEATON, ISAAC STANLEY. rec 1811. pp 382, 383

Deed dated 1811. DANIEL BAKER & SARAH his wife to JAMES CLARK JR. S 17, T 3, R 3. Signed DANIEL BAKER, SARAH BAKER. Witn: P. WILLIAMSON, DANL JONES. rec 1811. p 383

Deed dated 1799. JOHN CLEVES SYMMES to JOHN DOWNING, assignee of JOHN McCLAINE. Forfeiture for non-settlement of land by JOHN LINN of Jersey. Signed JOHN CLEVES SYMMES. Witn: JAS. CONN, JOH. TERRY. rec 1811. pp 383, 384

Deed dated 1810. CLARKSON FREEMAN to MOSES VAIL. S 5, T 2, R 3. Land entered by DAVID GREGORY, lately dec'd; heirs divided land into sixths; lot 3 to WILLIAM GREGORY as his share. Signed C. FREEMAN. Witn: HENRY WEAVER, JOHN AYERS. rec 1811. pp 384, 385

Deed dated 1809. EDMOND LISTON & ELIZABETH his wife to JOHN SCHENCK. S 1, T 2, R 3. Signed EDMOND LISTON, ELIZABETH LISTON. Witn: WILLIAM THOMAS, HENRY WEAVER. rec 1811. pp 385, 386

Deed dated 1810. JOHN SCHENCK & MARY his wife to SAMUEL SCHENCK. S 1, T 2, R 3. Signed JOHN SCHENCK, MARY (x) SCHENCK. Witn: STEPHEN GAREL, JAMES SIMCOCK rec 1811. pp 386, 387

Deed dated 1802. JOHN BALDWIN & ELIZABETH his wife of Hamilton Co, NW Ter'y to PETER WILLCOCKS of same. S 3, T 1, R 2. Signed JOHN BALDWIN, ELIZABETH (x) BALDWIN. Witn: J.R. BEATY, DANL PARSONS. rec 1811. pp 387, 388

Deed dated 1811. JAMES DUNN & NANCY his wife to PETER WILLCOCK. S 11, T 3, R 2. Signed JAS. DUNN, NANCY DUNN. Witn: JAMES DUNN JR, THOMAS BALDWIN. rec 1811. pp 388, 389

Deed dated 1809. JACOB POWERS & NANCY his wife to JOHN BARTON. S 13, T 3, R 3. Signed JACOB POWERS, NANCY (x) POWERS. Witn: ADAM LINN, ISC. S. SWEARINGEN. rec 1811. p 389

Deed dated 1810. ABRAHAM CHASE & ELIZABETH his wife of Millcreek Twp, Hamilton Co to VALLENTINE CHASE. S 5, T 4, R 1. Signed ABRAHAM CHASE, ELISABETH CHASE.

BUTLER COUNTY LAND RECORDS: BOOK B

Witn: JONATHAN W. LYON, LEWIS H. LEE. rec 1811. pp 389, 390

Deed dated 1811. PHILIP GORDON & NANCY his wife to JAMES SMILEY. S 13, T 4, R 2. Signed PHILIP (x) GORDON, NANCY (x) GORDON. Witn: JAMES SMITH, WM. BRODERICK. rec 1811. pp 390, 391

Deed dated 1811. JAMES DUNN & NANCY his wife to JAMES ELLIOTT. S 14, T 3, R 2. Signed JAS. DUNN, NANCY DUNN. Witn: JAMES DUNN JR, THOMAS BALDWIN. rec 1811. p 391

Deed dated 1811. JOSEPH PATTERSON & MARY his wife of Warren Co to DAVID RALSTON of same. S 17, T 3, R 3. Signed JOSEPH PATTERSON, MARY (x) PATTERSON. Witn: SAMUEL SERING, ENOS WILLIAMS. rec 1811. pp 391, 392

Quitclaim dated 1811. Heirs of RUDOLPH FLEENER to GEORGE KERSHNER & MARGARET his wife, late FLEENER. S 13 & 24, T 2, R 3. Signed GEORGE FLEENER, DANIEL FLEENER, STEPHEN (x) SLIPHER, ELIZABETH (x) SLIPHER, JACOB SLIPHER (german), SUSANNAH (x) SLIPHER, MARY M. FLEENER. Witn: JAMES SMITH, JACOB BAUM, DAVID FLEENER. rec 1811. pp 392, 393

Notice of Deposition dated 1811. To JOSEPH PEAK & WILLIAM ELLIOTT. JOHN CLEVES SYMMES to depose at request of JOHN EYERS (margin note: AYERS) concerning sale of S 1, T 2, R 3. Signed Court Justices STEPHEN WOOD, JAMES SILVER. rec 1811. p 393

Deposition dated 1811. DURAN WHITTLESEY stated he served notice on PEAK and ELLIOT. Signed ISAAC STANLEY, JP. Witn: STEPHEN WOOD, JAMES SILVER. rec 1811. p 393

Deed dated 1811. WILLIAM McCLELLAND, Sheriff of Butler Co, to JOHN SUTHERLAND & HENRY BROWN. Judgement obtained by JAMES SMITH against HENRY WASON. Seized Rossville outlots 16, 18, sold at auction. Signed WM. McCLELLAND, Sheriff. Witn: JAMES McBRIDE, WM. MURRAY. rec 1811. pp 394, 395

Deed dated 1811. WILLIAM McCLELLAND, Sheriff of Butler Co, to JOHN SUTHERLAND & HENRY BROWN. Judgement obtained by JOHN WINGATE against THOMAS McCULLOUGH. Seized S 1, T 1, R 3, sold at auction. Signed and witn above. rec 1811. pp 395, 396

BUTLER COUNTY LAND RECORDS: BOOK B

Deed dated 1811. AUDITORS apptd by court to WILLIAM STANLEY. WILLIAM GORDON obtained judgement against JAMES REED. Seized S 31, T , R 3; sold to NICHOLAS LONGWORTH of Cincinnati who assigned rights to Stanley. Signed JAMES SMITH. WM. McCLELLAN, JAMES HEATON. Witn: JAMES MILLS. rec 1811. pp 396, 397

Deed dated 1809. JOHN SUTHERLAND & HENRY BROWN to WILLIAM CORRY. Rossville lot 63. Signed JOHN SUTHERLAND, HENRY BROWN. Witn: WM. BOMBERGER JR, WM. PHARES. rec 1811. p 398

Deed dated 1811. ANDREW CHRISTY & ELISABETH his wife to ABRAHAM MILEY, late of PA. S 4, T 2, R 3. Signed ANDW. CHRISTY, ELISABETH (x) CHRISTY. Witn: ISAAC STANLEY, JOHN PARKER. rec 1811. pp 398, 399

Partition dated 1811. MOSES DRAKE & ELIZABETH his wife and THOMAS BAKER & LYDIA his wife to JOHN PRITCHARD. S 25, T 3, R 3 purchased jointly. Bounds of share given. Signed MOSES DRAKE, THOMAS BAKER, ELIZABETH (x) DRAKE, LYDIA (x) BAKER. Witn: HENRY WEAVER, JOHN MATTIX. rec 1811. pp 399, 400

Deed dated 1811. DANIEL PERREY & RHODA his wife to JAMES EMMERSON. S 3, T 5, R 2. Bound by land of WILLIAM TOLER, MARSH WILLIAMS. Signed DANIEL PERREY, RHODA (x) PERREY. Witn: EDWARD EMMERSON, MARSH WILLIAMS. rec 1811. pp 400, 401

Deed dated 1811. LEONARD RUSH & JEMIMA his wife of Warren Co to JOHN HORMEL SR of same. S 30, T 2, R 4. Signed LEONARD RUSH, JEMIMA RUSH. Witn: ENOS WILLIAMS, THOMAS (x) RUSH. rec 1811. pp 401, 402

Deed dated 1811. JOHN HORMEL & ELENOR his wife of Warren Co to DAVID PATTEN. S 30, T 2, R 4. Signed JOHN HORMER, ELENOR (x) HORMEL. Witn: ENOS WILLIAMS, JACOB MORRIS. rec 1811. pp 402, 403

Deed dated 1807. JOHN VAN NICE & ELIZABETH his wife to HUGH ABBA CRUMBA*. S 15, T 3, R 2. Signed JOHN VANNICE, ELIZABETH VANNICE. Witn: ISAAC PAXTON, MAGDALANA PAXTON. rec 1811. pp 403, 404 *possibly HUGH ABERCROMBIE?

Deed dated 1811. JAMES MOTT Esq of Middletown, Monmouth Co, NJ to SHORES STEPHENSON of same. ▪love and affection for nephew▪. S 35, T 3, R 2. Signed JAMES MOTT. Witn: EPHRAIM RYNO. rec 1811. pp 404, 405

BUTLER COUNTY LAND RECORDS: BOOK B

Quitclaim dated 1811. Heirs of RUDOLPH FLEENOR to GEORGE FLEENOR. S 13 & 24, T 2, R 3. Signed DANIEL FLEENER, STEPHEN (x) SLIPHER, ELIZABETH (x) SLIPHER, JACOB SLIPHER (german script), SUSANNAH (x) SLIPHER, GEORGE KERSHNER, MARGRET (x) KERSHNER, MARY M. (x) FLEENOR. Witn: JAMES SMITH, JACOB BAUM, DAVID FLEENER. rec 1811. pp 405, 406

Deed dated 1811. BENJAMIN D. DAVIS, tax collector of Fairfield Twp to Capt. ISAAC WILES. Hamilton lot 51. Signed BENJAMIN D. DAVIS, collector. Witn: THOS. BLAIR, JAMES McBRIDE. rec 1811. pp 406, 407, 408

Deed dated 1811. BENJAMIN ENYART & MARY his wife to THOMAS PATTON. S 12, T 2, R 3. Signed BENJAMIN ENYART, MARY (x) ENYART. Witn: JP JOHN AYERS, DAVID ENYART. rec 1811. pp 408, 409

Deed dated 1811. BENJAMIN ENYART & MARY his wife to SAMUEL CLARK. S 12, T 2, R 3. Signed and witn as above. rec 1811. pp 409, 410

Partition dated 1811. MOSES DRAKE & ELIZABETH his wife and JOHN PRITCHARD & RHODA his wife to THOMAS BAKER. S 25, T 3, R 3. Signed MOSES DRAKE, JOHN PRITCHARD, ELIZABETH (x) DRAKE, RHODAY (x) PRITCH- ARD. Witn: HENRY WEAVER, JOHN MATTIX. rec 1811. pp 410, 411, 412

Deed dated 1811. DAVID GARRIGUS & ABIGAIL his wife to ROBERT CAMPBELL. S 7, T 2, R 3. Signed DAVID GARRIGUS, ABIGAIL GARRIGUS. Witn: JEPTHA GARRIGUS, SOLOMON BEACH. rec 1811. pp 412, 413

Mortgage dated 1811. ROBERT CAMPBELL & RACHEL his wife to DAVID GARRIGUS. S 7, T 2, R 3. Signed ROB- ERT CAMPBELL, RACHEL (x) CAMPBELL. Witn: ISAAC STANLEY, MOSES CRUME. rec 1811. pp 413, 414

Deed dated 1811. DAVID GARRIGUS & ABIGAIL his wife to SOLOMON BEACH & JEPTHA GARRIGUS. S 15, T 1, R 2. Signed DAVID GARRIGUS, ABIGAIL GARRIGUS. Witn: JAMES HEATON, MARY HEATON. rec 1811. pp 414, 415

Mortgage dated 1811. SOLOMON BEACH & JEPTHA GARRIGUS to DAVID GARRIGUS. 5 bonds held on property above. Bound by land of JOHN MAXWELL, THOMAS ALSTON. Signed SOLOMON BEACH, JEPTHA GARRIGUS. Witn: JAMES HEATON, ISAAC STANLEY. rec 1811. pp 416, 417

Deed dated 1811. GEORGE SHUCK & MARY his wife of

BUTLER COUNTY LAND RECORDS: BOOK B

Hamilton Co to WALTER ARMSTRONG. S 34, T 3, R 1. Signed GEORGE SHOOK, MARY (x) SHOOK. Witn: EMMANUEL VANTREES, BRANT AGNEW. rec 1811. p 418

End of BOOK B; Start BOOK C

Deed dated 1804. ALLIS JOHN & MARGRET his wife to ISAAC JOHN. S 14, T 3, R 2. Bound by DAN'L SKINNER's land. Signed ELLIS JOHN, MARGRET JOHN. Witn: MICHAEL HILDEBRAND, DAVID (x) HILDEBRAND. rec 1800. p 1

Deed dated 1811. JOHN VAN NICE & ELIZABETH his wife to ABRAHAM LAREW. S 15, T 3, R 2. Signed JOHN VANNICE, ELIZABETH VANNICE. Witn: JAMES SMITH, WILL. BRODERICK. rec 1811. pp 1, 2

Deed dated 1811. ISAAC JOHNS & RHODA his wife to JAMES DALRYMPLE. S 14, T 3, R 2. Signed ISAAC JOHNS, RHODA JOHNS. Witn: FREDERICK SHAFF, THO. D. WHELAN. rec 1811. p 3

Deed dated 1811. PIERSON SAYRE & CATHARINE his wife to ABRAHAM MILEY. S 4, T 2, R 3. Signed PIERSON SAYRE, CATHARINE SAYER. Witn: JOHN MAHARD, MOSES FORNEY(?). rec 1811. pp 3, 4

Deed dated 1811. JAMES WITHROW & SARAH his wife to CHARLES SWEARINGEN. S 28,M T 3, R 3. Signed JAMES WITHROW, SARAH (x) WITHROW. Witn: WILL. BRODERICK, ALEXANDER MOORE. rec 1811. p 5

Deed dated 1806. JOAB REEVE & MARY his wife of Burlington Co, NJ, son and heir of JOHN REEVE the elder, decd, of Northampton Twp, county and state aforesaid, to JOHN REEVE, the younger, oldest son of John Reeve. S 19, T 3, R 3 owned by father as assignee of WILLIAM CLARK. Father's will dated 1-17-1794 filed at Trenton, NJ, directed land to be divided among his four children: SUSANNAH VANDEGRIFFE, wife of WILLIAM; EBER REEVE, JOHN REEVE, JOAB REEVE. Signed JOAB REEVE, MARY REEVE. Witn: JOSEPH EDWARDS, WM. H. BURR. rec 1811. pp 6, 7

Deed dated 1811. JACOB KEMP & MARY his wife to JOHN GEBHART. S 16, T 2, R 4. Signed JACOB KEMP, MARY KEMP. Witn: HENRY WEAVER, AARON VAIL. rec 1811. pp 8, 9

Deed dated 1811. JAMES WITHROW & SARAH his wife to BENONY GOBLE. S 28, T 3, R 3. Bound by land of

BUTLER COUNTY LAND RECORDS: BOOK C

JOSEPH BALDWIN, CHARLES SWEARINGEN, THOMAS POTTENGER. Signed JAMES WITHROW, SARAH (x) WITHROW. Witn: JOSEPH BALDWIN, JOHN SWEARINGEN. rec 1811. pp 9, 10

Notice dated 1811. To RALPH PHILLIPS or his atty JACOB BURNET. Deposition of JOHN CLEVES SYMMES to be taken regarding S 1, T 2, R 3. Signed STEPHEN WOOD, JAMES SILVER, associate judges, Butler Co Court of Common Pleas. rec 1811. p 10

Certificate dated 1811. JOHN AYERS swore he delivered above notice to Jacob Burnet. rec 1811. p 10

Deposition dated 1811. JOHN CLEVES SYMMES instructed surveyor ISRAEL LUDLOW to run a meridian line from southernmost point on the Ohio River Bank between the Miami Rivers; extend that line north six miles and set a marker. An east-west line to be run from the marker, establish a base line for later surveyors. Symmes' land rights extended only 15 miles north from the base line established by Ludlow. Signed JOHN CLEVES SYMMES. Witn: STEPHEN WOOD, JAMES SILVER. rec 1811. pp 10, 11

Deed dated 1811. MOSES VAIL & POLLY his wife to MICHAEL HAGEMAN. S 34, T 3, R 3. Signed MOSES VAIL, MARY VAIL. Witn: P.T. SCHENCK, JAMES McEWEN. rec 1811. pp 11, 12

Deed dated 1811. JAMES CLARK & ABIGAIL his wife to LEWIS W. GORDON. S 35, T 2, R 2. Signed JAMES CLARK, ABIGAIL CLARK. Witn: M. HUESTON, CHARLES CLARK. rec 1811. pp 12, 13

Deed dated 1811. SOLOMON LINE & SALOMA his wife to JACOB LINE. S 27, T 2, R 3 after "surveying off" land to JOHN LINE, DAVID LINE, ELIHU LINE; residue to Jacob. Signed SOLOMON LINE, SALOME (x) LINE. Witn: JAMES HEATON, JOHN VINNEDGE. rec 1811. pp 13, 14

Deed dated 1811. SOLOMON LINE & SALOME his wife to JONATHAN LINE. S 14, T 2, R 3. Signed SOLOMON (x) LINE, SALOME (x) LINE. Witn above. rec 1811. pp 14, 15

Deed dated 1811. SOLOMON LINE & SALOME his wife to DAVID LINE. S 27, T 2, R 3. Signed and witn as above. rec 1811. pp 15, 16

Deed dated 1811. SOLOMON LINE & SALOME his wife to ELIHU LINE. S 27, T 2, R 3. Signed and witn as

BUTLER COUNTY LAND RECORDS: BOOK C

previous entry. rec 1811. pp 16, 17

Deed dated 1811. SOLOMON LINE & SALOME his wife to JOHN LINE. S 27, T 2, R 3. Signed and witn as above. rec 1811. pp 17, 18

Deed dated 1811. ISAAC WILES & BETSY his wife to HENRY BROWN and JOHN SUTHERLAND. Hamilton lots 198, 200, 201. Signed ISAAC WILES, ELIZABETH WILES. Witn: ISAAC STANLEY, NOAH WADE. rec 1811. pp 18, 19

Deed dated 1811. ELIJAH BRUSH & ADELAIDE his wife of Detroit, Michigan Ter'y, to SAMUEL C. VANCE of Lawrenceburgh, IN Ter'y, and SINEUS PIERSON of Cincinnati, since decd. S 8, 18, 9, 19, 17 & 16, T 1, R 4. Signed E. BRUSH, ADELAIDE BRUSH. Witn: THOMPSON MAXWELL, GEO. McDOUGALL. rec 1811. pp 19, 20

Deed dated 1811. MATTHEW RICHARDSON & ANN his wife to ARCHEBALD ARMSTRONG, SAMUEL DAVIS & OLIVER SMITH for Presbyterian congregation on Seven Mile. S 23, T 5, R 2, to erect meeting house. Signed MATTH. RICHARDSON, ANN RICHARDSON. Witn: JP R. LYTLE, JOHN DOUGLASS. rec 1811. pp 20, 21

Deed dated 1811. AARON VAN CAMP SR of Green Co to ISAAC WATSON. Rossville lot 51. Signed AARON VAN CAMP SR. Witn: NOAH WADE, JAMES MILLS. rec 1811. pp 21, 22

Deed dated 1811. DAVID DUFFIELD & REBECCA his wife of Wayne Twp to JOHN HOFFMAN of same. S 17, T 3, R 3. Signed DAVID DUFFIELD, REB CAH DUFFIELD. Witn: WILLIS WHITSON. rec 1811. pp 22, 23

Deed dated 1811. JAMES WILSON of Boon(e) Co, KY to DAVID K. ESTE. Rossville lots 92, 93. Signed JAMES WILSON. Witn: JOHN SUTHERLAND JR, JACOB RICKART. rec 1811. pp 23, 24

Deed dated 1811. AMOS VALENTINE of Warren Co to JONATHAN DAYTON of NJ. S 10, T 3, R 3. Signed AMOS VALLANTINE. Witn: JAMES HEATON, P. WILLIAMSON. rec 1811. pp 24, 25

Deed dated 1809. MATTHEW WINTON & ELIZABETH his wife to ROBERT WINTON. S 5, T 2, R 3. Bound by land of JAMES PEERCE, PHILIP GORDEN. Signed M. WINTON, ELIZA WINTON. Witn: CHARLES SWEARINGEN, JOHN WINTON. rec 1811. pp 25, 26

BUTLER COUNTY LAND RECORDS: BOOK C

Deed dated 1809. JACOB POWERS & NANCY his wife to JOHN LINN. S 13, T 3, R 3. Signed JACOB POWERS, NANCY (x) POWERS. Witn: ADAM LINN SR, ISC. S. SWEARINGEN. rec 1811. pp 26, 27

Deed dated 1809. JACOB POWERS & NANCY his wife to ADAM LINN. S 13, T 3, R 3. Signed JACOB POWERS, NANCY (x) POWERS. Witn: JOHN LINN, ISC. S. SWEARGEN. rec 1811. pp 27, 28

Partition dated 1811. JOSEPH SPENCER & DIANNAH his wife of IN Ter'y to JACOB WHITENGER. Tenants in common on S 30, T 3, R 3. Whitenger to have NE quarter. Signed JOSEPH SPENCER, DIANNAH (x) SPENCER. Witn: BENJAMIN SMITH, CHARLES SWEARINGEN. rec 1811. pp 28, 29

Partition dated 1811. JACOB WHITENGER & ELIZABETH his wife to JOSEPH SPENCER. Tenants in common on S 30, T 3, R 3. Spencer to have SE quarter. Signed JACOB WHITENGER, ELIZABETH (x) WHITENGER. Witn as above. rec 1811. pp 29, 30

Deed dated 1809. ABRAHAM FREEMAN to MARGARET HAGEMAN Lot 5 in S 10, T 1, R 2. Signed ABRAHAM FREEMAN. Witn: H. RUNYAN, MICHAEL HAGEMAN. rec 1811. p 30

Mortgage dated 1811. WILLIAM HARLAN & HANNAH his wife to LAURENCE CAVANAUGH. Hamilton lot 213. Signed WM. HARLAN, HANNAH (x) HARLAN. Witn: DAN'L MILLIKIN, WM. MINOR. rec 1811. p 31

Deed dated 1811. DAVID MULFORD & HANNAH his wife to AMOS VALLENTINE of Warren Co. S 30, T 3, R 3. Signed DAVID MULFORD, HANNAH (x) MULFORD. Witn: P. WILLIAMSON, HANNAH WILLIAMSON. rec 1811. p 32

Deed dated 1811. WILLIAM THOMAS & MARGARATE his wife to JOHN BUSENBARK. S 1, T 2, R 3. Signed WILLIAM THOMAS, MARGARATE (x) THOMAS. Witn: ROBERT BUSENBARK, HENRY WEAVER. rec 1811. p 33

Power of Attorney dated 1804. JONATHAN DAYTON of NY apptd JOHN REILY as atty to make contracts, convey title & deliver money. Signed JONA. DAYTON. Witn: E. B. DAYTON, JOHN T. MARSH. rec 1811. pp 33, 34

Deed dated 1811. JAMES DUNN & NANCY his wife to WILLIAM CROOKS. S 11, T 3, R 2. Bound by land of DAVID SMITH, -- WILLCOCK, JOHN ELLIOTT. signed JAMES DUNN, NANCY DUNN. Witn: JAMES DUNN JR, THOMAS BALDWIN.

BUTLER COUNTY LAND RECORDS: BOOK C

rec 1811. pp 34, 35

Deed dated 1811. JAMES DUNN & NANCY his wife to JOHN ELLIOTT. S 11, T 3, R 2. Bound by land of JAMES EL- LIOTT, WM. SMITH, WM. CROOKS, JAMES MOOR & WILLIAM BALDWIN. Signed and witn as previous deed. rec 1811. pp 35, 36

Partition dated 1811. JOHN PRITCHARD & RHODA his wife & THOMAS BAKER & LYDIA his wife to MOSES DRAKE. Purchased S 22, T 3, R 3 in common, now dividing land. Signed JOHN PRITCHARD, THOMAS BAKER, RHODA (x) PRITCHARD, LYDIA (x) BAKER. Witn: HENRY WEAVER, JOHN MATTIX. JP ISAAC HOFF. rec 1811. pp 36, 37

Deed dated 1811. EBENEZER HEATON JR of Warren Co to JOHN HURST of same. S 12, T 2, R 3. Signed EBENEZER HEATON. Witn: IVORY H. CHADBOURN, DAVID SUTTON. rec 1811. pp 37,38

Quitclaim dated 1811. MARY HEATON, wife of DANIEL of Warren Co, to JOHN HURST. Yielded dower rights to S 12, T 2, R 3; she was moving. Signed MARY HEATON. Witn: DAN'L MILLIKIN, JAMES HEATON. rec 1811. pp 38, 39

Deed dated 1811. JOHN WITHROW & ANNA to ABRAHAM GRAFT. S 27 & 34, T 3, R 3. Signed JOHN WITHROW, ANNA (x) WITHROW. Witn: ISAAC STANLEY, TIMOTHY WOODRUFF SR. rec 1811. pp 39, 40

Deed dated 1810. WILLIAM OGLE & ELIZABETH his wife to CONROD DARR. S 28, T 5, R 2. Signed WILLIAM OGLE, ELIZABETH OGLE. Witn: J.F. ROYSDON, MATTH. RICHARDSON. rec 1811. pp 40, 41

Deed dated 1811. LAURENCE CAVENAUGH & ANN his wife of St. Clair Twp to WILLIAM HARLAN. Hamilton lot 213. Signed L. CAVNAUGH, ANNA CAVANAUGH. Witn: DAN'L MILLIKIN, WILLIAM MINOR. rec 1811. pp 41, 42

Deed dated 1811. JAMES DUNN & NANCY his wife to WILLIAM BALDWIN. S 11, T 3, R 2. Signed JAS. DUNN, NANCY DUNN. Witn: JAMES DUNN JR, THOMAS BALDWIN. rec 1811. pp 42, 43

Deed dated 1811. JAMES DUNN & NANCY his wife to WILLIAM WHITE. Money paid 1807 for S 11, T 3, R 2. Signed JAMES DUNN, NANCY DUNN. Witn: JOHN RICHMOND, WILLIAM CROOKS. rec 1811. pp 43, 44

BUTLER COUNTY LAND RECORDS: BOOK C

Deed dated 1811. ASHBEL KITCHEL & POLLY KITCHEL of Warren Co to ROBERT CRAIG. S 17, T 2, R 4; part of estate of JOHN KITCHEL decd. Signed ASHBEL KITCHEL, POLLY KITCHEL. Witn: DANIEL STRICKLAND, JOHN CAMPBELL. rec 1811. pp 44, 45

Deed dated 1811. WILLIAM CROOKS & AMEY his wife to WILLIAM MORRIS. S 11, T 3, R 2. Signed WILLIAM CROOKS, AMEY CROOKS. Witn: ELKANAH LANE, WILLIAM BALDWIN. JP JOHN DUNN. rec 1811. pp 45, 46

Deed dated 1810. USA to ARCHABALD BURNS. S 28, T 4, R 1. rec 1811. p 46

Mortgage dated 1811. ALEXANDER WILSON of St. Clair Twp to ALEXANDER WILSON JR. S 14 & 23, T 2, R 3. Signed ALEXANDER WILSON. Witn: JOHN JOHNSON, CHARLES SWEARINGEN. rec 1811. pp 47, 48

Deed dated 1811. GEORGE GILLESPIE JR of Warren Co to ROBERT FARES. S 11, T 2, R 4. Signed GEORGE GILLESPIE JR. Witn: JAMES McCASHEN, J. W. LANIER. rec 1811. pp 48, 49

Deed dated 1811. GEORGE GILLESPIE JR of Warren Co to JAMES RUSH. S 11, T 2, R 4. Signed and witn as above. rec 1811. p 49

Deed dated 1811. GEORGE GILLESPIE JR of Warren Co to JAMES MARSHALL. S 11, T 2, R 4. Signed and witn as above. rec 1811. pp 49, 50

Deed dated 1791. DR. CLARKSON FREEMAN of Somerset Co, NJ to EZRA FITZ FREEMAN of Middlesex Co, NJ. No S-T-R; warrant #295 signed by JOHN CLEVES SYMMES, dated 1788. Signed CLARKSON FREEMAN. Witn: ELIAS CAMPBELL, JOHN WILHOLMS. rec 1811. p 51

Mortgage dated 1811. WILLIAM McCLURE to ELIAS BOUDINOT. S 25, T 2, R 4. Signed W. McCLURE. Witn: JESSE HUNT, JAC. BURNET. rec 1811. pp 51, 52

Deed dated 1806. JUSTUS JONES & SARAH his wife of Champaign Co to WILLIAM WEBSTER. S 22, T 3, R 3. Signed JUSTUS JONES, SARAH (x) JONES. Witn: JOHN RUNYON, ABRAHAM JONES. rec 1811. pp 52, 53

Deed dated 1811. ANDERSON SPENCER & POLLY his wife to THOMAS BLAIR. Hamilton lots 49 & 50. Signed ANDERSON SPENCER, MEREY (x) SPENCER. Witn: JAMES MARTIN, J. or S. McCLAMMNOE. rec 1811. pp 53, 54

BUTLER COUNTY LAND RECORDS: BOOK C

Mortgage dated 1811. JAMES JOYCE of Hamilton Co to HOUGH BLAIR & CO. S 34, T 3, R 2; bound by land of DAVID WADE, JOEL WILLIAMS. Money to be paid JOSEPH HOUGH, THOMAS BLAIR, ROBERT CLARK or NEIL GILLISPIE. Signed JAMES JOYCE. Witn: ISAAC STANLEY, ISAAC (x) SMITH. rec 1811. pp 54, 55

Deed dated 1811. PEREGRINE ORNDORF & JANE his wife to THOMAS BLAIR. Rossville lots 82, 83, 88, 89. Signed PERRY GREE ORENDORFF, JANE ORENDORFF. Witn: ISAAC STANLEY, HENRY HESLY. rec 1811. pp 55, 56

Deed dated 1811. REUBEN REDER & REBECKEA his wife to FRAZEA HARRISON. S 24, T 3, R 2. Signed REUBEN REDER, REBEKAH REDER. Witn: MICH'L AYERS, ABIGAIL AYERS. rec 1811. pp 56, 57

Partition dated 1811. JACOB CASE & DORCAS his wife to THOMAS POUND. S 27, T 3, R 3. TP to have southwest corner. Signed JACOB (x) CASE, DORCAS (x) CASE. Witn: LEVI KINMAN, JACOB GOBLE. rec 1811. pp 57, 58

Partition dated 1811. THOMAS POUND & SARAH his wife to JACOB CASE. S 27, T 3, R 3. JC to have northwest corner. Signed THOMAS POUND, SARAH (x) POUND. Witn as above. rec 1811. pp 58, 59

Deed dated 1811. JACOB CASE & DORCAS his wife to JAMES WILSON. S 27, T 3, R 3. Signed JACOB (x) CASE, DORCAS (x) CASE. witn: JACOB GOBLE, WILLIAM DAILY. rec 1811. pp 59, 60

Deed dated 1811. JOSEPH BALDWIN & SARAH his wife to JONATHAN GOBLE. S 28, T 3, R 3. Signed JOSEPH BALDWIN, SARAH (x) BALDWIN. Witn: CATY SWEARINGEN, JANE WITHROW. rec 1811. pp 60, 61

Deed dated 1811. WILLIAM HERBERT & ELEANOR his wife to THOMAS BLAIR. Hamilton lots 187, 188. Signed WILLIAM HERBERT, ELEANOR HERBERT. Witn: JOS. HOUGH, DAN'L MILLIKIN. rec 1811. pp 61, 62

Deed dated 1811. ISAAC HART & SARAH his wife to HENRY GREEN. S 4, T 3, R 3. Signed ISAAC HART, SARAH (x) HART. Witn: JOSEPH GREEN, NATHAN STUBBS rec 1811 p63

Deed dated 1811. PHILIP KEMP & CATHERINE his wife to THOMAS MORGAN. S 16, T 2, R 4. Signed PHILIP KEMP, CATHERINE (x) KEMP. Witn: HENRY WEAVER, JACOB WEIDNER rec 1811. pp 63, 64

BUTLER COUNTY LAND RECORDS: BOOK C

Deed dated 1811. JACOB KEMP & MARY his wife to PHILIP KEMP. S 15 & 16, T 2, R 4. Signed JACOB KEMP, MARY (x) KEMP. Witn: HENRY WEAVER, AARON VAIL. rec 1811. pp 64, 65

Deed dated 1811. JOHN RICHARDSON & JANE his wife to ARMSTRONG BUCHANON. S 28, T 3, R 2. signed JOHN RICHARDSON, JEAN RICHARDSON. Witn: JOHN BROWN, RACHEL BROWN. rec 1811. pp 65, 66

Deed dated 1811. JOSEPH SPENCER & DIANNAH his wife of Wayne Co, IN Ter'y to BENJAMIN SMITH. S 30, T 3, R 3. Signed JOSEPH SPENCER, DIANNAH (x) SPENCER. Witn: JACOB WHITINGER, CHARLES SWEARINGEN. rec 1811. pp 66, 67

Certificate dated 1811. ABRAHAM F. FREEMAN signed deed conveying title to Cincinnati lot 51 as heir of ISAAC FREEMAN to MARTIN BAUM. rec 1811. p 67

Mortgage dated 1811. ANDREW ROWND, DANIEL ROWND & JACOB ROWND JR to JACOB ROUND SR. S 18, T 2, R 2. Signed ANDREW ROUND, DANIEL ROUND, JACOB ROWND. Witn: DANIEL MILLIKIN, JAMES HEATON. rec 1811. pp 67, 68

Deed dated 1811. ISAAC WILES to DAVID K. ESTE. Hamilton lot 106. Signed ISAAC WILES. Witn: JAMES MILLS CLINTON STACKHOUSE. rec 1811. pp 68, 69

Deed dated 1809. JOHN SUTHERLAND & HENRY BROWN to MICHAEL DALAROCK. Rossville lot 11. Signed JOHN SUTHERLAND, HENRY BROWN. Witn: WM. BOMBERGER JR, WM. PHARES JR. rec 1811. pp 69, 70

Deed dated 1811. JEDIDIAH T. TURNER of Casenovia, Madison Co, NY to CLARKSON FREEMAN of PA. S 36, T 3, R 3. Signed JEDIDIAH T. TURNER. Witn: JOHN MAYER, W. B. ROSS. rec 1811. pp 70, 71, 72

Deed date 1810. MOSES VAIL to CLARKSON FREEMAN of PA. S 5, T 2, R 3; formerly owned by DAVID GREGORY, lately decd. Divided into 6 shares, lot 3 set off to WILLIAM GREGORY as his share. Signed MOSES VAIL. Witn: HENRY WEAVER, JOHN AYERS, JAMES McEWEN. JP's statement: MARY VAIL, wife of Moses, relinquished dower rights. rec 1811. pp 72, 73

Quitclaim dated 1810. THOMAS COHOON of NY to JEDIDIAH T. TURNER of same. No S-T-R given. THOS. COHOON. Witn: JONAS JAY, D. LEDYARD. rec 1811. p 73

BUTLER COUNTY LAND RECORDS: BOOK C

Agreement dated 1810. THOMAS COHOON & JEDIDIAH T. TURNER divided property. TC recvd land bought of ROBERT JONES; JTT recvd land bought of JONATHAN DA(Y)TON; other property mentioned. No S-T-R given. Signed JEDIDIAH T. TURNER, THO. COHOON. Witn: JAMES LINPRY. rec 1811. pp 73, 74

Deed dated 1799. ELIAS BOUDINOT of Philadelphia by his agents: CORNELIUS R. SEDUM, ABIJAH HUNT & JACOB BURNET of Hamilton Co, NW Ter'y to WILLIAM McCLURE of same. S 25, T 1, R 4. Signed ELIAS BOUDINOT by CORNELIUS R. SEDAM, by ABIJAH HUNT and by JAC. BURNET. Witn: O.M. SPENCER, JOHN MAHARD. JP ROBT. BENHAM. rec 1811. pp 74, 75

Deed dated 1811. ELIAS BOUDINOT of Philadelphia by his agent JACOB BURNET of Hamilton Co to WILLIAM McCLURE of Dayton. S 25, T 2 (formerly called T 1), R 4. Signed ELIAS BOUDINOT by JAC. BURNET. Witn: JACOB WHEELER, L. WHEELER. rec 1811. pp 75, 76

Deed dated 1811. JOEL WILLIAMS & PHEBE his wife of Cincinnati to JOSEPH VAN HORNE of Mill Creek Twp, Hamilton Co. S 4, T 3, R 2 in Ross Twp. Signed JOEL WILLIAMS, PHEBE WILLIAMS. Witn: JOHN MAHARD, JOHN COX. rec 1811. pp 76, 77

Deed dated 1810. JONATHAN DAYTON of NJ to JOSEPH BLOOMFIELD, gov'r of NJ. S 20, T 2, R 3. Signed JONA. DAYTON. Witn: DAVID E. PATON. rec 1811. pp 77, 78

Deed dated 1811. UZAL EDWARDS & MARY his wife to JOSEPH HOHN. S 21, T 2, R 2. Signed UZAL EDWARDS, MARY EDWARDS. Witn: M. HUESTON, ALEXANDER McGILVRY. rec 1811. pp 78, 79

Deed dated 1811. JACOB LEWIS & DEBORAH his wife to JAMES H. PERSAL. Hamilton lot 185. Signed JACOB LEWIS, DEBORAH LEWIS. Witn: JAMES THOMPSON, DURAN WHITTELSEY. rec 1811. pp 79, 80

Mortgage dated 1811. JAMES DALRYMPLE to ISAAC JOHNS. S 14, T 3, R 2. Signed JAMES DALRYMPLE. Witn: THOS. D. WHELAN, ABIGAIL AYRES. rec 1811. pp 79, 80

Deed dated 1810. JOHN HUMES & **MARIA** his wife of Hamilton Co to RICHARD S. THOMAS of Warren Co. S 22, T 2, R 2. Signed JOHN HUMES, **MARIAH** HUMES. Witn: HEZEKIAH GLASSCOCK, PETER SPADER. JP THOMAS HIGGINS rec 1811. p 81

BUTLER COUNTY LAND RECORDS: BOOK C

Deed dated 1811. SAMUEL DILLON of Fairfield Twp to CHARLES WILKINS SHORT of Lexington Twp, Fayette Co, KY. S 22, T 2, R 2. DILLON bought mortgage of SENACA ROLLINS. Signed SAMUEL DILLON. Witn: JAMES HEATON. rec 1811. pp 82, 83

Deed dated 1811. JOHN VANNICE & ELIZABETH his wife to STEPHEN SLIFER. S 14, T 2, R 3. Bound by ALEXANDER WILSON's land. Signed JOHN VANNICE, ELIZABETH (x) VANNICE. Witn: ISAAC PAXTON, HENRY WEAVER. rec 1811. pp 83, 84

Deed dated 1811. JOHN CLEVES SYMMES of Hamilton Co to SAMUEL DILLON. S 1, T 2, R 3. Bound by land of JOHN AYERS, THOMAS VIRGIN. Mortgage given by WILLIAM LEGG JR bought by DILLON. Signed JOHN CLEVES SYMMES. Witn: JAMES HEATON, DAN MILLIKIN rec 1811. pp 84, 85

Mortgage dated 1811. SAMUEL DARKIES to DAVID K. ESTE. Hamilton lots 72, 73. Signed SAMUEL DARKIES. Witn: ABRAM COLWELL, JAMES McCLAMROCK. Clerk's margin note: mortgage canceled by POA of LOUISA K. ESTE, admtr of D.K. ESTE, mortgage record vol 58, p 138. rec 1811. p 85

Deed dated 1811. JOSEPH HOUGH & JEAN his wife to THOMAS BLAIR. Rossville lots 83, 88, 89. Signed JOSEPH HOUGH, JEAN (x) HOUGH. Witn: DAN'L. MILLIKIN JAMES J. BEELER. rec 1811. p 86

Deed dated 1811. SAMUEL C. VANCE & MARY his wife of Laurenceburgh, IN Ter'y to JOHN SUTHERLAND & HENRY BROWN. Hamilton lot 8. Signed SAMUEL C. VANCE, MARY M. VANCE. Witn: JOHN WHITWORTH, JOHN HALL. rec 1811. p 87

Deed dated 1807. JAMES & WILLIAM MURRY to OLIVER KELLY. S 32, T 3, R 3. Signed JAMES MURRY, <u>PAMELA</u> MURRY, WILLIAM MURRY. Witn: MARY KELLEY & JANE KELLEY. JP's note: ▪came JAMES MURRY & his wife <u>PERMELY</u> ▪ . rec 1811. pp 87, 88

Deed dated 1811. JONATHAN <u>SPINAGE</u> & ELIZABETH his wife to ISAAC WALTER. S 27, T 3, R 3. Signed JONATHAN <u>SPINNING</u>, ELIZABETH SPINNING. Witn: JP DANIL STRICKLAND. rec 1811. pp 88, 89

Deed dated 1810. JOHN SUTHERLAND & HENRY BROWN to MICHAEL DALAROCK. Rossville lot 20. Signed JOHN SUTHERLAND, HENRY BROWN. Witn: JAMES STEEL, JAMES BECK. rec 1811. pp 89, 90

BUTLER COUNTY LAND RECORDS: BOOK C

Deed dated 1811. JACOB CASE & DORCAS his wife to
ISAIAH LEIGH, late of NY City. S 27, T 3, R 3;
bound by land of JAMES WILSON, THOMAS POUND. Witn:
JACOB (x) CASE, DORCAS (x) CASE. Witn: LEVI KINMAN,
JACOB GOBLE. rec 1811. pp 90, 91

Deed dated 1811. JOSEPH HOUGH & JEAN his wife to
HENRY TRABER & JOHN TRABER. Hamilton lot 224. Signed
JOSEPH HOUGH, JEAN HOUGH. Witn: ISAAC STANLEY, JAMES
MILLS. rec 1811. pp 91, 92

Deed dated 1809. GEORGE HARLAND, tax collector of
Fairfield Twp to HUGH B. HAWTHORN. Hamilton lot 133.
Signed GEO. HARLAN. Witn: JOHN WINGATE, JAMES
MILLS. rec 1811. pp 92, 93

Deed dated 1810. JOHN WINGATE & EMMA WINGATE, admtrs
of JOHN TORRENCE to HUGH B. HAWTHORN. Hamilton lot
123. Signed JOHN WINGATE, EMMA WINGATE. Witn: NOAH
WADE, JAMES MILLS. rec 1811. pp 93, 94

Deed dated 1811. JAMES FINDLAY & JANE his wife of
Hamilton Co to MICHAEL MORNINGSTAR. S 6, T 1, R 5.
Signed JAMES FINDLAY, JANE FINDLAY. Witn: GEO. P.
TORRENCE, THOMAS HOOP(?). rec 1811. pp 94, 95

Deed dated 1811. ISAAC ANDERSON & EUPHEMIA his wife
of Hamilton Co to ROBERT ANDERSON. S 23, T 3, R 2.
Signed ISAAC ANDERSON, EUPHEMIA ANDERSON. Witn: JOHN
KINGERY, JOHN MAHARD. rec 1811. pp 95, 96

Deed dated 1811. JOSEPH CLIZBE of Amsterdam, Mont-
gomery Co, NY to IRA CLIZBE of same. S 15, T 3, R 3.
Signed JOSEPH CLIZBE. Witn: JEREMIAH FULLER, JAMES
ROSS. rec 1811. pp 96, 97

Deed dated 1811. WILLIAM NICHOLS to ANDERSON SPENCER
Hamilton lot 71. Signed WILLIAM NICKEL. Witn: DAN'L
MILLIKIN, JOHN (x) MURPHY. rec 1811. pp 97, 98

Deed dated 1811. JOSEPH HOUGH & JEAN his wife to
JAMES AYERS of Hamilton Co. Hamilton lots 76, 77.
Signed JOSEPH HOUGH, JEAN HOUGH. Witn: ISAAC STAN-
LEY, JAMES MILLS. rec 1811. pp 98, 99

Deed dated 1811. JAMES AYERS as above to DANIEL
SEWARD. Hamilton lots 76, 77. Witn: WILLIAM PHARES
JR, JOHN SUTHERLAND JR. rec 1811. p 99

Deed dated 1810. JOHN SUTHERLAND & HENRY BROWN to

BUTLER COUNTY LAND RECORDS: BOOK C

DANIEL SEWARD. Rossville outlot 17. Signed JOHN SUTHERLAND, HENRY BROWN. Witn: JAMES STEEL, JAMES BECK. rec 1811. p 100

Deed dated 1811. LEVI KINMAN & MARY his wife to HARMAN BARKALOO. S 18, T 3, R 3. Signed LEVI KINMAN MARY (x) KINMAN. Witn: ISAIAH LEIGH, JOHN SWEARINGEN. rec 1811. p 101

Mortgage dated 1811. HARMAN BARKELOO to LEVI KINMAN. Payment due 1813. Signed HARMAN BARKELOO. Witn: IZAAC CRUME, JOHN SWEARINGEN. rec 1811. pp 101, 102

Deed dated 1809. JOHN SUTHERLAND & HENRY BROWN to ROBERT TAYLOR & JOHN TAYLOR. Rossville lots 23, 28, 33, 38. Signed JOHN SUTHERLAND, HENRY BROWN. Witn: WM. BOMBERGER JR, WM. PHARES JR. rec 1811. p 103

Deed dated 1811. IRA CLIZBE of Amsterdam, Montgomery Co, NY to STEPHEN CRANE of Liberty Twp. S 15, T 3, R 3. Signed IRA CLIZBE. Witn: ISAAC LINDLY, JOHN WHITWORTH. rec 1811. pp 103, 104

Mortgage dated 1811. STEPHEN CRANE to IRA CLIZBE as above. S 15, T , R 3. Signed STEPHEN CRANE. Witn as above. rec 1811. pp 104, 105

Deed dated 1811. SAMUEL C. VANCE & MARY his wife of Lawrencebugh, IN Ter'y to CLARKSON FREEMAN of PA. S 16, T 1, R 4. Signed SAM'L. C. VANCE, MARY M. VANCE. Witn: JABEZ PERCIVAL, MOSES RUSSELL. rec 1811. pp 106, 107

Agreement dated 1806. JOHN YOUNG to convey deed to S 10, T 5, R 2 to SERAH YOUNG of Warren Co when patent is recvd from USA. Serah to make last payment due. Signed JOHN YOUNG, SERAH (x) YOUNG. Witn: ALEXANDER YOUNG, ANDREW YOUNG. rec 1811. p 107

Deed dated 1811. JOSEPH GASTON & MARTHA his wife to EZEKIEL McCONEL. S 27, T 2, R 2; once owned by WILLIAM TINDLE, sold to ABIJAH HUNT. Signed JOSEPH GASTON MARTHA GASTON. Witn: M. HUESTON, WM. ENYART. rec 1811. pp 107, 108

Plat of town of Orange. S 36, T 2, R 3. DAVID MULFORD, proprietor. rec 1811. p 109

Deed dated 1811. JOSEPH GASTON & MARTHA his wife to JOHN CAR*. S 27, T 2, R 2. Signed JOSEPH GASTON, MARTHA GASTON. Witn: M. HUESTON, WM. ENYART. rec

BUTLER COUNTY LAND RECORDS: BOOK C

1811. pp 110, 111. *KERR in deed text, margin note.

Deed dated 1811. HUGH B. HAWTHORN to JOHN SUTHERLAND. Hamilton lot 133. Signed HUGH B. HAWTHORN. Witn: JAMES SMITH, WM. PHARES JR. rec 1811. p 111

Deed dated 1811. JACOB KOUTZ & HANNAH his wife of Hamilton Co to JACOB HAWN of Warren Co. S 12. T 2, R 4. Signed JACOB KOUTZ, HANNAH KOUTZ. Witn: JOHN MAHARD, MOSES VAIL. rec 1811. pp 111, 112

Mortgage datd 1811. JAMES H. PARCEL & POLLY his wife to JACOB LEWIS. Hamilton lot 185; payment due 1813. Signed JAMES H. PARCEL, POLLY PARCEL. Witn: ISAAC STANLEY, SAMUEL GRAY. rec 1811. p 113

Deed dated 1811. ELIAS RUNYAN of Essex Co, NJ to JACOB LEWIS of Fairfield Twp. S 24, T 2, R 2. Signed ELIAS RUNYAN. Witn: HUGH McEOWN, LEWIS SMALLEY, QUUIN McCOY. rec 1811. pp 114, 115

Deed dated 1811. JOEL WILLIAMS & PHEBE his wife of Hamilton Co to SAMUEL DICK. No S-T-R; purchased from JACOB HIDAY & from ISAAC OGG. Signed JOEL WILLIAMS, PHEBE WILLIAMS. Witn: G. DICK, JOHN MAHARD. rec 1811. pp 115, 116

Manuscript of Symmes Purchase dated 1787. Entered into Butler County land records at the direction of JOHN CLEVES SYMMES. Land purchase and resale authorized by Congressional Act of 1787, dependant upon *frequency of the Indian irruptions may render the same impracticable*. Defines borders of tract, sets conditions of purchase and methods of payment by settlers. Signed JOHN CLEVES SYMMES. rec 1811. pp 116, 117, 118, 119, 120, 121, 122

Postscript to MS above dated 1811 Defines townships, land prices. Identifies sales agents. Signed JOHN CLEVES SYMMES. rec 1811. p 122

Deed dated 1811. WILLIAM P. BARKALOW & MARY his wife to BENJAMIN DUBOIS. S 33, T 2, R 5. Signed WM. P. BARKALOW, MARY BARKALOW. Witn: JP JAMES TAPSCOTT, ZEBULON BARKALOW. rec 1811. pp 122, 123

Mortgage dated 1811. BERIAH MaGOFFIN of Harrodsburgh, Mercer Co, KY to JOHN IMMICK. Hamilton lot 161. Signed BERIAH MAGOFFIN. Witn: JOHN SUTHERLAND, JOHN REILY. rec 1811. pp 123, 12

BUTLER COUNTY LAND RECORDS: BOOK C

Deed dated 1811. ISAAC STANLEY to EPHRAIM CATTERLIN. Hamilton lot 181. Signed ISAAC STANLEY. Witn: DAVID BEATY, JOHN REILY. rec 1811. pp 124, 125

Deed dated 1811. LEVI JENNINGS & ELIZABETH his wife of Montgomery Co to JACOB BELL. S 31 & 32, T 2, R 4. Signed LEVI JENNINGS, ELIZABETH (x) JENNINGS. Witn: HENRY WEAVER, DAVIS BALL. rec 1811. pp 125, 126

Deed dated 1811. MOSES DENMAN & ELIZABETH his wife to WILLIAM DENMAN. S 32 & 33, T 2, R 4. Signed MOSES DENMAN, ELIZABETH (x) DENMAN. Witn: AMOS DAVIS, HENRY WEAVER. rec 1811. pp 126, 127

Deed dated 1811. LEVI JENNINGS & ELIZABETH his wife of Montgomery Co to MOSES DENMAN. S 32 & 33, T 2, R 4. Bound by land of HENRY WEAVER, ISAAC HUFF, WILLIAM DENNISTON, ABRAHAM SIMPSON dec'd. Signed LEVI JENNINGS, ELIZABETH (x) JENNINGS. Witn: HENRY WEAVER, JACOB BELL. rec 1811. pp 127, 128

Deed dated 1811. THOMAS BLAIR & PEGGY his wife to WILLIAM HERBERT. Rossville lots 83, 88, 89. Signed THOS. BLAIR, PEGGY BLAIR. Witn: NOAH WADE, JOS. HOUGH, DAN'L. MILLIKIN. rec 1811. pp 128, 129

Deed dated 1811. JACOB BURNET & REBECCA his wife of Cincinnati to JACOB POWERS. S 33, T 2, R 2. Signed JAC. BURNET, REBECCA BURNET. Witn: ETHAN STONE, ROBT. WALLACE JR. rec 1811. pp 129, 130

Deed dated 1811. JOSEPH HOUGH & JEAN his wife to JOHN WINGATE. Hamilton lot 186. Signed JOSEPH HOUGH, JEAN (x) HOUGH. Witn: JAMES J. BEELER, DAN'L MILLIKIN. rec 1811. pp 130, 131

Deed dated 1811. LEVI JENNINGS & ELIZABETH his wife of Montgomery Co to JOHN BLUE. S 31, T 2, R 4. Signed LEVI JENNINGS, ELIZABETH (x) JENNINGS. Witn: HENRY WEAVER, DAVIS BALL. rec 1811. p 131

Deed dated 1811. ROBERT IRWIN & MARY his wife to JAMES MILLS. Rossville lot 61. Signed ROBERT IRWIN, MARY IRWIN. Witn: WILLIAM McCLELLAN, JAMES SMITH. rec 1812. p 132

Deed dated 1811. BERIAH MAGOFFIN of KY to WILLIAM HARLAN. Hamilton outlot 11. Signed BERIAH MAGOFFIN. Witn: JOHN REILY, L. CAVNAUGH. rec 1812. pp 132, 133

BUTLER COUNTY LAND RECORDS: BOOK C

Deed dated 1811. JACOB KEMP & MARY his wife to AARON VAIL. S 15, T 2, R 4. Signed JACOB KEMP, MARY (x) KEMP. Witn: HENRY WEAVER, JOHN McCAN. rec 1812. pp 133, 134

Deed dated 1811. AARON VAIL to RANDAL VAIL. S 21 & 22, T 2, R 4; bound by HUGH VAIL's land. Signed AARON VAIL. Witn: JOHN VANSICKLE, ELIAS POWERS. JP ISAAC HOFF. rec 1812. pp 134, 135

Deed dated 1811. RANDAL VAIL & MARIAH his wife to AARON VAIL. S 21 & 22, T 2, R 4; bound by ANDREW CLAWSON's land. Signed RANDAL VAIL, MARIAH (x) VAIL. Witn: JOHN VANSICKLE, ELIAS POWERS. rec 1812. pp 135, 136

Deed dated 1811. Admtrs of DAVID SLOAN to ELEANOR FLEMING. S 28, T 2, R 2. Bound by land of heirs of JOSEPH HUNTER. Signed STEPHAN CRANE, DAVID K. ESTE as admtrs. Witn: JAMES McBRIDE, JOSEPH HOUGH, JOHN WINGATE. rec 1812. pp 136, 137

Deed dated 1811. RACHEL SLOAN, widow of DAVID SLOAN to ELEANOR FLEMING, dau of ROBERT FLEMING. S 28, T 2, R 2. Signed RACHEL SLOAN. Witn: JAMES McBRIDE, JOHN WHITWORTH. rec 1812. pp 137, 138

Mortgage dated 1811. JOHN IMMICK to BERIAH MAGOFFIN. Hamilton lot 106. Signed JOHN IMMICK. Witn: JOHN REILY, JOHN SUTHERLAND. rec 1812. pp 138, 139

Deed dated 1811. ISAAC STANLEY to BERIAH MAGOFFIN of KY. Hamilton lot 161. Signed ISAAC STANLEY. Witn: JOHN SUTHERLAND, JAMES McBRIDE. rec 1812. pp 139, 140

Mortgage dated 1811. DAVID DAVIS to JOHN McEOWN. S 22, T 2, R 3. Payment due 1814. Signed DAVID DAVIS. Witn: JOHN VINNEDGE, JAMES HEATON. rec 1812. pp 140, 141

Power Of Attorney dated 1811. THOMAS CALDWELL, son of JAMES CALDWELL decd, ELIZABETH CALDWELL widow of JC, THOMAS RAMAGE & JANE his wife, dau of JC, all of NY City, apptd JAMES CALDWELL, another son of JC, as atty to convey land in S 22, T 3, R 2. Signed THOMAS CALDWELL, ELIZABETH (x) CALDWELL, THOMAS RAMAGE, JEAN RAMAGE. Witn: CHA. WHITE JR, ABM. A. SLOVER. rec 1812. pp 141, 142

Mortgage dated 1811. WILLIAM HARLAN to BERIAH MAGOFFIN of KY. Hamilton outlot 11. Signed WM. HARLAN.

BUTLER COUNTY LAND RECORDS: BOOK C

Witn: JOHN REILY, L. CAVENAUGH. rec 1812. pp 142, 143

Deed dated 1812. JOHN GARRISON & SUSANNAH his wife to NICHOLAS WHITINGER. S 19, T 3, R 3. Bound by land of SAMUEL DAVIS, SILAS GARRISON. Signed JOHN GARRISON, SUSANNAH (x) GARRISON. Witn: JAMES McKANE DAVID DUFFIELD. rec 1812. pp 143, 144

Deed dated 1811. MICHAEL PEARCE & PHEBE his wife to WILLIAM SQUIER. S 4 & 5, T 1, R 4. Signed MICHAEL PEARCE, PHEBE PEARCE. Witn: SQUIER LITTELL, HENRY WEAVER. rec 1812. pp 144, 145

Quitclaim dated 1812. ABRAHAM CALDWELL & ELIZABETH his wife and DAN CALDWELL & ANNE his wife, all of Butler Co and JAMES CALDWELL of NY to ROBERT CALDWELL. S 22, T 3, R 2. Signed ABRAHAM CALDWELL, ELIZABETH CALDWELL, DAN CALDWELL, ANNE (x) CALDWELL, JAMES CALDWELL. Witn: ABRAM R. COLWELL, MICHL. AYERS. rec 1812. p 146

Quitclaim dated 1812. ROBERT CALDWELL & MARY his wife, ABRAHAM CALDWELL & ELIZABETH his wife and DAN CALDWELL & ANNE his wife to JAMES CALDWELL of NY. S 22, T 3, R 2. Signed ROBERT CALDWELL, MARY (x) CALDWELL, ABRAHAM CALDWELL, ELIZABETH CALDWELL, DAN CALDWELL, ANNE (x) CALDWELL. Witn as above. rec 1812. p 147

Quitclaim dated 1812. ROBERT CALDWELL & MARY his wife, ABRAHAM CALDWELL & ELIZABETH his wife and JAMES CALDWELL by POA from heirs of NY City to DAN CALDWELL. Fourth part of S 22, T 3, R 2; POA rec Bk C, pp 141, 142, dated 1812. Signed ROBERT CALDWELL, MARY (x) CALDWELL, ABRAHAM CALDWELL, ELIZABETH CALDWELL, JAS. CALDWELL. Witn as above. rec 1812. pp 147, 148

Quitclaim dated 1812. ROBERT CALDWELL & MARY his wife, DAN CALDWELL & ANNE his wife and JAMES CALDWELL by POA from heirs of NY to ABRAHAM CALDWELL. A fourth part of S 22, T 3, R 2. Signed ROBERT CALDWELL, MARY (x) CALDWELL, DAN CALDWELL, ANNE (x) CALDWELL, JAS. CALDWELL. Witn as above. rec 1812. pp 148, 149

Deed dated 1811. DAVID MULFORD & HANNAH his wife to AMOS VALLENTINE of Warren Co. S 30, T 3, R 3. Signed DAVID MULFORD, HANNAH (x) MULFORD. Witn: P. WILLIAMSON, SAMUEL GREGORY. rec 1812. pp 150, 151

Deed dated 1811. GEORGE PAULB TORRENCE & MARY his

BUTLER COUNTY LAND RECORDS: BOOK C

wife to JACOB BURNET. S 10, T 2, R 3. Signed GEO. P. TORRENCE, MARY B. TORRENCE. Witn: MARY IRWIN, JANE FINDLAY. rec 1812. pp 151, 152

Deed dated 1811. MATTHEW RICHARDSON & ANN his wife to DAVID McMECHAN. S 23, T 5, R 2. Bound by WILLIAM MARTIN'S land. Signed MATTHEW RICHARDSON, ANN RICHARDSON. Witn: R. LYTLE, JNO. THOMPSON. rec 1812. pp 152, 153

Deed dated 1812. RICHARD McCAIN to THOMAS DILLON. No S-T-R; bounds only*. Signed RICHARD McCAINE. Witn: DAN'L MILLIKIN, SAMUEL MILLIKIN. rec 1812. pp 153, 154   *see following entry

Deed dated 1812. THOMAS DILLON & POLLY his wife to ELIHU WOODRUFF. ■tract surveyed to RICHARD McCAINE in S 30, T 2, R 2.■ Signed THOMAS DILLON, POLLY (x) DILLON. Witn: JAMES HEATON, SAM'L MILLER. rec 1812. pp 154, 155

Deed dated 1812. WILLIAM MURRAY & DEBORAH his wife to HANNAH BURKE. Hamilton lots 5 & 6. Signed WM. MURRAY, DEBBY MURRAY. Witn: JAMES McBRIDE, SAML McCULLAGH. rec 1812. pp 155, 156

Deed dated 1812. JONATHAN PIERSON & MALINDA his wife to JACOB RICKART. Hamilton lots 72 & 73. Signed JONATHAN PIERSON, MELILAD PIERSON. Witn: DANL. MILLIKIN THOS. BLAIR. rec 1812. pp 156, 157

Deed dated 1811. JACOB BURNET & REBECCA his wife of Hamilton Co. to EDWARD CORNTHWAITE. S 10, T 2, R 3. Signed JAC. BURNET, REBECCA BURNET. Witn: JOHN REILY JOHN SUTHERLAND. rec 1812. pp 157, 158

Deed dated 1811. ISAAC WOOD & JANE his wife to JAMES CLARK. S 18, T 3, R 3. Signed ISAAC WOOD, JANE (x) WOOD. Witn: HANNAH WILLIAMSON, P. WILLIAMSON. rec 1812. pp 158, 159

Deed dated 1808. LUDLOW PIERSON & ELEANOR his wife to ANDREW WILSON. Hamilton lot 9. Signed LUDLOW PIERSON ELENDER PIERSON. Witn: ISAAC STANLEY, STEPHEN SCUDDER. rec 1812. pp 159, 160

Mortgage dated 1811. DAVID McMECHAN of Milford Twp to MATTHEW RICHARDSON. S 23, T 5, R 2. Signed DAVID McMECHAN. Witn: R. LYTLE, JOHN THOMPSON. rec 1812. pp 160, 161

BUTLER COUNTY LAND RECORDS: BOOK C

Deed dated 1810. RALPH PHILLIPS & RUTH his wife of Hunterdon Co, NJ to WILLIAM McKIM of Salisbury Twp, Chester Co, PA. S 6, T 2, R 2. Signed RALPH PHILLIPS, RUTH PHILLIPS. Witn: L.W.K. PHILLIPS, ELIZA HENRY. rec 1812. pp 161, 162

Deed dated 1812. WARHAM STACY & JERUSHA his wife to JOSEPH WORTH. S 31, T 3, R 3. Signed WARHAM STACY, JERUSHA STACY. Witn: JOHN AYRES, WM. GRAY. rec 1812. pp 162, 163

Deed dated 1812. JOSEPH ELY & CATHERINE his wife to JOHN P. CRIST of Warren Co. S 8, T 1, R 5. Bound by land of JOHN McKEAN, MOSES VAIL, WILLIAM STREET. Signed JOSEPH ELY, CATHARINE ELY. Witn: WM. WILSON, HENRY WEAVER. rec 1812. pp 163, 164

Deed dated 1811. WILLIAM P. BARKALOW & MARY his wife to SAMUEL RHODES of Warren Co. No S-T-R: "tract where said WILLIAM now lives". Signed WM. P. BARKALOW, MARY BARKALOW. Witn: JAMES BARCALOW, HENRY WEAVER. rec 1812. pp 164, 165

Deed dated 1811. JAMES DUNN & NANCEY his wife to heirs of PINE PIERSON, decd. S 11, T 3, R 2. Bound by land of WM. BALDWIN, WM. CROOKS, PETER WILLCOCKS, WM. WHITE. Signed JAS. DUN, NANCEY DUNN. Witn: WILLIAM CROOKS, ANN RICHARDSON. rec 1812. pp 166, 167

Deed dated 1811. DAVID MULFORD to JOB MULFORD. S 36, T 3, R 3. Signed DAVID MULFORD. Witn: JACOB CLARK, UZAL BEACH. rec 1812. pp 167, 168

Deed dated 1811. DAVID MULFORD to JOHN MULFORD. S 36, T 3, R 3. Signed and witn as above. rec 1812. pp 168, 169

Mortgage dated 1811. CELADON SYMMES to SAMUEL HOWRY. S 34, T 2, R 2. Signed CELADON SYMMES. Witn: W. CORRY, JOHN WHITWORTH. rec 1812. pp 169, 170

Deed dated 1811. WILLIAM CORRY & ELEANOR his wife and JOHN REILY & NANCY his wife to LAURENCE CAVENAUGH Land in Hamilton town "whereon Fort Hamilton stood"; no lot number. Signed W. CORRY, JOHN REILY, ELEANOR CORRY, NANCY REILY. Witn: JAC. BURNET, JOHN WHITWORTH. JP J.H. WHITE. rec 1812. pp 170, 171

Deed dated 1807. JAMES HEATON & MARY his wife to AZARIAS THORN. Hamilton lot 9. Signed JAMES HEATON, MARY HEATON. Witn: ISAAC STANLEY, BENJAMIN RANDEL.

BUTLER COUNTY LAND RECORDS: BOOK C

rec 1812. pp 171, 172

Deed dated 1805. Admtrs of ISRAEL LUDLOW to SAMUEL CULBERTSON. Hamilton lots 33, 34, 121, 122, outlot 8; finalized sale begun 1795 by Ludlow. Signed CHARLOTTE CHAMBERS LUDLOW, JAMES FINDLAY. Witn: JOS. CONN SR, JAMES EWING. rec 1812. pp 172, 173, 174

Deed dated 1812. NATHAN PAGE & REBECCA his wife to STEPHEN SLIFER. S 12, T 2, R 3. Signed NATHAN PAGE, REBECCA (x) PAGE. Witn: LEONARD WEAVER, HENRY WEAVER. rec 1812. pp 174, 175

Deed dated 1812. WILLIAM ROBINSON to JOHN BEATY, JOHN ROBINSON & JAMES MORRISON, Trustees of Mt. Pleasant associate reformed congregation. S 18, T 3, R 3. Signed WILLIAM ROBINSON. Witn: ARTHUR ORR, JOHN MORROW. rec 1812. pp 175, 176

Deed dated 1809. MICHAEL PEARCE & PHEBE his wife of Lemon Twp to SAMUEL M. POTTER of same. S 6 in Lemon Twp, R 4. Signed MICHAEL PEARCE, PHEBE PEARCE. Witn ENOCH HAND, LEVI POTTER. rec 1812. pp 176, 177

Power of Attorney dated 1812. WILLIAM McNABB of Union Town, Fayette Co, PA appted ISRAEL WOODRUFF as atty to recover land and money from WILLIAM PATTON as admtr of JOHN McNABB, late of Hamilton. Signed WM. McNABB. Witn: JONATHAN ROWLAND. rec 1812. p 177

Mortgage datd 1812. JOSEPH HAYS & JAMES HINDS to ALEXANDER WARE of Warren Co. S 11 & 12, T 2, R 4. Signed JOSEPH HAYS, JAMES HINDS. Witn: L. REEDER, W.C. SCHENCK. rec 1812. p 178

Deed dated 1812. GEORGE SNIDER & SUSAN his wife to DANIEL MILLIKIN. Hamilton lot 211. Signed GEORGE SNIDER, SUSAN (x) SNIDER. Witn: JAMES HEATON, JAMES MILLS. rec 1812. p 179

Deed dated 1811. JOHN McEOWEN & JANE his wife to DAVID DAVIS. S 22, T 2, R 3. Signed JOHN McEOWEN, JANE McEOWEN. Witn: JAMES HEATON, JOHN VINNEDGE. rec 1812. pp 180, 181

Deed dated 1811. AZARIAS THORN & NANCEY his wife to LUDLOW PIERSON. Hamilton lot 23. Signed AZARIAS THORN, NANCEY THORN. Witn: ISAAC STANLEY, HENRY RHEA. rec 1812. p 181

Deed dated 1811. EBENEZER WILSON & ELIZABETH his

BUTLER COUNTY LAND RECORDS: BOOK C

wife to JAMES WILSON. S 23, T 3, R 3. Bound by land of DANIEL GOBLE, JAMES MAPES. Signed EBENEZER WILSON ELIZABETH (x) WILSON. Witn: P. WILLIAMSON, SALEM POCOCK. rec 1812. pp 182, 183

Deed dated 1812. JAMES WILSON to DANIEL RISK of Hamilton Co and JAMES CLARK. S 23, T 3, R 3. Signed JAMES WILSON. Witn: DAN'L MILLIKIN, JAMES HEATON. rec 1812. pp 183, 184

Deed dated 1812. HEZEKIAH SMITH & SUSAN his wife to JOHN SHANE. S 20, T 3, R 2; bound by WILLIAM NIXON's land. Signed HEZEKIAH SMITH, SUSAN SMITH. Witn: MICH'L. AYERS, PETER SMITH. rec 1812. pp 184, 185

Deed dated 1809. HENRY MILLER & EVE his wife to JAMES T. MORTON. S 20, T 3, R 2. Signed HENRY V. MILLER, EVE (x) MILLER. Witn: MICHAEL AYERS, ISC. S. SWEARINGEN. rec 1812. p 185

Deed dated 1808. ALLEN NIXON & MARGARET his wife to HENRY MILLER. S 20, T 3, R 2. Signed ALLEN (x) NIXON, MARGARET (x) NIXON. Witn: DANIEL (x) PERINE, ISC. S. SWEARINGEN. rec 1812. p 186

Deed dated 1812. JAMES T. MORTON & ABIGAIL his wife to HEZEKIAH SMITH. S 20, T 3, R 2. Signed JAMES T. MORTON, ABIGAIL (x) MORTON. rec 1812. p 187

Deed dated 1812. JOHN VANCE to PHILLIP DROLLINGER. S 9, T 2, R 2. Signed JOHN VANCE. Witn: DANL. MILLIKIN, JOAN MILLIKIN. rec 1812. pp 187, 188

Mortgage dated 1812. PHILIP DROLLINGER to JOHN VANCE. S 9, T 2, R 2; payment due 1814. Signed PHILIP DROLLINGER. Witn as above. rec 1812. p 189

Deed dated 1812. EDWARD MEEKS & DOROTHEA his wife to SAMUEL D. BOWMAN. S 23, T 3, R 2. Signed EDW. MEEKS, DOROTHEA C. MEEKS. Witn: JAMES LYON, JOHN SHARP. rec 1812. p 190

Deed dated 1812. JONATHAN LINE & JOANNA his wife to ELIHU LINE. S 14, T 2, R 3. Signed JONATHAN LINE, JOHANNAH (x) LINE. Witn: JOHN LINE, JOHN VINNEDGE. rec 1812. p 191

Deed dated 1812. JOSEPH ELY & CATHARINE his wife to RHEUBEN WOODWARD. S 5, T 1, R 5. Bound by land of WILLIAM WOODWARD, JOHN McKEAN. Signed JOSEPH ELY, CATHARINE ELY. Witn: WM. WILSON, HENRY WEAVER. rec

BUTLER COUNTY LAND RECORDS: BOOK C

1812. pp 192, 193

Deed dated 1812. BRICE VIRGIN & SARAH his wife to WILLIAM LEGG SR. S 2, T 2, R 3. Bound by land of JOEL WOODRUFF. Signed BRICE VIRGIN. SARAH (x) VIRGIN. Witn: JOHN AYERS, JOHN FREEMAN. rec 1812. pp 193, 194

Deed dated 1811. WILLIAM NICHOLS to SAMUEL ENYART. S 2, T 2, R 3. Signed WILLIAM NICKELS. Witn as above. rec 1812. pp 194, 195

Power of Attorney dated 1811. JOHN C. WINANS of Warren Co appted JOSHUA COLLETT of same to sell S 15, T 3, R 2. Signed JOHN C. WINANS. Witn: none. rec 1812. p 195

Deed dated 1812. JOHN C. WINANS, late of Warren Co to WILLIAM BELCH. S 15, T 3, R 2. Signed JOHN C. WINANS by JOSHUA COLLETT. Witn: TOBIAS (illegible), CLARISSA VAN HORNE. rec 1812. pp 196, 197

Deed dated 1812. JOHN VANNICE & ELIZABETH his wife to MICHAEL EARHEART. S 14, T 2, R 3. Signed JOHN VANNICE, ELIZABETH (x) VANNICE. Witn: GEORGE EARHEART, HENRY WEAVER. rec 1812. pp 197, 198

Deed dated 1812. DURAN WHITTLESEY & RUTH his wife to JOSHUA ELLIOTT. S 20, T 3, R 3. Signed DURAN WHITTLESEY, RUTH (x) WHITTLESEY. Witn: JOHN AYERS, IRA HUNT. rec 1812. pp 198, 199

Deed dated 1812. JOHN HURST & ELIZABETH his wife to NATHAN PAGE. S 12, T 2, R 3. Signed JOHN HURST, ELIZABETH (x) HURST. Witn: LEONARD WEAVER, HENRY WEAVER. rec 1812. pp 199, 200

Deed dated 1812. WILLIAM McCLELLAN, Sheriff, to WILLIAM LOWRY. In 1803, JEREMIAH BEATY obtained judgement against JOHN LOWRY. Beaty was given a mortgage on Lowry's land, S 14, T 3, R 3. Lowry died; CATHARINE LOWRY appted admtr. Land was seized to settle debt to Beaty; sold at auction. Signed WM. McCLELLAN Witn: JOHN BEATY, JOHN REILY. rec 1812. pp 201, 202

Deed dated 1812. WILLIAM LOWRY to DAVID WILLIAMSON. S 14, T 3, R 3. Signed WILLIAM LOWRY. Witn: JOHN BEATY, ARTHUR ORR. rec 1812. pp 202, 203

Deed dated 1812. WILLIAM LOWRY to ARTHUR ORR, both of Liberty Twp. S 14, T 3, R 3. Signed WILLIAM LOWRY

BUTLER COUNTY LAND RECORDS: BOOK C

Witn: GEORGE WILLIAMSON, P. WILLIAMSON. rec 1812. pp 203, 204

Deed dated 1806. USA to STEPHEN VAIL of Hamilton Co. S 22, T 2, R 4. rec 1812. p 204

Deed dated 1811. USA to STEPHEN VAIL. S 28 & 34, T 2, R 4. rec 1812. p 205

Deed dated 1811. JESSE HUNT & ELIZABETH his wife of Cincinnati for himself and as atty for ABIJAH HUNT, decd, to JOHN CLAPP. S 27, T 2, R 2. Bound by land of JOHN GASTIN. Signed JESSE HUNT, ELIZA. HUNT. Witn: GRIFFIN YEATMAN, W.C. ANDERSON. rec 1812. pp 205, 206

Deed dated 1812. JACOB BURNET & REBECCA his wife of Hamilton Co to WILLIAM WILSON of Ross Co. S 33, T 2, R 2. Signed JAC. BURNET, REBECCA BURNET. Witn: MATTHEW G. WALLACE, ETHAN STONE. rec 1812. pp 206, 207

Deed dated 1812. Admtrs of JOHN TORRENCE to WILLIAM BIGHAM. Hamilton lot 163. Signed JOHN WINGATE, AMMY WINGATE. Witn: ALEXANDER SACKETT, JAMES MILLS. rec 1812. pp 207, 208

Deed dated 1812. SHORES STEVENSON of Liberty Twp to JOHN FREEMAN of same. S 35, T 3, R 2. Signed SHORES STEVENSON. Witn: JOHN AYERS, WILLIAM LEGG. rec 1812. p 209

Deed dated 1800. SAMUEL SEWARD of Hamilton Co, NW Ter'y, to JOHN FREEMAN of same. S 5, T 2, R 2. Signed SAMUEL SEWARD. Witn: DANIEL SEWARD, ISAAC (x) SEWARD. rec 1812. p 210

Deposition dated 1812. ISAAC SEWARD swore he saw SAMUEL SEWARD sign and deliver above deed to FREEMAN; that DANIEL signed the deed as witness. Signed ISAAC (x) SEWARD. Witn: JP JOHN AYERS. rec 1811. p 210

Deed dated 1807. ABRAHAM FREEMAN to EZRA FREEMAN, atty at law. S 4, T 1, R 2, excluding land sold to JAMES BLACKBURN, DAVID BEATY. Signed ABRAHAM FREEMAN Witn: CORNELIUS THOMAS, JAMES CLARKSON. rec 1812 p211

Deposition dated 1811. CORNELIUS THOMAS swore ABRAHAM FREEMAN acknowledged deed above; that he saw JAMES CLARKSON sign as witness. Signed CORNELIUS THOMAS. Witn: JP JOHN AYERS. rec 1812. p 211

Deed dated 1809. USA to SAMUEL McCLEREY of Hamilton

BUTLER COUNTY LAND RECORDS: BOOK C

County. S 14, T 5, R 2. rec 1812. p 212

Deed dated 1811. SAMUEL SMITH & MARTHA his wife of Hamilton Co to MARGARET WARNOCK. S 4, T 5, R 2. Signed SAM'L SMITH, MARTHA SMITH. Witn: JOHN SMITH, JOAB COMSTOCK. rec 1812. pp 212, 213

Deed dated 1808. MATTHEW WINTON & ELIZA his wife to PHILIP GORDEN. S 5, T 2, R 3. Signed MATH. WINTON, ELIZA WINTON. Witn: none. rec 1812. pp 213, 214

Deed dated 1812. WILLIAM McCLEAN & ISABEL his wife of Wayne Twp to PHILIP GORDEN. S 30, T 3, R 3. Signed WM. McCLEAN, ISABEL McCLEAN. Witn: WM. McCLELLAN, WILLIAM WALLACE. rec 1812. pp 214, 215

Deed dated 1812. THOMAS HUNTER, tax collector of Fairfield Twp to NANCY DAVIS. Hamilton lot 139. Signed THOMAS HUNTER. Witn: JAMES McBRIDE, JOEL COLLINS. rec 1812. pp 215, 216

Deed dated 1811. DAVID REED & RUTH his wife and ROBERT CARRICK & RUTH his wife to JOHN MELLORY of Harrison Co, KY. S 2, T 2, R 4. Signed DAVID REED, RUTH (x) REED, ROBERT (x) CARRICK, RUTH (x) CARRICK. Witn: GRIFFIN YEATMAN, J. or I. SELLMAN. rec 1812. pp 26, 217

Deed dated 1809. JOHN SUTHERLAND & HENRY BROWN to JOHN LUDLOW of Hamilton Co. Rossville lot 22, outlot 32. Signed JOHN SUTHERLAND, HENRY BROWN. Witn: WM. BOMBERGER JR, WM. PHARES JR. rec 1812. pp 218, 219

Deed dated 1812. JOEL WILLIAMS & PHEBE his wife of Hamilton Co to JOHN RAINEY. S 34, T 4, R 2. Signed JOEL WILLIAMS, PHEBE WILLIAMS. Witn: JOHN MAHARD, ROBERT McCULLOUGH. rec 1812. pp 219, 220

Deed dated 1811. JACOB POWERS to DANIEL POWERS. S 20, T 2, R 2. Wife ELIZABETH named in text, no signature. Signed JACOB POWERS. Witn: M. HUESTON, JOHN BURGIN. rec 1812. pp 220, 221

Deed dated 1812. JOEL WILLIAMS & PHEBE his wife of Hamilton Co to WILLIAM MARTIN. S 20, T 4, R 2. Signed JOEL WILLIAMS, PHEBE WILLIAMS. Witn: JOHN COX, JOHN MAHARD. rec 1812. pp 221, 222

Deed dated 1812. EDWARD DYER to JOHN PRICE. S 8, T 4, R 2. Signed EDWARD DYER. Witn: ROBERT RUSSELL, JOHN MASON. rec 1812. p 222

BUTLER COUNTY LAND RECORDS: BOOK C

Deed dated 1799. SAMUEL SEWARD of Hamilton Co. NW Ter'y to ISAAC SEWARD of same. S 5, T 2, R 2. Signed SAMUEL SEWARD. Witn: ISC. S. SWEARINGEN, JOHN FREEMAN. rec 1812. pp 222, 223

Deposition dated 1812. JOHN FREEMAN swore SAMUEL SEWARD signed & delivered deed; that he saw ISAAC SWEARINGEN sign as witness. Signed JOHN FREEMAN. rec 1812. p 223

Deed dated 1812. DAVID MULFORD & HANAH his wife to OLIVER KELLY. S 36, T 3, R 3. Signed DAVID MULFORD, HANAH (x) MULFORD. Witn: JOSEPH HUFFMAN, HENRY (x) BOLLEN. rec 1812. pp 223, 224

Deed dated 1812. JOHN SUTHERLAND & NANCY his wife and HENRY BROWN & CATHARINE his wife to SAMUEL GRAY. Rossville lot 10. Signed JOHN SUTHERLAND, NANCY R. SUTHERLAND, HENRY BROWN, KITTY P. BROWN. Witn: SAMUEL SCOTT, JOHN FOLKERTH. rec 1812. pp 225, 226

Deed dated 1812. JONATHAN DAYTON of NJ to SKILMAN AUGUR. S 7, T 2, R 3. Signed JONA. DAYTON by atty ELIAS I. DAYTON. Witn: GRIFFIN YEATMAN, JACOB ROSENCRANS. rec 1812. p 226

Deed dated 1812. Sons & daus, heirs of JAMES LOWRY of Montgomery Co to JOHN SUTHERLAND & HENRY BROWN. Hamilton lot 136. Signed JAMES LOWRY, ROSANNAH LOWRY WILLIAM LOWRY. Witn: JOHN FOLKERTH, SAMUEL WATSON. rec 1812. pp 226, 227

Deed dated 1812. SKILMAN ALGUR to JACOB ROSENCRANS. S 2, T 2, R 3. Signed SKILMAN ALGER, CATY ALGER. Witn: DAVID WADE, ETHAN STONE. JP's note: •SKILMAN ALGER & CATY ALGER, his wife•. rec 1812. pp 228, 229

Deed dated 1812. JOHN FREEMAN & ELIZABETH his wife to JACOB ROSENCRANS. S 5, T 2, R 2. Signed JOHN FREEMAN, ELIZABETH FREEMAN. Witn: JOHN AYERS, BRICE VIRGIN. rec 1812. pp 229, 230

Deed dated 1812. DANIEL McCLELLAN & BETSEY his wife to JAMES McINTIRE. S 15, T 2, R 4. Signed DANIEL McCLELLAN, BETSEY McCLELLAN. Witn: JABES TUTTLE, BENJAMIN BRIDGE. rec 1812. pp 230, 231

Deed dated 1811. LEVI JENNINGS & ELIZABETH his wife of Montgomery Co to DAVIS BALL. S 31 & 32, T 2, R 4. Signed LEVI JENNINGS, ELIZABETH (x) JENNINGS. Witn: HENRY WEAVER, JACOB BELL. rec 1812. pp 231, 232

BUTLER COUNTY LAND RECORDS: BOOK C

Deed dated 1812. DAVID MULFORD & HANNAH his wife to PETER SHAFER. S 36, T 3, R 3. Signed DAVID MULFORD, HANNAH (x) MULFORD. Witn: SAMUEL POSELL, WM. PERRY. rec 1812. pp 232, 233

Deed dated 1812. DAVIS BALL & POLLY his wife to JONATHAN CLARK. S 31, T 2, R 4. Signed DAVIS BALL, POLLY (x) BALL. Witn: HENRY WEAVER, WILLIAM HAYS. rec 1812. pp 233, 234

Deed dated 1812. Admrs of JOHN CHAMBERLAIN to SAMUEL CALDWELL. Finalize 1807 sale of S 32, T 2, R 5. Signed JOHN N.C. SCHENCK, JAMES TAPSCOTT. Witn: ALEXANDER WEAR, JAMES W. LANIER. rec 1812. pp 234, 235, 236

Deed dated 1806. Admrs of ISRAEL LUDLOW to GEORGE HARLAN. Hamilton lot 226. Signed CHARLOTTE CHAMBERS LUDLOW, JAMES FINDLAY, JOHN LUDLOW, SINEUS PIERSON. Witn: N.C. FINDLAY, JOHN MAHARD. rec 1812. pp 236, 237

Deed dated 1812. WILLIAM McCLELLAN, Sheriff, to WILLIAM BIGHAM. In 1809, Bigham obtained judgements against GEORGE HARLAN. Hamilton lots 225, 226 were seized, sold at auction. Signed WM. McCLELLAN. Witn: JAMES McBRIDE, ISAAC STANLEY. rec 1812. pp 238, 239, 240 (p 239/240 bound out of order)

Deed dated 1812. ABEL STOUT & THEODOCIA his wife to WILLIAM SUTTON. S 20, T5, R 2. Signed ABEL STOUT, THEODOCIA STOUT. Witn: THOMAS COOCH, JOHN REILY. JP MARSH WILLIAMS. rec 1812. pp 240, 241

Deed dated 1811. USA to JOSEPH DUNGAN of Warren Co. S 36, T 4, R 1. rec 1812. p 241

Deed dated 1812. TOBIAS BARCALOW & ELIZABETH his wife to DANIEL BARKALOW of NJ. S 14, T 2, R 4. Signed TOBIAS BARCALOW, ELIZABETH BARCALOW. Witn: DAVID WILLIAMSON, HENRY WEAVER. rec 1812. pp 241, 242

Note dated 1812. JOHN CLEVES SYMMES •acknowledged the within deed of conveyance•. No names, S-T-R given. Signed JOHN MAHARD. Clerk's margin note: J.C. SYMMES to E. ALLEN. rec 1812. p 242

Deed dated 1812. ADAM NELSON & NANCEY his wife to WILLIAM NELSON. S 24, T 4, R 1. Signed ADAM NELSON NANCEY (x) NELSON. Witn: J.H. WHITE, JOHN POARCES. rec 1812. p 243

BUTLER COUNTY LAND RECORDS: BOOK C

Deed dated 1812. JOHN HAHN & ELIZABETH HAHN of Hamilton Co to MICHAEL HAHN. S 27, T 2, R 2. Signed JOHN HAHN, ELIZABETH HAHN. Witn: JAMES McBRIDE, STEPHEN CORBLY. rec 1812. pp 243, 244

Deed dated 1811. WILLIAM McCLURE & MARTHA his wife of Montgomery Co to BENJAMIN VANCLIEF. S 25, T 2, R 4. Signed W. McCLURE, MARTHA McCLURE. Witn: HENRY WEAVER, JAMES PIPER. rec 1812. pp 245, 246

Deed dated 1812. JOHN HALL & ISAAC MOSS to JOHN RITCHEY JR, late of Hamilton Co. S 23. R 4, R 2. Signed JOHN HALL, ISAAC MOSS. Witn: JOHN REILY, JOHN WHITWORTH. rec 1812. pp 246, 247

Deed dated 1812. WILLIAM ELLIOTT to MICAJAH ELLIOTT, son of said WM. S 23, T 3, R 2. Signed WILLIAM ELLIOTT. Witn: JOHN AYERS, EDWARD ALLDREDGE. rec 1812. pp 247, 248

Deed dated 1812. JOHN HALL to GEORGE FLEENOR & DANIEL FLEENOR. S 19, T 1, R 4. Signed JOHN HALL. Witn JOHN REILY, JOHN WHITWORTH. rec 1812. pp 248, 249

Deed dated 1812. **WAREHAM** STACY & JARUSHA his wife to BAZEL HARRISON. S 31, T 3, R 3. Signed **WARHAM** STACY JARUSHA STACY. Witn: JOHN AYERS, SOLOMON DILLY. rec 1812. pp 249, 250, 251

Deed dated 1812. ARTHUR ST. CLAIR JR & FRANCES his wife of Hamilton Co to SAMUEL SCOTT. S 16, T 2, R 3. Signed AR. ST. CLAIR JR, FRANCES H. ST.CLAIR. Witn: JOHD. SPINNING, GEORGE HOWARD. rec 1812. pp 251, 252

Mortgage dated 1812. SAMUEL SCOTT to ARTHUR ST. CLAIR of Cincinnati. S 16, T 2, R 3. Signed SAMUEL SCOTT. Witn: JOHN REILY, JOHN WHITWORTH. rec 1812. pp 254, 255

Deed dated 1812. WILLIAM McCLELLAN, sheriff, to MATTHEW G. WALLACE. In 1807, ARTHUR ST. CLAIR obtained judgement against THOMAS McCULLOUGH. Hamilton lot 69 seized, sold for debt. Signed WM. McCLELLAN. Witn: JAMES McBRIDE, ISAAC STANLEY. rec 1812. pp 254, 255

Deed dated 1810. USA to JAMES CHARLTON, assignee of SAMUEL LEE. S 33, T 3, R 1. rec 1812. pp 255, 256

Deed dated 1812. SAMUEL SEWARD SR & ANNY his wife to TIMOTHY WOODRUFF. S 5, T 2, R 2. Signed SAMUEL SEWARD ANNY (x) SEWARD. Witn: JOHN AYERS, DAVID MULFORD.

BUTLER COUNTY LAND RECORDS: BOOK C

rec 1812. pp 256, 257

Deed dated 1812. VALLNTIN CHASE & ELIZABETH his wife of Reily Twp to JAMES CROOKS, SAMUEL CROOKS, ABRAHAM LEE & JOHN MORRIS, Trustees of Indian Creek Baptist Church. S 5, T 4, R 1. Signed VALLENTINE CHASE, BETSEY CHASE. Witn: J.H. WHITE, ABRAHAM JONES. rec 1812. pp 257, 258

Deed dated 1812. ANDREW BROWN & PHEBE his wife to EZEKIEL JOHNSON. S 12, T 5, R 2. Signed ANDREW BROWN, PHEBE (x) BROWN. Witn: JOHN GLINES, MATTH. RICHARDSON. rec 1812. pp 258, 259

Deed dated 1809. JOHN SUTHERLAND & HENRY BROWN to SAMUEL ASTON. Rossville lot 32. Signed JOHN SUTHERLAND, HENRY BROWN. Witn: WM. BOMBERGER JR, WM. PHARES JR. rec 1812. pp 260, 261

Deed dated 1812. GEORGE HOFFMAN & ELIZABETH his wife to JACOB HOFFMAN. S 2, T 2, R 3. Signed GEORGE (x) HOFFMAN, ELIZABETH (x) HOFFMAN. Witn: JAMES SMITH, OWEN DAVSLY?. rec 1812. pp 261, 262

Deed dated 1812. GEORGE HOFFMAN & ELIZABETH his wife to ISAAC HOFFMAN. S 2, T 2, R 3. Signed GEORGE (x) HOFFMAN, ELIZABETH (x) HOFFMAN. Witn: JAMES SMITH, OWEN DAREY. rec 1812. pp 262, 263

Deed dated 1812. GEORGE HOFFMAN & ELIZABETH his wife to JOHN HOFFMAN. S 2, T 2, R 3. Signed and witn as above. rec 1812. pp 263, 264

Deed dated 1812. GEORGE HOFFMAN & ELIZABETH his wife to ABRAHAM HOFFMAN. S 2, T 2, R 3. Signed and witn as above. rec 1812. pp 264, 265

Deed dated 1812. GEORGE HOFFMAN & ELIZABETH his wife to ISAAC HOFFMAN. S 2, T 2, R 3. Signed and witn as above. rec 1812. pp 265, 266

Deed dated 1812. JOHN MATSON & MARY his wife of Hamilton Co to DAVID FRANCIS. S 31, T 3, R 2. Signed JOHN MATSON, RICHARD HARRIS. rec 1812. pp 267, 268

Deed dated 1812. JOHN BRALSFORD to BENJAMIN BRALSFORD, son of John. S 13, T 3, R 3. Signed JOHN BRELSFORD. Witn: JOHN BRELSFORD JR, HENRY WEAVER. rec 1812. pp 268, 269

Deed dated 1811. JOSEPH BAIRD and JANE his wife to

BUTLER COUNTY LAND RECORDS: BOOK C

PIERSON BRELSFORD. S 12, T 3, R 3; money paid by PB or by JOHN BRELSFORD on his behalf. Signed JOSEPH BAIRD, JANE BAIRD. Witn: BENJAMIN VAN CLEIF, HENRY WEAVER. rec 1812. pp 269, 270

Deed dated 1812. USA to JOHN VANNICE. S 11, T 2, R 3. rec 1812. pp 270, 271

Deed dated 1812. HENRY TAYLOR & ELIZABETH his wife to ZACHARIAH PARISH. S 36, T 5, R 2. Signed HENRY TAYLOR, ELIZABETH (x) TAYLOR. Witn: MATTH. RICHARDSON, REBECCA RICHARDSON. rec 1812. pp 271, 272.

Deed dated 1801. DAVID ENOCH & NANCY his wife of Hamilton Co, NW Ter'y to MATTHEW HUESTON of same. S 35, T 2, R 2. Signed DAVID ENOCH, NANCY ENOCH. Witn: HEZEKIAH BROADBURY, JAMES BROADBURY. rec 1812. pp 272, 273

Deed dated 1812. MATTHEW HUESTON & CATHARINE his wife to JOHN R. SCHENCK of Warren Co. S 35, T 2, R 2. Signed M. HUESTON, CATHARINE HUESTON. Witn: DANL. MILLIKIN, JAMES HEATON. rec 1812. pp 273, 274

Deed dated 1811. ELIAS BOUDINOT by his agent JACOB BURNET to JOSEPH HENDERSON. S 20, T 2, R 4. Signed E. BOUDINOT by JAC. BURNET, agent. Witn: ROBT. WALLACE JR, WILLIAM IRWIN JR. rec 1812. pp 275, 276

Deed dated 1812. JOHN CLEVES SYMMES to FREDERICK ALLENDORF. S 27, T 3, R 2. FREDERICK ALLENDORF, an early volunteer settler, died. His son FREDERICK complied with terms in father's stead for 7 yrs; now able to claim title. Signed JOHN CLEVES SYMMES, registrar. Witn: JONATHAN CUSLETON, JAS. S. BRUYN JR rec 1812. pp 276, 277

Deed dated 1812. RICHARD McCAIN to FREDERICK BLUE. S 30, T 2, R 2. Bound by land of ROBERT FLEMING, ELIHU WOODRUFF and heirs of SAMUEL ALEXANDER. Signed RICHARD McCAIN. Witn: DAN'L MILLIKIN, SAM'L MILLIKIN. rec 1812. pp 277, 278

Plat of Prince Town dated 1812. S 2, T 2, R 3 in Liberty Twp. SAMUEL ENYART, proprietor. rec 1812. pp 278, 279

Deed dated 1812. JOEL WILLIAMS & PHEBE his wife of Hamilton Co to JOHN LIVINGSTON. S 14, T 1, R 2; subject to encumbrance of dower rights of AGNESS DAVIS,

BUTLER COUNTY LAND RECORDS: BOOK C

widow of JOHN DAVIS. Signed JOEL WILLIAMS, PHEBE WILLIAMS. Witn: GRIFFIN YEATMAN, JACOB PIATT. rec 1812. pp 279, 280

Deed dated 1812. ANDREW WILSON & SALLY his wife to NICHOLAS DAVIS. Hamilton lot 9. Signed ANDW. WILSON SALLY (x) WILSON. Witn: JAMES SMITH. rec 1812. pp 280, 281

Deed dated 1812. NICHOLAS DAVIS & NERIAH his wife to SAMUEL GARVER. Hamilton lot 9. Signed NICHOLAS DAVIS NARIAH (x) DAVIS. Witn: ARABEL GREER, ISAAC STANLEY rec 1812. p 281

Deed datd 1812. WILLIAM COOLEY & NANCEY his wife to SIMEON BROADBERRY. S 33, T 5, R 2; surveyed by ELEAZAR HOAG. Signed WILLIAM COOLEY, NANCEY (x) COOLEY. Witn: JAMES JOHNSTON, ENOS CAMPBELL. rec 1812. pp 281, 282, 283

Deed dated 1812. ABRAHAM LAREW to BENJAMIN LAREW. S 15, T 3, R 2. Bound by land of MARCOLM ANDRE, HUGH ABERCRUMBIE. Signed ABRAHAM LAREW. Witn: MICHAEL AYERS, BENJAMIN STONE. rec 1812. pp 283, 284

Deed dated 1811. USA to JOHN HALL & ISAAC MOSS, assignees of THOMAS AUTOR. S 23, T 4, R 2. rec 1812. p 284

Lease dated 1812. JOHN STONEBREAKER, farmer, to NATHAN GRIFFITH & KATHERINE his wife. No S-T-R. Griffith to have lifetime possession for rent of $1/yr. Signed JOHN STONEBREAKER (german script). Witn: JOHN RAINEY, SAMUEL RAINEY. rec 1812. pp 284, 285

Deed dated 1811. JOHN BROWN & ANN his wife of Franklin Co, IN Ter'y to SAMUEL SMITH. S 32, T 3, R 2. Signed JOHN BROWN, ANN BROWN. Witn: JOHN ALLEN SR, SAMUEL BROWN. rec 1812. pp 285, 286

Deed dated 1807. SAMUEL READING of KY to CORNELIUS STEPHENSON. S 7, T 3, R 2. Signed SAM. READING. Witn: ISC. S. SWEARINGEN, DAVID CURD. rec 1812. pp 286, 287

Deed dated 1812. CORNELIUS STEPHENSON & PHEBE his wife to DAVID WILLIAMSON, all of Liberty Twp. S 7, T 3, R 2. Signed CORNELIUS (x) STEPHENSON, PHEBE (x) STEPHENSON. Witn: P. WILLIAMSON, HEZEKIAH WILLIAMSON rec 1812. pp 287, 288

BUTLER COUNTY LAND RECORDS: BOOK C

Deed dated 1812. Exctr of STEPHEN VAIL to WILLIAM SPINNING. Finalize 1804 sale of Middletown lot 14. Stephen died 1 Sept, 1808, leaving minor heirs. Signed AARON VAIL. Witn: ZADOK SEXTON. rec 1812. pp 288, 289

Deed dated 1812. ELIAS BOUDINOT of NJ by JACOB BURNET, his agent to JOHN HOLMES. S 13, T 2, R 4. Signed ELIAS BOUDINOT by JAC. BURNET. Witn: ABIGAIL M. STONE, ETHAN STONE. rec 1812. pp 289, 290

Deed dated 1812. ABRAHAM HARTZELL & EVE his wife to SAMUEL SHERARD. S 25, T 3, R 3. Signed ABRAHAM HARTZELL (german script), EVE HARTZELL. Witn: ANDW. CHEW, #2 (german script). rec 1812. pp 291, 292

Deed dated 1812. LEWIS W. GORDON & ELEANOR his wife of Campbell Co, KY to HEZEKIAH BROADBERRY. S 35. T 2, R 2. Signed LEWIS W. GORDON, ELANOR GORDON. Witn: GRIFFIN YEATMAN, HEZEKIAH BROADBERRY JR. rec 1812. pp 292, 293

Deed dated 1812. BERIAH McGOFFIN & JANE his wife of Mercer Co, KY to WILLIAM RIDDLE. Hamilton lot 150. Signed BERIAH MAGOFFIN, JANE MAGOFFIN. Witn: THOS. ALLIN JR, S. McFEE. rec 1812. pp 293, 294

Deed datd 1812. WILLIAM MURRAY & DEBORAH his wife to RICHARD BIRCH. Lot 6 in S 1, T 1, R 3. Signed WM. MURRAY, DEBBY MURRAY. Witn: DAN'L MILLIKIN, DD. K. ESTE. rec 1812. pp 294, 295

Deed dated 1812. ABRAHAM HARTZELL & EVE his wife to CHRISTOPHER SMITH. S 25, T 3, R 3. Signed ABRAHAM HARTZELL (german script), EVE C. HARTZELL. Witn: EDWARD HUNT, ANDW. CHEW. rec 1812. pp 295, 296

Mortgage dated 1812. GARRET VAN NEST to TRUMAN BLACKMAN of Cincinnati. S 18, T 2, R 4. Signed GARRET VANNEST. Witn: JOHN MAHARD, MARGARET KING. rec 1812. pp 296, 297

Deed dated 1812. ISAAC WILES & ELIZABETH his wife to RICHARD BIRCH SR. Outlot 19 as laid out by CORNELIUS R. SEDAM; adjoins land of said Richard. Signed ISAAC WILES, ELIZABETH (x) WILES. Witn: DAVID K. ESTE, JAS. L. BENHAM. rec 1812. pp 297, 298

Deed dated 1812. USA to MATTHIAS ROLL of Warren Co. S 17 & 18, T 4, R 2. rec 1812. p 299

BUTLER COUNTY LAND RECORDS: BOOK C

Deed dated 1812.   PHINEAS McCRAY & SARAH his wife to
EBENEZER HEATON.   S 35, T 3, R 4.   Signed PHINEAS (x)
McCRAY, SARAH (x) McCRAY.   Witn: WILLIAM McCREA,
HENRY WEAVER.   rec 1812.   pp 299, 300

Deed dated 1812.   Exctr of STEPHEN VAIL to JOSEPH
HAVELAN.   Middletown lot 20; finalize sale begun
1807.   Signed AARON VAIL.   Witn: JOHN HUESTON, SAML.
POWELL.   rec 1812.   pp 300, 301, 302

Deed dated 1812.   JOSEPH HAVELAN & LYDIA his wife to
ISAAC WALTZ.   Middletown lot 20.   Signed JOSEPH HEAV-
ILAN, LYDIA HEAVILAN.   Witn: HIRAM POTTER, HENRY
WEAVER.   rec 1812.   pp 302, 303

Deed dated 1812.   SAMMUEL SEWARD SR & ANNY his wife
to BYRUM SEWARD.   S 5, T 2, R 2.   Signed SAMUEL SEW-
ARD, ANNY (x) SEWARD.   Witn: JOHN AYERS, DAVID
MULFORD.   rec 1812.   pp 303, 304

Deed dated 1812.   ABRAHAM HARTZELL & EVE his wife to
JOHN MATTIX.   S 25, T 3, R 3.   Signed ABRAHAM HURT-
ZELL, EVE C. HURTZELL.   Witn: MICHAEL AYERS, EDWARD
HURT JR.   rec 1812.   pp 304, 305

Deed dated 1811.   JOHN PRITCHARD & RHODA his wife to
JOHN MATTIX.   S 25, T 3, R 3.   Signed JOHN PRITCHARD,
RHODA (x) PRITCHARD.   Witn: HENRY WEAVER, MOSES
DRAKE.   rec 1812.   pp 305, 306

Deed dated 1812.   JOAB COMSTOCK of Hamilton Co to
ELIZABETH WHIPPLE, his oldest dau.   S 28, T 3, R 2.
Bound by land of WILLIAM ANTHONY and heirs of ASA
HERVY.   Signed JOAB COMSTOCK.   Witn: JAMES COMSTOCK,
JAMES SCOTT.   rec 1812.   pp 306, 307

Deed dated 1812.   SAMUEL SEWARD & ANNY his wife to
SAMUEL SEWARD JR.   S 5, T 2, R 3.   Signed SAMUEL
SEWARD, ANNY (x) SEWARD.   Witn: JOHN AYERS, DAVID
MULFORD.   rec 1812.   pp 307, 308

Deed dated 1812.   JOHN VZ. DAVIS & NANCY his wife to
DAVID GRIFFIS.   S 32, T 3, R 3.   Bound by land of
DANIEL WOODRUFF, WILLIAM & ARTHUR LEGG, GEORGE LEE,
MATTHEW MARKLAND.   Signed JOHN VZ. DAVIS, NANCY
DAVIS.   Witn: JOHN AYERS, ARTHUR LEGG.   rec 1812.   pp
308, 309

Deed dated 1812.   Excr of STEPHEN VAIL to JAMES HEATH
Finalize 1805 sale of Middletown lot 32.   Signed AARON
VAIL.   Witn: JOHN HUESTON.   rec 1812.   pp 310, 311

BUTLER COUNTY LAND RECORDS: BOOK C

Deed dated 1812. Excr of STEPHEN VAIL to NICHOLAS YEAGER. Finalize 1805 sale of Middletown lot 33. Signed and witn as above. rec 1812. pp 311, 312

Deed dated 1812. JAMES CLARK & ALETHIA his wife to PIERSON SAYRE. S 17, T 3, R 3. Signed JAMES CLARK, ALETHIA CLARK. Witn: P. WILLIAMSON, JOHN VANDIKE. rec 1812. p 313

Deed dated 1812. RALPH PHILLIPS of NJ to JAMES MILLS. S 8, T 2, R 3. Signed RALPH PHILLIPS. Witn: DAN'L MILLIKIN, CHARLES ESTE. rec 1812. pp 313, 314

Deed dated 1812. WILLIAM McCLELLAN, Sheriff, to JOSEPH HOUGH. In 1809, DAVID E. WADE obtained judgement against admrs of JOHN TORRENCE; seized Hamilton lots 124, 125, 126. Signed WM. McCLELLAN. Witn: M. HUESTON, JAMES WITHROW. rec 1812. pp 315, 316, 317

Mortgage dated 1812. JACOB BENNET to JOHN & HENRY TREBER. S 35, T 5, R 2; payment due 1813. Signed JACOB BENNET. Witn: ROBERT ANDERSON, JOHN DUNN. rec 1812. pp 317, 318

Deed dated 1812. Admtrs of WILLIAM SYMMES to DANIEL SYMMES of Hamilton Co. S 9, T 2, R 2. Bound by land of RHEUBEN CARTER, ARCHIBALD STARK. Signed CELADON SYMMES, JOSEPH F. RANDOLPH. Witn: DAVID L. CARNEY, DAVID OLIVER. rec 1813. pp 318, 319,, 320

Notice dated 1812. Relinquishment of dower rights by REBEKAH SYMMES, widow of Wm., for above property. rec 1813. p 320

Deed dated 1812. USA to MATTHIAS ROLL of Warren Co. S 13, R 4, R 1. rec 1813. p 320

Deed dated 1812. ANDREW CHRISTY of Clinton Co to NOAH LONG. S 4, T 2, R 3. *together with ELIZABETH his wife*. Signed ANDREW CHRISTY, no wife's signature. Witn: JAMES HEATON, DAVID MULFORD. rec 1813. pp 321, 322

Deed dated 1812. THOMAS BLAIR & PEGGY his wife to BENJAMIN PERSAILS. Hamilton lot   28. Signed THOS. BLAIR, PEGGY BLAIR. Witn: A. BLAIR, R. LYTLE.   rec 1813. p 323

Deed dated 1812. SAMUEL AYRES & ANNA his wife to MICHAEL DELAROCK. Rossville outlot 2. Signed SAMEUL AYERS, ANNA AYERS. Witn: WM. STUART, JAMES MILLS.

BUTLER COUNTY LAND RECORDS: BOOK C

rec 1813. pp 323, 324, 325

Deed dated 1812. JAMES CLARK & ABIGAIL his wife to JAMES CARLISLE. S 36, T 2, R 2. Signed JAMES CLARK, ABIGAIL CLARK. Witn: ISAAC STANLEY, BENJAMIN PURSAIL. rec 1813. pp 325, 326

Notice dated 1812. Hamilton lots 22, 35, 40, 52, 139 23 & 24, 178 to be sold for taxes. Signed THOS HUNTER Collector. Witn: JAMES MILLS. rec 1813. p 326

Deed dated 1813. JAMES MILLS & SARAH his wife to JOSEPH BROOKS. S 8, T 2, R 3. Signed JAMES MILLS, SARAH MILLS. Witn: DAN'L MILLIKIN, ALEXANDER SACKETT rec 1813. pp 326, 327, 328

Deed dated 1813. JAMES MILLS & SARAH his wife to ELIJAH LONGFELLOW. S 8, T 2, R 3. Signed JAMES MILLS, SARAH MILLS. Witn: JAMES HEATON, JAMES SMITH. rec 1813. pp 328, 329

Deed dated 1812. AARON HOUGHHAM SR & ELIZABETH his wife to ANDREW HAMILTON. S 1, T 2, R 3. Signed AARON HOUGHHAM, ELIZABETH HOUGHHAM. Witn: DANIEL COLLVER, SAMUEL SCHENCK. rec 1813. pp 330, 331

Deed dated 1812. ROBERT DOUGLAS & JANE his wife to ROBERT TAYLOR. Rossville outlots 15 & 24. Signed ROBERT DOUGLASS, JANE (x) DOUGLASS. Witn: MARSH WILLIAMS, JOHN WILLIAMS. rec 1813. pp 331, 332

Deed dated 1812. JOHN SUTHERLAND & NANCY his wife to DAVID K. ESTE. Hamilton lot 103. Signed JOHN SUTHERLAND, NANCY R. SUTHERLAND. Witn: ISAAC STANLEY, DAVID LUSK or TUSK. rec 1813. pp 332, 333

Deed dated 1812. RALPH PHILLIPS of NJ to RICHARD JACQUES. S 8, T 2, R 3. Signed RALPH PHILLIPS. Witn DD. K. ESTE, CHARLES ESTE. rec 1813. pp 333, 334

Mortgage dated 1812. RICHARD JAQUES & SALLY his wife to RALPH PHILLIPS. S 8, T 2, R 3. Signed RICHARD JAQUES, SALLY JAQUES. Witn as above. rec 1813. pp 334, 335

Deed dated 1812. HENRY BURCH & MARY ANN his wife of Morgan Twp to BENJAMIN McCLEAVE of same. S 10, T 3, R 1. Signed HENRY (x) BURCH, MARY ANN (x) BURCH. Witn: JAMES SHIELDS, WM. McCLEAVE, SUSANNA (x) JENKINS. JP WILLIAM JENKINS. rec 1813. pp 335, 336, 337

BUTLER COUNTY LAND RECORDS: BOOK C

Mortgage dated 1813. JAMES CARLISLE to JAMES CLARK. S 36, T 2, R 2. Payment due 1817. Signed JAMES CARLISLE. Witn: JAMES HEATON, ISAAC STANLEY. rec 1813. pp 337, 338

Deed dated 1812. Auditors of Court to SHOBAL VAIL. Judgement obtained by STEPHEN VAIL against non-resident EDWARD STEIN. Middletown lot 15 seized; writ served by constable JOSEPH HENRY. Sold at auction. Signed ROBERT FERRES, WM. SQUIER, JOSEPH LUMMIS. Witn: GEORGE RUSSELL, HENRY WEAVER. rec 1813. pp 338, 339

Deed dated 1812. Exctr of STEPHEN VAIL to SHOBAL VAIL. Finalize 1805 sale of "the mill seat adj. to town of Middletown"; no S-T-R given. Signed AARON VAIL. Witn: JOHN VANSICKLE, HUGH VAIL. rec 1813. pp 339, 340, 341

Deed dated 1813. SHORES STEVENSON to SAMUEL SEWARD. S 35, T 2, R 3. Signed SHORES STEVENSON. Witn: JOHN AYRES, ANNA AYRES. rec 1813. pp 341, 342

Deed dated 1812. Admtrs of WILLIAM SYMMES to WILLIAM WILSON. Rossville lots 95, 96. Signed CELADON SYMMES, JOSEPH F. RANDOLPH. Witn: JOHN REILY, JOHN WHITWORTH. rec 1813. pp 342, 343

Deed dated 181. WILLIAM WILSON & PEGGY his wife to JAMES MILLS. Rossville lots 95 & 96. Signed WILLIAM WILSON, MARGARET WILSON. Witn: JAMES SMITH, JAMES VANSANT. rec 1813. p 343

Deed dated 1813. CELADON SYMMES & PHEBE his wife to DANIEL MILLIKIN. Hamilton outlots 29, 30, 32, 33 & 34. Signed CELADON SYMMES, PHEBE SYMMES. Witn: M. HUESTON, ROBT. B. MILLIKIN. rec 1813. pp 344, 345

Deed dated 1812. SHORES STEVENSON of Liberty Twp to MIKEL PAUGH. S 35, T 3, R 2; part of tract granted to JAMES MOTT of NJ. Signed SHORES STEVENSON. Witn: JOHN AYERS, JOHN FREEMAN. rec 1813. pp 345, 346

Deed dated 1812. DAVID GRIFFIS & POLLY his wife to MATHEW MARKLAND*. S 32, T 3, R 3. Signed DAVID GRIFFIS, POLLY GRIFFIS. Witn: JOHN AYERS, JOHN C. AYERS. rec 1813. pp 346, 347 *MARKLIN in deed text

Deed dated 1808. BENJAMIN RANDLE & ELENDER his wife of Wayne Twp to WILLIAM McCLEAN. S 31, T 3, R 3. Signed BENJ. RANDLE, ALLA RANDLE. Witn: JAMES MILLS

BUTLER COUNTY LAND RECORDS: BOOK C

JAMES PEAIRS. rec 1813. pp 347, 348

Bill of sale dated 1813. WILLIAM MURRAY to MICHAEL MURRAY of Liberty Twp. Livestock, household goods. Signed WILLIAM MURRAY. Witn: WM. MURRAY, JOHN VINNEDGE. rec 1813. p 348

Deed dated 1812. Admtrs of BENJAMIN YOUNGS TO PHILIP YOUNGS. Finalize 1808 sale of S 4, T 4, R 2; BENJ. died leaving minor heirs. Signed ELIZABETH YOUNGS, ABIJAH YOUNGS. Witn: ENOS HURIN, CONSTANCE SMITH. rec 1813. pp 349, 350

Deed dated 1813. JOHN MERRILL & SARAH his wife to JAMES CUMMINS, all of Liberty Twp. S 1, T 2, R 3; bound by land of JOHN AYERS, SAMUEL ENYART, JAMES MURTHY, ASHBEL WALLEN. signe JOHN MERRILL, SARAH MERRILL. Witn: JOHN AYERS, SAMUEL ENYART. rec 1813. pp 350, 351

Deed dated 1813. SAMUEL ENYART & ANNA his wife to JOSEPH PEAK. Princetown lot 18. Signed SAMUEL ENYART, ANNA ENYART. Witn: JAMES MURPHY, JOHN AYERS. rec 1813. p 351

Deed dated 1811. ALBERT BONTA & NANCY his wife to JOSEPH ASTON SR & JOSEPH ASTON JR. S 31, T 3, R 4. Signed ALBERT BONTA, NANCY BONTA. Witn: SUSAN WEAVER, HENRY WEAVER. rec 1813. pp 351, 352

Bond dated 1810. JOHN PATTERSON to SAMUEL POTTENGER. Promise to convey deed to S 32, T 3, R 3 by Oct, 1812. Signed JOHN PATTERSON. Witn: MATH. WINTON, ROBT. BRODERICK. rec 1813. pp 352, 353

Power of Attorney dated 1813. JOHN WINGATE appted CHARLES BRUCE and/or ISAAC WILES to collect debts, convey deeds. Signed JOHN WINGATE. Witn: JOHN REILY, DANL MILLIKIN. rec 1813. p 353

Deed dated 1812. THOMAS COOCH SR & HANNA his wife to MOSES TEAGARDEN. S 29, T 5, R 2. Signed THOS. C. COOCH, HANNA COOCH. Witn: HANNA SANKEY, ELIZA COOCH, MATTH. RICHARDSON. rec 1813. pp 354, 355

Deed dated 1813. JOHN WINGATE & EMMA his wife to JOHN CALDWELL. Hamilton lot 82. Signed JOHN WINGATE by CHS. BRUCE & ISAAC WILES, attys, AMMA WINGATE. rec 1813. p 355

BUTLER COUNTY LAND RECORDS: BOOK C

Deed dated 1812. Extr of STEPHEN VAIL to JAMES PIPER Finalize 1806 sale of Middletown lot 17. Signed AARON VAIL. Witn: JOHN HUSTON. rec 1813. pp 356, 357

Deed dated 1812. Extr of STEPHEN VAIL to JAMES PIPER Finalize 1806 sale of Middletown lot 18. Signed and witn as above. rec 1813. pp 357, 358

Mortgage dated 1812. JOHN R. SCHENCK of Warren Co to MATTHEW HUESTON. S 34 & 35, T 2, R 2. Signed JOHN R. SCHENCK. Witn: DANL MILLIKIN, JAMES HEATON. rec 1813. pp 358, 357

Deed dated 1813. JOSEPH HOUGH & JANE his wife to JAMES McBRIDE. Hamilton lots 124, 125, 126. Signed JOSEPH HOUGH, JANE (x) HOUGH. Witn: JAMES MILLS, HENRY HESLY. rec 1813. pp 359, 360

Prenuptial agreement dated 1813. ROBERT FLEMING & ELIZABETH McCOLLOUGH to marry soon. Each retains the right to make a will disposing of property owned prior to wedding. If deceased intestate, the property goes to heirs as if the marriage had not taken place. Elizabeth to have no dower rights. JAMES McBRIDE a third party to agreement; no duty defined. Signed ROBERT FLEMING, ELIZABETH McCLAUGH, JAMES McBRIDE. Witn: WILLIAM EARLY, JACOB LINE, JOHN SHREDER (german script). rec 1813. pp 360, 361, 362

Deed dated 1812. USA to PETER KUN of Hamilton Co. S 13, T 5, R 2. rec 1813. p 362

Deed dated 1813. MATHEW VANDUYN SR to IRA HUNT. S 6, T 2, R 2 in Liberty Twp; bound by land of MARTIN VANDUYN JR, RALPH PHILLIPS or WILLIAM McKIMM, ISAAC SEWARD, JOHN GARD and land once owned by JOHN FREEMAN. Signed MATTHEW VANDUYN SR. Witn: JOHN AYERS, DAVID CONGER. rec 1813. p 363

Bill of sale dated 1813. SETH ARNET to WILLIAM MURRAY. Livestock, bed & bedding. Signed SETH (x) ARNET. Witn: GEORGE HARLAN, CLINTON STACKHOUSE. rec 1813. pp 363, 364

Deed dated 1811. MOSES DENMAN & ELIZABETH his wife to CHRISTOPHER WAGONER. S 32, T 2, R 4. Signed MOSES DENMAN, ELIZABETH (x) DENMAN. Witn: AMOS DAVIS, HENRY WEAVER. rec 1813. pp 364, 365

Power of Attorney dated 1812. JOHN PATTERSON of Maury Co, TN apptd his son JOHN PATTERSON as atty to

BUTLER COUNTY LAND RECORDS: BOOK C

collect debts, convey title to SAMUEL POTTENGER land which "I sold before I left that state." Signed JOHN PATTERSON. Witn: JOHN HODGE, WM. FRIERSON. rec 1813. pp 365, 366

Deed dated 1813. ELIZABETH HARVEY to ISAIAH BALL & DENNIS BALL. S 21, T 2, R 3 except a graveyard on the south side; bound by land of WILLIAM PATTON. PATRICK MOORE, SAMUEL KENEDY, TIMOTHY WOODRUFF. Signed ELIZABETH (x) HERVEY. Witn: JOHN REILY, WM. G. ARMSTRONG. rec 1813. pp 366, 367

Deed dated 1808. ZOPHAR BALL & ELIZABETH his wife to ISAIAH BALL & DENNIS BALL. S 21, T 3, R 3; bound by JAMES LYON, PATRICK MOORE, SAMUEL KENNEDY, TIMOTHY WOODRUFF. Signed ZOPHAR BALL, ELIZABETH (x) BALL. Witn: JAMES McBRIDE, JOHN REILY. rec 1813. pp 367,368

Deed dated 1813. Marshal of Ohio to WILLIAM BIGHAM. In 1808, GEORGE BECKHAM & JACOB REES obtained judgement from THOMAS McCOLLOCK. Marshal seized 4 acres with grist and saw mill in S 27, T -, R 3; sold for debt. Signed THOMAS STEEL, deputy marshal for LEWIS CASE, marshal, Ohio dist. Witn: STEPHEN MACFARLAND, WILLIAM HARRIS. rec 1813. pp 368, 369, 370

Deed dated 1813. STEPHEN ARMSTRONG & RUTH his wife to JAMES MAPES, all of Reily Twp. S 35, T 4, R 1. Signed STEPHEN ARMSTRONG, RUTH (x) ARMSTRONG. Witn: AARON POWERS, CHARLES STEWART. rec 1813. pp 370, 371

Deed dated 1813. AARON POWERS & MARTHA his wife to STEPHEN ARMSTRONG. S-T-R as above. Signed AARON POWERS, MARTHA POWERS. Witn: JAMES MAPES, CHARLES STEWART. JP JOHN BURK. rec 1813. p 371

Deed dated 1813. JOHN WINGATE & EMMA his wife to JOHN JENKINS. Hamilton lot 186. Signed JOHN WINGATE by CHARLES BRUCE & ISAAC WILES, attys, AMMA WINGATE. Witn: JAMES McCLAMROE, ABRAM COLWELL. rec 1813. pp 372, 373.

Deed dated 1811. DAVID K. ESTE to SAMUEL DARCOS. Hamilton lots 72, 73. Signed DD. K. ESTE. Witn: JAMES McCLAMROE, ABRAM COLWELL. rec 1813. pp 372, 373

Deed dated 1813. JONATHAN HIGGINS & MARGARET his wife to DAVID BLACKBURN. S 7, T 4, R 2. Signed JONATHAN HIGGINS, MARGARET (x) HIGGINS. Witn: JOHN REILY, MATTH. RICHARDSON. rec 1813. pp 373, 374

BUTLER COUNTY LAND RECORDS: BOOK C

Deed dated 1813. DAVID BLACKBURN & MARTHA his wife to WILLIAM McMANUS. S 7, T 4, R 2. Signed DAVID (x) BLACKBURN, MARTHA (x) BLACKBURN. Witn: JOHN REILY, JOHN WHITWORTH. rec 1813. pp 374, 375

Deed dated 1813. JONATHAN HIGGINS & MARGARET his wife to JOHN JOHNSTONE. S 7, T 4, R 2. Signed JONATHAN HIGGINS, MARGARET (x) HIGGINS. Witn as above. rec 1813. pp 375, 376

Deed dated 1812. EDWARD COEN & MARGARET his wife of Ross Twp to his son, THOMAS COEN. S 31, T 3, R 2: bound by land of WILLIAM JONES, MAURICE JONES. Signed EDWARD COEN, MARGARET (x) COEN. Witn: JAMES SHIELDS, JP WILLIAM D. JONES. rec 1813. pp 376, 377

Deed dated 1813. MAXWELL PARKISON & MAHALA his wife of Morgan Twp to SAMUEL JOHNSTONE of Reily Twp. S 6, T 4, R 1. Signed MAXWELL PARKISON, MAHALA PARKISON. Witn: JP KING DEARMOND, WILLIAM PARKISON. rec 1813. pp 377, 378

Deed dated 1812. EDWARD COEN & MARGARET his wife of Ross Twp to his son, HUGH COEN. S 31, T 3, R 2; bound by land of heirs of JAMES COEN, DAVID FRANCIS. Signed and witn as above. rec 1813. pp 378, 379

Deed dated 1813. MAXWELL PARKISON & MAHALA his wife of Morgan Twp to WILLIAM PARKISON of Reily Twp. S 6, T 4, R 1. Signed MAXWELL PARKISON, MAHALA PARKISON. Witn: JP KING DEARMOND, SAMUEL JOHNSON. rec 1813. pp 379, 380

Deed dated 1813. JOHN MILLER & PHEBE his wife of 10th twp, Franklin Co, IN Ter'y to THOMAS WHITE. S 14, T 5, R 1. Signed JOHN MILLER, PHEBE (x) MILLER. Witn: JP LEVI LEE, Oxford Twp. rec 1813. pp 380, 381

Deed dated 1812. PHENIAS McCRAY & SARAH his wife to JACOB EMRICK. S 35, T 3, R 4. Signed PHENIAS (x) McCRAY, SARAH (x) McCRAY. Witn: WILLIAM McCREA, HENRY WEAVER. rec 1813. pp 381, 382

Deed dated 1813. JOHN CLEVES SYMMES of North Bend, Hamilton Co to MICHAEL AYERS of Liberty Twp. S 14, T 3, R 2. Signed JOHN CLEVES SYMMES. Witn: GRIFFIN YEATMAN, ROBT. WARWICK. rec 1813. pp 382, 383

Deed dated 1812. CELADON SYMMES & PHEBE his wife to JOHN R. SCHENCK. S 34, T 2, R 2. Witn: JOSEPH F. RANDOLPH, ARTHUR WILSON. rec 1813. pp 383, 384

BUTLER COUNTY LAND RECORDS: BOOK C

Mortgage dated 1812. DAVID GRIFFITHS to OLIVER ORMSBY S 32, T 3, R 3; bound by land of DANIEL WOODRUFF, WILLIAM & ARTHUR LEGG, GEORGE LEE, DANIEL GRIFFITH, JAMES McCLELAN. Payment due 1815. Signed DAVID GRIFFITHS. Witn: JOHN MAHARD, N. LONGWORTH. rec 1813. pp 384, 385

Deed dated 1813. JONATHAN DAYTON of NJ to JACOB HUSSAM. S 0, T 2, R 3. Signed JONA. DAYTON by ELIAS I. DAYTON. Witn: CHAS. K. OSMON. rec 1813. pp 385, 386

Deed dated 1813. ANDERSON SPENCER & MARY his wife to EPHRAIM MORGAN of Hamilton Co. Hamilton lot 71. Signed ANDERSON SPENCER, MARY (x) SPENCER. Witn: R. LYTLE, BENJAMIN DAVIS. rec 1813. pp 386, 387

Deed dated 810. THOMAS COOCH & HANNAH his wife to GEORGE MERICLIN. S 29, T 5, R 2. Signed THOS. COOCH HANNAH COOCH. Witn: WILLIAM PRICE, ANN PRICE. rec 1813. pp 387, 388

Deed dated 1809. USA to ELIJAH BRUSH, assignee of JACOB BURNET. S 8, 18, 9, 19, 17 & 16, T 1, R 4. rec 1813. p 388

Deed dated 1812. JOHN HALL & ISAAC MOSS to JOHN REILY. S 23, T 4, R 2. Signed JOHN HALL, ISAAC MOSS. Witn: MATTHIAS ROLL, JP JOEL COLLINS. rec 1813. p 389

Deed dated 1813. Admtrs of ISRAEL LUDLOW to Commissioners of Butler Co: JAMES SILVER, BENJAMIN STITES, DANIEL SUTTON. During his lifetime, IL agreed to donate land for courthouse (Hamilton lots 95, 96, 97, 98) and land for a church and graveyard (Hamilton lots 13, 14, 15, 16, 29, 30, 31, 32). Commis'rs appted Hamilton as the seat of government. Ludlow died Jan 21, 1804 without completing transaction, now being finalized. Signed JAMES FINDLAY, JOHN LUDLOW. Witn: GRIFFIN YEATMAN, THO. SLOO? JR. rec 1813. pp 389, 390, 391

Mortgage dated 1813. JOHN JENKINS to OLIVER ORMSBY. Hamilton lot 186. Signed JOHN (x) JENKINS. Witn: JOHN REILY, WM. G. ARMSTRONG. rec 1813. pp 391, 392

Mortgage dated 1813. JOHN CALDWELL to OLIVER ORMSBY of Pittsburg, PA. Hamilton lot 82. Signed JOHN CALDWELL. Witn as above. rec 1813. pp 3392, 393

BUTLER COUNTY LAND RECORDS: BOOK C

Deed dated 1813. JOHN HALL of Rossville to JAMES REED, house carpenter. S 18, T 1, R 4; bound by land of GEORGE & DANIEL FLEENOR, M. DOUGHTY, E. BOYLES. Signed JOHN HALL. Witn: JOHN REILY, WM. G. ARMSTRONG rec 1813. pp 393, 394

Deed dated 1812. WILLIAM McCLELLAN, sheriff, to Commissioners of Butler Co. In 1809, Commissioners obtained judgement against GEORGE HARLAN, JOHN WINGATE & WILLIAM DILLON. Seized Hamilton lot 195; sold to Commissioners. Signed WM. McCLELLAN. Witn: JAMES McBRIDE, M. HUESTON. rec 1813. pp 394, 395, 396

Deed dated 1811. ELIAS BOUDINOT by JACOB BURNET, agent to JAMES MORRISON. S 20, T 2, R 4. Signed ELIAS BOUDINOT by JACOB BURNET. Witn: ROBT. WALLACE JR, WILLIAM IRWIN JR. rec 1813. pp 396, 397

Deed dated 1812. THOMAS ROBERTS & ANN his wife of Wayne Co, IN Ter'y to SAMUEL ROBINS. S 8, T 3, R 3. Signed THOMAS ROBERDS, ANN ROBERTS. Witn: DAVID HOOVER, CATARINE HOOVER. rec 1813. p 397

Deed dated 1812. JOSEPH EVANS & ESTHER his wife of Montgomery Co to CHARLES SWEARINGEN. S 20, T 3, R 3. Signed JOSEPH EVANS, ESTHER (x) EVANS. Witn: JOHN HALDERMAN, ISAAC MILLER. rec 1813. pp 397, 398. 399

Deed dated 1812. ROBERT MORRIS & ABIGAIL his wife to EDWARD HUNT. S 25, T 3, R 3. Signed ROBERT MORRIS, ABIGAIL (x) MORRIS. Witn: JOHN MORRIS, HENRY WEAVER. rec 1813. pp 399, 400

Deed dated 1813. JOSEPH SMITH & ELIZABETH his wife to ISAAC CONOROE. S 6, T 3, R 3. Signed JOSEPH (x) SMITH, ELISABETH SMITH. Witn: JOHN CONOROE, SAMUEL HUNT. rec 1813. p 400

Deed dated 1813. JOSEPH SMITH & ELIZABETH his wife to JOHN CONOROE. S 6, T 3, R 3. Signed JOSEPH (x) SMITH, ELISABETH SMITH. Witn: ISAAC CONOROE, SAMUEL HUNT. rec 1813. p 401

Deed dated 1813. Admtrs of ISRAEL LUDLOW to SAMUEL W. MORRISON. Hamilton lot 109. Signed CHARLOTTE CHAMBERS RISK, JOHN LUDLOW, JAMES FINDLAY. Witn: GRIFFIN YEATMAN, THOS SLOO? JR. rec 1813. pp 401, 402

Power of Attorney dated 1813. SAMUEL W. MORRISON appted THOMAS BLAIR to collect debts, sell Hamilton

BUTLER COUNTY LAND RECORDS: BOOK C

lot 109. Signed SAM. W. MORRISON. Witn: JAMES SMITH, JOHN CASSIDY. rec 1813. pp 402, 403

Deed dated 1813. SAMUEL W. MORRISON to JOHN SUTHERLAND. Hamilton lot 109. Signed SAMUEL W. MORRISON by THOS. BLAIR, atty. Witn: ANDERSON SPENCER, ISAAC MOSS. rec 1813. pp 403, 404.

Deed dated 1813. Admtrs of ISRAEL LUDLOW to THOMAS BLAIR & HUGH WILSON. Hamilton lot 85. CHARLOTTE CHAMBERS RISK, JOHN LUDLOW, JAMES FINDLAY. Witn: GRIFFIN YEATMAN, THO. SLOO? JR. rec 1813. pp 404, 405

Partition dated 1813. HUGH WILSON & SARAH his wife to THOMAS BLAIR. North half of Hamilton lot 85. Signed HUGH WILSON, SARAH WILSON. Witn: ANDREW HUNTER, ISAAC STANLEY. rec 1813. pp 405, 406

Partition dated 1813. THOMAS BLAIR & PEGGY his wife to HUGH WILSON. South half of Hamilton lot 85. Signed THOS. BLAIR, PEGGY BLAIR. Witn: ISAAC STANLEY, WILLARD M. SMITH. rec 1813. p 406

Mortgage dated 1813. RICHARD BIRCH SR & RICHARD BIRCH JR to CORNELIUS R. SEDAM of Hamilton Co. S 1, T 1, R 3. Signed RICHARD BIRCH SR, R. BIRCH. Witn: OLIVER H. HENRY, ISAAC STANLEY. rec 1813. p 407

Deed dated 1810. DAVID DUFFIELD & REBECCA his wife to JOSEPH EVANS. S 17, T 3, R 3. Signed DAVID DUFFIELD, REBCAH DUFFIELD. Witn: JAMES STARKEY, LEVI KINMAN. rec 1813. p 408

Deed dated 1813. JOHN HARDEN & CATHARINE his wife to ROBERT SEGERSON. S 25, T 3, R 3. Signed JOHN (x) HARDEN, CATHARINE (x) HARDEN. Witn: HENRY WEAVER, ISABELAH FULLERTON. rec 1813. pp 408, 409

Deed dated 1812. THOMAS COOCH & HANNA his wife to CORNELIUS HINDSEY & JONATHAN THOMPSON, Deacons of the regular Baptist Church called Mt. Bethel in Milford Twp. S 32, T 5, R 2. Signed THOMAS COOCH, HANNA COOCH. Witn: HANNA SANKEY, ELIZA COOCH. rec 1813. pp 409, 410

Deed dated 1813. JOHN CLEM SR & SUSANNA his wife to WILLIAM WOOD. S 1, T 4, R 1. Signed JOHN CLEM, SUSANNA (x) CLEM (both in german script). Witn: WILLIAM CURRY, LEMUEL LEMMON. rec 1813. pp 410, 411

Deed dated 1813. BOSTON STONEBREAKER & SUSANNAH his

BUTLER COUNTY LAND RECORDS: BOOK C

wife to GEORGE SHAFER. S 2, T 3, R 2; bound by land of DAVID SMITH. Signed BOSTON STONEBREAKER (german script) SUSANNAH (x) STONEBREAKER. Witn: JOHN RAINEY JR, SAMUEL RAINEY. JP JOHN RAINEY. rec 1813. pp 411, 412

Deed dated 1812. Exctr of STEPHEN VAIL to JONAS SMALLEY SR. Finalize 1806 sale of Middletown lot 38. Signed AARON VAIL. Witn: ZADOCK SEXTON. rec 1813. pp 412, 413

Deed dated 1809. JOHN WINGATE, Sheriff, to ANDREW LEWES. In 1818, JOHN BRADFORD obtained judgement against JOHN WATSON. S 11, T 2, R 4 seized, sold of debt. Signed JOHN WINGATE. Witn: NOAH WADE, DAVID K. ESTE. rec 1813. pp 414, 415

Deed dated 1813. GEORGE <u>CHESTERTON</u> & CHARITY his wife to ISAAC SELLERS. S 26, T 2, R 2; bound by land of HUGH HALL, WILLIAM SLAYBACK. Signed GEORGE (x) <u>CHERSON</u>, CHARITY (x) CHESTERTON. Witn: JP JOHN McGILLIARD, ROBERT GUTHRIE. rec 1813. pp 415, 416

Deed dated 1813. HUGH HALL & NANCY his wife to GEORGE CHESTERTON. S 26, T 2, R 2; once owned by JACOB POWERS & NANCY his wife. Witn as above. rec 1813. p 416

Deed dated 1799. JOHN CLEVES SYMMES to JOHN SINNERD. WILLIAM SINNERD, ABRAHAM SINNERD and THOMAS SINNERD, sons of THOMAS SINNARD SR, dec'd, of Hamilton Co. SINNARD SR was the assignee of JOHN WELSH, who was the assignee of FERDINAND BROKAW, the assignee of DAVID GRUMMON who purchased the forfeiture of JAMES GRUMMON the volunteer settler in S 10, T 2, R 2. Signed JOHN C. SYMMES. Witn: SARAH PRINCE, JAS. MAGILL. rec 1813. pp 417, 418

Deed dated 1813. JOHN SUTHERLAND & NANCY his wife to THOMAS BLAIR. Hamilton lot 109. Signed JOHN SUTHERLAND, NANCY R. SUTHERLAND. Witn: LEWIS LAING, ISAAC STANLEY. rec 1813. p 418

Deed dated 1813. ANDERSON SPENCER & POLLY his wife to JOSEPH HOUGH. Hamilton lot 71. Signed ANDERSON SPENCER, POLLY (x) SPENCER. Witn: ISAAC STANLEY, WILLARD M. SMITH. rec 1813. p 419

Deed dated 1813. STEPHEN ARMSTRONG & RUTH his wife to CHARLES STEWART. S 35, T 4, R 1; bound by land of witn. Signed STEHPEH ARMSTRONG, RUTH (x) ARMSTRONG.

BUTLER COUNTY LAND RECORDS: BOOK C

Witn: AARON POWERS, JAMES MAPES. rec 1813. pp 419, 420

Deed dated 1813. NOAH LONG & SARAH his wife to ABRAHAM MILEY JR. S 4, T 2, R 3; bound by land of JOHN McGARY. Signed NOAH (x) LONG, SARAH (x) LONG. Witn: ANN WEAVER, HENRY WEAVER. rec 1813. pp 420, 421

Deed dated 1813. ARTHUR W. ELLIOTT & POLLY his wife to JOSHUA ELLIOTT, all of Liberty Twp. S 20, T 3, R 3. Signed ARTHUR W. ELLIOTT, POLLY ELLIOTT. Witn: NICHOLAS CURTIS, P. WILLIAMSON. rec 1813. pp 420, 421

Mortgage dated 1813. SAMUEL FRAZY of Hamilton Co to JOSHUA ELLIOTT. S 20, T 3, R 3. Payment due 1815. Signed SAMUEL FRAZY. Witn: P. WILLIAMSON, JOHN MORROW. rec 1813. pp 422, 423

Deed dated 1812. ROBERT WARWICK & SARAH his wife of Hamilton Co to SAMUEL HYNDMAN. S 10, T 2, R 2; purchased from JOHN LYON. Signed ROBT. WARWICK, SARAH WARWICK. Witn: HATFIELD WILLIAMS, JAMES COGY. rec 1813. pp 423, 424

Deed dated 1813. WILLIAM McCLELLAN, sheriff to JAMES F. MORTON. In 1811, JACOB LOPER obtained judgement against ISAAC WILES. Hamilton lot 51 seized, sold for debt. Signed WM. McCLELLAN. Witn: JOHN WHITWORTH, WM. G. ARMSTRONG. rec 1813. pp 424, 425

Deed dated 1811. Admtrs of JOHN TORRENCE to JAMES MILLS JR. Rossville outlot 9. Signed JOHN WINGATE, AMMA WINGATE. Witn: J.H. WHITE, NOAH WADE. rec 1813. pp 425, 426

Deed dated 1813. Admtrs of ISRAEL LUDLOW to LAURENCE CAVENAUGH. Hamilton lot 134. Signed CHARLOTTE CHAMBERS RISK, JOHN LUDLOW, JAMES FINDLAY. Witn: GRIFFIN YEATMAN, THOS SLOOP?. rec 1813. pp 426, 427, 428

Deed dated 1813. WILLIAM CORRY & ELEANOR his wife of Cincinnati to JOHN REILY. Hamilton lot 87, Rossville lot 63. Signed WILLIAM CORRY, ELEANOR CORRY. Witn: ELY ELDER, JOHN MAHARD. rec 1813. pp 428, 429

Deed dated 1813. JAMES MARTIN JR, son and heir of JAMES MARTIN to LAURENCE CAVENAUGH. One seventh share of S 25, T 5, R 2; where *ANNA MARTIN, widow of

BUTLER COUNTY LAND RECORDS: BOOK C

JAMES, now resides"; bound by MATTHEW RICHARDSON, WILLIAM MARTIN. Signed JAMES MARTIN JR. Witn: JOHN REILY, ISAAC STANLEY. rec 1813. pp 429, 430

Deed dated 1813. Admtrs of ISRAEL LUDLOW to LAURENCE CAVENAUGH. Hamilton outlot 18. Signed CHARLOTTE CHAMBERS RISK, JOHN LUDLOW, JAMES FINDLAY. Witn: GRIFFIN YEATMAN, THOS ?. rec 1813. pp 430, 431, 432

Deed dated 1811. JAMES DUNN & NANCY his wife to JAMES MOORE. S 11 & 14, T 3, R 2; bound by land of JOHN DUNN, JAMES ELLIOTT, JOHN ELLIOTT. Signed JAS. DUNN, NANCEY DUNN. Witn: JAMES DUNN JR, THOMAS BALDWIN. Rec 1813. pp 432, 433

Deed dated 1813. ISAAC HOFF & CATHARINE his wife to WILLIAM TEITSORT. S 29, T 2, R 4. Signed ISAAC HOFF CATHARINE HOFF. Witn: ABRAM TEITSORT, JOHN DINE. rec 1813. pp 433, 434

Deed dated 1813. ISAAC HOFF & CATHARINE his wife to JOHN DINE. S 29, T 2, R 4. Signed ISAAC HOFF CATHARINE HOFF. Witn: ABRAM TEITSORT, WILLIAM TEITSORT. rec 1813. pp 434, 435

Deed dated 1813. DAVID K. ESTE to JAMES REED. Rossville lot 78. Signed DAVID K. ESTE. Witn: JOHN HALL, ROBT. FLEMING. rec 1813. pp 435, 436

Deed dated 1813. WILLIAM NELSON & BARBARA his wife to JOHN SMITH. S 20, T 4, R 2. Signed WILLIAM NELSON, BARBARY NELSON. Witn: J.H. WHITE, JOHN BURKE. rec 1813. pp 437, 438

Mortgage dated 1813. SQUIER LITTELL & MARY his wife and STEPHEN GARD & RACHEL his wife to MARGARET RANDLE S 5, T 1, R 4 "on which Gard now resides" and "property of S. Littell lying...in section aforesaid". Signed SQUIER LITTELL, MARY LITTELL, STEPHEN GARD, RACHEL GARD. Witn: PHEBE PARCE, HENRY WEAVER. rec 1813. pp 438, 439

Deed dated 1807. USA to ABRAHAM CHASE. S 5, T 4, R 1. rec 1813. pp 439, 440

Deed dated 1807. USA to ABRAHAM CHASE. S 5, T 4, R 1. rec 1813. p 440

Deed dated 1809. USA to ABRAHAM CHASE. S 6, T 4, R 1. rec 1813. p 441

BUTLER COUNTY LAND RECORDS: BOOK C

Deed dated 1813. ELIZABETH FLEMING, late widow of THOMAS McCULLOUGH, and ROBERT FLEMING, now husband of Elizabeth, to WILLIAM BIGHAM. S 27, T -, R 3; 4 acres containing a grist and saw mill. Signed ELIZABETH FLEMING, ROBT. FLEMING. Witn: OLIVER H. HENRY ISAAC STANLEY. rec 1813. pp 441, 442

Deed dated 1813. WILLIAM McCLELLAN, sheriff to STEPHEN D. DAY of NJ. DAVID PECK sued on a deed of mortgage made by SAMUEL SEWARD to ▪said DANIEL PECK▪ for a seventh part of S 19, T 3, R 3. Property seized, sold for debt. Signed WM. McCLELLAN. Witn: JOHN WHITWORTH, WM. G. ARMSTRONG. rec 1813. pp 442, 443, 444

Deed dated 1813. HENRY WEAVER & SUSAN his wife to HENRY ALLEN. Money paid by ALLEN or by ABRAHAM VANSICKLE on his behalf. S 27 & 28, T 2, R 4. Signed HENRY WEAVER, SUSAN WEAVER. Witn: ABRAHAM TEITSORT, PETER TEITSORT. rec 1813. pp 444, 445

Deed dated 1813. JOHN HORMELL & ELINOR his wife of Warren Co to THEOPHILUS EAGLESFIELD. S 30, T 2, R 4. Signed JOHN HORMELL, ELENOR HORMELL. Witn: JP ENOS WILLIAMS, AARON SOUTHARD. rec 1813. pp 446, 447

Deed dated 1813. THOMAS POWERS & MARY his wife to HENRY ALLEN. S 27 & 28, T 2, R 4; bound by land of NOAH LONG, JOHN VANSICKLE. Signed THOMAS POWERS, MARY POWERS. Witn: HENRY WEAVER, DANIEL SALLE. rec 1813. pp 447, 448

Deed dated 1813. Heirs of ROBERT SMITH of Shelby CO, KY by DAVID K. ESTE, atty to MATTHEW MARKLAND. Finalize sale begun 1810 for S 32, T 3, R 3, ▪lately owned and occupied by JAMES McCLELLAN▪. Smith died leaving minor heirs; ELIZABETH SMITH appted admtr. Este appted by court to convey deed. Signed DD. K. ESTE. Witn: JOHN WHITWORTH, WM. G. ARMSTRONG. rec 1813. pp 448, 449, 450

Deed dated 1813. Admtrs of STEPHEN VAIL to WILLIAM SIMONTON. Finalize sale beguen 1805 for Middletown lot 48. Signed AARON VAIL. Witn: JOSEPH TREEN. rec 1813. pp 451, 452

Deed dated 1812. Trustees of S 16, T 2, R 3 to HENRY ALLEN. Lease for mill seat and lot for benefit of school, term of 99 yrs. Signed SAMUEL ENYART, PATRICK MOORE and DENNIS BALL, trustees. Witn: JOHN AYERS, JOHN MERRILL. rec 1813. pp 452, 453, 454

BUTLER COUNTY LAND RECORDS: BOOK C

Deed dated 1809. ANDREW VAGNER & MARY his wife of Lemon Twp to CHRISTOPHER VAGNER. S 7, T 2, R 4. Signed ANDW. (x) VAGNER, MARY (x) VAGNER. Witn: ANN (x) SIMPSON, HENRY WEAVER. rec 1813. pp 454, 455

Deed dated 1812. CHRISTOPHER VAGNER & ELIZABETH his wife to MOSES DENMAN. S 7, T 2, R 4. Signed CHRISTOPHER (x) VAGONER*, ELIZABETH (x) VAGONER. Witn: MARY (x) DENMAN, HENRY WEAVER. rec 1813. pp 455, 456
*possibly this name is WAGGONER, spelled as it would be pronounced in German.

End of Book C; start Book D

Deed dated 1813. ISAAC MARTIN & MARY his wife of Madison Twp to DANIEL STRICKLAND of Lemon Twp. S 6, R 4 "in twp aforesaid". Bound by land of ENOCH HAND. RUSSEL POTTER, ANDREW HAMILTON, DUIEL CULVER. Signed ISAAC MARTIN, MARY MARTIN. Witn: JAMES HEATH, JONATHAN MARTIN. rec 1813. pp 1, 2

Deed dated 1813. SILAS GARRISON & ANNE his wife of Wayne Twp to THUNES SPEER. S 19, T 3, R 3. Bound by land of SAMUEL DAVIS, JOHN KNIP, MOSES CRUME. Signed SILAS GARRISON, ANNE (x) GARRISON. Witn: HARMON BARKLOW, MATTH. RICHARDSON. rec 1813. pp 2, 3

Deed dated 1813. ELIHU WOODRUFF & MARGARET his wife to JOSEPH KENNEDY of Campbell Co, KY. S 30, T 2, R 2. Signed ELIHU WOODRUFF, MARGARET WOODRUFF. Witn: ISAAC STANLEY, MARY HEATON. rec 1813. pp 3, 4

Power of Attorney dated 1813. ALEXANDER WILSON of Montgomery Co apptd brother JOHN WILSON as atty to collect money, convey title, since AW was moving. Signed ALEXANDER WILSON. Witn: WM. M. SMITH, JOHN FOLKERTH. rec 1813. pp 4, 5

Deed dated 1813. THOMAS POWERS & MARY his wife to NOAH LONG, assignee of JOHN BARRET. S 28, T 2, R 4. Bound by JOHN VANSICKLE's land. Signed THOS. POWERS, MARY POWERS. Witn: HENRY WEAVER, DANIEL SALLE. rec 1813. pp 5, 6

Deed dated 1813. JOSEPH WILLIAMSON & MARY his wife to JOHN R. SCHENCK. S 15, T 2, R 4. Signed JOSEPH WILLIAMSON, MARY (x) WILLIAMSON. Witn: CARLTON WALDO, DAVID WOOLVERTON. rec 1813. pp 6, 7, 8

Deed dated 1813. JOHN SUTHERLAND & NANCY his wife to JOHN HALL. Rossville lots 5, 6, 41, 50. Signed JOHN

BUTLER COUNTY LAND RECORDS: BOOK D

SUTHERLAND, NANCY R. SUTHERLAND. Witn: ISAAC STANLEY, JAS. DUNN. rec 1813. pp 8, 9

Deed dated 1813. JONATHAN HIGGINS & MARGARET his wife to WILLIAM MURRAY in trust for ELIZABETH FLEMING, late McCULLOUGH. S 7, T 4, R 2. Bound by land of DAVID BLACKBURN, JOHN JOHNSON. Signed JONATHAN HIGGINS, MARGARET (x) HIGGINS. Witn: JAMES HEATON, JAMES SMITH. rec 1813. pp 9, 10

Deed dated 1813. THEOPHILUS EAGLEFIELD & PHEBE his wife to DAVID CRANE. S 30, T 2, R 4. Money to be paid by Crane or AARON SOUTHARD on his behalf. Signed THEOPHILUS EAGLEFIELD, PHEBE EAGLEFIELD. Witn: AARON SOUTHARD, HENRY WEAVER. rec 1813. pp 11, 12

Deed dated 1813. DAVID CRANE & ELIZABETH his wife to RICHARD V. V. CRANE. S 30, T 2, R 4. Signed DAVID CRANE, ELIZABETH (x) CRANE. Witn: LEONARD WEAVER, HENRY WEAVER. rec 1813. pp 12, 13

Deed dated 1813. WILLIAM McCLELLAN, sheriff, to JOHN WILSON & ALEXANDER WILSON. HENRY LOGAN obtained judgement against ALEXANDER WILSON. Seized S 14 & 23, T 2, R 3; sold at auction to JW & AW. Signed WM. McCLELLAN. Witn: JP DANIEL MILLIKIN, WM. G. ARMSTRONG. rec 1813. pp 13, 14, 15

Deed dated 1811. JOSEPH BAIRD & JANE his wife to GEORGE KELLY. S 12, T 3, R 3. Signed JOSEPH BAIRD, JANE BAIRD. Witn: BENJAMIN VAN CLEEF, HENRY WEAVER. rec 1813. pp 15, 16

Deed dated 1812. NATHANIEL BELL & MARY his wife to GEORGE KELLY. S 1, T 3, R 3. Signed NATHANIEL BELL, MARY (x) BELL. Witn: JOSEPH WEBB, SAMUEL HUNT. rec 1813. pp 16, 17, 18

Deed dated 1813. DAVID WILLIAMSON & MARY his wife to DAVID SNODGRASS of Warren Co. S 7, T 3, R 3 in Liberty Twp. Signed DAVID WILLIAMSON, MARY WILLIAMSON. Witn: ARTHUR ORR, JACOB DEARDORF. rec 1813. pp 18, 19

Deed dated 1807. JAMES MARSHALL & FANNY his wife to PATRICK MAHAN. S 7, T 3, R 3. Signed JAMES (x) MARSHALL, FANNY MARSHALL. Witn: ISAAC S. SWEARINGEN, BARBARA SWEARINGEN. rec 1813. pp 19, 20

Deed dated 1813. ADRAN HAGERMAN SR & MICA his wife of Hamilton Co to MARIAH ANDERSON. S 7, T 3, R 3.

BUTLER COUNTY LAND RECORDS: BOOK D

Signed ADRIAN HAGAMAN, MICHA (x) HAGEMAN. Witn: THOS HIGGINS, SIMON HAGEMAN. rec 1813. pp 20, 21

Deed dated 1806. USA to JOHN VAN NEST of Hamilton Co. S 18, T 2, R 4. rec 1813. p 21

Deed dated 1813. THOMAS BURKE & ELIZABETH his wife to OBEDIAH WILLIVER. S 26, T 4, R 1. Signed THOMAS BURKE, ELIZABETH BURKE. Witn: JOHN ISRAEL, JOHN (x) RUSSEL. rec 1813. pp 22, 23

Deed dated 1813. SAMUEL STITES & MARTHA his wife of Green Co to JOHN McCLEAN. S 12, T 3, R 3. Signed SAMUEL STITES, MARTHA STITES. Witn: JAMES CLARK, WM. GOUDY. rec 1813. pp 23, 24

Deed dated 1813. HENRY WEAVER & SUSAN his wife to JOHN VANSICKLE. S 28, T 2, R 3. Signed HENRY WEAVER, SUSAN WEAVER. Witn: ISAAC HOFF, THOS POWERS. rec 1813. pp 24, 25

Deed dated 1813. CORNELIUS R. SEDAM of Hamilton Co to RICHARD BIRCH SR & ROBERT BIRCH JR of Fairfield Twp. S 1, R 3 in Ffld Twp. Signed CORNS. R. SEDAM. Witn: OLIVER H. HENRY, ISAAC STANLEY. rec 1813. pp 25, 26

Deed dated 1812. STEPHEN CRAIN & POLLY his wife of Liberty Twp to WILLIAM WEBSTER of same. S 15, T 3, R 3. Signed STEPHEN CRANE, MAY CRANE. Witn: P. WILLIAMSON, MARY (x) MARTIN. rec 1813. pp 27, 28

Deed dated 1813. PETER KEEN & JEMIMA his wife of Colerain Twp (Hamilton Co) to JAMES WILLSON of St. Clair Twp. S 13, T 5, R 2. Bound by ANDREW BROWN's land. Signed PETER KEEN, JEMIMA KEEN. Witn: WM. MURRAY, ISAAC STANLEY. rec 1813. pp 28, 29

Deed dated 1813. THOMAS BLAIR & MARGARET his wife to JAMES WILSON. Hamilton lots 85, 86 and lot 2 in CORNELIUS SEDAM's plat in S 1, T 1, R 3. Signed THOS BLAIR, MARGARET BLAIR. Witn: JOEL COLLINS, WILLIAM GREENLEE. rec 1813. pp 30, 31

Mortgage dated 1813. JOHN EMERICK & MARY his wife to PHINEAS McCREA. S 1, T 2, R 4. Paymt due in 3 yrs. Signed JOHN EMERICK (german script), 2d signature illegible. Witn: WILLIAM McCREA, HENRY WEAVER. rec 1813. pp 31, 32, 33

Deed dated 1813. ISAAC HOFF & CATHARINE his wife to

BUTLER COUNTY LAND RECORDS: BOOK D

JOHN TEITSORT. S 29, T 2, R 4. Signed ISAAC HOFF, CATHARINE HOFF. Witn: JOHN DINE, WILLIAM TEITSORT. rec 1813. pp 33, 34

Deed dated 1813. SAMUEL GRAY & MARGARET his wife to JAMES MILLS. Rossville lot 10. Signed SAMUEL GRAY, MARGARET GRAY. Witn: JAMES HEATON, ISAAC STANLEY. rec 1813. pp 34, 35

Deed dated 1813. SAMUEL D. BOWMAN & CHARLOTTE his wife to ROBERT CARTER. S 23, T 3, R 2. Bound by JOHN JAMISON's land. Signed SAMUEL D. BOWMAN, CHARLOTTE (x) BOWMAN. Witn: JNO. DUNN, JOHN TUCKER. rec 1813. pp 35, 36

Deed dated 1813. RICHARD WATTS & ELCE his wife to EMMA QUICK, widow. S 22, T 2, R 4. Signed RICHARD (x) WATTS, ELCE (x) WATTS. Witn: PLATT B. DICKSON, ISRAEL WATTS. rec 1813. pp 36, 37, 38

Deed dated 1813. JOHN CLEVES SYMMES of Hamilton Co to WILLIAM ENYART. S 15, T 2, R 2. Signed JOHN CLEVES SYMMES. Witn: DANIEL MAYS, GRIFFIN YEATMAN. rec 1813. pp 38, 39

Deed dated 1813. JOHN CLEVES SYMMES of Hamilton Co to GEORGE VANEST, assignee of THOS. McEWEN, dec'd. S 5, T 2, R 2. SILAS CONDIT owned balance of section. Signed JOHN CLEVES SYMMES. Witn: DANIEL MAYS, GRIFFIN YEATMAN. rec 1813. pp 39, 40, 41

Deed dated 1813. JAMES McCLELLAN JR to GEORGE KIRKPATRICK SR. S 28, T 4, R 2. Signed JAMES McCLELLAN JR. Witn: WM McCLELLAN, JOSEPH TREEN. rec 1813. pp 41, 42

Deed dated 1813. EBENEZER PADDOCK & KAZIA his wife to JAMES DRAKE. S 36, T 3, R 3. Signed EBENEZER PADDOCK, KAZIA PADDOCK. Witn: RICHD. V.V. CRANE, HENRY WEAVER. rec 1813. pp 42, 43

Deed dated 1813. BYRAM SEWARD & PHEBY his wife to STEPHEN SCUDDER. S 5, T 2, R 2. Surveyed by SAMUEL SEWARD SR; bound by SAMUEL SEWARD JR's land. Signed BYRAM (x) SEWARD, PHEBE (x) SEWARD. Witn: JOHN AYERS, NATHAN WALLEN. rec 1813. pp 43, 44

Deed dated 1813. DAVID GARRIGUS & ABIGAIL his wife to JONATHAN LEWIS. S 7, T 2, R 3. Bound by land of WILLIAM FRAZER, WILLIAM DAVID. Signed DAVID GARRIGUS, ABIGAIL (x) GARRIGUS. Witn: JOHN WHITWORTH,

BUTLER COUNTY LAND RECORDS: BOOK D

JOHN JOHNSON.   rec 1813.   pp 44, 45, 46

Deed dated 1813.   LAWRENCE CAVENAUGH & ANN his wife to SOLOMON MOORE of Hamilton Co. Hamilton lot 134. Signed LAWRENCE CAVENAUGH, ANN CAVENAUGH. Witn: ASAHEL MORDOCK, ISAAC STANLEY.   rec 1813.   pp 46, 47

Deed dated 1813.   EBENEZER PADDOCK JR & NANCY his wife to SAMUEL POTTINGER. S 36, T 3, R 3. Signed EBENEZER PADDOCK, NANCY (x) PADDOCK. Witn: (illeg) FERGUSON, CHARLES SWEARINGEN.   rec 1813.   pp 47, 48

Deed dated 1813.   JONATHAN DAYTON & SUSAN his wife of NJ to BENJAMIN MEGIE* of Rhaway Twp, Essex Co, NJ. S 10, T 3, R 3. Signed JONA. DAYTON, SUSAN DAYTON. rec 1813.   pp 48, 49, 50 *name could possibly be BENJAMIN McGEE or BENJAMIN M. GEE.

Deed dated 1813.   ISRAEL WATTS & MARY his wife to JOHN SHAFER. Middletown lot 20. Signed ISRAEL WATTS MARY (x) WATTS. Witn: ISAAC ROBY, JOB MULFORD.   rec 1813.   pp 50, 51

Deed dated 1813.   NATHAN POPEJOY & <u>MARY</u> his wife to JAMES AYERS. S 5, T 2, R 3. Bound by DAVID HIRAM GREGORY's land. Signed NATHAN POPEJOY, <u>POLEY</u> POPEJOY. Witn: JAMES CUMMINS, (illeg) CORTMEL.   rec 1813.   pp 51, 52, 53

Deed dated 1812.   AARON VAIL, excr of STEPHEN VAIL to JAMES AYRES. Middletown lot 34. STEPHEN died before completing sale, left minor heirs; will named SHOBAL VAIL & AV as excrs. Signed AARON VAIL. Witn: JOHN HUSTON, JP DANIEL STRICKLAND.   rec 1813.   pp 53, 54, 55

Deed dated 1797.   JOHN CLEVES SYMMES of NW Ter'y to DANIEL PERINE of Washington Co, PA, assignee of WILLIAM PERINE, his father. S 7, T 3, R 2. Signed JOHN CLEVES SYMMES. Witn: DANIEL PIERSON, SIMEON MARSH. rec 1813.   pp 55, 56

Deed dated 1813.   MOSES DENMAN & ELIZABETH his wife to JOHN GUNCKEL. S 32, T 2, R 4. Signed MOSES DENMAN ELIZABETH (x) DENMAN. Witn: FREDERICK WOLF, HENRY WEAVER.   rec 1813.   pp 56, 57, 58

Deed dated 1813.   MOSES VAIL & MARY his wife to JACOB WEIDNER. S 10, T 4, R not given. Signed MOSES VAIL, MARY VAIL. Witn: HENRY WEAVER, ABRAHAM TEITSORT. JP JAMES LANIER.   rec 1813.   pp 59, 60

BUTLER COUNTY LAND RECORDS: BOOK D

Deed dated 1810. JAMES FERGUSON & JANE his wife of Hamilton Co to JOHN & WILLIAM PEARSON of same. S 22, T 3, R 3. Signed JAMES FERGUSON, JANE FERGUSON. Witn: NATH'L REED, ETHAN STONE. rec 1813. pp 60, 61

Deed dated 1813. JOHN PIERSON & ELIZABETH his wife and WILLIAM PIERSON & HULDA his wife of Cincinnati to MOSES BONNEL of same. S 22, T 3, R 3. Signed JOHN PEARSON, ELIZA PEARSON, WILLIAM PEARSON, HULDA (x) PEARSON. Witn: JOHN MAHARD, WM. HAMILTON. rec 1813. pp 61, 62

Deed dated 1813. JONATHAN PIERSON & MATILDA his wife to JOSEPH HOUGH. Hamilton lots 72, 73. Signed JONATHAN PIERSON, MATILDA PIERSON. Witn: ISAAC STANLEY, NICHOLAS DAVIS. rec 1813. pp 63, 64

Deed dated 1801. USA to SAMUEL DICK. S 9, T 3, R 2. rec 1813. pp 64, 65

Deed dated 1810. JOHN SUTHERLAND & HENRY BROWN to SAMUEL DICK. Rossville lot 39. Signed JOHN SUTHERLAND, HENRY BROWN. Witn: JAMES STEEL, JAMES BECK. rec 1813. pp 65, 66

Deed dated 1809. JOHN SUTHERLAND & HENRY BROWN to SAMUEL DICK. Rossville lot 8, 18, 43, 44, 47, 52, 66, 73, 86. Signed JOHN SUTHERLAND, HENRY BROWN. Witn: WM BOMBERGER JR, WM PHARES JR. rec 1813. pp 66, 67

Deed dated 1809. JOHN SUTHERLAND & HENRY BROWN to SAMUEL DICK. S 31 & 36, T 4, R 2. Signed JOHN SUTHERLAND, HENRY BROWN. Witn: WM BOMBERGER JR, WM PHARES JR. rec 1813. pp 69, 70

Deed dated 1813. WILLIAM HERBERT & ELEANOR his wife to JACOB LINGLE. Rossville lot 89. Signed WILLIAM HERBERT, ELEANOR HERBERT. Witn: DANL MILLIKIN, J.C. McMANIS, CATHARINE SNAPP. rec 1813. pp 70, 71

Deed dated 1810. GEORGE PAUL TORRENCE to WILLIAM McCLELLAND. S 10 & 15, T 2, R 3. Signed GEORGE PAULL TORRENCE. Witn: JOHN MAHARD, JAMES McBRIDE. rec 1813. pp 72, 73

Deed dated 1813. RICHARD BIRCH to JAMES WILSON. Lot 6 in S 1, T 1, R 3. Signed RICHD. BIRCH. Witn: JOHN REILY, ISAAC STANLEY rec 1813. pp 73, 74

Deed dated 1813. WILLIAM McCLELLAN & MARY his wife

BUTLER COUNTY LAND RECORDS: BOOK D

to FOSTER FIELDS & SAMUEL FIELDS JR in trust for their parents SAMUEL FIELDS & LOVIA his wife, late FOSTER. Money paid by THOMAS FOSTER of Lycoming Co, PA, exctr of JAMES FOSTER of Northumberland, PA. S 10 & 25, T 2, R 3. After parents' demise, land to be shared among heirs: DORCAS HAHN late FOSTER, SARAH FIELDS, JOHN FOSTER, DANIEL FOSTER, LOVIA FOSTER, RACHEL FOSTER, STEPHEN FOSTER, FREEBORN FOSTER. Signed WM. McCLELLAN, MARY McCLELLAN. Witn: JOHN FOSTER, JAMES MILLS. rec 1813. pp 74, 75, 76

Deed dated 1812. EZRA FITZ FREEMAN to AARON BIGELOW. S 4, T 1, R 2 conveyed to AB in 1811. Deed incorrectly defined southern boundary, interfering with land of JAMES BLACKBURN. Signed EZRA FITZ FREEMAN. Witn: JAMES HEATON, DAN'L MILLIKIN. rec 1813. pp 76, 77

Deed dated 1813. EZRA FITZ FREEMAN to AARON BIGELOW. S 4, T 1, R 2. Signed EZRA F. FREEMAN. Witn: WM. MURRAY, ISAAC STANLEY. rec 1813. pp 78, 79

Deed dated 1813. YORK FREEMAN & JUDE his wife to AARON BIGELOW. S 4, T 1, R 2. Signed YORK (x) FREEMAN, JUDE (x) FREEMAN. Witn: WM. MURRAY, ISAAC STANLEY. rec 1813. pp 79, 80

Deed dated 1813. Surviving admtrs of ISRAEL LUDLOW to THOMAS C. KELSEY & WILLARD M. SMITH. Hamilton lot 109. Signed CHARLOTTE CHAMBERS RISK, JOHN LUDLOW, JAMES FINDLAY. Witn: GRIFFIN YEATMAN, THOS. HOO JR. rec 1813. pp 80, 81, 82

Deed dated 1813. PHINEAS McCREA & SARAH his wife to JOHN EMRICK. S 1, T 2, R 4. Signed PHINEAS (x) McCREA, SARAH (x) McCREA. Witn: MARTIN EARHART, HENRY WEAVER. rec 1813. pp 82, 83

Deed dated 1813. GEORGE VANNEST & LENCHY his wife to WILLIAM PATTON. S 5, T 2, R 2. Signed GEORGE VAN NEST, LINCHY (x) VAN NEST. Witn: JOHN AYERS, JOHN VANNEST. rec 1813. pp 83, 84

Deed dated 1813. BENONY GOBLE & SARAH his wife to WILLIAM SMITH. S 28, T 3, R 3. Signed BENONY GOBLE, SARAH (x) GOBLE. Witn: JOHN SWEARINGEN, ABNER GOBLE. rec 1813. pp 84, 85, 86

Deed dated 1813. ISAIAH BALL & PHEBE his wife and DENNIS BALL & MARGARET his wife to ELIZABETH HARVEY. S 21, T 2, R 3. Bound by land of WILLIAM PATTON, PATRICK MOORE, SAMUEL KENNEDY, TIMOTHY WOODRUFF.

BUTLER COUNTY LAND RECORDS: BOOK D

Signed ISAIAH BALL, DENNIS BALL, PHEBE (x) BALL, MARGARET (x) BALL. Witn: JOHN REILY, WM. G. ARMSTRONG JOHN VINNIDGE. rec 1813. pp 86, 87

Deed dated 1813. HENRY BROWN & CATHARINE his wife of Montgomery Co to JOHN SUTHERLAND. Hamilton lots 121, 122, 136, 147, 148, 197, 198, 200, 201, 223 and Hamilton outlots 8, 9, 16, 19, 20 & 28; S 2 & 3, T 1, R 3. Signed HENRY BROWN, CATHARINE P. BROWN. Witn: P. PATTERSON, FRANCIS PATTERSON. rec 1813. pp 88, 89

Deed dated 1813. WILLIAM McCLELLAN & MARY his wife to JOHN SUTHERLAND. S 1, T 2, R 3, lot 7. Signed WM. McCLELLAN, MARY M. McCLELLAN. Witn: ISAAC STANLEY, WM. MURRAY. rec 1813. pp 89, 90, 91

Deed dated 1812. JOHN REILY & NANCY his wife to JOHN SUTHERLAND & HENRY BROWN. S 31 & 32, T 2, R 3 (Rossville outlot 29). Signed JOHN REILY, NANCY REILY. Witn: MARSH WILLIAMS, WM. McCLELLAN. rec 1813. pp 91, 92

Deed dated 1813. JOHN HALL of Rossville to JOHN SUTHERLAND. S 18, T 1, R 4. Bound by land of JOHN HALL, JAMES REED, M. DOUGHTY, E. BOYLES. Signed JOHN HALL. Witn: JOHN REILY, JOHN WHITWORTH. rec 1813. pp 93, 94

Deed dated 1813. JOHN GREER & <u>ELEANOR</u> his wife to JOHN SUTHERLAND. Hamilton lots 111, 112. Signed JOHN GREER, ELINOR GREER. Witn: JAMES P. RAMSEY. rec 1813. pp 94, 95

Deed dated 1813. HENRY BROWN & CATHARINE his wife of Montgomery Co to JOHN SUTHERLAND. S 31, 32 T 2, R 3; S 36, T 4, R 2. Signed HENRY BROWN, CATHARINE P. BROWN. Witn: P. PATTERSON, FRANCIS PATTERSON. rec 1813. pp 95, 96, 97

Deed dated 1813. Admtrs of ISRAEL LUDLOW to JOHN SUTHERLAND. Hamilton lot 107. Signed JAMES FINDLAY, JOHN LUDLOW. Witn: GRIFFIN YEATMAN, THOS FLOO JR. rec 1813. pp 97, 98, 99

Mortgage dated 1813. NICHOLAS HOGAN to JOHN SUTHERLAND. Hamilton lot 37. Signed NICHOLAS HOGAN. Witn: JOHN REILY, WM. G. ARMSTRONG. rec 1813. pp 99, 100, 101

Deed dated 1813. RICHARD WATTS & <u>ELCE</u> his wife to DAVID HEATON. S 22, T 2, R 4. Signed RICHARD (x)

BUTLER COUNTY LAND RECORDS: BOOK D

WATTS, ELICE (x) WATTS. Witn: PLATT B. DICKSON, ISRAEL WATTS. rec 1813. pp 101, 102

Deed dated 1813. JAMES ELLIOTT & MARGARET his wife to JAMES MILLS. Rossville lot 85. Signed JAMES ELLIOTT, MARGARET ELLIOTT. Witn: ISAAC STANLEY, JOHN WILSON. rec 1813. pp 103, 104

Deed dated 1813. MICHAEL PIERCE & PHEBE his wife to JONATHAN CLARK. S 6, T 1, R 4. Signed MICHAEL PEARCE PHEBE PEARCE. Witn: JOHN PEARCE, HENRY WEAVER. rec 1813. pp 104, 105

Deed dated 1812. USA to RICHARD WALLS. S 22, T 2, R 4. rec 1813. pp 105, 106

Deed dated 1811. RICHARD CAMPBELL & RACHEL his wife to DAVID GARRIGUS. S 7, T 2, R 3. Signed RICHARD CAMPBELL, RACHEL (x) CAMPBELL. Witn: ISAAC STANLEY, WILLIAM (x) MARTIN. rec 1813. pp 106, 107

Deed dated 1813. JOHN GREER & ELEANOR his wife to ABSOLOM GOODENOUGH. Hamilton lot 3. Signed JNO. GREER, ELINOR GREER. Witn: HARRIETT CARLISLE, ISAAC STANLEY. rec 1813. pp 07, 108, 109

Deed dated 1805. JOEL WILLIAMS & PHEBE his wife to ABRAHAM MONTANYE. S 20, T 3, R 2. Signed JOEL WILLIAMS, PHEBE WILLIAMS. Witn: SIMON M. STOCKDELL, JOHN MAHARD. rec 1813. pp 107, 108, 109

Deed dated 1813. RUTH REED, admtr of DAVID REED, to JOHN MALLORY. S 19, T 2, R 4. Bound by land of ROBERT CARRICK. Contract begun 1811; Reed left minor heirs. Signed RUTH (x) REED. Witn: JAMES TANNEHILL, ROBERT (x) CARRICK. rec 1813. pp 110, 111, 112, 113

Deed dated 1812. JOHN PATTERSON of Fayette Co, PA to ISAAC KING. S 18, T 3, R 3. Signed JOHN PATTERSON. Witn: A. OLIPHANT, WM. CUNNINGHAM. rec 1813. pp 113, 114

Deed dated 1812. JOHN PATTERSON of Fayette Co, PA to THOMAS KING. S 18, T 3, R 3. Signed and witn as above. rec 1813. pp 113, 114

Deed dated 1813. JOHN PIERSON & ELIZABETH his wife and WILLIAM PIERSON & HULDA his wife to DENNIS KELLY. S 22, T 3, R 3. Signed JOHN PIERSON, ELIZA PIERSON, WILLIAM PIERSON, HULDA (x) PIERSON. Witn: JOHN MAHARD, WM. HAMILTON. rec 1813. pp 116, 117, 118

BUTLER COUNTY LAND RECORDS: BOOK D

Deed dated 1812. Admtrs of WILLIAM SYMMES to JOHN SUTHERLAND & HENRY BROWN. Rossville lot 34. Signed CELADON SYMMES, JOSEPH F. RANDOLPH. Witn: JOHN REILY, JOHN WHITWORTH. rec 1813. pp 118, 119

Deed dated 1813. JOHN CLEVES SYMMES to JOHN (S or C) POTTS. S 15 & 16, T 2, R 2. Signed JOHN CLEVES SYMMES Witn: J. CLEVES SHORT. rec 1813. pp 118, 119

Deed dated 1813. BENJAMIN PERSAILS & ELIZABETH his wife to MARGARET McDONALD. Hamilton lot 28. Signed BENJAMIN PURSAIL, ELIZABETH PURSAIL. Witn: JOHN GILLESPIE, ISAAC STANLEY. rec 1813. pp 121, 122

Deed dated 1813. JOSHUA ELLIOTT & ELIZABETH his wife to SAMUEL FRAZY, Hamilton Co. S 20, T 3, R 3. Signed JOSHUA ELLIOTT, ELIZABETH (x) ELLIOTT. Witn: P. WILLIAMSON, JOHN MORROW. rec 1813. pp 122, 123, 124

Deed dated 1813. ROBERT ROSSBROUGH & MARY his wife to WILLIAM NIXON. S 9, T 4, R 2. Signed ROBT. ROSEBROUGH, MARY (x) ROSEBROUGH. Witn: JAMES JOHNSON, SARAH JOHNSTON. rec 1813. pp 124, 125

Deed dated 1813. THOMAS HUNTER, tax collector of Fairfield Twp to NANCY DAVIS. Hamilton lot 139. Signed THOMAS HUNTER. Witn: WM. CORRY, ISAAC STANLEY. rec 1813. pp 127, 128

Deed dated 1812. ELIHU LINE & NANCY his wife to JONATHAN LINE. S 27, T 2, R 3. Signed ELIHU LINE, NANCY (x) LINE. Witn: JOHN LINE, JOHN VINNEDGE. rec 1813. pp 127, 128

Deed dated 1813. ALEXANDER AYERS to JAMES MARTIN. S 31, T 3, R 4. Signed ALEX'R. AYERS. Witn: ABRAHAM SOUTHARD, HENRY WEAVER. rec 1813. pp 129, 130

Deed dated 1813. ALBERT BONTA & NANCY his wife to ALEXANDER AYRES. S 31, T 3, R 4. Signed ALBERT BONTA, NANCY BONTA. Witn: JOHN MARTIN, HENRY WEAVER. rec 1813. pp 130, 131, 132

Mortgage dated 1812. DANIEL WOODRUFF to JACOB BARNET of Cincinnati. S 32, T 3, R 3. Signed DANIEL WOODRUFF Witn: JOHN MAHARD, ANN MAHARD. rec 1813. pp 132, 133

Deed dated 1812. USA to RICHARD WATTS. S 28 & 34, T 2, R 4. rec 1813. p 134

BUTLER COUNTY LAND RECORDS: BOOK D

Deed dated 1813.   DANIEL PERRY & RHODA his wife of Millford Twp to SAMUEL BOURN of same. S 3, T 5, R 2. Bound by land of JAMES EMMERSON, JONATHAN COOPER, MARSH WILLIAMS, WILLIAM COOPER. Signed DANIEL PERRY, RHODA (x) PERRY. Witn: MARSH WILLIAMS, BENJAMIN BOURN. rec 1813. pp 134, 135, 136

Deed dated 1813. ARCHIBALD STARK & ELEANOR his wife to JOSEPH H. McMAHON*. S 9, T 2, R 2. Signed ARCHIBALD STARK, NELLY STARK. Witn: ISAAC STARK, JOHN BURK. rec 1813. pp 136, 137, 138 *clerk's margin note gives name as McMAKEN

Deed dated 1813. JOSEPH McMAKEN & ELIZABETH his wife to JOSEPH H. McMAKEN, his son. S 26, T 4, R 2. Signed JOSEPH McMAKEN, ELIZABETH (x) McMAKEN. Witn: JOHN CAMPBELL, JOHN McMAKEN. rec 1813.   pp 138, 139

Deed dated 1813. THOMAS KYLE & SARAH his wife to JAMES KYLE. S 28, T 3, R 3. Signed THOMAS KYLE, SARAH KYLE. Witn: SAMUEL KYLE, P. WILLIAMSON. rec 1813. pp 139, 140

Deed dated 1813. THOMAS KYLE & SARAH his wife to SAMUEL KYLE. S 28, T 3, R 3. Signed THOMAS KYLE, SARAH KYLE. Witn: JAMES KYLE, P. WILLIAMSON. rec 1813. pp 140, 141

Mortgage dated 1813. WILLIAM PATTON to GEORGE VANNEST. S 5, T 2, R 2. Signed WILLIAM PATTON. Witn: WILLIAM WILLIAMSON, JOHN AYERS. rec 1813. pp 142, 143

Deed dated 1813. JOHN SUTHERLAND & NANCY his wife to JOHN SUTHERLAND JR. Hamilton lots 111, 112. Signed JOHN SUTHERLAND, NANCY R. SUTHERLAND. Witn: WM. W. PHARES, SAMUEL SCOTT. rec 1813. pp 143, 144, 145

Deed dated 1813. RUFUS ENYART & SALLY his wife to DANIEL THOMPSON. S 9, T 2, R 2. Bound by land of LEVI MOORE, DAVID URMSTON, JOHN LINE. Signed RUFUS ENYART, SARAH (x) ENYART. Witn: WM. STANBERRY, ZACARIAH CARLISLE. rec 1813. pp 145, 146

Deed dated 1813. GEORGE SHAFER & BETSEY his wife to WILLIAM STEWART. S 2, T 3, R 2; bound by land of DAVID SMITH.   Signed GEORGE SHAFER (german script), BETSEY (x) SHAFER. Witn: WM. MURRAY, DAN'L MILLIKIN. rec 1813. pp 146, 147

Deed dated 1813. SAMUEL ENYART & ANNA his wife of Princetown to JACOB L. CONKLIN. Princetown lots 4,

BUTLER COUNTY LAND RECORDS: BOOK D

10, 11. Signed SAMUEL ENYART, ANNA ENYART. Witn: JOHN AYERS, HUMPHREY NICHOLS. rec 1813. pp 147, 148

Deed dated 1811. SAMUEL DILLON to JOSEPH PEAK. S 1, T 2, R 3. Signed SAMUEL DILLON. Witn: JAMES HEATON, WILLIAM HARLAN. rec 1814. p 149

Deed dated 1813. DAVID LONG & SARAH his wife to NOAH LONG. S 20, T 2, R 4. Signed DAVID (x) LONG, SARAH (x) LONG. Witn: ALEX'R. AYERS, HENRY WEAVER. rec 1814. pp 149, 150, 151

Deed dated 1813. WILLIAM HERBERT & ELEANOR his wife, HENRY CRUSE & SUSAN his wife and JACOB LINGLE & MARY his wife to JOHN NELSON. Rossville lot 82. Signed WILLIAM HERBERT, ELEANOR HERBERT, HENRY CRUSE (german script) SUSAN (x) CRUSE, JACOB LINGLE (german script) MARY (x) LINGLE. Witn: DAN'L MILLIKIN, A.C. McMANNIS, CATHARINE SNAPP. rec 1814. pp 151, 152

Deed dated 1813. PHILIP **MUCHNER** & MARY his wife to WILLIAM CURRYER. S 22, T 3, R 3. Signed PHILIP **MUTCHNER**, MARY MUTCHNER. Witn: P. WILLIAMSON, SALEM POCOCK. rec 1814. pp 153, 154

Mortgage dated 1813. AMOS WHITE JR of Hamilton Co to GEORGE CRANE. S 17, T 5, R 2. Bound by land of ABRAHAM WHITE. Signed AMOS WHITE. Witn: MARSH WILLIAMS, ROBERT CRANE. rec 1814. pp 154, 155

Deed dated 1811. THOMAS **TOLBIN** & KEZIAH his wife of Wayne Twp to THOMAS FOX of same. (TOLBERT in deed text) S 9, T 3, R 3. Signed THOMAS TOLBERT, KEZIAH (x) TOLBERT. Witn: JOHN PA--, KEZIAH ORR. rec 1814. pp 155, 156, 157

Deed dated 1813. ISAAC STANLEY to ABSALOM GOODENOUGH Hamilton lot 3. Signed ISAAC STANLEY. Witn: JOHN WHITWORTH, WM. G. ARMSTRONG. rec 1814. pp 157 158

Deed dated 1807. ABRAHAM FREEMAN JR to ISAAC HAGEMAN S 10, T 2, R 1. Signed ABRAHAM F. FREEMAN. Witn: JOHN CASSIDY, OBADIAH SCHENCK. rec 181. pp 158, 159

Deed dated 1812. ALBIN SHAW & EUNICE his wife to SWITHIN CHANDLER. Lots 4, 5 & 6 in the partition of a land tract formerly property of JOHN SHAW, decd. Bound by land of SAMUEL DICK, DAVID E. WADE, RUBEN ROOD & HULDAH his wife. Signed ALBIN SHAW, EUNICE SHAW. Witn: JUDAH WILLEY, MICHAEL SHALEE. rec 1814. 159, 160, 161

BUTLER COUNTY LAND RECORDS: BOOK D

Deed dated 1814. SWITHIN CHANDLER & RACHEL his wife to SARAH CHANDLER. Lot 6 as above. Signed SWITHIN CHANDLER, RACHL CHANDLER. Witn: none. rec 1814. pp 161, 162

Deed dated 1813. JOHN SUTHERLAND & NANCY his wife to THOMAS C. KELSEY & WILLARD M. SMITH (WILLIAM in deed text). Rossville lot 40. Signed JOHN SUTHERLAND, NANCY R. SUTHERLAND. Witn: JOHN REILY, WM. W. PHARES. rec 1814. pp 162, 163, 164

Deed dated 1813. JOHN CLEVES SYMMES to JOHN NOBLE CUMMINS of Newark, NJ, agent for widow and heirs of Rev. PHILIP STOCKTON of NJ. S 23, T 2, R 2. Signed JOHN CLEVES SYMMES. Witn: GRIFFIN YEATMAN, J. CLEVES SHORT. rec 1814. pp 164, 165

Deed dated 1813. Admtrs of ISRAEL LUDLOW to JOHN SUTHERLAND. Hamilton lot 197. Signed CHARLOTTE CHAMBERS RISK, JOHN LUDLOW, JAMES FINDLAY. Witn: GRIFFIN YEATMAN, THOS. FLOO JR. rec 1814. pp 165, 166, 167

Deed dated 1813. Admtrs of ISRAEL LUDLOW to JOHN SUTHERLAND. Hamilton lot --. Signed CHARLOTTE CHAMBERS RISK, JOHN LUDLOW, JAMES FINDLAY. Witn: GRIFFIN YEATMAN, THOS. FLOO JR. rec 1814. pp 167, 168

Deed dated 1813. Admtrs of ISRAEL LUDLOW to JOHN SUTHERLAND. Hamilton lot 234. Signed CHARLOTTE CHAMBERS RISK, JOHN LUDLOW, JAMES FINDLAY. Witn: GRIFFIN YEATMAN, THOS. FLOO JR. rec 1814. pp 168, 169, 170

Deed dated 1813. Admtrs of ISRAEL LUDLOW to JOHN SUTHERLAND. Hamilton lot 108. Signed CHARLOTTE CHAMBERS RISK, JOHN LUDLOW, JAMES FINDLAY. Witn: GRIFFIN YEATMAN, THOS. FLOO JR. rec 1814. pp 170, 171

Deed dated 1813. JOEL WILLIAM & PHEBY his wife of Cincinnati to JOSEPH VANHORN. S 5, T 3, R 2. Signed JOEL WILLIAM, PHEBE WILLIAMS. Witn: JOHN MAHARD, JAMES GIBSON. rec 1814. pp 171, 172, 173

Deed dated 1813. STEPHEN CAMPBELL of Ross Twp to FRANCIS KELSHAMMER (or HELSHAMMER) of same. S 33, R 3, R 2. Signed STEPHEN CAMPBELL. Witn: JUDAH WILLEY. rec 1814. pp 173, 174

BUTLER COUNTY LAND RECORDS: BOOK D

Deed dated 1814. MOSES CRUME, JOHN MARKS, GEORGE EARHART, MICHAEL EARHART as atty for JOHN DOUGHTY, SAMUEL ROBBINS and JACOB HUFFMAN to JOHN WITHROW. S 34, T 3, R 3. Signed MOSES CRUME (and his wife) SARAH CRUME, JOHN MARKS (and his wife) REBECCA MARKS, GEORGE EARHART (and his wife) MARY EARHART, MICHAEL EARHART (german script), SAMUEL ROBBINS (and his wife) JANE ROBBINS, JACOB HOFFMAN (and his wife) ELIZABETH HOFFMAN. Witn: NATHAN STUBBS, MATTH. RICHARDSON. rec 1814. pp 17, 175, 176

Deed dated 1814. WILLIAM SIMONTON of Middletown to EZEKIEL McCLURE of same. ▪lot 49▪. Signed WM. SIMONTON. Witn: JOHN HUESTON, ROBT. BROWN. rec 1814. pp 176, 177

Deed dated 1812. AARON VAIL, exctr of STEPHEN VAIL, to SAMUEL McCLURE. Middletown lot 37. Signed AARON VAIL. Witn: JOHN HUESTON, EZEKIEL McCLURE. rec 1814. pp 177, 178, 179

Deed dated 1814. WILLIAM HERBERT & ELEANOR of Rossville to JOHN NELSON of same. Rossville lots 83, 88. Signed WILLIAM HERBERT, ELEANOR HERBERT. Witn: AZUR R. MILLS, JAMES MILLS. rec 1814. pp 179, 180

Mortgage dated 1813. WILLIAM CURRYER to PHILIP MUCHNER. S 22, T 3, R 3. Signed WILLIAM CURRYER. Witn: P. WILLIAMSON, SALEM POCOCK. rec 1814. pp 180, 181

Deed dated 1813. JAMES ARMSTRONG & ISABELLA his wife to JOHN HIGGINS BROWN ARMSTRONG, an infant, if he lives to 21 yrs; if deceased before 21, to SARAH B. ADAMSON of Hamilton Co. Hamilton lots 57 & 135. Signed JAMES ARMSTRONG, ISABELLA (x) ARMSTRONG. Witn: SAMUEL J. BROWN, ENOS WILLIAMS. rec 1814. pp 182, 183

Deed dated 1814. AUDITORS of Court to JOSEPH F. RANDOLPH. RUFUS ENYART obtained judgement against NATHANIEL MARTIN. Seized S 9, T 2, R 3. Signed WM. MURRAY, JOHN SUTHERLAND, JAMES McBRIDE. Witn: JOHN REILY, DAVID LATHAM. rec 1814. p 183, 184, 185, 186

Deed dated 1814. DANIEL THOMPSON of Licking Co to JOSEPH F. RANDOLPH. S 9, T 2, R 3. Signed DANIEL THOMPSON. Witn: ANDERSON SPENCER, JOHN REILY. rec 1814. pp 186, 187

Deed dated 1813. JOHN VANNICE & ELIZABETH his wife to ISAAC PAXTON. S 11, T 2, R 3. Signed JOHN

BUTLER COUNTY LAND RECORDS: BOOK D

VANNICE, ELIZABETH (x) VANNICE. Witn: HENRY WEAVER, JAMES McGINNIS. rec 1814. pp 187, 188, 189

Power of Attorney dated 1814. CHRISTIAN BORTH, soldier in 19th Regt, US Infantry at Hamilton, appted Lt. GEORGE W. STALL as atty to recover sums from PETER LOVE of Cincinnati, GEORGE WALKER of same, JOHN SUTHERLAND "and other persons". Signed CHRISTIAN BORTH. Witn: J.C. McMANIS, JOHN SIMMONS. rec 1814. pp 189, 190

Deed dated 1813. MATTHIAS ROLL & MARY his wife to JOSEPH ROLL. S 13, T 4, R 1. Signed MATTHIAS ROLL, MARY ROLL. Witn: JAMES JOHNSTON, SARAH JOHNSTON. rec 1814. pp 190,191

Deed dated 1813. JOSEPH KITCHELL & RACHEL his wife to DAVID BAKER, both of Hamilton Co. S 13, T 4, R 1. Signed JOSEPH KITCHELL, RACHEL KITCHELL. Witn: EPHRAIM SCUDDER, JOSEPH THOMPSON. rec 1814. pp 191, 192

Deed dated 1813. SAMUEL ENYART & ANNA his wife to LEVI WALLER. Princetown lot 6. Signed SAMUEL ENYART, ANNA ENYART. Witn: JAMES MURPHY, JOHN AYERS. rec 1814. pp 192, 193

Deed dated 1813. JACOB L. CONKLING to AARON AUSTIN. Princetown lot 4. Signed JACOB L. CONKLING. Witn: JOHN BREES, JOHN AYERS. rec 1814. pp 193, 194

Deed dated 1813. DAVID GIBSON & AGNES DAVIS, admtrs of JOHN DAVIS of Hamilton Co to SAMUEL DAVIS. John and Samuel, tenants in common on S 14 & 15, T 1, R 2; in 1802, at Colerain Twp, Hamilton Co, John gave a quitclaim. He died, leaving minor heirs; in 1813, title can be conveyed. Signed DAVID GIBSON, AGNES (x) DAVIS. Witn: JOHN REILY, JAC. BURNET. rec 1814. pp 194, 195, 196, 197

Deed dated 1812. AARON VAIL, exctr of STEPHEN VAIL, to JOHN HUESTON. Middletown lot 35. Purchased 1808 before SV died. Signed AARON VAIL. Witn: SAMUEL POWELL. rec 1814. pp 197, 198, 199

Deed dated 1813. JOHN HUESTON to WILLIAM HARVEY. Middletown lot 35. Signed JOHN HUESTON. Witn: WALTER THOMAS, THOMAS M. FOO. rec 1814. p 199

Deed dated 1813. JACOB CLARK & SALLY his wife of Lemon Twp to WILLIAM HARVEY. Middletown lot 39. Signed JACOB CLARK, SALLY (x) CLARK. Witn: JP

BUTLER COUNTY LAND RECORDS: BOOK D

JAMES CLARK, JAMES BARNET. rec 1814. pp 199, 200, 201

Deed dated 1813. HENRY WEAVER & SUSAN his wife to THOMAS POWERS. S 27 & 28, T 2, R 4. Signed HENRY WEAVER, SUSAN WEAVER. Witn: ISAAC HOFF, WM. HARVEY. rec 1814. pp 201, 202

Deed dated 1813. WILLIAM OGLE & ELIZAH his wife to WILLIAM DOUGLASS. S 2 7 28, T 2, R 4. Bound by land of CONROD DARR, ROBERT OGLE. Signed WILLIAM OGLE, ELIZA (x) OGLE. Witn: MATTH. RICHARDSON, SAMUEL YOUNG. rec 1814. pp 202, 203

Deed dated 1813. SIMEON BROADBERRY to JOSEPH HAINS. S 27, T 5, R 2. Signed SIMEON BROADBERRY. Witn: JESSE SIMPSON, JOSEPH GRAY, MATTH. RICHARDSON. rec 1814. pp 204, 205

Deed dated 1813. JOHN MATSON & MARY his wife of Hamilton Co to EVAN JONES. S 31, T 3, R 2. Signed JOHN MATSON, MARY MATSON. Witn: JP JAMES SILVER, PALLAS MORGAN. rec 1814. pp 205, 206

Deed dated 1812. ALBIN SHAW & EUNICE his wife to JUSTUS KIRBY. S 33, T 3, R 2. Signed ALBIN SHAW, EUNICE SHAW. Witn: WARREN (x) HUNGERFORD, JUDAH WILLEY. rec 1814. pp 206, 207

Deed dated 1813. RICHARD WATTS & ELICE his wife to BENJAMIN BRIDGE. S 22, T 2, R 4. Bound by land of DAVID HEATON, EMMA QUICK. Signed RICHARD (x) WATTS, ELICE (x) WATTS. Witn: PLATT B. DICKSON, ISRAEL WATTS. rec 1814. pp 208, 209

Mortgage dated 1814. Admtrs of ISRAEL LUDLOW to JAMES McBRIDE. Hamilton lot 110, ordered by Orphan's Court. Signed JOHN LUDLOW for CHARLOTTE CHAMBERS RISK & JAMES FINDLAY, JOHN LUDLOW for himself. Witn: JOHN REILY, JOHN WHITWORTH. rec 1814. pp 209, 210

Deed dated 1814. SHOBAL VAIL & MARY his wife to THOMAS MACKLIN. Middletown lot 25. Signed SHOBAL VAIL, MARY VAIL. Witn: HUGH VAIL, EZEKIEL BALL. rec 1814. pp 210, 211

Deed dated 1814. SAMUEL SMITH of Philadelphia, guardian of minor heirs of ROBERT IRVIN of same, by his atty DAVID K. ESTE to CLARKSON FREEMAN of Lancaster Co, PA. No S-T-R; land in Madison Twp bound by ELIJAH BRUSH's property. Signed DAVID K. ESTE. Witn: JAMES HEATON, JAMES SMITH. rec 1814. pp 211, 212, 213

BUTLER COUNTY LAND RECORDS: BOOK D

Deed dated 1812. AARON VAIL, exctr of STEPHEN VAIL, to ELISHA WADE. SV died 1808, leaving minor heirs. Signed AARON VAIL. Witn: JOHN VANSICLE, HUGH VAIL. rec 1814. pp 213, 214, 215

Deed dated 1813. WILLIAM REED & REBECKAH his wife to ISRAEL WATTS. No S-T-R: bound by land of ADAM DICKEY. Signed WILLIAM REED, REBECKAH (x) REED. Witn: DAVID MULFORD, WILLIAM HARVEY. rec 1814. pp 215, 216

Deed dated 1814. ROBERT TAYLOR & CATY his wife to JOHN SUTHERLAND. Rossville lots 23, 28, 33, 38. Signed ROBERT TAYLOR, CATY TAYLOR. Witn: ISAAC STANLEY, JAMES P. RAMSEY. rec 1814. pp 216, 217

Deed dated 1814. Heirs of WILLIAM MARKS to GEORGE EARHEART. S 34, T 3, R 3. Bound by land of - PRICE, JAMES WITHROW, JOHN WITHROW. Signed MOSES CRUME, JOHN MARKS, MICHAEL EARHEART (german script), JACOB (x) HOFFMAN, SAMUEL ROBINS, SARAH CRUME, REBECCA (x) MARKS, ELIZABETH (x) HOFFMAN, JANE (x) ROBINS. Witn: NATHAN STUBBS, MATTH. RICHARDSON. rec 1814. pp 218, 219

Mortgage dated 1813. SAMUEL BOUM of Milford Twp to DANIEL PERRY of same. S 3, T 5, R 2. Bound by land of JAMES EMMERSON, JONATHAN COOPER. Signed SAMUEL BOUM. Witn: MARSH WILLIAMS, BENJAMIN BOUM. rec 1814. pp 220, 221

Deed dated 1810. SAMUEL ENYART & ANNA to JOHN HUTSON. Hamilton lot 89. Signed SAMUEL ENYART, ANNA ENYART. Witn: JOHN VINNEDGE, ROSANNAH VINNEDGE. rec 1814. pp 221, 222, 223

Deed dated 1814. JOHN JOHNSON & ELIZABETH his wife to WILLIAM MURRAY in trust for ELIZABETH FLEMING, late McCULLOUGH. S 7, T 4, R 2. Signed JOHN JOHNSTON, ELIZABETH (x) JOHNSTON. Witn: JAMES JOHNSTON, JONATHAN LIMPUS. rec 1814. pp 223, 224

Deed dated 1814. WILLIAM STEWART of Hanover Twp to PHILIP SHAFER of same. S 32, T 4, R 2. Signed WM. STUART. Witn: SAMUEL RAINEY, JP JOHN RAINEY. rec 1804. pp 224, 225

Deed dated 1810. JOHN SUTHERLAND & HENRY BROWN to JAMES SMITH GREER. Rossville lot 19. Signed JOHN SUTHERLAND, HENRY BROWN. Witn: JAMES STEELE, JAMES BECK. rec 1814. pp 225, 226

BUTLER COUNTY LAND RECORDS: BOOK D

Deed datd 1813. WILLIAM WELLS of Springfield, Muskingum Co to ELEANOR GREER. S 28, T 2, R 2. Signed WILLIAM WELLS. Witn: JOHN REILY, WM. G. ARMSTRONG. rec 1814. pp 227, 228

Deed dated 1814. HUGH B. HAWTHORN to WILLIAM ROBESON. Hamilton lot 123. Signed HUGH B. HAWTHORN. Witn: ISAAC STANLEY, SAMUEL GRAY. rec 1814. pp 228, 229

Deed dated 1814. ABRAHAM FREEMAN JR & CATY his wife to MICHAEL HAGERMAN. S 35, T 3, R 3. Signed ABRAHAM FREEMAN, CATY FREEMAN. Witn: ROSANNAH (x) VINNEDGE, JOHN VINNEDGE. rec 1814. pp 229, 230

Deed dated 1813. JOEL WILLIAMS & PHEBE his wife of Cincinnati to HENRY MILLER. S 20, R 2 in Liberty Twp. Signed JOEL WILLIAMS, PHEBE WILLIAMS. Witn: JACOB IRWIN, JOHN MAHARD. rec 1814. pp 231, 232

Deed dated 1813. HIRAM MARTIN To WILLIAM NICOL of Cincinnati. S 13, T 4, R 2. Signed HIRAM MARTIN. Witn: JONAH MARTIN, ETHAN STONE. rec 1814. pp 232, 233

Deed dated 1814. JOHN SUTHERLAND & NANCY his wife to YORK FREEMAN (a man of color). Lot 5 in S 1, T 1, R 3. Signed JOHN SUTHERLAND, NANCY R. SUTHERLAND. Witn: JAMES HEATON, ISAAC STANLEY. rec 1814. pp 233, 234, 235

Deed dated 1813. JOSEPH HOUGH & JANE his wife to MATTHEW WINTON. Hamilton lot 84. Signed JOSEPH HOUGH, JANE HOUGH. Witn: ROBERT WINTON, JAMES McBRIDE. rec 1814. pp 235, 236

Deed dated 1814. MATTHEW WINTON & ELIZABETH his wife to ROBERT WINTON. S 5, T 2, R 3. Signed MATTHEW WINTON, ELIZA WINTON. Witn: EDWARD CORNTHWAITE, WM. BROWN. rec 1814. pp 236, 237, 238

Deed dated 1813. GARRET VANNEST & JANE his wife to ALBERT BANTA of Warren Co. S 12, T 2, R 4. Signed GARUT VANNEST, JANE VANNEST. Witn: SAML CAMPBELL, JAMES W. LANIER. rec 1814. pp 238, 239

Deed dated 1813. MOSES VAIL & MARY his wife of Warren Co to ALBERT BANTA of same. S 12, T 2, R 4. Signed MOSES VAIL, MARY VAIL. Witn: CHARLES LANG, J. W. LANIER. rec 1814. pp 240, 241

BUTLER COUNTY LAND RECORDS: BOOK D

Deed dated 1813. THOMAS KYLE & SARAH his wife to DANIEL WOODMANSEE. S 28, T 3, R 3. Signed THOMAS KYLE, SARAH KYLE. Witn: SAMUEL KYLE, P. WILLIAMSON. rec 1814. pp 241, 242

Deed dated 1814. JOHN SUTHERLAND & NANCY his wife and ABRAHAM HUFF & MAGDALANE his wife to FRANCIS WALDRON. S 2, T 1, R 4 & S 32, T 2, R 4. Signed JOHN SUTHERLAND, NANCY R. SUTHERLAND, ABRAHAM HUFF, MAGDALANE (x) HUFF. Witn: HENRY WEAVER, JAMES MILLS. rec 1814. pp 243, 244

Deed dated 1814. ISAAC HOFF & CATHARINE his wife to JOHN GUNCKLE. Money to be paid by JOHN GUNCKLE or PATTEN BROCAW. S 29, T 2, R 4. Signed ISAAC HOFF, CATHARINE HOFF. Witn: #1 (german script), HENRY WEAVER. rec 1814. pp 244, 245

Plat dated 1814. Darrtown in S 28, T 5, R 2. CONRAD DARR, proprietor. Witn: MATTH. RICHARDSON. rec 1814. pp 246, 247

Deed dated 1814. JOHN SUTHERLAND & NANCY his wife to ABRAHAM HUFF. S 2, T 1, R 4. Signed JOHN SUTHERLAND, NANCY R. SUTHERLAND. Witn: JOHN E. SCOTT, JAMES MILLS. rec 1814. pp 247, 248

Deed dated 1814. SHOBAL VAIL & MARY his wife to JOHN WINGATE of Hamilton Co. Middletown lot 25. Signed SHOBAL VAIL, MARY VAIL. Witn: RANDAL VAIL, JAMES AYERS. rec 1814. pp 248, 249

Deed dated 1814. JOHN GREER & <u>ELEANOR</u> to JACOB RICKART. S 28, T 2, R 2. Signed JOHN GREER, <u>ELINOR</u> GREER. Witn: ISAAC STANLEY, JOHN McGONIGLE. rec 1814. pp 249, 250

Deed dated 1814. JACOB RICKART & DELILAH his wife to ELEANOR GREER. S 38, T 2, R 2. Signed JACOB RICKART, DELILAH RICKART. Witn: ISAAC STANLEY, JOHN McGONIGLE. rec 1814. pp 250, 251

Deed dated 1813. HENRY MILLER & EVE to JAMES DALRIMPLE. S 20, T 3, R 2. Signed HENRY (x) MILLER, EVE (x) MILLER. Witn: BESEY DRESKELL, JP MICHAEL AYERS. rec 1814. pp 251, 252, 253

Deed dated 1804. DANIEL PAUGH, DANIEL PRINE, MICHAEL AYERS, JAMES THOMPSON and DAVID <u>LEMMON</u> to JOSEPH McMAHON. S 21, T 3, R 2. Signed DAVID LAYMAN, MICHAEL AYERS, DAN'L PRINE, DAN'L PAUGH, JAMES THOMPSON. Witn:

BUTLER COUNTY LAND RECORDS: BOOK D

JOHN SHINER, HENRY RUNYAN. rec 1814. pp 253, 254

Deed dated 1813. NICHOLAS WHITINGER & SARAH his wife to JOHN KNIPE of Wayne Co, Indiana Ter'y. S 19, T 3. R 3. Bound by land of SILAS GARRISON, SAMUEL DAREIS. JOHN KIRKPATRICK. Signed NICHOLAS WHITINGER, SARAH (x) WHITINGER. Witn: JACOB WHITINGER, BROWN WILSON. rec 1814. pp 255, 256

Deed dated 1814. JOHN KNIPE & SOPHIA his wife of Butler Co to BENJAMIN HINDS of PA. S 19, T 3, R 3. Signed JOHN KNIPE, SOPHIA (x) KNIPE. Witn: SAML DAVIS, CHARLES SWEARINGEN. rec 1814. pp 256, 257, 258

Deed dated 1814. JOSEPH WILLIAMSON & MARY his wife to JOHN R. SCHENCK. S 15, T 2, R 4. Signed JOSEPH WILLIAMSON, MARY (x) WILLIAMSON. Witn: EZEKIEL BALL, CHRENEYANCE SCHENCK. rec 1814. pp 258, 259

Deed dated 1814. THOMAS COEN & NANCY his wife to SAMUEL BROWN. S 31, T 3, R 2. Bound by land of MAURICE JONES, WILLIAM D. JONES, JOSEPH BROWN, EDWARD COEN. Signed THOMAS (x) COEN, NANCY COEN. Witn: WM D. JONES, EDWARD COEN. rec 1814. pp 260, 261

Deed dated 1814. GEORGE KELLY & ELIZABETH his wife to ELIJAH HORNER, weaver. S 1, T 3, R 3. Signed GEORGE KELLY, ELIZABETH (x) KELLY. Witn: DANIEL PAGE, JACOB OVERPECK. rec 1814. pp 261, 262

Deed dated 1813. USA to SAMUEL HUNT of Warren Co. S 2, T 3, R 3. pp 262, 263

Deed dated 181. SHOBAL VAIL & MARY his wife to JOHN CUMMINGS. S 28, T 2, R 4. Witn: RANDAL VAIL, JAMES AYERS. rec 1814. pp 263, 264

Quitclaim dated 1813. ROBERT CORRICK & RUTH his wife to JOHN MALLORY. Paymt on S 19, T 2, R 4 made by DAVID REED, "late of Butler Co". Signed ROBERT (x) CORRICK, RUTH (x) CORRICK. Witn: JP JAMES CLARK, JAMES TANNEHILL. rec 1814. pp 265, 266

Deed dated 1814. SAMUEL POTTINGER & SARAH his wife to BENONY GOBLE. S 36, T 3, R 3. Signed SAMUEL POTTINGER, SARAH (x) POTTINGER. Witn: SAMUEL POTTINGER JR, ABNER GOBLE. rec 1814. pp 266, 267

Deed dated 1814. ELIAS BOUDINOT by his atty JACOB BURNET to JOHN LARIMORE. S 14, T 2, R 4. Signed

BUTLER COUNTY LAND RECORDS: BOOK D

ELIAS BOUDINOT by JAC. BURNET. Witn: JAMES SMITH, WILLIAM WALLACE. rec 1814. pp 268, 269

Deed date 1806. USA to JOSEPH LORIMORE of Hamilton Co. S 14, T 2, R 4. rec 1814. p 269

Deed dated 1814. JAMES ROBESON & JANE to JOHN P. FINKLE. S 8, T 2, R 4. Signed JAMES ROBISON, JANE ROBISON. Witn: JAMES CLARK, JAMES ROBISON JR. rec 1814. pp 270, 271

Deed dated 1814. JOHN GREER & ELEANOR his wife to HUGH B. HAWTHORN & JACOB BAYMILLER of Cincinnati. Hamilton lots 111, 112. Signed JOHN GREER. ELINOR GREER. Witn: ISABELLA GREER, ISAAC STANLEY. rec 1814. pp 271, 272

Deed dated 1814. SHOBAL VAIL & MARY his wife to WILLIAM SIMONTON. Middletown lot 46. Signed SHOBAL VAIL, MARY VAIL. Witn: HUGH VAIL, THOMAS CILLEY. rec 1814. pp 273, 274

Deed dated 1814. SHOBAL VAIL & MARY his wife to WILLIAM SIMONTON. Middletown lots 29 & 30. Signed SHOBAL VAIL, MARY VAIL. Witn: HUGH VAIL, THOMAS McLARN. rec 1814. pp 274, 275

Deed dated 1813. THOMAS HUNTER, tax collector of Fairfield Twp to DANIEL SEWARD. Hamilton lot 40. Signed THOMAS HUNTER. Witn: ISAAC STANLEY, THOMAS STONE. rec 1814. pp 276, 277

Deed dated 1814. DRAKE RANDOLPH & SARAH his wife of Fairfield Twp to NIMROD RANDOLPH of same. Land formerly belonged to SAMUEL RANDOLPH of NJ, given by will to Drake Randolph. S 24, T 2, R 2. Signed DRAKE RANDOLPH, SARAH RANDOLPH. Witn: JOHN AYERS, LEWIS ENYART. rec 1814. pp 277, 278

Deed dated 1813. DAVID K. ESTE & STEPHEN CRANE, admtrs of DAVID SLOAN, to THOMAS C. KELSEY & WILLARD M. SMITH. Hamilton lot 25. Signed DAVID K. ESTE, STEPHEN CRANE. Witn: D. WADE, WM. CORRY. rec 1814. pp 278, 279, 280

Deed dated 1814. ROBERT FLEMING to JAMES WARD. S 12, T 2, R 2. Signed ROBT. FLEMING. Witn: DANL. MILLIKIN, DANIEL WOODMAYER. rec 1814. pp 280, 281

Deed dated 1814. GEORGE LOY & NANCY his wife to BENJAMIN I. DUBOIS. S 5, T 1, R 5. Signed GEORGE LOY

BUTLER COUNTY LAND RECORDS: BOOK D

(german script), NANCY (x) LOY. Witn: DANIEL DuBOIS, J. W. LANIER. rec 1814. pp 281, 282, 283

Deed dated 1814. SAMUEL CALDWELL & ELIZABETH his wife of Warren Co to GEORGE LOY. S 32, T 2, R 5. Signed SAMUEL CALDWELL, ELIZABETH CALDWELL. Witn: DANIEL DuBOIS, J. W. LANIER. rec 1814. pp 284, 285

Deed dated 1814. JAMES TAPSCOTT to JOHN N.C. SCHENCK admtrs of JOHN CHAMBERLAIN to GEORGE LOY. S 32, T 2. R 5. Signed JAMES TAPSCOTT, JOHN N.C. SCHENCK. Witn: HELENA LANIER, J.W. LANIER. rec 1814. pp 285, 286.287

Deed dated 1813. JAMES RUGLASS & ELIZABETH his wife of Lemon Twp to JOHN KERR of same. S 7, T 2, R 4. Signed JAMES RUGLASS, ELIZABETH (x) RUGLASS. Witn: JAMES STEWART, HENRY (x) BOWLING. rec 1814. pp 287, 288

Deed dated 1812. DANIEL SKINNER & ISABEL his wife of Warren Co to ABRAHAM HARTZEL. S 20, T 3, R 2. Signed DANIEL SKINNER, ISSABEL SKINNER. Witn: JONAH TAYLOR, JP MICH'L AYERS. rec 1814. pp 289, 290

Deed dated 1814. ANDREW CORNELIUSON of Wayne Twp to JAMES SHARARD of same. S 24, T 3, R 3. Signed ANDREW CORNELIUSON. Witn: MASH (x) CORNELIUSON, SAMUEL HUNT. rec 1814. pp 290, 291

Deed dated 1814. ANDREW CORNELIUSON of Wayne Twp to MASH CORNELIUSON of same. S 24, T 3, R 3. Signed ANDREW CORNELIUSON. Witn: JAMES SHERARD, SAMUEL HUNT. rec 1814. pp 291, 292

Deed dated 1814. ANDREW CORNELIUSON of Wayne Twp to GEORGE HATFIELD. S 24, T 3, R 3. Signed ANDREW CORNELIUSON. Witn: MASH (x) CORNELIUSON, SAMUEL HUNT. rec 1814. pp 293, 294

Deed dated 1810. USA to ANDREW CORNELIUSON, assignee of JONATHAN ROBINS. S 23, T 3, R 3. rec 1814. p 295

Deed dated 1812. JOHN THOMPSON & MARY his wife to NATHAN STUBBS. S 2, T 3, R 3. Signed JOHN THOMPSON, MARY (x) THOMPSON. Witn: JESSE OVERMAN, SAMUEL HUNT. rec 1814. pp 295, 296

Deed dated 1814. HENRY THOMPSON & NANCY his wife to LEWIS LAING. Rossville lot 3. Signed HENRY THOMPSON, NANCY (x) THOMPSON. Witn: ISAAC STANLEY, JAS. WITSON. rec 1814. pp 296, 297

BUTLER COUNTY LAND RECORDS: BOOK D

Deed dated 1800. JOHN SUTHERLAND & NANCY his wife to HENRY THOMPSON. Rossville lot 3. Signed JOHN SUTHERLAND, NANCY R. SUTHERLAND. Witn: HUGH B. HAWTHORN WM. MURRAY. rec 1814. pp 297, 298, 299

Deed dated 1814. SAMUEL JONES & MARY his wife of Miami Co to NATHAN STUBBS. S 3, T 3, R 3. Signed SAMUEL JONES, MARY JONES. Witn: THOS. T. MOORE, SAMUEL HUNT. rec 1814. pp 299, 300

Deed dated 1813. JOHN DAVIS SR of Milford Twp to JOHN DAVIS JR. S 6, T 5, R 2. Signed JOHN (x) DAVIS. Witn: JOHN HAMMER, MARSH WILLIAMS. rec 1814. pp 300, 301

Deed dated 1813. JOHN V.L. DAVIS to DAVID GRIFFIS. S 32, T 3, R 3. Signed JOHN V.L. DAVIS. Witn: RICHD. HALL, JOSEPH TREEN. rec 1814. pp 301, 302

Deed dated 1814. ISAAC STANLEY to ELEANOR GREER. Hamilton lot 162. Signed ISAAC STANLEY. Witn: JAMES MILLS, JOHN REILY. rec 1814. pp 302, 303, 304

Deed dated 1806. ELEANOR MOORE to ELEANOR GREER, wife of JOHN GREER *one of the daus of said Eleanor*. Hamilton lots 111, 112. Signed ELEANOR (x) MOORE. Witn: JOHN REILY, THOS. McCULLOUGH. rec 1814. pp 304, 305

Deed dated 1814. WILLIAM PLASKET of the Indiana Ter'y, atty for heirs of WILLIAM PLASKET, to JOHN CUMMINS. Heirs: WILLIAM PLASKET, SAMUEL PLASKET, ROBERT L. PLASKET, JOHN FISLER & ELIZABETH his wife, JOHN KELLY & MARTHER his wife. S 18, T 3, R 2. Signed WILLIAM PLASKET, *atty for heirs at law of WILLIAM PLASKET, decd*. Witn: JP THO. HIGGINS, EZEKIEL McAULEY. rec 1814. pp 305, 306

Deed dated 1814. WILLIAM PLASKET of the Indiana Ter'y, atty for heirs of WILLIAM PLASKET, to JAMES CUMMINS. S 18, T 3, R 2. Signed and witn as above. rec 1814. pp 307, 308

Power of Attorney dated 1813. SAMUEL PLASKET et al, residing in Clark Co, IN Ter'y, appt WILLIAM PLASKET as atty to convey land in S 18, T 3, R 2. Signed SAMUEL PLASKET, ROBT. L. PLASKET, JOHN FISLER, ELIZABETH FISLER, JOHN KELLY, MARTHA KELLY. Witn: JOHN FISLER. rec 1814. pp 308, 309

Deed dated 1814. WILLIAM McCINSTRAY & CATY his wife

BUTLER COUNTY LAND RECORDS: BOOK D

to BENJAMIN D. DAVIS. S 4, T 3, R 2. Bound by JOHN McCINSTRAY' land. Signed WILLIAM (x) McKINSTRY, CATY (x) McKINSTRY. Witn: ISAAC STANLEY, ROBERT TAYLER. rec 1814. pp 309, 310

Deed dated 1813. JOHN SUTHERLAND & NANCY his wife to NICHOLAS HORNER. Hamilton lot 37. Signed JOHN SUTH- ERLAND, NANCY R. SUTHERLAND. Witn: JOHN BAXTER, ISAAC STANLEY. rec 1814. pp 310, 311

Deed dated 1814. SAMUEL STITES & WILLIAM GOUDY of Green Co to JOHN McCLEAN. S 12, T - R 3, adjoined by land of heirs of WIDOW LOWRY, dec, & JAMES STUART. Signed SAMUEL STITES, WILLIAM GOUDY. Witn: JAMES CLARK, WILLIAM H. CLARK. rec 1814. pp 312, 313

Deed dated 1813. EDWARD DYER & JANE his wife of Montgomery Co to OWEN HATFIELD of same. S 8, T 4, R 2. Signed EDWARD DYER, JANE DYER. Witn: JAMES RUSSELL, WHITELY HATFIELD. rec 1814. pp 313, 314

Deed dated 1813. MATTHEW HUESTON & CATHARINE his wife to JOHN SUTHERLAND. S 1, T 1, R 3, lots 11 & 16. Signed M. HUESTON, CATHARENE HUESTON. Witn: DAN. MILLIKIN, NANCY REILY. rec 1814. pp 314, 315, 316

Deed dated 1813. JOHN SUTHERLAND & NANCY his wife to HENRY BROWN of Dayton. Rossville lots 55, 56. Signed JOHN SUTHERLAND, NANCY R. SUTHERLAND. Witn: DANL. MILLIKIN, JAMES L. RAMSEY. rec 1814. pp 316, 317

Quitclaim dated 1814. ANTHONY LOGAN & JANE his wife, JAMES McCLURE, MARTHA McCLURE and DAVID McCLURE & RUTHY his wife, all of Montgomery Co to JOHN McCLURE. S 25, T 2, R 4. Signed ANTHONY LOGAN, JANE LOGAN, JAMES McCLURE, MARTHA McCLURE, DAVID McCLURE, RUTHY McCLURE. Witn: JOHN McCLURE JR, ROBERT ELLIOT. rec 1814. pp 317, 318, 319

Deed dated 1814. ALLEN CULLUM to ROBERT LEGISON. S 25, T 3, R 3. Signed ALLEN CULLUM. Witn: JOHN AYERS, SAMUEL ENYART. rec 1814. pp 319, 320

Deed dated 1814. JACOB LINE & RUTH his wife to JOHN SUTHERLAND. S 26, T 2, R 3. Signed JACOB LINE, RUTH (x) LINE. Witn: JAMES HEATON, ISAAC STANLEY. rec 1814. pp 320, 321

Deed dated 1814. USA to WILLIAM PHARES. S 10, T 3, R 3. rec 1814. pp 321, 322

BUTLER COUNTY LAND RECORDS: BOOK D

Deed dated 1813. MELYN BAKER & PRUDENCE his wife to SAMUEL WOODMANSEE. S 33, T 3, R 3. Bound by BENJAMIN SCUDDER's land. Signed MELYN BAKER, PRUDENCE (x) BAKER. Witn: JP JOHN AYERS, BETSEY (x) AYERS. rec 1814. pp 322, 323

Deed dated 1814. WILLIAM McCLELLAN & MARY his wife to JOHN SUTHERLAND. S 32, T 2, R 3; formerly owned by JAMES WILKINS. Signed WILLIAM McCLELLAN, MARY McCLELLAN. Witn: DAVID VANCE, ISAAC STANLEY. rec 1814. pp 323, 324, 325

Deed dated 1814. JOHN CLEVES SYMMES to ELLIS JOHN. S 14, T 3, R 2. Signed JOHN CLEVES SYMMES. Witn: THOMAS HENDERSON, GRIFFIN YEATMAN. rec 1814. pp 325, 326

Deed dated 1813. EDWARD MECKS & DOROTHEA his wife to THOMAS JOHNS. S 23, T 3, R 2. Bound by land of WILLIAM HARPER, STEPHEN GANO, WILLIAM ELLIOTT, SAML D. BROWN. Signed EDWARD MEEKS, DOROTHEA (x) MEEKS. Witn: JAMES LYON, JACOB ARNOLD. rec 1814. pp 326, 327

Deed dated 1813. SAMUEL D. BOWMAN & CHARLOTTY his wife to THOMAS JOHNS. S 23, T 3, R 2. Signed SAMUEL D. BOWMAN, CHARLOTTY (x) BOWMAN. Witn: MICHAEL AYERS, RICHARD BOWMAN. rec 1814. pp 327, 328

Deed dated 1814. SAMUEL DICK & MARTHA his wife to JAMES MILLS. Rossville lot 26. Signed SAMUEL DICK, MARTHA DICK. Witn: THOS. BLAIR, ISAAC STANLEY. rec 1814. pp 328, 329, 330

Deed dated 1814. JAMES MILLS & SARAH of Rossville to GEORGE W. STALL. Rossville lot 4. Signed JAMES MILLS, SARAH MILLS. Witn: GEORGE KENNARD, ISAAC STANLEY. rec 1814. pp 330, 331

Deed dated 1814. THOMAS DONNALD & ELIZABETH his wife to MOSES BREES. S 3, T 2, R 3. Signed THOMAS DONNALD ELIZABETH DONNALD. Witn: WM. HUNT, JOHN VINNEDGE. rec 1814. pp 331, 332, 333

Deed dated 1814. JAMES RUSSELL & ESTHER his wife to MARY RUSSELL. S 10, T 2, R 4. Bound by land of MEEKER SQUIRE, purchased from JOSEPH PARKS. Signed JAMES RUSSELL, ESTHER (x) RUSSELL. Witn: EZEKIEL BALL, SHOBAL VAIL. rec 1814. pp 333, 334

Deed dated 1813. REBECCA CORNELL to JAMES McCLEMROCK Rossville lot 71. (Deed book reversed order of buyer

BUTLER COUNTY LAND RECORDS: BOOK D

& seller) Signed JAMES McCARNMROCK. Witn: WILLIAM CORNELL, JAMES SMITH. rec 1814. pp 334, 335, 336

Deed dated 1813. JAMES MILLS & SARAH to AZZUR REED MILLS. Rossville lot 61. Signed JAMES MILLS, SARAH MILLS. Witn: DANL. MILLIKIN, ALEXANDER SACKETT. rec 1814. pp 336, 337

Deed dated 1813. DAVID FRAZER & SARAH his wife to THOMAS ALBRED of Preble Co. S 5, T 5, R 2. Signed DAVID FRAZER, SARAH (x) FRAZER. Witn: MARSH WILLIAMS, A. HAMMES. rec 1814. pp 337, 338, 339

Deed dated 1814. DAVID K. ESTE & STEPHEN CRANE, admtrs of DAVID SLOAN, to DANIEL SEWARD. Hamilton lot 39. Signed DAVID K. ESTE, STEPHEN CRANE. Witn: D. WADE, WM. CORRY. rec 1814. pp 339, 340

Deed dated 1814. JONATHAN LINE & JOANNA to JOHN LINE. S 27, T 2, R 3. Signed JONTHAN LINE, JOHANNAH (x) LINE. Witn: HANNAH (x) BURK, ISAAC STANLEY. rec 1814. pp 340, 341, 342

Deed dated 1814. ABSOLEM GOODENOUGH & SARAH his wife to GEORGE W. STALL, US Army. Hamilton lot 3. Signed ABSOLEM GOODENOUGH, SARAH (x) GOODENOUGH. Witn: WM. WALLACE, ISAAC MOSS. rec 1814. pp 342, 343

Deed dated 1814. ISAAC MOSS to GEORGE W. STALL of US Army. Hamilton lots 187, 188. Signed ISAAC MOSS. Witn: JAMES HEATON, ISAAC STANLEY. rec 1814. pp 343, 344

Deed dated 1812. JOHN CLEVES SYMMES to DANIEL SYMMES of Cincinnati. S 9, T 2, R 2. Signed JOHN CLEVES SYMMES. Witn: H. GOODWIN, JOHN TIBLELS. rec 1814. pp 344, 345, 346

Deed dated 1813. CELADON SYMMES & JOSEPH RANDOLPH, admtrs of WILLIAM SYMMES, to DANIEL SYMMES. S 9, T 2, R 2. Signed CELADON SYMMES, JOSEPH F. RANDOLPH. Witn: ALEXANDER IRWIN, DANIEL F. SYMMES. rec 1814. pp 346, 347

Deed dated 1814. SAMUEL C. VANCE & MARY, his wife of Cincinnati to CLARKSON FREEMAN of PA. No S-T-R; land in Madison Twp. Signed SAM. C. VANCE, MARY M. VANCE. Witn: STEPHEN WOOD, MARGARET ELIZA VANCE. rec 1814. pp 347, 348, 349

Deed dated 1814. SAMUEL SMITH of Philadelphia, admtr

BUTLER COUNTY LAND RECORDS: BOOK D

of RICHARD IRWIN, on behalf of minor children of
Irwin, to CLARKSON FREEMAN. Title to land now held
by SAMUEL VANCE; obligated to convey title as
directed. Map of land on p. 350. Signed SAMUEL
SMITH. Witn: RICHD. PETERS JR, WILLIAM M. MILLS.
rec 1814. pp 349, 350

Description of land above by surveyor HENRY WEAVER.
p 351.

Deed dated 1796. JOHN POINDEXTER, house carpenter,
to JOHN HAMILTON, merchant. Hamilton lot 163.
Signed JOHN POINDEXTER. Witn: ROBERT SPROUL, WILLIAM SCOTT. rec 1814. p 351

Affadavit dated 1814. WILLIAM SCOTT testified Hamilton lot 163 sold to POINDEXTER by JOHN WINGATE. rec
1814. pp 351, 352

Assignment of title dated 1796. JOHN WINGATE to JOHN
POINDEXTER. Hamilton 163. Signed JOHN WINGATE.
Witn: ROBERT SPROUL, WILLIAM SCOTT. rec 1814. p 352

Deed dated 1814. JAMES WILSON & JANE his wife to
ISAAC WILES. S 1, T 1, R 3, lot 6. Signed JAMES
WILSON, JANE WILSON. Witn: ISAAC STANLEY, ROSS
SMILEY. rec 1814. pp 352, 353

Deed dated 1813. JAMES McBRIDE, tax collector of the
First District, to WILLIAM McCLELLAN. In 1806,
Fairfield tax collector AARON GOFORTH sold S 32, T 2,
R 3 to PETER F. SCHENCK, a tract entered by JAMES
WILKINS. PFS assigned right to McCLELLAN who presented certificate to JAMES HEATON, surveyor of
Butler Co. In 1809, Heaton laid out plot in S 32, T
2, R 3 for McClellan: rights to property confirmed.
Signed JAMES McBRIDE, collector. Witn: WM. MURRAY,
WM. M. PHARES. rec 1814. pp 353, 354, 355

Deed dated 1811. JOHN WINGATE & EMMA WINGATE, admtrs
of JOHN TORRENCE to JOHN SUTHERLAND & HENRY BROWN.
Rossville lot 19. Signed JOHN WINGATE, AMMA WINGATE.
Witn: ABRAM COLWELL, JAMES MILLS. rec 1814. pp
355, 356, 357

Deed dated 1813. ABNER ENOCH & ELIZABETH his wife
to ROBERT BROWN. S 29, T 2, R 4. Signed ABNER
ENOCH, ELIZABETH ENOCH. Witn: JAMES SUTTON JR,
HENRY WEAVER. rec 1814. pp 357, 358

Deed dated 1813. ABNER ENOCH & ELIZABETH his wife

BUTLER COUNTY LAND RECORDS: BOOK D

to ROBERT BROWN. S 29, T 2, R 4. Signed and witn as previous. rec 1814. pp 358, 359, 360

Deed dated 1814. ANDERSON SPENCER & MARY his wife to WILLIAM PHARES JR. Hamilton lot 71. Signed ANDERSON SPENCER, MERCY (x) SPENCER. Witn: JAMES WILSON, ISAAC STANLEY. rec 1814. pp 360, 361

Deed dated 1814. WILLIAM SQUIER & SARAH his wife to JAMES HEATON. Hamilton lot 165. Signed WM. SQUIER, SARAH (x) SQUIER. Witn: EZRA F. FREEMAN, ELLIS LANIER. rec 1814. pp 361, 362

Deed dated 1814. JOHN CLARK & SARAH his wife to WILLIAM SQUIER. S 32, T 2, R 4. Signed JOHN CLARK, SARAH (x) CLARK. Witn: LYIA SIMPSON, HENRY WEAVER. rec 1814. pp 363, 363

Deed dated 1812. HENRY HOUSE & ANN his wife to WILLIAM SQUIER. S 32, T 2, R 4. Signed HENRY HOUSS, ANN HOUSS. Witn: LEONARD WEAVER, HENRY WEAVER. rec 1814. pp 363, 364, 365

Deed dated 1813. REBECCA SYMMES, late FITZ RANDOLPH, to WILLIAM SQUIRE. Hamilton lot 165. Signed REBECCA SYMMES. Witn: JAMES HEATON, MATTH. RICHARDSON. rec 1814. pp 365, 366

Deed dated 1812. JANE RUNYAN of Piscataway Twp, Middlesex Co, NJ to JACOB LEWIS. S 24, T 2, R - in Symmes Purchase, formerly belonged to ELIAS RUNYAN of Morris Co, NJ. Jane a lawful heir of Elias. Signed JANE RUNYAN. Witn: ABRAHAM CONILL, ELIZA DENN. rec 1814. pp 366, 367

Deed dated 1814. WILLIAM HARLAN & HANNAH his wife to THOMAS BLAIR. Hamilton lot 11. Signed WM. HARLAN, HANNAH (x) HARLAN. Witn: ISAAC STANLEY, LEVI (x) McDONALD. rec 1814. pp 368, 369

Deed dated 1814. JOB DeCAMP & MARY his wife to ROBERT IRWIN. S 25, T 4, R 2. Signed JOB (x) DeCAMP MARY (x) DeCAMP. Witn: AZARIAS THORN, JAMES MILLS. rec 1814. pp 369, 370

Quitclaim & partition dated 1814. ARCHIBALD ARMSTRONG & REBECCA his wife, CORNELIUS KINSEY & SARAH his wife, and WILLIAM KINSEY & ELIZA his wife purchased S 9, T 5, R 2 in common; now dividing into shares. Signed ARCHIBALD ARMSTRONG, CORNELIUS KINSEY

BUTLER COUNTY LAND RECORDS: BOOK D

WILLIAM KINSEY, REBECCA ARMSTRONG, SARAH KINSEY, ELIZA KINSEY. rec 1814. pp 370, 371, 372, 373

Deed dated 1814. JAMES SUTTON JR & NANCY his wife to ELIZABETH CANFIELD. S 29, T 2, R 4. Signed JAMES SUTTON JR, NANCY SUTTON. Witn: EZEKIEL BALL, PHEBE BALL. rec 1814. pp 373, 374

Deed dated 1814. ABNER ENOCH & ELIZABETH his wife to DANIEL McDANIEL. S 29, T 2, R 4. Signed ABNER ENOCH, ELIZABETH ENOCH. Witn: ESEKIEL BALL, DAVID WOOLVERTON. rec 1814. pp 375, 376

Deed dated 1814. JOHN SUTHERLAND & NANCY his wife to HENRY LONG of PA. Hamilton lot 36. Signed JOHN SUTHERLAND, NANCY R. SUTHERLAND. Witn: GEORGE R. BIGHAM, ISAAC STANLEY. rec 1814. pp 376, 377

Deed dated 1814. ELEXIS BURK & ELIZABETH his wife to HENRY LONG of Mifflin Co, PA. S 22, T 4, R 1. Signed ALEXIS BURK, ELIZABETH BURK. Witn: JOHN BURK, DANL BIGHAM. rec 1814. pp 378, 379

Deed dated 1813. JOHN KERR & JANE his wife to JAMES RUGLESS. S 7 T 2, R 4. Signed JOHN KERR, JANE (x) KERR. Witn: JNO. McCRACKIN, DAVID LOGAN. rec 1814. pp 379, 380

Deed dated 1814. JOSEPH HOUGH & JANE his wife to ABSALOM GOODENOUGH. Hamilton lot 71. Signed JOSEPH HOUGH, JEAN (x) HOUGH. Witn: ISAAC STANLEY, MARY JACKSON. rec 1814. pp 380, 381, 382

Quitclaim dated 1814. WILLARD W. SMITH & HARRIET his wife to THOMAS C. KELSEY. Hamilton lot 109 & Rossville lot 40. Signed WILLARD W. SMITH, HARRIET SMITH. rec 1814. pp 382, 383

Deed dated 1814. JOSEPH HOUGH & JANE his wife to DAVID K. ESTE. Hamilton lots 72, 73. Signed JOSEPH HOUGH, JANE (x) HOUGH. Witn: DANL. MILLIKIN, SAM. MILLIKIN. rec 1814. pp 383, 384, 385

Deed dated 1813. JACOB LINE & RUTH his wife to DAVID K. ESTE. Hamilton lots 189, 190. Signed JACOB LINE, RUTH (x) LINE. Witn: OLIVER H. HENRY, JOHANNES ? (german script). rec 1814. pp 385, 386

Deed dated 1813. JOHN LUDLOW & SUSAN to DAVID K. ESTE. Hamilton lot 104. Signed JOHN LUDLOW, SUSAN LUDLOW. Witn: JAMES LYON, JOHN LUDLOW JR. rec

BUTLER COUNTY LAND RECORDS: BOOK D

1814. pp 386, 387

Deed dated 1814. Admtrs of ISRAEL LUDLOW to DAVID K. ESTE. Hamilton lot 105. Signed CHARLOTTE CHAMBERS RISK, JOHN LUDLOW, JAMES FINDLAY. Witn: GRIFFIN YEATMAN, THOS. COOS. rec 1814. pp 387, 388

Deed dated 1814. JAMES HEATON & MARY to WILLIAM HERBERT. Hamilton lot 203. Signed JAMES HEATON, MARY HEATON. Witn: POLLY (x) VINNEDGE, ISAAC STANLEY. rec 1814. pp 388, 389

Deed dated 1814. ISAAC PAXTON & MAGDALAIN his wife to DANIEL STRICKLAND. S 11, T 2, R 3. Signed ISAAC PAXTON, MAGDALAIN (x) PAXTON. Witn: JOHN VANNICE, ISAAC STANLEY. rec 1814. pp 389, 390

Deed dated 1814. JOHN SUTHERLAND & NANCY his wife to ISAAC PAXTON & HENRY WALLACE. Hamilton lot 136. Signed JOHN SUTHERLAND, NANCY R. SUTHERLAND. Witn: GEORGE R. BIGHAM, ISAAC STANLEY. rec 1814. pp 390, 391

Mortgage dated 1814. RICHARD BIRCH JR to JOHN SUTHERLAND. S 1, T 1, R 3 in Fairfield Twp. Signed R. BIRCH. Witn: D. K. ESTE, DANL MILLIKIN. rec 1814. pp 391, 392, 393

Deed dated 1814. JOHN WINGATE & EMMA WINGATE, late EMMA TORRENCE, admtrs of JOHN TORRENCE, to JOHN SUTHERLAND. Hamilton lot 160. Signed JOHN WINGATE, **AMMA** WINGATE. Witn: JOSIAH H. WEBB, JOHN MAHARD. rec 1814. pp 393, 394

Deed dated 1814. JOHN LODER & ISABELLA to JAMES MANAGHAN. S 31, T 3, R 3. Signed JOHN LODER, ISABELLA (x) LODER. Witn: JOHN AYERS, WILLIAM LEGG JR. rec 1814. pp 394, 395, 396

Deed dated 1814. JOHN REILY & JOHN HUTSON to Trustees of the town of Hamilton. Reily's lot 88, Hutson's lot 89 each to donate equal portions to form an alley. Signed JOHN REILY, JOHN (x) HUTSON. Witn: JAMES McBRIDE, WM. GREENLEE. rec 1814. pp 396, 397

Deed dated 1814. JOHN SUTHERLAND & NANCY his wife to JACOB BURNET of Cincinnati. Rossville lot 8. Signed JOHN SUTHERLAND, NANCY R. SUTHERLAND. Witn: DANIEL KEYT, ISAAC STANLEY. rec 1814. pp 397, 398

Deed dated 1814. JOHN SUTHERLAND & NANCY his wife and ABRAHAM HUFF & MAGDALANE his wife to ADAM DICKEY.

BUTLER COUNTY LAND RECORDS: BOOK D

S 32, T 2, R 4. Signed JOHN SUTHERLAND, NANCY R. SUTHERLAND, ABRAHAM HUFF, MAGDALANE (x) HUFF. Witn: HENRY WEAVER, JAMES MILLS. rec 1814. pp 398, 399

Deed dated 1814. JOHN HUTSON & RUTH his wife to JOHN CALDWELL. Hamilton lot 89. Signed JOHN (x) HUTO, RUTH (x) HUTSON. Witn: MICHAEL AYERS, #2 german script. rec 1814. pp 399, 400

Deed dated 1813. JOHN BECKET & MARY his wife to JOHN CALDWELL. S 28, T 3, R 2. Signed JOHN BECKET, MARY (x) BECKET. Witn: none. JP MICHAEL AYERS. rec 1814. pp 400, 401, 402

Deed dated 1814. JONATHAN LINE & JOANNA his wife to JOHN CALDWELL. S 27, T 2, R 3. Signed JONATHAN LINE, JOANNA (x) LINE. Witn: JAMES HEATON, MARY HEATON. rec 1814. pp 402, 403

Deed dated 1814. ELIHU WOODRUFF & MARGRET his wife to JOHN CALDWELL. S 30, T 2, R 2. Signed ELIHU WOODRUFF, MARGRET WOODRUFF. Witn: HUGH B. HAWTHORN, ISAAC STANLEY. rec 1814. pp 403, 404

Mortgage dated 1814. FRANCIS KELSHEIMER & MARGARET his wife to STEPHEN CAMPBELL. S 33, T 3, R 2. Signed FRANCIS (x) KELSHEIMER, MARGARET (x) KELS- HEIMER. Witn: JP JOAB COMSTOCK, FRANCIS KELSHEIMER. rec 1814. pp 404, 405

Deed dated 1814. ROBERT IRWIN & MARY his wife to WILLIAM WALLACE. S 7, T 2, R 3. Bound by land of heirs of THOMAS McCULLOUGH, dec. Signed ROBERT IRWIN, MARY IRWIN. Witn: ROBT. TAYLOR, JAMES MILLS. rec 1814. pp 405, 406, 407

Deed dated 1814. MOSES BREES & ANNA his wife to JAMES CUMMINS. S 3, T 2, R 3. Signed MOSES BREES, ANNA BREES. Witn: WM. HUNT, JOHN VINNEDGE. rec 1814. pp 407, 408

Deed dated 1814. MICHAEL HAGEMAN to JOHN HOUGHLAND. S 34, T 3, R 3. Signed MICHAEL HAGEMAN. Witn: JAMES HEATON, ISAAC HAWLEY. rec 1814. pp 408, 409

Deed dated 1814. IRA HUNT to MATTHEW VANDUYN SR. S 6, T 2, R 2. Signed IRA HUNT. Witn: JOHN AYERS, SARAH (x) AYERS. rec 1814. pp 409, 410

Deed dated 1814. JACOB BURNET & REBECCA his wife of

BUTLER COUNTY LAND RECORDS: BOOK D

Cincinnati to JOSEPH GASTON, son & devisee of JAMES GASTON, dec. S 33, T 2, R 2 purchased by James, now conveyed per instructions in James' will. Signed JAC. BURNET, REBECCA BURNET. Witn: ISAAC G. BURNET, JOHN MAHARD. rec 1814. pp 411, 412

Mortgage dated 1813. GOIKUM VAN VALKINBURGH of Crosby Twp, Hamilton Co to JAMES McNUTT of Ross Twp. Security: distillery and lease; lists stills, apparatus, notes due 1815. Signed GOIKUM VAN VALKINBURGH. Witn: JAMES SHIELDS, JANE SHIELDS. rec 1814. pp 412, 413

Deed dated 1814. SAMUEL CLARK & MARTHY to FREDERICK FEATHERLAND. S 12, T 2, R 3. Bound by PAUL SANDERS' land. Signed SAMUEL CLARK, MARTHY (x) CLARK. Witn: JOHN AYERS, BENJAMIN ENYART. rec 1814. pp 413, 414

Deed dated 1814. JOHN **ROBESON** & JANE his wife of Turtle Creek Twp, Warren Co to JAMES KENNEDY. S 18 in Lemon Twp. Signed JOHN **ROBINSON**, JANE ROBINSON. Witn: P. WILLIAMSON, JOHN D. ROBISON. rec 1814. pp 414, 415

Deed dated 1814. GEORGE W. STALL of US Army & MARIAH B. his wife to MICHAEL DELARAC. Rossville lot 4. Signed G.W. STALL, BARBARA STALL. Witn: ALEX. DELARAC, ISAAC STANLEY. rec 1814. pp 415, 416

Deed dated 1814. Butler Co Commissioners to HUGH B. HAWTHORN & JACOB BAYMILLER. S 1, T 1, R 3, lot 9. Signed JAMES BLACKBURN, WILLIAM ROBESON, MATTH. RICHARDSON. rec 1814. pp 417, 418

Deed dated 1812. USA to WILLIAM MURRAY. S 28, T 4, R 2. rec 1814. pp 418, 419

Deed dated 1812. USA to WILLIAM MURRAY. S 26, T 4, R 2. rec 1814. p 419

Deed dated 1814. JONATHAN PIERSON & MATILDA his wife to JAMES T. MORTON. Hamilton lot 54. Signed JONATHAN PIERSON, **METILDA** PIERSON. Witn: BENJ. D. DAVIS, ISAAC STANLEY. rec 1814. pp 419, 420

Deed dated 1814. WILLIAM COOLEY & NANCY to WILLIAM BELL. S 9, T 4, R 2. Signed WILLIAM COOLEY, NANCY (x) COOLEY. Witn: MATTH. RICHARDSON, REBECCA RICHARDSON, JOHN REILY. rec 1814. pp 421, 422

Mortgage dated 1814. SAMUEL BROWN & MARY of Ross Twp

BUTLER COUNTY LAND RECORDS: BOOK D

to THOMAS COEN of same. No S-T-R; land on waters of Paddy's Run, Ross Twp. Signed SAMUEL BROWN, MARY BROWN. Witn: WILLIAM D. JONES, EDWARD COEN. Margin note: COEN assigned note to DAVID FRANCIS who acknowledged satisfaction, 1815. rec 1814. pp 422, 423

Deed dated 1814. SAMUEL SCOTT to ISAAC FAULKNER. Rossville lot 42. Signed SAMUEL SCOTT. Witn: ISAAC STANLEY, DAVID CONNER. rec 1814. pp 423, 424.

Deed dated 1814. WILLIAM McMANUS & REBECCA his wife to JOHN C. McMANUS & ISAAC FALCONER. S 7, T 4, R 2. Signed WILLIAM McMANUS, REBECCA McMANUS. Witn: JAS. DUNN, JAMES MILLS. rec 1814. pp 425, 426

Deed dated 1813. JOHN DAVIS SR to JOHN DAVIS JR. S 19, T 2, R 4 entered by JAMES MORRISON, assigned to DAVIS SR in 1810. Selling half of property to DAVIS JR for $1, subject to lease entered into by MORRISON. Signed JOHN (x) DAVIS SR. Witn: JAMES(x) MORRISON, C.N. MASHWEGAT, JOHN LAU. rec 1814. pp 426, 427

Deed dated 1814. WILLIAM MURRAY & DEBORAH his wife to BARTHOLOMEW WICKART. S 26, T 4, R 2. Signed WM. MURRAY, DEBBY MURRAY. Witn: DANL. MILLIKIN, ALEX. DELARAC. rec 1814. pp 427, 428

Deed dated 1812. ELIZABETH McCULLOUGH, widow of THOMAS McCULLOUGH, to MATTHEW G. WALLACE. Hamilton lot 69. Signed ELIZABETH McCULLOUGH. Witn: JAMES HEATON, JAMES McBRIDE. rec 1814. pp 428, 429

Deed dated 1814. WILLIAM SQUIER & SARAH his wife to JOHN CLARK. S 32, T 2, R 4. Signed WM. SQUIER, SARAH (x) SQUIER. Witn: ELLIS SQUIER, HENRY WEAVER. rec 1814. pp 429, 430, 431

Deed dated 1814. JOHN N. CUMMINS of Essex Co, NJ by his agent WILLIAM C. SCHENCK to DANIEL ANDERS. S 4, T 2, R 2. Signed JOHN N. CUMMINS by WM. C. SCHENCK, agent. Witn: ALEXR. M. WAUGH, J. W. LANIER. rec 1814. pp 431, 432

Deed dated 1810. WILLIAM OGLE & ELIZABETH to ROBERT OGLE. S 28, T 5, R 2. Signed WILLIAM OGLE, ELIZABETH OGLE. Witn: J. ROYSDEN, MATTH. RICHARDSON. rec 1814. pp 432, 433, 434

Deed dated 1811. JONATHAN DAYTON of NJ to DAVID MULFORD. S 36, T 3, R 3. Signed JONA. DAYTON by atty ELIAS I. DAYTON. Witn: JOHN WHITWORTH, JOHN REILY.

BUTLER COUNTY LAND RECORDS: BOOK D

rec 1814. pp 434, 435

Deed dated 1814. WILLIAM NICOL of Hanover Twp to THOMAS COOPSTICK of Lemon Twp. S 11, T 2, R 4. Signed WM. NICOL. Witn: J.C. McMANUS, JAMES HEATON. rec 1814. pp 435, 436

Mortgage dated 1814. THOMAS COOPSTICK to WILLIAM NICOL. S 11, T 2, R 4. Paymt due 1817. Signed THOMAS (x) COOPSTICK. Witn: as above. rec 1814. pp 437, 438

Deed dated 1814. TOBIAS BARCALOW & ELIZABETH his wife to SAMUEL McCREA. S 2, T 2, R 4. Signed TOBIAS BARCALOW, ELIZABETH BARCALOW. Witn: ARTHUR POLHEMUS, HENRY WEAVER. rec 1814. pp 438, 439

Deed dated 1811. ELIAS BOUDINOT by JACOB BURNET, his agent, to PETER TIEGLER, late of PA. S 14, T 2, R 4. Signed ELIAS BOUDINOT by JAC. BURNET. Witn: WILLIAM IRWIN JR, JAMES F. GRISWOLD. rec 1814. pp 439, 440

Deed dated 1814. MATTHEW WINTON & ELIZA to EDWARD CORNTHWAITE. S 5, T 2, R 3. Reserved right for ROBERT WINTON to build a mill dam. Signed MATTH. WINTON, ELIZA WINTON. Witn: ROBERT WINTON, WM. BROWN, CHARLES SWEARINGEN. rec 1814. pp 440, 441, 442

Deed dated 1812. JOHN SMITH & ELIZABETH his wife of Hamilton Co to BAZEL HARRISON. S 32, T 3, R 3. Signed JOHN SMITH by FIELDING LOWRY his agent, ELIZA-BETH SMITH. Witn: WM. G. ARMSTRONG, A.D. SMITH. rec 1814. pp 442, 443

Deed dated 1814. JOHN HALL to CORNELIUS W. HALL. No S-T-R; bound by land of BENJAMIN LONG, WILLIAM WHITE. Signed JOHN HALL. Witn: JP JOSEPH GASTON, HUGH HALL. rec 1814. pp 445, 446

Deed dated 1813. ABRAHAM WHITE & MARY his wife of Milford Twp to AMOS WHITE JR. S 17, T 5, R 2. Signed ABRAHAM WHITE, MARY (x) WHITE. Witn: MARSH WILLIAMS, ROBERT CRANE. rec 1814. pp 446, 447

Deed dated 1814. SOLOMON BEACH & SARAH his wife of Hamilton Co to DAVID GARRIGUS. S 15, T 1, R 2. Signed SOLOMON BEACH, SARAH BEACH. Witn: JAMES HEATON, JAMES H. PARCEL. rec 1814. pp 447, 448

Deed dated 1814. DAVID K. ESTE to JOHN SUTHERLAND.

BUTLER COUNTY LAND RECORDS: BOOK D

Rossville outlot 13. Signed D.K. ESTE. Witn: DANL. MILLIKIN, JOHN RITCHEY. rec 1814. p 449

Deed dated 1813. JOSEPH H. McMAKEN & JANE his wife to ARCHIBALD STARK. S 26, T 4, R 2. Signed JOSEPH H. McMAKEN, JANE McMAKEN. Witn: ISAAC STANLEY, JOHN BURK. rec 1814. pp 450, 451

Deed dated 1814. ARCHIBALD STARK & ELEANOR his wife to JOHN SUTHERLAND. S 26, T 4, R 2. Signed ARCHIBALD STARK, NELLY STARK. Witn: PETER F. FRELAND, ISAAC STANLEY. rec 1814. pp 451, 452

Deed dated 1814. JOB MULFORD & EUPHEFINIA his wife, JOHN MULFORD & MARY his wife, EDMUND ALRIDGE & JANE his wife to OLIVER KELLY. No S-T-R; bound by land of CLARKSON FREEMAN. Signed JOB MULFORD, EUPHEFINIA MULFORD, JOHN MULFORD, MARY MULFORD, EDMUND ALRIDGE, JANE ALRIDGE. Witn: JAMES CLARK, HENRY THOMPSON. rec 1814. pp 452, 453

Quitclaim dated 1814. CHARLES REED & CLOEY his wife to ISAAC ROBY. An interest in the real estate of ELIAS ROBY, decd: "my wife's part" of S 17, T 3, R 3 where the widow of Roby now lives. Signed CHARLES REED, CLOEY (x) REED. Witn: JAMES CLARK, CATHARINE KING. rec 1814. pp 453, 454

Deed dated 1814. ROBERT LYTLE & MARGARET his wife to MARY BONE, his dau. S 24, T 5, R 2. Signed R. LYTLE, MARGARET (x) LYTLE. Witn: MATTH. RICHARDSON, HANNAH LYTLE. rec 1814. pp 454, 455

Deed dated 1812. USA to JONATHAN BEALE. S 2, T 3, R 2. rec 1814. p 456

Deed dated 1814. ROBERT LYTLE & MARGARET to JOHN BONE. S 24, T 5, R 2. Signed R. LYTLE, MARGARET (x) LYTLE. Witn: MATTH. RICHARDSON, HANNAH LYTLE. rec 1814. pp 456, 457

Quitclaim dated 1813. Heirs of WILLIAM KYLE to ANN & MARGARET KYLE. S 6, T 1, R 3. William being without issue, the heirs are his brothers and sisters: JOHN KYLE, MARY BUCKLES wife of WILLIAM of KY, JOSEPH and JAMES KYLE of the Indiana Ter'y, ELIZABETH JOHNSTON widow of DAVID of KY, AGNES WATSON wife of JOHN, ANN & MARGARET KYLE. Signed JOHN (x) WATSON, AGNES (x) WATSON, JOSEPH KYLE, JAMES KYLE, ELIZABETH JOHNSTON, JOHN LYLE (probably clerical error; should be KYLE).

BUTLER COUNTY LAND RECORDS: BOOK D

Witn: JOHN REILY, WM. G. ARMSTRONG. rec 1814. pp 457, 458, 459

Deed dated 1813. USA to WILLIAM EVANS. S 28, T 3, R 1. rec 1814. p 459

Deed dated 1814. ANDREW McGARVEY & NANCY his wife of Nelson Co, KY to DAVID THOMPSON. Hamilton lot 177. Signed ANDREW (x) McGARVEY, NANCY (x) McGARVEY. Witn: J. LEWIS, R. HUBBARD. rec 1814. pp 460, 461

Deed dated 1814. DAVID THOMAS THOMPSON & ELIZABETH his wife to ROBERT IRWIN. Hamilton lot 177. Signed DAVID (x) THOMPSON, ELIZABETH (x) THOMPSON. Witn: JAMES McBRIDE, ISAAC STANLEY. rec 1814. pp 461, 462

Quitclaim dated 1814. Heirs of JAMES JOHNSON to THOMAS & SAMUEL JOHNSON. S 28, T 3, R 2. Signed JOHN JOHNSON, JANE (x) GILL, FREDERICK SHAFF, SARAH (x) SHAFF. Witn: MICHAEL AYERS, ABIGAIL AYERS. rec 1814. pp 462, 463

Deed dated 1809. JOHN SUTHERLAND & HENRY BROWN to BENJAMIN THOMPSON. Rossville lot 29. Signed JOHN SUTHERLAND, HENRY BROWN. Witn: WM. BOMBERGER, WM. PHARES JR. rec 1814. pp 464, 465

Deed dated 1814. BENJAMIN THOMPSON & PEGGY to ROBERT IRWIN of St. Clair Twp. Rossville lots 25, 26, 29, 35, 36 and outlot 10. Signed BENJAMIN THOMPSON, PEGGY (x) THOMPSON. rec 1814. pp 465, 466

Deed dated 1809. JOHN SUTHERLAND & HENRY BROWN to BENJAMIN THOMPSON. Rossville lots 25, 26, 35, 36. Signed JOHN SUTHERLAND, HENRY BROWN. rec 1814. pp 466, 467, 468

Deed dated 1814. Auditors of court to WILLIAM SQUIER & WILLIAM McCLANE. SQUIER granted judgement against GEORGE TROXELL. House and Middletown lot 6 seized. Lot bound by land of JAMES PIPER. Damages for detention granted to DANIEL STRICKLAND, JOSEPH HAYS, WILLIAM SIMONTON. Lot sold to Squier & McClane. Signed ROBT. FARRIS, JAMES HEATH, JOHN TAYLOR. rec 1814. pp 468, 469, 470

Deed dated 1814. WILLIAM SPINNING & HANNAH his wife to WILLIAM McCLANE. Middletown lot 14. Signed WILLIAM SPINNING, HANNAH SPINNING. Witn: EZEKIEL BALL, EZEKIEL B. McCLURE. rec 1814. pp 470, 471

BUTLER COUNTY LAND RECORDS: BOOK D

Deed dated 1811. SAMUEL DICK & MARTHA his wife to JOEL WILLIAMS of Cincinnati. No S-T-R: "part of the fourth quarter of T 1, R 2...a tract appropriated for satisfying military warrants for service." Signed SAMUEL DICK, MARTHA E. DICK. Witn: JOHN MAHARD, ALEXANDER KIRKPATRICK. rec 1814. pp 471, 472, 473

Deed dated 1807. JOHN CLEVES SYMMES to WILLIAM HARPER, assignee of ISAAC S. SWEARINGEN. S 23, T 3, R 2: purchased originally by EDWARD MEEKS of NY state, forfeited for non-improvement. Signed JOHN CLEVES SYMMES. Witn: BENJAMIN STEWART, WILLIAM RUFFIN. rec 1814. pp 473, 474.

Deed dated 1813. DANIEL SYMMES of Hamilton Co to JACKSON AYERS. S 36, T 2, R 2. Signed DANIEL SYMMES. Witn: PEYTON SYMMES, DAVID OLIVER. rec 1814. pp 474, 475, 476

Bill of Sale dated 1814. GOIKIM VANVALKINBURGH of Ross Twp to JOHN RICHMOND JR. Money paid by Richmond: $102 to JAMES McBRIDE, $43.87 to JOHN REEVES, $11.37 to KING DEARMOND. Selling personal propty: a still, loom, horses and wagon, etc. Signed GOIKIM VANVAL-KINBURGH. Witn: JOHN (x) HERRON, JOHN RICHMOND. rec 1814. pp 477, 478

Deed dated 1814. ABRAHAM TEITSORT & MARGARET his wife to DAVID CRANE. S 29, T 2, R 4. Signed ABRAHAM TEITSORT, MARGARET TEITSORT. Witn: ABRAHAM HALL, HENRY WEAVER. rec 1814. pp 477, 478

Deed dated 1814. CLARKSON FREEMAN of Lancaster, PA to PETER GOOD of Conistogoe Twp, Lancaster Co, PA. S 5, T 2, R 3 & S 16, T 1, R 4. Signed C. FREEMAN. Witn: JACOB DUCHMAN, CHRISTIAN MUSSELMAN, PHILIP GLOVINGER. rec 1814. pp 478, 479, 480, 481, 482

Deed dated 1813. DAVID LONG & SARAH his wife to HENRY WEAVER. S 20, T 2, R 4. Signed DAVID (x) LONG, SARAH (x) LONG. Witn: ALEXR. AYERS, JAMES FLOWERS. rec 1814. pp 482, 483

Deed dated 1814. WILLIAM TAYLOR & JAMES BECKET to SAMUEL FRAREY. S 10, T 4, R 2. Signed WILLIAM TAYLOR, JAMES BECKET. Witn: M. HUESTON, CHARLES McMANUS. rec 1814. pp 483, 484

pp 487, 488 bound out of order

Deed dated 1814. JOHN SUTHERLAND & NANCY his wife to

BUTLER COUNTY LAND RECORDS: BOOK D

ROBERT IRWIN. S 32 & 32, T 2, R 3. Rossville outlot 11. Signed JOHN SUTHERLAND, NANCY R. SUTHERLAND. Witn: JAMES P. RAMSEY, ISAAC STANLEY. rec 1814. pp 485, 486

Deed dated 1814. WILLIAM H. HARRISON & JOHN CLEVES SHORT of Cincinnati to JOHN MAXWELL. 2 9. R 1, R 2. Signed WILLIAM H. HARRISON, J. CLEVES SHORT. Witn: DAVID BEATY JR, JABEZ RICHARDS. rec 1814. pp 486, 487

Deed dated 1814. DANIEL DOTY & BETSY to WILLIAM SQUIER. S 27, T 2, R 4. Signed DANIEL DOTY, BETSY DOTY. Witn: HENRY WEAVER, EZEKIEL BALL. rec 1814. pp 487, 488, 489

Deed dated 1814. WILLIAM C. KEEN & ANDREW STEWART to JAMES THROCKMORTON.* Hamilton lot 52. Signed WM. C. KEEN, ANDW. STEWART. Witn: JOHN REILY, JOHN VINNEDGE. rec 1814. pp 489, 490 * see following deed

Deed dated 1814. JAMES B. THOMAS & WILLIAM THOMAS to JAMES F. MORTON.* Hamilton lot 51. Signed JAMES B. THOMAS, WILLIAM THOMAS. Witn: ISAAC STANLEY, ISAAC HAWLEY. rec 1814. pp 490, 491 *possibly Throckmorton?

Deed dated 1813. USA to JOHN SMITH of PA. S 20, R 4, R 1. rec 1814. pp 495, 496

Deed dated 1814. MATTHIAS ROLL & MARY his wife to WILLIAM S. STEWART. S 18, T 4, R 2. Signed MATTHIAS ROLL, MARY ROLL. Witn: JAMES JOHNSTON, SARAH JOHNSTON. rec 1814. pp 492, 493

Deed dated 1812. JOHN MULFORD & MARY his wife to HENRY HOUSE. Orange town lot 22. Signed JOHN MULFORD, MARY MULFORD. Witn: DAVID MULFORD, JAMES (x) CROCKET. rec 1814. pp 493, 494

Deed dated 1812. WILLIAM SQUIER & SARAH his wife to HENRY HOUSE. S 5, T 1, R 4. Signed WM. SQUIER, SARAH (x) SQUIER. Witn: LEONARD WEAVER, HENRY WEAVER. rec 1814. pp 495, 496

Deed dated 1814. NOAH WILLEY of Crosby Twp, Hamilton Co to NOAH WILLEY JR of same. S 33, T 3, R 2. Signed NOAH WILLEY. Witn: WILLIAM D. JONES, EVAN JONES. rec 1814. pp 496, 497

Mortgage dated 1814. JOHN TRIM of Springfield Twp, Hamilton Co to DANIEL POWERS of Fairfield Twp. S 20, T 2, R 2. Signed JOHN TRIM. Witn: JOS. GASTON, MARTHA GASTON. rec 1814. pp 497, 498, 499

BUTLER COUNTY LAND RECORDS: BOOK D

Deed dated 1810. ISAAC VANDUYN & LYDIA to ISAAC SEWARD. S 6, T 2, R 2. Signed ISAAC VANDUYN, LYDIA (x) VANDUYN. Witn: ISRAEL WOODRUFF, TIMOTHY WOODRUFF. rec 1814. pp 499, 500

Deed dated 1814. JOHN VANNICE & ELIZABETH his wife to SAMUEL SCOTT. S 14, T 2, R, 3. Signed JOHN VAN NICE, ELIZABETH VAN NICE. Witn: WILL. BRODERICK, HENRY WEAVER. rec 1814. pp 500, 501

Deed dated 1814. JAMES WILSON & JANE his wife to SAMUEL ROBBINS of Wayne Twp. S 13, T 5, R 2. Signed JAMES WILSON, JANE WILSON. Witn: JAMES WITHEROE, ISAAC STANLEY. rec 1814. pp 502, 503

Deed dated 1814. DAVID LONG & SARAH his wife to GIDEON LONG, his son. S 20, T 2, R 4. Signed DAVID (x) LONG, SARAH (x) LONG. Witn: ANN WEAVER, HENRY WEAVER. rec 1814. pp 503, 504

Deed dated 1814. WILLIAM ELLIOTT to THOMAS DONALD. S 1, T 2, R 3. Signed WILLIAM ELID. Witn: JOHN AYERS, JONAH SUTTON. rec 1814. pp 504, 505

Deed dated 1814. THOMAS WHITE of Oxford Twp to THOMAS BURK of Reily Twp. S 14, T 5, R 1. Signed THOS. WHITE. Witn: JAMES McBRIDE, ISAAC STANLEY. rec 1814. pp 505, 506, 507

Deed dated 1814. WILLIAM W. PHARES to JOHN SUTHERLAND. Hamilton lot 71. Signed WM. W. PHARES. Witn: JOHN E. SCOTT, ISAAC STANLEY. rec 1814. pp 507, 508

Deed dated 1814. JOSEPH HOUGH & JANE his wife to ROBERT FLEMING. Hamilton lot 71. Signed JOSEPH HOUGH, JANE (x) HOUGH. Witn: ISAAC STANLEY, ANDERSON SPENCER. rec 1814. pp 508, 509

Deed dated 1814. SHOBAL VAIL & MARY his wife to WILLIAM GARRET. Middletown lot 43. Signed SHOBAL VAIL, MARY VAIL. Witn: JAMES HEATH, SAMUEL POWELL. rec 1814. pp 509, 510, 511

Deed dated 1814. SHOBAL VAIL & MARY his wife to WILLIAM GARRET. Middletown lot 26. Signed and witn as above. rec 1814. pp 511, 512

Deed dated 1812. SAMUEL ENYART & ANNA his wife to MATTHEW MARKLAND. Princetown lot 24. Signed SAMUEL ENYART, ANNA ENYART. Witn: JOHN NEWHOUSE, JOHN AYERS. rec 1814. pp 512, 513

BUTLER COUNTY LAND RECORDS: BOOK D

Deed dated 1814.   JOHN SUTHERLAND & NANCY his wife to WILLIAM W. PHARES. Hamilton 197. Signed JOHN SUTHERLAND, NANCY R. SUTHERLAND. Witn: JOHN E. SCOTT, ISAAC STANLEY.   rec 1814.   pp 513, 514, 515

Deed dated 1814.   HENRY BROWN & KITTY his wife of Montgomery Co to JOHN SUTHERLAND. Hamilton lots 119, 120. Signed HENRY BROWN, KITTY P. BROWN. Witn: JOHN ANDERSON, JAMES P. RAMSEY. rec 1814. pp 515, 516

Deed dated 1814.   JOHN GREER & ELEANOR his wife to ISAAC STANLEY. Hamilton lots 111, 112. Signed JOHN GREER, ELINOR GREER. Witn: JAMES MILLS, JOHN RUTEY. rec 1814.   pp 516, 517

Deed dated 1810.   JOHN VAN NICE & ELIZABETH his wife to MALCOLM ANDRE, late of Centre Co, PA. S 15, T 3, R 2. Signed JOHN VANNICE, ELIZABETH (x) VANNINCE. Witn: JOHN CALDWELL, SOLOMON (x) SIMONS. rec 1814. pp 517, 518, 519

Deed dated 1813.   JOHN PATTERSON of Murry Co, TN to SAMUEL POTTENGER. S 32, T 3, R 3. Signed JOHN PATTERSON. Witn: P. LARSH, CHARLES SWEARINGEN.   rec 1814.   pp 519, 520

Deed dated 1813.   JOHN PATTERSON & CONSTANT of Humphreys Co, TN to SAMUEL POTTENGER. S 32, T 3, R 3. Signed JOHN PATTERSON, CONSTANT (x) PATTERSON. Witn: WM. H. BURTON, DAVID H. BURTON. rec 1814. pp 520, 521

Deed dated 1814.   THOMAS BLAIR & PEGGY his wife to WILLIAM RIDDLE. Lot #14, as laid out by CORNELIUS R. SEDAM. Signed THOS. BLAIR, PEGGY BLAIR. Witn: ISAAC HAWLEY, ISAAC STANLEY. rec 1814. pp 521, 522

Deed dated 1814.   MATTHIAS ROLL & MARY his wife to REUBEN BLACKFORD. S 18, T 4, R 5. Signed MATTHIAS ROLL, MARY ROLL. Witn: JAMES JOHNSTON, SARAH JOHNSTON.   rec 1814.   pp 522, 523

Deed dated 1814.   RICHARD WATTS to his beloved son, RICHARD WATTS JR.   All goods, chattels and real estate; no S-T-R given.   Signed RICHARD WATTS. Witn: DANIEL DOTY, ABRAHAM TEITSORT. rec 1814. pp 523, 524

Deed dated 1814.   SAMUEL W. BEELER & AMELIA his wife to ANDERSON SPENCER. Hamilton outlots 13, 14. Signed SAMUEL W. BEELER, AMELIA BEELER. Witn: JOHN GREER, ISAAC STANLEY. rec 1814. pp 524, 525

BUTLER COUNTY LAND RECORDS: BOOK D

Deed dated 1814. ANDERSON SPENCER & POLLY his wife to THOMAS BLAIR. Hamilton outlots 13, 14. Signed ANDERSON SPENCER, POLLY (x) SPENCER. Witn: JAMES WILSON, ISAAC STANLEY. rec 1814. pp 525, 526

Plat of Brownstown dated 1814. HENRY HOUSS, proprietor. S 5, T 1, R 4. Witn: HENRY WEAVER. rec 1814. p 527

Deed dated 1814. RICHARD WATTS & ALICE to DAVID ENYART. S 28 & 34, T 2, R 4. Signed RICHARD (x) WATTS, ALICE (x) WATTS. Witn: JOHN TAYLOR, HENRY WEAVER. rec 1814. pp 528, 529

Deed dated 1814. ELIHU HAMMER & ELIZABETH his wife to ABRAHAM CLARK. S 5, T 5, R 2. Signed ELIHU HAMMER ELIZABETH (x) HAMMER. Witn: PHINIAS ROSS, ETHAN STONE. rec 1814. pp 529, 530

Deed dated 1814. ABEL SLAYBACK to THOMAS BLAIR. Hamilton lot 197. Signed ABEL SLAYBACK. Witn: JOHN DUNN ISAAC HAWLEY. rec 1814. pp 531, 532

Deed dated 1814. SAMUEL W. MORRISON to THOMAS BLAIR. Hamilton lot 109. Signed SAM. W. MORRISON. Witn: ISAAC HAWLEY, ISAAC STANLEY. rec 1814. p 532

Deed dated 1814. JOHN REILY & NANCY his wife to WILLIAM C. KEEN & ANDREW STEWART. Hamilton lot 52. Signed JOHN REILY, NANCY REILY. Witn: SAMUEL DAVIS JR, JOHN VINNEDGE. rec 1814. pp 532, 533, 534

Deed dated 1814. JOHN MURPHEY & SUSANNA his wife to BENJAMIN FULKERSON. S 2, T 2, R 3. Signed JOHN (x) MURPHY, SUSANNA (x) MURPHY. Witn: HENRY WEAVER, DAVID CLARKSON, J. CONKLING, ETHAN STONE. rec 1814. pp 534, 535

Deed dated 1814. JAMES MURPHY & EUNICE his wife to BENJAMIN FULKERSON. S 2, T 2, R 3. Bound by PETER MURPHY's land. Signed JAMES MURPHY, UNIS (x) MURPHY. Witn: JOHN AYERS, DAVID MARTIN. rec 1814. pp 535, 536

Deed dated 1814. DAVID LONG & SARAH his wife to his son DAVID LONG JR. S 20, T 2, R 4. Signed DAVID (x) LONG, SARAH (x) LONG. Witn: ANN WEAVER, HENRY WEAVER. rec 1814. pp 36, 537

Deed dated 1809. JOHN McDONALD of Fairfield Twp to ISAAC GIBSON JR. S 33, T 2, R 2. Signed JOHN McDONALD. Witn: DAVID BEATY, JOHN R. BEATY. rec 1814.

BUTLER COUNTY LAND RECORDS: BOOK D

pp 537, 538

Deed dated 1814. JONATHAN PIERSON & MATILDA his wife to JAMES CLARK. Hamilton lot 54. Signed JONATHAN PIERSON, MATILDA PIERSON. Witn: JOHN BURK, ISAAC STANLEY. rec 1814. pp 538, 539

Deed dated 1812. JAMES MURPHY & EUNICE his wife to SAMUEL ENYART & JOHN LODER. S 2, T 2, R 3. Signed JAMES MURPHY, EUNICE (x) MURPHY. Witn: JOHN MERRILL, JOHN DANNIST. rec 1814. pp 539 (the second), 540

Deed dated 1814. GEORGE P. TORRENCE & MARY his wife to ROBERT RICHEY. S 10 & 15, T 2, R 3. Signed GEO. P. TORRENCE, MARY B. TORRENCE. Witn: LEWIS WHITEMAN JOHN MAHARD. rec 1814. pp 540, 541

Deed dated 1814. WILLIAM CROOKS SR & ANNY his wife to WILLIAM CROOKS JR. S 11, T 3, R 2. Signed WILLIAM CROOKS, ANNY CROOKS. Witn: JOHN DUNN, WILLIAM MORRIS. rec 1814. pp 542, 543

Deed dated 1814. BAZEL HARRISON & MARTHA his wife to JAMES MURPHY. S 32, T 3, R 3. Signed BAZEL HARRISON, MARTHA (x) HARRISON. Witn: JOHN AYERS, ABRM. P. THOMAS. rec 1814. pp 542, 543

Deed dated 1814. ROBERT IRWIN & MARY his wife of St. Clair Twp to ROBERT TAYLOR. Rossville lot 29. Signed ROBERT IRWIN, MARY IRWIN. Witn: JAMES MILLS, WILLIAM SUTHERLAND. rec 1814. p 544

Deed dated 1814. JACOB BELL & SARAH his wife to DANIEL HESS of Lancaster Co, PA. S 31 & 32, T 2, R 4. Signed JACOB BELL, SARAH (x) BELL. Witn: WILLIAM WOLLARS, BENJAMIN MARSHALL. rec 1814. pp 545, 546

Mortgage dated 1814. SAMUEL FRAREY of Hamilton to WILLIAM TAYLOR. S 10, T 4, R 2. Signed SAMUEL FRAREY Witn: M. HUESTON, CHARLES McMANUS. rec 1814. pp 546, 547

Deed dated 1814. PHINEAS McCRAY & SARAH his wife to ROBERT BROWN. S 36, T 3, R 4. Signed PHINEAS (x) McCRAY, SARAH (x) McCRAY. Witn: HENRY WEAVER, LEONARD WEAVER. rec 1814. pp 547, 548

Deed dated 1812. WILLIAM McCLELLAN, sheriff, to JOHN REILY. Admtrs of estate of JOHN TORRENCE (AMMA TORRENCE & JOHN WINGATE) recovered judgement against THOMAS McCULLOUGH; Hamilton lot 22 seized, sold to

BUTLER COUNTY LAND RECORDS: BOOK D

Reily. Signed WM. McCLELLAN. Witn: ISAAC STANLEY, JAMES CLARK. rec 1814. pp 548, 549, 550, 551

Deed dated 1814. THOMAS HUNTER, tax collector of Fairfield Twp, to JOHN REILY. Hamilton lot 22 seized. Signed THOMAS HUNTER. Witn: JAMES McBRIDE, ISAAC STANLEY. rec 1814. pp 551, 552

Deed dated 1814. THOMAS HUNTER, tax collector of Fairfield Twp, to JOHN REILY. Hamilton lot 52 seized. Signed THOMAS HUNTER. Witn: JAMES McBRIDE. ISAAC STANLEY. rec 1814. pp 552, 553, 554

Deed dated 1814. WILLIAM H. HARRISON & J. CLEVES SHORT to THOMAS ALSTON. S 9, T 1, R 2. Signed WILLIAM HENRY HARRISON, J.C. SHORT. Witn: THOMAS ANDERSON, GRIFFIN YEATMAN. rec 1814. pp 555, 556

Deed dated 1814. JOHN CLEVES SYMMES of Hamilton Co to heirs of ISAAC FREEMAN. S 10, T 1, R 2 sold to Freeman, measured short acreage. Land in S 35, T 2, R 2 given as compensation; bound by land of HEZEKIAH BROADBERRY, JOSEPH WALKER. Heirs: ABRAHAM FREEMAN JR JOHN FREEMAN, SARAH CASSIDY widow of JOHN CASSIDY, OBADIAH SCHENCK, husband of ABIGAIL formerly FREEMAN. Signed JOHN CLEVES SYMMES. Witn: THOMAS HENDERSON, JOHN MAHARD. rec 1814. pp 556, 557, 558

Deed dated 1814. JAMES KERCHEVAL to JAMES WITHRO. S 31, T 3, R -. Bound by JARVIS HUFFAM's land. Signed JAS. KERCHEVAL. Witn: ISAAC STANLEY, JAMES CLARK. rec 1814. pp 558, 559

Deed dated 1814. JOHN SUTHERLAND JR to HUGH B. HAW-THORN. Hamilton lots 111, 112. Signed JOHN SUTHER-LAND JR. Witn: DAVID VANCE, ISAAC STANLEY. rec 1814. pp 559, 560

Deed dated 1814. ISAAC S. PATTON & ELIZABETH his wife to JOHN CARSON. S 25, T 2, R 4. Signed ISAAC S. PATTON, ELIZABETH (x) PATTON. Witn: WM. HARVEY, JOHN CARSON. rec 1814. pp 560, 561

Deed dated 1813. WILLIAM SMITH to JOSEPH CILLEY. S 15, T 3, R 2. Signed WILLIAM SMITH. Witn: JOHN RICHMOND JR, JAMES SMITH. rec 1814. pp 560, 561

Deed dated 1814. JOSEPH EVANS & ESTHER his wife of Montgomery Co to MORDICAH CARTER of Warren Co. S 20, T 3, R 3. Signed JOSEPH EVANS, ESTHER EVANS. Witn: JOHN HOLDERMAN, ABEL PEARSON, MOSES EVANS. rec 1814.

BUTLER COUNTY LAND RECORDS: BOOK D

pp 563, 564

Deed dated 1810. USA to JOHN McCORMICK. S 17, T 3, R 3. rec 1814. p 564

Deed dated 1812. USA to WILLIAM JONES. S 21, T 3, R 3. rec 1814. pp 564, 565

Deed dated 1813. USA to WILLIAM JONES. S 21. T 3, R 3. rec 1814. p 565

Deed dated 1813. USA to WILLIAM JONES. S 17, T 3, R 3. rec 1814. pp 565, 566

Deed dated 1814. DANIEL DOTY & BETSEY his wife of Lemon Twp to WILLIAM SIMONTON of Middletown. S 27, T 2, R 4. Signed DANIEL DOTY, BETSEY DOTY. Witn: HENRY WEAVER, SAMUEL C. CHRISTY. rec 1814. pp 566, 567

Deed dated 1814. DANIEL OSBORN & REBECKAH his wife of Franklin Co, IN Ter'y, to WILLIAM SIMONTON. S 27, T 2, R 4. Signed DANIEL OSBORN, REBECKAH (x) OSBORN. Witn: MATTHEW NICOL, JOHN WILSON. rec 1814. pp 567, 568, 569

Deed dated 1812. USA to JOHN SCHNIBLY & JOHN MILLER. S 9, T 2, R 4. rec 1814. p 569

Deed dated 1812. GEORGE SMOCK & MARGARET of Somerset NJ to PETER POAST. S 12, T 2, R 4. Signed GEORGE SMOCK, MARGARET SMOCK. Witn: JACOB KIRKPATRICK, DICKINSON MILLER. rec 1814. pp 569, 570, 571

Deed dated 1814. JAMES FINDLAY & JANE his wife to WILLIAM WILLSON. S 6, T 1, R 5. Signed JAMES FINDLAY, JANE FINDLAY. Witn: GEO. P. TORRENCE, GRIFFIN YEATMAN. rec 1814. pp 571, 572

Deed dated 1814. WILLIAM WILSON & RUTH his wife to MICHAEL VANTUYL. S 6, T 1, R 5. Signed WM. WILSON, RUTH WILSON. Witn: JOHN MAUGH, HENRY WEAVER. rec 1814. pp 572, 573

Deed dated 1814. JOHN SUTHERLAND & NANCY his wife to AZURE REED MILLS. Rossville outlot 11. Signed JOHN SUTHERLAND, NANCY R. SUTHERLAND. Witn: R. BIRCH, ISAAC STANLEY. rec 1814. pp 573, 574

Deed dated 1814. JOSEPH HASLET & ELIZABETH his wife to JAMES MILLS JR. S 17, T 2, R 3. Signed JOSEPH HASLET, ELIZABETH (x) HASLET. Witn: JAMES SMITH,

BUTLER COUNTY LAND RECORDS: BOOK D

ANTHONY HINCLE. rec 1814. pp 574, 575

Deed dated 1812. USA to JOSEPH HAZLET, assignee of JAMES HAZLET. S 17, T 2, R 3. rec 1814. p 575

Deed dated 1814. JOHN BELT to JESSE WALDEN. S 11, T 3, R 1 in Morgan Twp. Signed JOHN BELT. Witn: WILLIAM D. JONES, JAMES SHIELDS. rec 1814. pp 576, 577

Deed dated 1814. JAMES HEATON & MARY his wife to CELICIA HERBERT. Hamilton lot 165. Signed JAMES HEATON, MARY HEATON. Witn: J.C. McMANUS, ISAAC STANLEY. rec 1814. pp 577, 578

Deed dated 1814. SAMUEL McCLURE & MARY his wife to ENOCH D. JOHN. Middletown lot 37. Signed SAMUEL McCLURE, MARY (x) McCLURE. Witn: JAMES HEATON, EZEKIEL BALL. rec 1814. pp 578, 579

Deed dated 1814. EZEKIEL McCLURE to JOSHUA MUMMY of Franklin Co, IN Ter'y. Middletown lot 49. Signed EZEKIEL B. McCLURE. Witn: EZEKIEL D. JOHN , WILLIAM SPINNING. rec 1814. pp 579, 580

Deed dated 1814. BAZEL HARRISON & MARTHA his wife to JAMES MURPHY. S 31, R , R 3. Signed BAZEL HARRISON, MARTHA (x) HARRISON. Witn: JOHN AYERS, JOHN C. AYERS rec 1814. pp 580, 581

Deed dated 1814. ABSOLEM GOODENOUGH & SALLY his wife to NICHOLAS DAVIS. Hamilton lot 71. Signed ABSOLEM GOODENOUGH, SALLY (x) GOODENOUGH. Witn: ISAAC STANLEY, ISAIAH GOODENOUGH. rec 1814. pp 581, 582

Bill of Sale dated 1814. JACOB KEEN to RICHARD GAINS. Personal propt'y, livestock. Signed JACOB KEENE. Witn: WILLIAM GRANT. rec 1814. pp 582, 583

Deed dated 1813. JOSEPH L. McMAHON & ELIZABETH his wife to JOSEPH L. McMAHON JR, his nephew. S 26, T 4, R 2. Signed JOSEPH McMAKIN, ELIZABETH (x) McMAKIN. Witn: ANDREW McMAKEN. rec 1814. pp 583, 584, 585

Mortgage dated 1814. WILLIAM McCLANE & MARGARET his wife & WILLIAM SQUIER & SARAH his wife to WILLIAM SPINNING. Middletown lot 16. Signed WM. McCLAIN, MARGARET McCLAIN, WM. SQUIER, SARAH (x) SQUIER. Witn: EZEKIEL BALL, EZEKIEL B. McCLURE. rec 1814. pp 585, 586

Deed dated 1814. USA to JACOB MILLER. S 7, T 1, R

BUTLER COUNTY LAND RECORDS: BOOK D

4. rec 1814. p 586

Deed dated 1812. USA to JACOB MILLER & STEPHEN CLARK. S 26, T 3, R 3. rec 1814. 586, 587

Deed dated 1814. JOHN CLEVES SYMMES to WILLIAM HENRY HARRISON, Major Gen'l, US Army & JOHN CLEVES SHORT of Cincinnati. S 7 & 11, T 4, R 1; S 21, T 3, R 2; S 20, T 3, R 2; S 6, T 4, R 2; S 34, T 4, R 1; S 22, T 2, R 2; S 18, T 4, R 2; S 34, T 4, R 2; S 12, T4, R 1; S 14, T 5, R 1; S 1, T 2, R 4; S 7, T 2, R 4; S 25, T 3, R 4; S 17, T 3, R 3, S 31, T 3, R 2, S 17, T 5, R1; S 34, T 4, R 3, S 31, T 3, R 4. Signed JOHN CLEVES SYMMES. Witn: JOHN MAHARD, MARGARET McCREA. rec 1814. pp 587, 588, 589

Deed dated 1814. JOHN WINGATE & AMMA his wife of Cincinnati to JOHN H. PIATT. Middletown lot 25. Signed JOHN WINGATE, AMMA WINGATE. Witn: ALFRED REYNOLDS, ETHAN STONE. rec 1814. pp 589, 590, 591

Deed dated 1814. JOHN SUTHERLAND & NANCY his wife to SARAH MILLS. Rossville lots 84, 87. Signed JOHN SUTHERLAND, NANCY R. SUTHERLAND. Witn: AZZUR R. MILLS, ISAAC STANLEY. rec 1814. pp 591, 592

Deed dated 1814. RICHARD WATTS & ALISE his wife to MOSES BREES. S 28 & 34, T 2, R 4. Signed RICHARD (x) WATTS, ALICE (x) WATTS. Witn: JOHN TAYLOR, HENRY WEAVER. rec 1814. pp 592, 593

Deed dated 1814. Board of Commissioners, Butler Co to HUGH WILSON. S , T 1, R 3, lot 4. Signed WILLIAM ROBESON, JOSEPH HENDERSON, JOSEPH HOUGH. Witn: JOHN REILY, ISAAC STANLEY. rec 1814.. pp 595, 596

Mortgage dated 1814. ELIAS MOORE & ELIZABETH his wife to NATHAN PAGE. S 12, T 2, R 3. Signed ELIAS (x) MOORE, ELIZABETH (x) MOORE. Witn: DANIEL MILLI- KIN, JAMES McBRIDE. rec 1814. pp 596, 597

Deed dated 1814. NATHAN PAGE & REBECCA his wife to ELIAS MOORE. S 12, T 3, R 3. Signed NATHAN PAGE, REBECCA (x) PAGE. Witn: DANIEL MILLIIKIN, JAMES McBRIDE. rec 1814. pp 597, 598

Deed dated 1814, ISAAC WILES & ELIZABETH his wife to JAMES WILSON. Hamilton lot 3. Signed ISAAC WILES, ELIZABETH (x) WILES. Witn: NICHOLAS HOGAN, ISAAC STANLEY. rec 1814. p 599

BUTLER COUNTY LAND RECORDS: BOOK D

Quitclaim dated 1814. Heirs of JOHN DOTY to SAMUEL CLARK. S 18, T 2, R 2; to compensate "our brother SAMUEL CLARK" for land taken in lawsuit with ELIHU WOODRUFF. Signed DANIEL DOTY (and his wife) BETSEY DOTY, STEPHANUS CLARK (and his wife) BETSEY (x) CLARK, ZINA DOTY (and his wife) SARAH (x) DOTY. Witn: ALEXANDER CARNS, JAMES CLARK. rec 1814. p 600

Quitclaim dated 1814. Heirs of JOHN DOTY to ZINA DOTY. No S-T-R; bound by land of JACOB ROWAN, STEPHANUS CLARK and on the north, by R 3 line. Signed DANIEL DOTY, BETSEY DOTY, STEPHANUS CLARK, BETSEY (x) CLARK, SAMUEL CLARK, JANEY CLARK. Witn: CONRAD COOK, LEWIS ENYART. rec 1814. pp 600, 601

Quitclaim dated 1814. SAMUEL CLARK & his wife JANEY late DOTY to Heirs of JOHN DOTY. S --, T 2, R 2; part of deed given in 1805 by JOHN DOTY. Signed SAMUEL CLARK, JANEY CLARK. Witn: ALEXR. CARNS, JAMES CLARK. rec 1814. pp 601, 602

Deed dated 1814. SAMUEL ENYART & ANNA his wife to BENJAMIN ENYART. Princetown lots 19, 20, 26. Signed SAMUEL ENYART, ANNA ENYART. Witn: AARON AUSTEN, JOHN AYERS. rec 1814. pp 602, 603

Deed dated 1814. MICHAEL WOLF & ANN his wife to ELIHU CRANDLE. S 10, T 4, R 2. Signed MICHAEL WOLF, ANN WOLF. Witn: WILLIAM CARTER, JAMES JOHNSON. rec 1814. pp 603, 604

Deed dated 1814. BENJAMIN HAWKINS & OLIVE his wife to WILLIAM HOLLINGSWORTH. S 5, T 3, R 3. Signed BENJAMIN HAWKINS, OLIVE HAWKINS. Witn: JESSE GREENE, SAMUEL HUNT. rec 1814. pp 605, 606

Deed dated 1814. DANIEL POWERS & ABIGAIL his wife to JOHN TRIM of Hamilton Co. S 20, T 2, R 2. Signed DANIEL POWERS, ABIGAIL (x) POWERS. Witn: JOSEPH GASTON, MARTHA GASTON. rec 1814. pp 608, 609

Deed dated 1814. ABRAM MILEY SR & CATHRINE his wife to JOHN MILEY. S 4, T 2, R 3. Signed ABRAM (x) MILEY, CATHRINE (x) MILEY. Witn: DAVID BRADBERRY, WILLIAM GRIFFIN. rec 1814. pp 609, 610

Deed dated 1814. ABRAM MILEY JR & SUSANNA his wife to JOHN MILEY. S 4, T 2, R 3. Signed ABRAM (x) MILEY JR, SUSANNA (x) MILEY. Witn: WILLIAM HAYS, ELISHA SWINDLES. rec 1814. pp 611, 612

BUTLER COUNTY LAND RECORDS: BOOK D

Deed dated 1814. ABRAHAM LOWRY & RACHEL his wife to JOHN P. FINKLE. S 12, T 3, R 3. Signed ABM. LOWRY, RATCHEL (x) LOWRY. Witn: JAMES CLARK, STEPHEN JONES. rec 1814. pp 612, 613

Deed date 1814. JOHN HANCOCK SR & NANCY his wife to JOHN HANCOCK JR. S 1, T 4, R 1. Signed JOHN HANCOCK, NANCY (x) HANCOCK. Witn: SAMUEL BEELER JR, JAMES J. BEELER. rec 1815. pp 613, 614

Deed dated 1814. JONATHAN PIERSON & MATILDA his wife to ABSOLEM GOODENOUGH. Hamilton lot 54. Signed JONATHAN PIERSON, MATILDA PEIRSON. Witn: ISAAC STANLEY, DANIEL BROKAW. rec 1815. pp 614, 615

Deed dated 1815. JACOB BENNET to MATTHEW HUESTON. S 35, T 5, R 2. Signed JACOB BENNET. Witn: JOHN REILY, JOHN WINTON. rec 1815. pp 615, 616

Deed dated 1814. SAMUEL DAVIS & SUSAN his wife of Wayne Twp to his mother MARTHA DAVIS. S 14, T 1, R 2 Signed SAML. D. DAVIS, SUSAN DAVIS. Witn: MATTH. RICHARDSON, JOHN C. CRUME. rec 1815. pp 616, 617, 618.

Deed dated 1814. PETER METZGER & BARBARA his wife of St. Clair Twp to PETER GREEN. No S-T-R; land in St. Clair bound by DANIEL FLEENER's property. Signed PETER METZGER, BARBARA (x) METZGER. Witn: JAMES SMITH, JACOB SLIFER. rec 1815. pp 618, 619

Deed dated 1814. WILLIAM LEGG SR & CASSANDRA his wife to RUNEY CLAWSON. S 2, T 2, R 3. Signed WILLIAM LEGG, CASSANDRA (x) LEGG. Witn: JOHN VINNEDGE, ROSANA VINNEDGE. rec 1815. pp 619, 620

Deed dated 1814. DAVID CRANE & ELIZABETH his wife to ABRAHAM HALL. S 29, T 2, R 4. Signed DAVID CRANE, ELIZABETH (x) CRANE. Witn: CORNELIUS HIGGINS, HENRY WEAVER. rec 1815. pp 620, 621, 622

Deed dated 1814. ISAAC MARTIN & MARY his wife of Madison Twp to WILLIAM SQUIER of same. S 5, T 1, R 4. Signed ISAAC MARTIN, MARY MARTIN. Witn: LEONARD WEAVER, HENRY WEAVER. rec 1815. pp 622, 623

Deed dated 1814. WILLIAM HARVEY & ISABELLA his wife to ROBERT JOHN. Middletown lot 35. Signed WM. HARVEY, ISABELLA HARVEY. Witn: JAMES CLARK, JOSEPH FREEN. rec 1815. pp 623, 624

BUTLER COUNTY LAND RECORDS: BOOK D

Deed dated 1814. ARTHUR ST. CLAIR JR & FRANCES his wife to HENRY BALSER. S 21, T 2, R 3. Signed AR. ST. CLAIR JUN., FRANCES H. ST. CLAIR. Witn: ICHD. SPINING, ETHAN STONE. rec 1815. pp 624, 625

Deed dated 1815. WILLIAM C. KEEN & RACHEL his wife and ANDREW STEWART & ISABELLA his wife to JOSEPH F. RANDOLPH. Hamilton lot 52. Signed ANDW. STEWART, ISABELLA STEWART, WM. C. KEEN, RACHEL (x) KEEN. Witn: ZEROBABEL COLBY, JOHN AYERS. rec 1815. pp 625, 626, 627

Deed dated 1814. Sheriff of Butler Co to MATTHEW WINTON. JOHN HAMILTON obtained judgement against JOHN GREER. Hamilton outlot 3 seized, sold at auction. Signed JAMES McBRIDE, Sheriff. Witn: DAN'L MILLIKIN, GEORGE STONEBRAKER. rec 1815. pp 627m 628, 629, 630

Deed dated 1815. ROBERT IRWIN & MARY his wife to HENRY LONG of PA. S 32, T 2, R 1. Signed ROBERT IRWIN, MARY IRWIN. Witn: JAMES CUMMINS, JAMES MILLS. rec 1815. pp 630, 631

Deed datd 1814. SAMUEL SEWARD JR & ANNA his wife to ISAAC SEWARD. S 5, T 2, R 2. Signed SAMUEL SEWARD JR, ANNA SEWARD. Witn: JAMES HEATON, BYRAM SEWARD. rec 1815. pp 631, 632

Bill of Sale dated 1815. BENJAMIN STITES to AARON ETHERTON & JOSEPH SALER of Hamilton Co. Crops, livestock, etc. Signed BENJAMIN STITES. Witn: AARON ATHERTON, HENRY (x) BROADBERRY. rec 1815. pp 632, 633

Deed dated 1814. JOHN C. WINANS & ELIZA his wife of Warren Co to ARTHUR ELLIOTT JR. S 21, T 3, R 3. Signed JOHN C. WINANS, ELIZA B. WINANS. Witn: ENOS WILLIAMS, ELI W. MINOR. rec 1815. pp 633, 634

Deed dated 1812. USA to AARON SHRADER, assignee of DAVID BEATY JR. S 26, T 2, R 3. rec 1815. p 634

Deed dated 1814. JAMES P. MORTON to JAMES B. THOMAS & WILLIAM THOMAS. Hamilton lot 51. Signed JAMES P. MORTON. Witn: ISAAC HAWLEY, ISAAC STANLEY. rec 1815. p 635

Deed dated 1814. JAMES CARLISLE & HARRIET his wife to JAMES CLARK. S 36, T 2, R 2. Signed JAMES CARLISLE, HARRIET CARLISLE. Witn: ISAAC STANLEY,

BUTLER COUNTY LAND RECORDS: BOOK D

LEVI (x) McDONALD. rec 1815. pp 636, 637

Deed dated 1815. WILLIAM GARRET & ELIZABETH his wife to THOMAS AYERS of Hartfort Co, MD. Middletown lot 26. Signed WILLIAM GARRET, ELIZABETH (x) GARRET. Witn: WM. HARVEY, JOHN GARRET. rec 1815. pp 637, 638

Deed dated 1813. JOHN DAVIS SR of Green Twp, Greene Co, PA to beloved dau SARAH MORRISON & s/n/law BENJAMIN MORRISON. S 19, T 2, R 4 given "hereunto moving". Signed JOHN DAVIS. Witn: PETER MYERS, ASCHEY MORRISON. rec 1815. pp 638, 639

Deed dated 1813. JOHN FREEMAN & ELIZABETH his wife to JOHN FREEMAN JR. S 26, T 2, R 4. Bound by land of JOSHUA BUTLER. Signed JOHN (x) FREEMAN, ELIZABETH (x) FREEMAN. Witn: HENRY WEAVER, ELISHA SUTTON. rec 1815. pp 639, 640

Deed dated 1814. JOHN FREEMAN & ELIZABETH his wife to JOHN FREEMAN JR. S 26, T 2, R 4. Bound by land of WILLIAM HARVEY. Signed JOHN (x) FREEMAN. (ELIZABETH mentioned, no signature). Witn: WILLIAM HARVEY, JACOB CAMPBELL. rec 1815. pp 640, 641

Deed dated 1815. STEPHEN SCUDDER & ELIZABETH his wife to WILLIAM JOHNSON. S 5, T 2, R 2. Signed STEPHEN SCUDDER, ELIZABETH (x) SCUDDER. Witn: JOHN AYERS, JOHN REED JR. rec 1815. pp 641, 642

Deed dated 1814. CLARKSON FREEMAN of PA to ABRAHAM FREEMAN. S 35, T 3, R 3. Signed C. FREEMAN. Witn: W.B. ROSS, CHRIS. STAUFFER. rec 1815. p 643

Deed dated 1814. STEPHEN CRANE & MARY his wife to BENJAMIN BARBEE. S 15, T 3, R 3. Signed STEPHEN CRANE, MARY CRANE. Witn: P. WILLIAMSON, JOHN BOYD. rec 1815. pp 643, 644

Deed dated 1809. JOHN CLEVES SYMMES to SAMUEL HARPER of Liberty Twp. S 17, T 3, R 2. Signed JOHN CLEVES SYMMES. Witn: JESSE REEDER, HUGH MOORE. rec 1815. pp 645, 646

Deed dated 1815. WILLIAM PATTON to PHILIP McGONIGLE. Hamilton lot 151. Signed WILLIAM PATTON. Witn: JAMES HEATON, WILLIAM BIGHAM. rec 1815. pp 646, 647

Deed dated 1815. WILLIAM PATTON & JANE his wife to PHILIP McGONIGLE. Hamilton lot 151. Signed and witn as above. (no wife's signature) rec 1815. pp 647, 648

BUTLER COUNTY LAND RECORDS: BOOK D

Deed dated 1815. BENJAMIN HAWKINS by his atty, JOSEPH HOLLINGSWORTH to JAMES HAWKINS. S 8, T 3, R 3. Signed BENJAMIN HAWKINS by JOSEPH HOLLINGSWORTH. Witn: MATTHEW RICHARDSON, MATTHEW I. RICHARDSON. rec 1815. pp 648, 649

Power of Attorney dated 1815. BENJAMIN HAWKINS appted JOSEPH HOLLINGSWORTH as atty to convey land title. Signed BENJAMIN HAWKINS. Witn: SAMUEL PLATT, SAMUEL HUND. rec 1815. pp 649, 650

Deed dated 1815. BENJAMIN HAWKINS & OLIVE his wife to JOSEPH HOLLINGSWORTH. S 5, T 3, R 3 & S 8, T 3, R 3. Signed BENJAMIN HAWKINS, OLIVE HAWKINS. Witn: JAMES HARPER, JAMES HAWKINS. rec 1815. pp 650, 651

Deed dated 1815. JOSEPH ORSBORN & LYDIA his wife of Franklin Co, Indiana Ter'y to ABRAHAM TEITSORT. S 29, 33, T 2, R 4. Signed JOSEPH ORSBORN, LYDIA (x)ORSBORN ESTHER TEITSORT. Witn: ISAAC HOFF, HENRY WEAVER. JP's note: ESTHER TEITSORT, late ESTHER ORSBORN, relinquishes dower rights. rec 1815. pp 651, 652

Deed dated 1815. PETER TEITSORT SR & ESLE his wife to ISAAC THOMPSON. S 29, T 4, R 2. Signed PETER TEITSORT, ESTHER TEITSORT. Witn: ISAAC HOFF, HENRY WEAVER. rec 1815. pp 652, 653, 654

Deed dated 1814. Sheriff to JOSEPH POTTER. Damages assessed against WILLIAM NICOL, a private in Capt. IRA HUNT's company, for neglect of duty by officers of 1st Regt, 2d Battn, 3d Brigade of 1st Divsn, OH militial. Hamilton lot 12 seized, sold at auction. Signed JAMES McBRIDE, Sheriff. Witn: DANL. MILLIKIN, JAMES MILLS. rec 1815. pp 654, 655, 656

Deed dated 1814. JOHN DAVIS JR & JANE his wife of Milford Twp to AARON BIGGS of Summer Twp, Preble Co. S 6, T 5, R 2. Signed JOHN DAVIS JR, JANE DAVIS. Witn: MATTH. RICHARDSON, BETSEY SIMPSON. rec 1815. pp 656, 657

Deed dated 1814. JOHN MANSON & ELIZABETH his wife to JOHN ZIMMERMAN of Preble Co. S 21, T 6, R 2. Signed JOHN MANSON, ELIZABETH (x) MANSON. Witn: MATTH. RICHARDSON, D.C. HOPE. rec 1815. pp 657, 658

Deed dated 1814. ALBERT BANTA & NANCY his wife of Warren Co to GEORGE & JOSEPH McDOUGLE of Hamilton Co. S 12, T 2, R 4. Signed ALBERT BANTA, NANSE BANTA. Witn: SAML. CAMPBELL, JAMES W. LANIER. rec 1815.

BUTLER COUNTY LAND RECORDS: BOOK D

pp 658, 659, 660

Deed dated 1814. JAMES CLARK & ALETHA his wife to DAVID RISK of Hamilton Co. S 23, T 3, R 3. Signed JAMES CLARK, ALETHA CLARK. Witn: P. WILLIAMSON, JAMES STEWART. rec 1815. pp 660, 661

Deed dated 1815. SAMUEL DICK & MARTHEW his wife to JOHN McCLOSKY & JAMES BEATY. S 28, T 4, R 2. Signed SAMUEL DICK, MARTHEW DICK. Witn: JP JOHN DURRAS, BENJAMIN PINE. rec 1815. pp 661, 662

Deed dated 1813. JOHN SUTHERLAND & NANCY his wife to JOEL KENNEDY. Hamilton lot 114. Signed JOHN SUTHERLAND, NANCY R. SUTHERLAND. Witn: SAMUEL SCOTT, JAMES RAMSEY. rec 1815. pp 662, 663

Deed dated 1808. SETH GARD & MARY his wife of Springfield Twp, Hamilton Co to GEORGE SUTTON of St.Clair Twp S 2, T 4, R 2. Signed SETH GARD, MARY (x) GARD. Witn: PETER KEEN, MOSES ARGO. rec 1815. pp 663, 664

Deed dated 1814. THOMAS DONALD & ELIZABETH his wife to WILLIAM HUNT. S 1, T 2, R 3. Signed THOMAS DONALD ELIZABETH DONALD. Witn: JOHN AYERS, JAMES DONALD. rec 1815. pp 664, 665

Deed dated 1815. WILLIAM HUNT & MARGRET his wife of Hamilton Co to JAMES CUMMINGS. S 1, T 2, R 3. Signed WM. HUNT, MARGARET HUNT. Witn: ANDW. BRANNON, JOHN MAHARD. rec 1815. pp 666, 667

Deed dated 1815. PHILIP McGONIGLE & CATY his wife to WILLIAM PATTON. Hamilton lots 151, 152. Signed PHILIP McGONIGAL, CATY (x) McGONIGAL. Witn: JAMES HEATON, WILLIAM BIGHAM. rec 1815. pp 667, 668

Deed dated 1814. EVAN JONES of Ross Twp to JOSEPH BROWN of same S 31, T 3, R 2; bound by land of DAVID FRANCIS, WILLIAM D. JONES. Signed EVAN JONES. Witn: JAMES SHIELDS, JOHN SMITH. rec 1815. pp 668 669, 670

Deed dated 1814. EDWARD COEN & MARGARET his wife of Ross Twp to SAMUEL BROWN of same. S 31, T 3, R 2. Signed EDWARD COEN, MARGARET (x) COEN. Witn: JP WM. D. JONES, SARAH JONES. rec 1815. pp 670, 671

Deed dated 1813. WILLIAM McCINTRAY & CATY his wife to JOHN McCINTRAY. S 4, T 4, R 2. Bound by land of GEORGE BOYER. Signed WILLIAM (x) McCINTRAY,

BUTLER COUNTY LAND RECORDS: BOOK D

CATY (x) McCINTRAY. Witn: DANL MILLIKIN, ROBT. B. MILLIKIN. rec 1815. pp 671, 672

Deed dated 1814. HENRY HALL & MARY his wife to WILLIAM WOOD. S 1, T 4, R 1. Signed HENRY (x) HALL, MARY (x) HALL. Witn: ELEAZAR HOAG, JOHANNES (german script). rec 1815. pp 672, 673

Deed dated 1814. HENRY HALL & MARY his wife to HENRY CLEM. S 1, T 4, R 1. Signed and witn as above. rec 18115. pp 674, 675

Deed dated 1814. JOHN CALDWELL & ELIZABETH his wife to WILLARD M. SMITH. Hamilton lot 82. Signed JOHN CALDWELL, ELIZABETH CALDWELL. Witn: IRA MILLER, ISAAC STANLEY. rec 1815. pp 675, 676

Deed dated 1810. JOHN STONEBRAKER & REBECCA his wife to SABASTON STONEBRAKER, farmer. S 34, T 4, R 2. Signed JOHN STONEBRAKER (german script) REBECCA (x) STONEBRAKER. Witn: NATHAN GRIFFITH, NINIAN BEATY. rec 1815. pp 676, 677

Deed dated 1815. DAVID CONKLING to STEPHEN McFARLAND S 24, T 4, R 1. Signed DAVID CONKLIN. Witn: SAMUEL DILLON, ETHAN STONE. rec 1815. pp 677, 678

Deed dated 1813. CORNELIUS R. SEDAM to Board of Commissioners, Butler Co. Land to erect courthouse given in appreciation to Butler Co. S 1, T 1, R 3. Signed CORNELIUS R. SEDAM. Witn: JOHN REILY, WM. CORRY. rec 1815. pp 678, 679

Deed dated 1811. ELIAS BOUDINET to THOMAS McADAMS. S 21, T 2, R 4. Signed ELIAS BOUDINOT by JAC. BURNET, agent. Witn: ROBT. WALLACE JR, WILLIAM IRWIN JR. rec 1815. pp 679, 680

Deed dated 1813. JOHN MILLS & SARAH his wife to JAMES DENNY. S 1, T 2, R 4. Signed JOHN MILLS, SARAH (x) MILLS. Witn: JOSEPH BANKER, JOHN (x) LUCAS. rec 1815. pp 681, 682

Deed dated 1815. JOHN LUCAS & JEMIMA his wife to MICHAEL TEMPLE JR. S 12, T 2, R 4. Signed JOHN LUCAS, JEMIMA (x) LUCAS. Witn: JAMES LEE, HENRY WEAVER. rec 1815. pp 682, 683

Deed dated 1815. STEPHEN McFARLAND & CATHARINE his wife of Cincinnati to DAVID CONKLING of Hamilton Co.

BUTLER COUNTY LAND RECORDS: BOOK D

S 24, T 4, R 1. Signed STEPHEN MacFARLAND, CATHARINE McFARLAND. Witn: SAMUEL DILLON, ETHAN STONE. rec 1815. pp 683, 684

Deed dated 1813. WILLIAM SQUIER to MOSES DENMAN. S 5, T 1, R 4. Signed WM. SQUIER. Witn: WILLIAM HUTCHIN, HENRY WEAVER. rec 1815. pp 684, 685

Deed dated 18--. WILLIAM DENMAN & MARY his wife to MOSES DENMAN. S 32, 33, T 2, R 4. Signed WILLIAM DENMAN, MARY (x) DENMAN. Witn: HENRY WEAVER, CHRISTOPHER (x) WAGONER. rec 1815. pp 685, 686

Deed dated 1814. ABRAHAM HARTZEL & EVE his wife to WILLIAM WILLIS. S 20, T 3, R 2. Signed ABRAHAM HARTZEL, EVE B. HARTZEL. Witn: MICHAEL AYERS, DANIEL (x) PERRINE. rec 1815. pp 687, 688

Deed dated 1815. JONATHAN CONNERY to ELLIS JOHN. S 14, T 3, R 2; bound by land of MICHAEL HILDERBRAND, BENJAMIN DECKER. Signed JONATHAN CONNERY. Witn: JOHN AYERS, JOHN JOHN. rc 1815. pp 688, 689

Deed dated 1815. HENRY HOUSS & ANN his wife to JOHN CLARK. Brownstown lots 14, 15, 27. Signed HENRY HOUSS, ANN HOUSS. Witn: THOMAS CARLE, HENRY WEAVER. rec 1815. pp 689, 690

Mortgage dated 1814. ROBERT SIGERSON to ALLEN CULLUM. S 25, T 3, R 3. Signed ROBERT SIGERSON. witn: JOHN AYERS, SAMUEL ENYART. rec 1815. pp 690, 691

Deed dated 1814. JOHN SUTHERLAND & NANCY his wife and ABRAHAM HUFF & MAGDALEN his wife to WILLIAM HARVEY & WILLIAM PATTON. S 32, T 2, R 4. Signed JOHN SUTHERLAND, NANCY R. SUTHERLAND, ABRAHAM HUFF, MAGDALEN (x) HUFF. Witn: HENRY WEAVER, JAMES MILLS. rec 1815. pp 691, 692

Deed dated 1815. NANCY DAVIS to ISAAC MOSS. Hamilton lot 139. Signed NANCY DAVIS. Witn: JOS. S. BENHAM, DANIEL MILLIKIN. rec 1815. pp 693, 694

Bill of Sale dated 1814. JAMES VAUGHN of Fairfield Twp to WILLIAM MURRAY. Horses. Signed JAMES (x) VAUGHN. Witn: DANIEL MILLIKIN, JAMES McBRIDE. rec 1815. p 694

Deed dated 1814. ELIJAH WILKINSON & ELIZABETH his wife to SAMUEL WILKINSON. S 14, T 2, R 2; formerly

BUTLER COUNTY LAND RECORDS: BOOK D

owned by JOHN WILKINSON, decd. Signed ELIJAH WILKINSON, ELIZABETH WILKINSON. Witn: JOHN GASTON, E. McCONNEL. rec 1815. p 695

Deed dated 1815. JOHN SUTHERLAND & NANCY his wife to MICHAEL DELARAC. Rossville lot 23. Signed JOHN SUTHERLAND, NANCY R. SUTHERLAND. Witn: DANL. MILLIKIN, JOSEPH HOUGH. rec 1815. pp 696, 697

Deed dated 1807. JOSEPH POWERS & SALOME his wife to DANIEL PARSON. S 3, T 1, R 2. Signed JOSEPH POWERS, SALOME (x) POWERS. Witn: MATTHEW HUSTON, JOHN THORNBERRY. rec 1815. pp 697, 698

Certificate. In 1801, JAMES WHALEN purchased S 20, T 2, R 2 at public sale. Signed JAMES SMITH, Sheriff. Whalen assigned rights to THOMAS ALSTON on behalf of THOMAS KING. Signed JAMES WHALEN. Witn: THOMAS ALSTON, THOMAS WHALEN. rec 1815. pp 698, 699

Quitclaim dated 1814. GASPAR PHRANER & RUTH his wife of Queen's Co, NY, ZEBEDEE PHRANER, JEMIMA WHITEHEAD and WILLIAM PRICE & HANNAH his wife, all of Essex Co, NJ to UZAL EDWARDS. S 19, T 3, R 3. Signed GASPAR PHRANER, RUTH PHRANER, ZEBEDEE PHRANER, WILLIAM PRICE, HANNAH (x) PRICE, JEMIMA WHITEHEAD. Witn: JOHN MASTON, WILLIAM LUDLOW. rec 1815. pp 699, 700, 701

Deed dated 1813. GEORGE CHESTERSON & CHARITY his wife to PHILIP C. HILE. No S-T-R. Signed GEORGE CHESTERTON,, CHARITY (x) CHESTERTON. Witn: JOHN McGILLIARD, ROBT. GUTHRIE. rec 1815. pp 701, 702, 703

Deed dated 1814. STEPHEN CRANE & MARY his wife to PHEBE CRANE of Sycamore Twp, Hamilton Co. S 15, T 3, R 3. Signed STEPHEN CRANE, MARY CRANE. Witn: P. WILLIAMSON, DAVID TULLIS. rec 1815. pp 702, 703

Deed dated 1814. SILAS CONDIT & ELIZABETH his wife of Newark Twp, Essex Co, NJ to UZAL EDWARDS. S 19, T 3, R 3. Signed SILAS CONDIT, ELIZABETH CONDIT. Witn: AARON MUNN. rec 1815. pp 703, 704

Deed dated 1814. STEPHEN S. DAY & SALLY his wife of Orange Twp, Essex Co, NJ to SILAS CONDIT. S 19, T 3, R 3. Signed STEPHEN S. DAY, SALLY DAY. Witn: JAMES CAMP. rec 1815. p 705

Deed dated 1815. ROBERT RICHEY & MARTHA his wife to THOMAS RICHEY. S 15, T 2, R 3. Signed ROBERT RICHEY,

BUTLER COUNTY LAND RECORDS: BOOK D

MARTHA (x) RICHEY. Witn: JAMES HEATON, MARY HEATON. rec 1815. pp 706, 707

Deed dated 1815. DAVID ALEXANDER to HEZEKIAH BROADBERRY. S 30, T 2, R 2. Signed DAVID ALEXANDER. Witn: JAMES HEATON, WILLIAM ALEXANDER. rec 1815. pp 707, 708

Deed dated 1815. EBENEZER HEATON & ANN his wife to MICHAEL VANTYLE. S 35, T 3, R 4. Signed EBENEZER HEATON, ANN HEATON. Witn: HENRY WEAVER, #2 german script. rec 1815. pp 708, 709

Deed dated 1814. ABNER ENOCH & ELIZABETH his wife to DAVID WOOLVERTON. S 29, T 2, R 4. Signed ABNER ENOCH, ELIZABETH ENOCH. Witn: EZEKIEL BALL, DANIEL McDONALD. rec 1815. pp 709, 710, 711

Deed dated 1815. MATTHEW G. WALLACE & DEBORAH his wife to JOHN P. FINKLE. S 12, T 3, R 3. Signed MATTHEW G. WALLACE, DEBORAH WALLACE. Witn: ABRAHAM LOWRY, WM. HARVEY. rec 1815. pp 711, 712

Deed dated 1815. RICHARD N.V. CRANE & MARY his wife to GEORGE BENNET. S 30, T 2, R 4. Signed RICHARD N.V. CRANE, MARY CRANE. Witn: LEONARD WEAVER, HENRY WEAVER. rec 1815. pp 712, 713

Deed dated 1814. SAMUEL MATTIX & ELEANOR his wife to GEORGE BENNET. S 30, T 2, R 4. Signed SAMUEL MATTIX, ELEANOR (x) MATTIX. Witn: GILES MARTIN, HENRY WEAVER. rec 1815. pp 713, 714

Deed dated 1814. JOHN KEMP & ELIZABETH his wife to ABRAHAM MARTS. S 4, T 2, R 4. Signed JOHN KEMP, ELIZABETH (x) KEMP. Witn: ARTHUR P. THOMAS, HENRY WEAVER. rec 1815. pp 714, 715, 716

Deed dated 1814. JOHN KEMP & ELIZABETH his wife to CHRISTOPHER REED. S 4, T 2, R 4. Signed JOHN KEMP, ELIZABETH (x) KEMP. Witn: ARTHUR POLHEMUS, HENRY WEAVER. rec 1815. pp 716, 717

End of Book D; Start Book E

Book E has been xerox copied and reduced in page size. Reading is difficult, but preferable to the retyped ledgers, spellings altered by guesswork.

Mortgage datd 1814. SAMUEL BROWN to EDWARD COEN. S 31, T 3, R 2 in Ross Twp. Signed SAMUEL BROWN. Witn:

BUTLER COUNTY LAND RECORDS: BOOK E

RACHEL BROWN, WM. D. JONES. rec 1815. pp 1, 2

Deed dated 1815. Admtr of JOHN LOWRY JR to JAMES STUART. S 12, T 3, R 3. Signed FLEMING LOWRY. Witn JP JAMES CLARK, WILLIAM H. CLARK. rec 1815. pp 2, 3

Deed dated 1815. THOMAS SWIFT & REBECCA his wife to ANDREW HAMILTON. S 1, T 2, R 3. Signed THOMAS SWIFT REBECCA SWIFT. Witn: JOHN SUTHERLAND, DAVID PUGH. rec 1815. pp 4, 5

Deed dated 1814. RICHARD WATTS & ALICE his wife to JOHN TAYLOR. S 28, T 2, R 4; bound by land of DANIEL DOTY, HUGH VAIL. Signed RICHARD (x) WATTS, ALICE (x) WATTS. Witn: DAVID ENYART, HENRY WEAVER. rec 1815. pp 5, 6

Deed dated 1813. HUGH VAIL to JOHN TAYLOR. S 28, T 2, R 4. Signed HUGH VAIL. Witn: DANIEL TAYLOR, HENRY WEAVER. rec 1815. pp 6, 7

Deed dated 1814. DAVIS BALL & MARY his wife to MICHAEL PEARCE. S 31, T 2, R 4. Signed DAVIS BALL, MARY (x) BALL. Witn: HENRY WEAVER, SARAH BALL. rec 1815. pp 7, 8, 9

Deed dated 1815. JOHN BLUE & MARY his wife to MICHAEL PEARCE. S 31, T 2, R 4. Signed JOHN BLUE, MARY (x) BLUE. Witn: DAVID (x) DAVIS, HENRY WEAVER. rec 1815. pp 9, 10

Deed dated 1815. EBENEZER PADDOCK & KEZIA his wife to MICHAEL PEARCE. S 36, T 3, R 3; bound by land of JAMES DRAKE. Signed EBENEZER PADDOCK, KEZIA (x) PADDOCK. Witn: WILLIAM PADDOCK, HENRY WEAVER. rec 1815. pp 10, 11

Mortgage date 1814. ARTHUR ELLIOTT to JOHN C. WINANS S 21, T 3, R 3. Signed ARTHUR W. ELLIOTT. Witn: RICHARD VESBRYCK, MATTHIAS CORWIN JR. rec 1815. p 12

Deed dated 1815. JAMES McBRIDE, sheriff, to WILLIAM R. WRIGHT. S 31, T 3, R 4. Land belonged jointly to JOSEPH ASHTON the elder & to JOSEPH ASHTON the younger. After the death of JOSEPH the younger, the land could not be partitioned equitably; sale ordered by Court. JOSEPH the younger's heirs were his minor son and daus, MARTHA, CATHARINE, JOSEPH, SARAH & MARY ASHTON. Signed JAMES McBRIDE. Witn: THOMAS FREEMAN, WM. CORRY. rec 1815. pp 12, 13, 14, 15

BUTLER COUNTY LAND RECORDS: BOOK E

Deed dated 1812. Admtrs of ISRAEL LUDLOW to THOMAS C. KELSEY. Hamilton lot 110. Signed JOHN LUDLOW for CHARLOTTE RISK, for JAMES FINDLAY and for himself. Witn: JOHN REILY, JOHN WHITWORTH. rec 1815. pp 15, 16

Deed dated 1815. LAURENCE CAVENAUGH & ANNA his wife late ANNA MARTIN, dau of JAMES MARTIN decd, to JOHN SUTHERLAND. One equal seventh part of land now held by ANNA MARTIN, widow of JAMES. Signed LAURENCE CAVENAUGH, ANNA CAVENAUGH. Witn: EPHRAIM CATTERLIN, ISAAC STANLEY. rec 1815. pp 16, 17

Deed dated 1814. LAURENCE CAVENAUGH & ANNA his wife to JOHN SUTHERLAND. S 23, T 4, R 2; one seventh of land held by ANNA MARTIN, purchased from JAMES MARTIN JR, son of JAMES decd. Signed and witn as above. rec 1815. pp 17, 18, 19

Deed dated 1815. JOHN SUTHERLAND & NANCY his wife to JAMES YOUNG. S 23, T 4, R 2; one seventh part, respecting dower rights of ANNA MARTIN. Signed JOHN SUTHERLAND, NANCY R. SUTHERLAND. Witn: DANIEL MILLIKIN, JOSEPH HOUGH. rec 1815. pp 19, 20

Deed dated 1814. ARCHIBALD TALBOT & POLLY his wife, a dau & heir of JAMES MARTIN, to JAMES YOUNG. S 23, T 4, R 2; one seventh part, bound by land of WILLIAM MARTIN, MATTHEW RICHARDSON. Signed ARCHIBALD TALBOT, POLLY TALBOT. Witn: JOHN E. SCOTT, ISAAC STANLEY. rec 1815. pp 20, 21, 22

Deed dated 1813. JOSEPH STEELE & AGNESS his wife to JAMES YOUNG. One seventh part of estate of JAMES MARTIN, decd, of Milford Twp: S 23, T 4, R 2. Signed JOSEPH STEELE, AGNESS STEELE. Witn: JOHN McMAHON, MATTH. RICHARDSON. rec 1815. pp 22, 23

Agreement dated 1813. ANDREW YOUNG with JAMES YOUNG. Andrew to deliver good deed for S 12, T 5, R 2 when patent is obtained. Signed ANDREW YOUNG, JAMES YOUNG. Witn: ALEXANDER YOUNG. rec 1815. p 24

Deed dated 1814. NANCY DAVIS to RICHARD DAVIS. Hamilton lot 139. Signed NANCY DAVIS. Witn: JAMES T. MORTON, ISAAC STANLEY. rec 1815. pp 24, 25

Deed dated 1815. RICHARD D. DAVIS to M.S. PETITT of Hamilton Co. Hamilton lot 139. Signed RICHARD D. DAVIS. Witn: THOS. RAWLINS, ANN RAWLINS. rec 1815. pp 25, 26, 27

BUTLER COUNTY LAND RECORDS: BOOK E

Deed dated 1815. WILLIAM C. KERR & ANDREW STUART to JOHN C. McMANUS. Hamilton lot 52. Signed WM. C. KERR, ANDW. STEWART. Witn: JAMES HEATON, MARY HEATON. rec 1815. pp 27, 28

Deed dated 18--. JOHN WINGATE, sheriff, to JACOB BURNET of Cincinnati. Admtrs of CHARLES AVERY, dec'd, (JOHN ARMSTRONG, ROBERT CALDWELL, ANDREW BURT) obtained judgement against JAMES SMITH. Hamilton outlots 1 & 2 seized, sold for debt. Signed JOHN WINGATE. Witn: JOHN REILY, SAMUEL DAVIS JR. rec 1815. pp 28, 29, 30, 31

Deed dated 1814. AARON BAKER & HANNAH his wife of Montgomery Co to GEORGE ROBY. Baker gave deed dated 1809, rec Bk B, pp 168, 169. Description of bounds not correct. Quitclaim for additional land in S 17, T3, R 3. Signed AARON BAKER, HANNAH BAKER. Witn: MOSES SIMPSON, JOHN FOLKERTH. rec 1815. pp 31, 32

Deed dated 1815. GEORGE ROBY & NAOMI his wife to PIERSON SAYRE. S 17, T 3, R 3; bound by land of AARON RICHARDSON, JOSEPH PATTERSON, JOHN CARSON. Signed GEORGE ROBY, NAOMI ROBY. Witn: JP JAMES CLARK, ANN SAYRE. rec 1815. pp 32, 33

Deed dated 1815. PIERSON SAYRE & CATHARINE his wife to GEORGE ROBY. S 11, T 3, R 3; bound by land of JAMES STEWART, ESTHER THOMAS. Signed PIERSON SAYRE, CATHARINE SAYRE. Witn: JAMES CLARK, ANN SAYRE. rec 1815. pp 34, 35

Mortgage dated 1815. HENRY CONKLING to AARON GARD. S 2, T 4, R 2; bound by land of ZACARIAH PARRISH, DAVID SUTTON, M. HUESTON. Signed HENRY CONKLING. Witn: M. HUESTON, JOSHUA McDOWELL. rec 1815. pp 35,36

Deed dated 1815. AARON GARD & GINNE his wfie to HENRY CONKLING. S 2, T 4, R 2, surveyed by ISAAC HAWLEY. Signed AARON GARD, GINNE (x) GARD. Witn as above. rec 1815. pp 36, 37

Deed dated 1812. GEORGE SUTTON & HANNAH his wife to AARON GARD. S 2, T 4, R 2. Signed GEORGE SUTTON, HANNAH SUTTON. Witn: JP JAMES JOHNSON, SARAH JOHNSON. rec 1815. pp 37, 38, 39

Mortgage dated 1815. ZACARIAH PARRISH to GEORGE SUTTON. S 2, T 4, R 2; bound by land of H. CONKLIN, GARD PARRISH, DAVID SUTTON, A. GARD. Signed ZACARIAH PARRISH. Witn: M. HUESTON, AARON GARD. rec 1815.

BUTLER COUNTY LAND RECORDS: BOOK E

pp 39, 40

Deed dated 1815. ELISHA WADE & NANCY his wife of (illegible) Co, IN Ter'y to JOSEPH HAYS. S 22, T 2, R 4. Signed ELISHA WADE, NANCY (x) WADE. Witn: JACOB WEIDNER, HENRY WEAVER. rec 1815. pp 40, 41

Power of Attorney revocation dated 1808. ELIAS BOUDINOT revoked POA dated 1797 granted to ABIJAH HUNT, since removed to New Orleans, CORNELIUS SEDAM & JACOB BURNET. Signed ELIAS BOUDINOT. Witn: A. PRINTARD, SUSAN F. SMITH. rec 1815. pp 41, 42

Power of Attorney dated 1818? ELIAS BOUDINOT, now of Burlington, NJ appted JACOB BURNET to collect debts, convey deeds. Signed and witn as above. rec 1815. pp 42, 43

Deed dated 1815. DAVID CONNER & NANCY his wife of Rossville to JOHN SUTHERLAND. S 31, T 2, R 3; bound by land of SAMUEL DICK. Signed DAVID CONNER, NANCY CONNER. Witn: JOHN WINTON, JOHN REILY, MOSES SCOTT. rec 1815. pp 43, 44, 45

Deed dated 1810. NICHOLAS JONES & LYDIA his wife to JOSEPH COLEBY SR of Hamilton Co. S 14, T 2, R 2. Signed NICHOLAS (x) JONES, LYDIA (x) JONES. Witn: CALEB WALKER, JAMES WALKER. rec 1815. pp 45, 46

Deed dated 1815. JAMES ROSS to JOSEPH WILSON & JAMES WILSON. Rossville outlot 29. Signed JAS. ROSS. Witn: ISAAC WILES, JAMES HEATON. rec 1815. pp 46, 47

Bill of Sale dated 1814. JAMES ANDREW of Ross Twp to PETER MOUDY. Livestock, household goods; money paid by ALEC MOUDY. Signed JAMES ANDREW. Witn: WILLIAM McGOMERY, DEBORE (x) WHITINER. JP WILLIAM D. JONES. rec 1815. pp 47, 48

Deed dated 1815. JOHN C. WINANS & ELIZA B. his wife of Warren Co to JOSEPH McCLUNG of Baltimore Co, MD. S 21, T 3, R 3. Signed JOHN C. WINANS, ELIZA B. WINANS. Witn: SAMUEL BLACKBURN, ENOS WILLIAMS. rec 1815. pp 48, 49, 50

Deed dated 1814. Butler County commissioners to Rev. MATTHEW G. WALLACE. S 1, T 1, R 3; lot 4 in CORNELIUS SEDAM's plat. Signed WILLIAM ROBISON, JOSEPH HENDERSON, JOSEPH HOUGH. Witn: JOHN REILY, ISAAC STANLEY. rec 1815. pp 50, 51

BUTLER COUNTY LAND RECORDS: BOOK E

Deed dated 1815.   JACKSON AYERS & ELIZABETH his wife
to MATTHEW G. WALLACE. S 36, T 2, R 2. Signed JACK-
SON AYERS, ELIZABETH AYERS. Witn: E. McCONNEL, NIMROD
P. RANDOLPH. JP JOSEPH GASTON. rec 1815. pp 51, 52

Deed dated 1815.   ISAAC VANDYN & LYDIA his wife to
SAMUEL SEWARD SR. Princetown lot 9 in Liberty Twp.
Signed ISAAC VANDYN, LYDIA VANDYN. Witn: JOHN
AYERS, JOHN C. AYERS. rec 1815. p 53

Deed dated 1815.   ROBERT BROWN & RACHEL his wife to
DANIEL McDONALD. S 29, T 2, R 4. Signed ROBERT
BROWN, RACHEL BROWN. Witn: HENRIETTA (x) BAILY,
EZEKIEL BALL. rec 1815. pp 53, 54, 55

Deed dated 1815.   JOSEPH COLEBY SR & MARGERY his wife
to ISAAC COLEBY. S 14, T 2, R 2. Signed JOSEPH
COLEBY, MARGERY (x) COLEBY. Witn: EZEKIEL WALKER,
JAMES WALKER. JP JOHN McGILLIARD. rec 1815. pp 55, 56

Deed dated 1815.   ABSALOM GOODENOUGH & SARAH his wife
to NICHOLAS DAVIS. Hamilton lot 54. Signed ABSALOM
GOODENOUGH, SARAH (x) GOODENOUGH. Witn: JAMES
HEATON, ROBT. B. MILLIKIN. rec 1815. pp 56, 57

Deed dated 1814.   CONRAD DARR & CATHARINE his wife to
OBADIAH WILLEVER. Darrtown lot 103. Signed CONRAD
DARR, CATHARINE DARR. Witn: MATTH. RICHARDSON,
DAVID WALDRON. rec 1815. pp 57, 58

Deed dated 1815.   THOMAS BURK to OBADIAH WILLEVER. S
16, T 4, R 1. Signed THOMAS (x) BURK. Witn: JOHN
BURK, REBECCA (x) BURK. rec 1815. pp 59, 60

Deed dated 1815.   JOHN GREER & ELEANOR his wife to
JONATHAN PIERSON. Hamilton lot 70. Signed JOHN
GREER, ELINOR GREER. Witn: JOS. S. BENHAM, JAMES
HEATON. rec 1815. pp 60, 61

Deed dated 1815.   DAVID CONKLING of Cincinnati to
MOSES BONNELL of same. S 24, T4, R 1. Signed DAVID
CONKLING. Witn: TIMOTHY COLLARD, JOHN FREEMAN. rec
1815. pp 61, 62

Mortgage dated 1815. JAMES STUART to FLEMING LOWRY.
S 12, T -, R 3. Payment due 1818. Signed JAMES
STEWART. Witn: JAMES CLARK, JOSEPH STEWART. rec
1815. pp 62, 63, 64

Deed dated 1814.   JAMES SUTTON JR & NANCY his wife to

BUTLER COUNTY LAND RECORDS: BOOK E

MATTHEW NICOL. S 29, T 2, R 4; bound by land of
JAMES ROISAL. Signed JAMES SUTTON JR, NANCY SUTTON.
Witn: EZEKIEL BALL, PHEBE BALL. rec 1815. pp 64, 65

pages 65, 66 bound upside down, out of order

Plat of Millville dated 1815. S 4, T 3, R -. JOSEPH
VAN HORNE, proprietor. rec 1815. p 66

Deed dated 1815. DAN CALDWELL & ANN his wife to
ABRAHAM CALDWELL. S 22, T 3, R 2. Signed DAN CALD-
WELL, ANNA (x) CALDWELL. Witn: none. rec 1815. pp
67, 68

Deed dated 1815. JOEL WILLIAMS & PHEBE his wife of
Cincinnati to heirs of DANIEL BROSIUS, his son and
daus: CATHARINE KEMPBELL wife of GEORGE; ELIZABETH
McCLOSKEY wife of JOHN; MARGARET BROSIUS, SARAH BRO-
SIUS & DANIEL BROSIUS. S 3, T 3, R 2; dower rights
reserved by widow ELIZABETH, now wife of JOHN RAINEY.
Suit brought against WILLIAMS and heirs of BROSIUS by
THOMAS MOORHEAD & JOHN MOORHEAD, heirs of ROBT. MOOR-
HEAD, decd; reason unexplained. Signed JOEL WILLIAMS
PHEBE WILLIAMS. Witn: JACOB WHITE, JOHN MAHARD.
rec 1815. pp 68, 69, 70

Deed dated 1815. ROBERT PATTERSON & FLORA his wife
to ABRAHAM GRAFT. S 26, T 3, R 3. Signed ROBERT
PATTERSON, FLORA PATTERSON. Witn: ANDREW CORNELIUS-
ON, HENRY WEAVER. rec 1815. pp 70, 71

Deed dated 1815. ISAAC VANDYN & LYDIA his wife to
WILLIAM JOHNSON. Princetown outlot 8. Signed ISAAC
VANDYN, no wife's signature. Witn: JOHN AYERS, JOHN
C. AYERS. rec 1815. pp 71, 72

Deed dated 1815. WILLIAM JOHNSTON to JAMES CUMMINS.
Princetown outlot 8. Signed WILLIAM (x) JOHNSON.
Witn: DANL. MILLIKIN, NIMROD F. RANDOLPH. rec 1815.
pp 72, 73

Deed dated 1814. THEOPHILUS EAGLESFIELD & PHEBE his
wife to DANIEL SALLE. S 30, T -, R 4. Signed THEOPH-
ILUS EAGLESFIELD, PHEBE EAGLESFIELD. Witn: LEONARD
WEAVER, HENRY WEAVER. rec 1815. pp 73, 74

Deed dated 1814. WILLIAM McCLELLAN, sheriff, to
SMITH THOMPSON. In 1811, JAMES MAXWELL obtained
judgement against JOSEPH THOMPSON. Seized S 2, T 3, R
3; sold at auction. Signed WM. McCLELLAN. Witn:
JAMES SMITH, WM. MURRAY. rec 1815. pp 74, 75, 76, 77

BUTLER COUNTY LAND RECORDS: BOOK E

Deed dated 1815. WILLIAM JOHNSON to ISAAC VANDYN. S 5, T 2, R 2; bound by land of BYRAM SEWARD, SAMUEL SEWARD JR, SAMUEL SEWARD SR. Signed WILLIAM (x) JOHNSTON. Witn: JOHN AYERS, SAMUEL SEWARD. rec 1815. pp 77, 78

Deed dated 1812. SAMUEL ENYART & ANNE his wife to ISAAC VANDYN. Princetown lot 8 in Liberty Twp. Signed SAMUEL ENYART, ANNA ENYART. Witn: JOHN NEWHOUSE, JOHN AYERS. rec 1815. pp 78, 79

Deed dated 1812. SAMUEL ENYART & ANNA his wife to ISAAC VANDYN. Princetown lot 9. Signed and witn as above. rec 1815. pp 79, 80

Deed dated 1814. EDWARD BEBB & MARGARET his wife to minor heirs of BRISON BLACKBURN: JAMES, HAMILTON, MARY & BRYSON BLACKBURN, all of Montgomery Twp, Butler Co (no Montgomery Twp in Butler). No S-T-R given; land in Morgan Twp. Dower rights given to ESTHER BLACKBURN, mother of minors. Signed EDWARD BEBB, MARGARET BEBB. Witn: JP WILLIAM JINKINS, LOT ABRAHAM. rec 1815. pp 80, 81, 82

Deed dated 1813. JAMES MILLS & SARAH his wife to heirs of JAMES PIERCE, decd, sons and daus: JOSEPH, PEGGY, ELISHA, JAMES, BENJAMIN, ELIZA & JOHN PIERCE. S 8, T 2, R 3; now in possession of ELIZABETH PIERCE widow of James. Signed JAMES MILLS, SARAH MILLS. Witn: SQUIER LITTELL, HENRY WEAVER. rec 1815. pp 82, 83

Deed datd 1814. WILLIAM LEGG & SUSANNA his wife to BENJAMIN VANGORDEN. S 2, T 2, R 3, except that sold to JOSEPH YEATS; bound by BENJAMIN FULKERSON's land. Signed WILLIAM LEGG, SUSANNA (x) LEGG. Witn: JOHN AYERS, SAMUEL ENYART. rec 1815. pp 83, 84, 85

Mortgage datd 1815. JAMES ROSS to JAMES MILLS. Rossville lot 90. Signed JAS. ROSS. Witn: JAMES HEATON, BENJAMIN PURSAIL. rec 1815. pp 85, 86

Assignment datd 1815. JAMES MILLS sold above mortgage to SAMUEL DICK. Witn: JAMES HEATON, SAMUEL MORRISON. rec 1815. p 86

Mortgage dated 1810. CORNELIUS THOMAS to ISAAC WILES. S 24, T 2, R 2. Signed CORNELIUS THOMAS. Witn: JAMES HEATON, JONATHAN LINE. rec 1815. pp 88, 89

BUTLER COUNTY LAND RECORDS: BOOK E

Deed dated 1815. MATTHEW ORBISON & JANE his wife to GEORGE BURKET & ANDREW SMITH. S 31, T 3, R 3. Signed MATTHEW ORBISON, JANE (x) ORBISON. Witn: MATTH. RICHARDSON, REBECCA RICHARDSON. rec 1815. pp 88, 89

Quitclaim dated 1815. ANDREW SMITH & ELEANOR his wife to GEORGE BURKET. All interest in land above. Signed ANDREW SMITH, ELEANOR SMITH. Witn: MATTH. RICHARDSON, JOHN GIBSON. rec 1815. pp 89,90

Deed dated 1814. DAVIS BALL & MARY his wife to DAVID ENYART. S 32, T 2, R 4; bound by JONATHAN SIMPSON's land. Signed DAVIS BALL, MARY (x) BALL. Witn: HENRY WEAVER, MICHAEL PEARCE. rec 1815. pp 90, 91

Deed dated 1814. AMOS WHITE & MARY his wife of Hamilton Co to JOHN WHITE. S 8, T 5, R 2. Signed AMOS WHITE, MARY (x) WHITE. Witn: JP JONATHAN PITMAN, LEVI WHITE. rec 1815. pp 91, 92

Deed dated 1814. AMOS WHITE & MARY his wife as above to EDWARD WHITE. S 8, T 5, R 2. Signed & witn as above. rec 1815. pp 93, 94

Deed dated 1815. ABRAHAM WILLIAMS & ELIZA his wife to JONATHAN PITMAN. S 5, T 5, R 2. Signed ABRAHAM WILLIAMS, ELIZA H. WILLIAMS. Witn: JOHN LILLY, ETHAN STONE. rec 1815. pp 94, 95

Deed dated 1811. ELIAS BOUDINOT by JACOB BURNET his agent to JOHN SINKEY or LINKEY. S 25, T 2, R 4: bound by land of JOHN CARSON. Signed ELIAS BOUDINOT by JB. Witn: ETHAN STONE, ISAAC S. PATTON. rec 1815. pp 95, 96

Deeddated 1814. JOHN CARSON & LEAH his wife to ARCHIBALD CAMPBELL. S 25, T 2, R 4. Signed JOHN CARSON, LEAH (x) CARSON. Witn: WM. HARVEY, ALEXANDER CARSON. rec 1815. pp 96, 97, 98

Deed dated 1811. ELIAS BOUDINOT to JACOB KINDELSPECKER, late of PA. S 20, T 2, R 4. Signed ELIAS BOUDINOT by JACOB BURNET his agent. Witn: WILLIAM IRWIN JR, JAMES F. GRISWOLD. rec 1815. pp 98, 99

Deed dated 1815. JACOB KINDELSPECKER & SARAH his wife to DERRICK BARKALOW of Warren Co. S 20, T 2, R 4. Signed JACOB KINDELSPERYER, SARAH (x) KINDELSPERYER. Witn: GEORGE SHELLHOUSE, HENRY WEAVER. rec 1815. pp 99, 100, 101

BUTLER COUNTY LAND RECORDS: BOOK E

Deed dated 1815. SALEM POCOCK to DANIEL POCOCK. S 20, T 3, R 3. Signed SALEM POCOCK. Witn: JOHN AYERS DANIEL WOODRUFF. rec 1815. pp 101, 102

Deed dated 1815. USA to JAMES POCOCK. S 26, T 3, R 3. rec 1815. p 102

Deed dated 1815. USA to SALEM & DANIEL POCOCK. S 26, T 3, R 3. rec 1815. p 103

Deed dated 1815. ALLEN NIXON & MARGRET his wife of Warren Co to JAMES McMANAMAN (in text & clerk's margin note: McMANAMY). S 20, T 3, R 2. Signed ALLEN (x) NIXON, MARGRET (x) NIXON. Witn: JP PATRICK MALOY, GEORGE NIXON. rec 1815. pp 103, 104

Deed dated 1812. WILLIAM BUTLER & MAHITABLE his wife of Cincinnati to ALEXANDER McCALL of same. S 0, T 2, R 2. Signed WM. BUTLER, MAHITABLE (x) BUTLER. Witn: THOMAS SCOTT, SOLOMON LANGDON. rec 1815. pp 104, 105, 106

Deed dated 1815. OBADIAH SCHENCK & ABBY his wife to WILLARD M. SMITH. A fourth part of S 35, T 2, R 2; bound by JOSEPH WALKER's land. Signed OBADIAH SCHENCK ABBEY SCHENCK. Witn: WILLIAM SCHENCK, JOSEPH GASTON. rec 1815. pp 106, 107

Quitclaim dated 1800. DANIEL NELSON & HESTER his wife to JOHN McDONALD, all of Hamilton Co, NW Ter'y. Capt. JOHN McDONALD of Colerain Twp, now decd, entered forfeiture in S 33, T 2, R 2, since conveyed to heirs: ESTER NELSON wife of DANIEL; MARGRATE EWING wife of SAMUEL; JOHN McDONALD; REBECCA McDONALD. Rights granted to John. Signed DANIEL NELSON, ESTHER (x) NELSON. Witn: DAVD. BEATY, WILLIAM MITCHELL. rec 1815. pp 107, 108 (see next 2 deeds)

Quitclaim dated 1800. SAMUEL EWING & MARGRATE his wife and REBECCA McDONALD to JOHN McDONALD, all of Hamilton Co, NW Ter'y. Land above; rights yielded. Signed SAMUEL EWING, MARGRATE (x) EWING, REBECCA (x) McDONALD. Witn: WILLIAM MITCHELL, JAMES McGITH. rec 1815. pp 108, 109

Deed dated 1796. JOHN CLEVES SYMMES to JOHN McDONALD. S 33, T 2, R 2; land forfeited by DANIEL MASK; McDONALD a volunteer settler. Signed JOHN CLEVES SYMMES. Witn: BENJAMIN MORSE, WILLIAM MORFIT. rec 1815. pp 109, 110, 111

BUTLER COUNTY LAND RECORDS: BOOK E

Deed dated 1815. JOHN FREEMAN & HARRIET his wife to WILLARD M. SMITH. S 35, T 2, R 2. Signed JOHN FITS FREEMAN, HARRIET FREEMAN. Witn: JAMES HEATON, TREPHENICE SWEET. rec 1815. pp 111, 112

Deed dated 1815. WILLIAM HARVEY & ISABELLA his wife to JOHN P. FINKLE. Middletown lot 39. Signed WM. HARVEY, ISABELLA HARVEY. Witn: JAMES CLARK, JOSEPH FAIRE. rec 1815. pp 112, 113

Quitclaim dated 1814. Heirs of JOHN TAYLOR of Oxford Twp to EASTER TAYLOR, widow of John. Oxford outlots 33, 34. Signed ROBERT TAYLOR, JOHN SAMPLE (& his wife) ANY SAMPLE, WM. TAYLOR (& his wife) POLLY TAYLOR. Witn: JAMES MILLS, JOHN GRAY. rec 1815. p 114

Deed dated 1815. JACOB SLIFER & SUSANNA his wife to JACOB WM. DECHANT. S 24, T 2, R 3, except land sold to PETER METZGAR. Signed JACOB (x) SLIFER, SUSANNA (x) SLIFER. Witn: JAMES HEATON, JAMES REED. rec 1815. pp 115, 116

Deed dated 1815. JAMES REED to JACOB WM. DECHANT. S 18 & 19, T 1, R 4. Signed JAMES REED. Witn: JACOB HARTZEL, JAMES HEATON. rec 1815. pp 116, 117

Deed datd 1815. PETER METZGER & BARBARA his wife to JACOB WM. DECHANT. No S-T-R; "conveyed to me by JACOB SLIFER" less land previously sold to PETER GREEN rec Bk D, pp 618, 619. Signed PETER METSGOR, BARBARA (x) METSGOR. Witn: JAMES HEATON, JAMES REED. rec 1815. pp 117, 118, 119

Deed dated 1814. JACOB SLIFER & SUSANNAH his wife of St. Clair Twp to PETER METSGER. Land conveyed to Slifer by release from Fleenor heirs; rec Bk B, pp 372, 373. Signed JACOB (x) SLIFER, SUSANNA (x) SLIFER. Witn: JOHN SMITH, PETER V. GREEN. rec 1815. pp 119, 120

Quitclaim dated 1814. Heirs of WILLIAM STANLEY of Cincinnati to WILLIAM STANLEY HATCH of same. Cincinnati lots 52, 54, 77, 79; Columbia lot 22 in Hamilton Co; Franklin lot 96 and S 28, T 4, R 2 in Warren Co; 262 acres in Athens Co; S 15, T 2 in Symmes Purchase; 70 acres in military warrant 3474 issued to LEONARD COOPER; 4 shares in Cincinnati Mill Stream Company; lot 97 in Williamsburg, KY. Signed JACOB MERRILL (& his wife) ANNA MERRILL of Whitstown, Oneida Co, NY, JAMES STANLEY JR (& his wife) DIANTHA (x) STANLEY of Cassonovia, Madison Co, NY. Witn:

BUTLER COUNTY LAND RECORDS: BOOK E

FREDERICK STANLEY, JACOB M. MERRILL. rec 1815. pp 121, 122

Deed dated 1815. JOHN LUCAS & JEMIMA his wife to JOHN TEMPLE. S 12, T 2, R 4. Signed JOHN LUCAS, no wife's signature. Witn: JAMES LEE, HENRY WEAVER. rec 1815. pp 122, 123

Deed dated 1815. BENJAMIN D. DAVIS & JANE his wife to JOHN McCINSTRAY. S 4, T 4, R 2. Signed BENJAMIN D. DAVIS, JANE (x) DAVIS. Witn: MATTH. RICHARDSON, MATTHEW J. RICHARDSON. rec 1815. pp 124, 125

Deed dated 1815. ISAAC LINDLEY & ABIGAIL his wife to HIRAM LINDLEY. S 12, T 4, R 1. Signed ISAAC LINDLEY, ABIGAIL LINDLEY. Witn: JP J. M. DORSEY, ALEXANDER (x) ABEL. rec 1815. pp 126, 127, 128

pp 128, 129 bound out of order

Deed dated 1814. MARK HARRIS of Hamilton Co to JEMIMA FRENCH. Middletown lot 19. Signed MARK HARRIS. Witn: NATHL. FRENCH, WM. CLARK. rec 1815. pp 128, 129

Deed dated 1815. JAMES MOREHOUSE & MARY his wife of Champaign Co to JAMES SCHANK of Warren co. S 10, T 2, R 4. Signed JAMES MOREHOUSE, MARY MOREHOUSE. Witn: MARTHA CRAWFORD, WILLIAM CRAWFORD. rec 1815. pp 129, 130

Deed dated 1812. JOHN DAVIS, weaver & SARAH his wife of Millford Twp to JEMIMA WRIGHT, widow. S 6, T 5, R 2. Signed JOHN DAVIS, SARAH (x) DAVIS. Witn: MARSH WILLIAMS, WILLIAM McCREARY. rec 1815. pp 130, 131

Deed dated 1815. PETER GREEN & POLLY his wife to JACOB WM DECHANT, late of PA. Land in St. Clairs Twp conveyed by PETER METZGER, rec Bk D, pp 618, 619. Signed PETER GREEN, POLLY (x) GREEN. Witn: JAMES HEATON, PAUL BONNEL. rec 1815. pp 132, 133

Deed dated 1815. WILLIAM STUART to JOHN SIMONTON.. S 17, T 3, R 2. Signed WM. STUART. Witn: WM. KEEN, JAMES HEATON. rec 1815. pp 133, 134

Deed dated 1814. MICHAEL KERGAN of NY City & ELIZABETH his wife, formerly ELIZABETH CALDWELL, widow & exctr of JAMES CALDWELL, to ABRAM R. COLWELL of Urbani, OH. S 22, T 3, R 2 part of estate. Signed MICHAEL (x) KERGAN, ELIZABETH (x) KERGAN. Witn:

BUTLER COUNTY LAND RECORDS: BOOK E

B. LIVINGSTON, #2 illeg. rec 1815. pp 134, 135, 136

Deed dated 1815. FREDERICK ALLENDORF & NANCY his wife to JOHN R. BECKET. S 27, T 3, R 2. Signed FREDERICK (x) ALLENDORF, NANCY (x) ALLENDORF. Witn: JAMES HEATON, GERSHAM NORRIS. rec 1815. pp 136, 137

Deed dated 1806. JOHN DOTY to DANIEL DOTY. S 18, T 2, R 2. Signed JOHN DOTY. Witn: WILLIAM P. DOTY, ZINA DOTY. rec 1815. pp 138, 139

Deed dated 1815. ROBERT LYTLE & MARGARET his wife of Milford Twp to JAMES SCOTT & WILLIAM ROBESON, Trustees of Concord Congregation. S 24, T 5, R 2; land for a meeting house. Signed R. LYTLE, MARG. LYTLE. Witn: MATTH. RICHARDSON, PHILIP PETERS. rec 1815. pp 139, 140

Deed dated 1815. JOHN PHILIPS FINKLE & CATHARINE his wife to WILLIAM HARVEY. S 12, T 3, R 3. Signed JOHN P. FINKLE, CATHARINE FINKLE (german script). Witn: JAMES CLARK, JAMES ROBESON. rec 1815. pp 140, 141

Deed dated 1815. JAMES AYERS & JULIA his wife to ROBERT CLARK. Middletown lot --. Signed JAMES AYERS, JULIA AYERS. Witn: JOHN FOLKERTH, JP WM. HARVEY. rec 1815. pp 141, 142, 143

Deed dated 1815. ROBERT CLARK & ELIZA his wife to WILLIAM HARVEY. Middletown lot 34. Signed ROBERT CLARK, ELIZA (x) CLARK. Witn: JAMES CLARK, JOHN HOLMES. rec 1815. pp 143, 144

Deed dated 1815. WILLIAM ROBESON & MARY his wife to WILLIAM BUCKHANNON. S 25, T 5, R 2. Signed WILLIAM ROBESON, MARY ROBESON. Witn: MATTH. RICHARDSON, JAMES ROBESON. rec 1815. pp 144, 145, 146

Deed dated 1815. BENJAMIN LAREW to WILLIAM VANHISE. S 15, T 3, R 2; bound by HUGH ABERCROMBIE's land. Signed BENJAMIN LAREW. Witn: SAMUEL SEWARD JR, SAMUEL AYERS. rec 1815. pp 146, 147

Deed dated 1814. ENOCH D. JOHN of Franklin Co, IN Ter'y to EZEKIEL B. McCLURE. Middletown lot 37. Signed ENOCH D. JOHN. Witn: WILLIAM SPINNING, WM. HARVEY. rec 1815. pp 147, 148

Deed dated 1814. MOSES CONNER & MARY his wife to THOMAS R. SMILEY. Rossville lot 77. Signed MOSES (x) CONNER, MARY (x) CONNER. Witn: JOHN REILY,

BUTLER COUNTY LAND RECORDS: BOOK E

SAMUEL DAVIS JR. rec 1815. pp 148, 149

Deed dated 1815. THOMAS B. SMILEY & POLLY his wife to WILLIAM RAINEY. Rossville lot 77. Signed THOMAS B. SMILEY, POLLY SMILEY. Witn: JAMES HEATON, NIMROD F. RANDOLPH. rec 1815. pp 149, 150, 151

Deed dated 1815. JOHN E. SCOTT to PIERSON SAYRE. Hamilton lot 120. Signed JOHN E. SCOTT. Witn: JAMES HEATON, ISAAC MOSS. rec 1815. pp 151, 152

Deed dated 1815. JOSEPH HOUGH & JANE his wife and THOMAS BLAIR & PEGGY his wife to AMSEY AYERS. S 14, T 4, R 2. Signed JOSEPH HOUGH, THOS. BLAIR, JANE (x) HOUGH, PEGGY BLAIR. Witn: JAMES HEATON, SAMUEL AYERS. rec 1815. pp 152, 153

Mortgage dated 1815. WM. C. KEEN & ANDREW STEWART to THOMAS BLAIR & JAMES HEATON. Hamilton lot 52. Signed WM. C. KEEN, ANDREW STEWART. Witn: JOSEPH F. RANDOLPH, ISAAC HAWLEY. rec 1815. pp 153, 154, 155

Deed dated 1815. WILLIAM SUTHERLAND JR to JOSEPH WILSON & JAMES WILSON. Rossville lot 75. Signed WILLIAM SUTHERLAND. Witn: JAMES HEATON, BENJ. D. PAR---. rec 1815. pp 155, 156

Deed dated 1812. USA to AARON SACKETT of Hamilton Co. S 23, T 4, R 2. rec 1815. p 156

Mortgage dated 1815. JOSEPH GAILBRAITH to JOHN P. FINKLE. Middletown lot 39. Payment due 1817. Signed JOSEPH GAILBREATH. Witn: WM. HARVEY, EZEKIEL McCLURE. rec 1815. pp 157, 158

Deed dated 1814. Heirs of WILLIAM McCLURE, decd, of Dayton to ROBERT EWING. S 25, T 2, R 4. Signed JOHN McCLURE, ANTHONY LOGAN (& his wife) JANE LOGAN, JAMES McCLURE, MARTHA McCLURE by their attys DAVID McCLURE and JAMES STEELE, DAVID McCLURE (& his wife) RUTH McCLURE for themselves. Witn: JOHN KING, JOHN FOLKERTH. All signees of Montgomery Co. rec 1815. pp 158, 159, 160

Deed dated 1815. PIERSON SAYRE & CATHARINE his wife to JOHN H. PIATT of Hamilton Co. S 7, T 3, R 3; bound by land of AARON RICHARDSON, JOSEPH PATTERSON, JOHN CARSON. Signed PIERSON SAYRE, CATHARINE SAYRE. Witn: FRANCES G. HOPKINS, GRIFFIN YEATMAN. rec 1815. pp 160, 161, 162

BUTLER COUNTY LAND RECORDS: BOOK E

Deed dated 1814. JOSEPH KELLY & KEZIA his wife to ELIJAH HORNER. S 1, T 3, R 3. Signed JOSEPH KELLY, KEZIA (x) KELLY. Witn: NATHAN STUBBS, SAMUEL HUNT. rec 1815. pp 162, 163

Deed dated 1815. WILLIAM ANTHONY & FANNY his wife to MICHAEL WILKINS of IN Ter'y. S 18, T 4, R 1. Signed WILLIAM ANTHONY, FANNY (x) ANTHONY. Witn: JP JOHN BURK, JOSHUA HARRIS. rec 1815. pp 164, 165

Deed dated 1814. SHOBAL VAIL & MARY his wife to JONATHAN MARTIN. Middletown lot 7. Signed SHOBAL VAIL, MARY VAIL. Witn: JAMES HEATH, SAMUEL POWELL. rec 1815. pp 165, 166

Deed dated 1814. WILLIAM SQUIER & SARAH his wife of Madison Twp to ISAAC MARTIN of same. S 5, T 1, R 4. Signed WM. SQUIER, SARAH (x) SQUIER. Witn: SQUIER LITTELL, STEPHEN GARD. rec 1815. pp 166, 167

Power of Attorney dated 1813. Heirs of WILLIAM McCLURE appted DAVID McCLURE & JAMES STEELE to sell S 25, T -, R 4. Signed JOHN McCLURE, ANTHONY LOGAN, JANE LOGAN, JAMES McCLURE, MARTHA McCLURE. Witn: JOHN MCCLURE, ALEXANDER LOGAN. rec 1815. pp 167, 168

Deed dated 1815. JAMES SUTTON JR & NANCY his wife of Franklin Co, IN Ter'y to ROBERT BROWN. S 29, T 2, R 4; bound by land of DAVID WOOLVERTON. Signed JAMES SUTTON, NANCY SUTTON. Witn: JAMES LIVISTON, NANCY LIVISTON. rec 1815. pp 168, 169, 170

Mortgage dated 1815. ROBERT BROWN to JAMES SUTTON of IN Ter'y. Payment on above land due 1815. Signed ROBT. BROWN. Witn: JAMES HEATON, CHS. BRUCE. rec 1815. pp 170, 171

Deed dated 1815. CELICIA WILCOX, late CELICIA HERBERT, to DAVID CORWIN of Warren Co. Hamilton lot 165. Signed CELICIA WILLCOX. Witn: DANL MILLIKIN, UOL HAMAN. rec 1815. pp 171, 172

Deed dated 1814. GEORGE HOFFMAN & ELIZABETH his wife to DANIEL HERSHMAN of Rockingham Co, VA and JOSEPH RYCRAFT. S , T 2, R 3. Signed GEORGE (x) HOFFMAN, ELIZABETH (x) HOFFMAN. Witn: JAMES SMITH, ROBERT RITCHEY. rec 1815. pp 173, 174

Deed dated 1814. THOMAS BLAIR & PEGGY his wife to ABEL SLAYBACK. Hamilton outlots 11, 13 & 14. Signed THOMAS BLAIR, PEGGY BLAIR. Witn: JP JOHN DUNN,

BUTLER COUNTY LAND RECORDS: BOOK E

ISAAC HAWLEY. rec 1815. pp 174, 175

Deed dated 1815. ABEL SLAYBACK & AMELIA his wife to JOHN CALDWELL. Hamilton outlots 11, 13 & 14. Signed ABEL SLAYBACK, AMELIA E. SLAYBACK. Witn: SAMUEL BOYLES, JAMES HEATON. rec 1815. pp 175, 176

Deed dated 1815. JOSEPH HOUGH & JANE his wife and THOMAS BLAIR & PEGGY his wife to ISAAC AYERS. S 14, T 4, R 2. Signed JOSEPH HOUGH, THOS. BLAIR, JANE (x) HOUGH, PEGGY BLAIR. Witn: JAMES HEATON, SAMUEL AYERS. rec 1815. pp 176, 177, 178

Deed dated 1815. JOHN FREEMAN to THOMAS FREEMAN. S 26, T 2, R 4. Signed JOHN (x) FREEMAN. Witn: JOHN (x) VANSCHOYCK, HENRY WEAVER. rec 1815. pp 178, 179

Deed dated 1814. STEPHEN GARD & RACHEL his wife to THOMAS FREEMAN. S 26, T 2, R 4; bound by land of JOSHUA BUTLER, JOHN FREEMAN JR. Signed STEPHEN GARD, RACHEL GARD. Witn: SQUIER LITTELL, WILLIAM MORRIS. rec 1815. pp 179, 180

Deed dated 1815. HUGH **ABERCROMBIE** & ROSANA his wife to ABEL SLAYBACK. S 15, T 3, R 2. Signed HUGH **ABBER-CROMBIE**, ROSANA (x) ABBERCROMBIE. Witn: MICHAEL AYERS, BENJAMIN LAREW. rec 1815. pp 181, 182

Deed dated 1815. JOHN PHILLIPS & MARY his wife of Maidenhead, NJ to ABEL SLAYBACK of West Windford Twp, Middlesex Co, NJ. S 9, T 3, R 2; adj land of RALPH W. HUNT, JARIAMIAH SMITH. Signed JOHN PHILLIPS, MARY PHILLIPS. Witn: JOS. W. VANCLEVEE, R. L. SAUSBERRY. rec 1815. rec 1815. pp 182, 183, 184

Deed dated 1815. Heirs of DAVID MULFORD to JOHN P. FINKLE. Land & sawmill in Lemmon Twp: S 36, T 2, R 3. Signed HANNAH (x) MULFORD (widow of David); JOHN MULFORD (& his wife) MARY (x) MULFORD; JOB MULFORD (& his wife) AFFE (x) MULFORD; EDMUND ALLRIDGE (& his wife) JANE ALLRIDGE. Witn: WM. TANEHILL, PATRICK SHIELDS. rec 1815. pp 124, 125, 126

Deed dated 1815. Heirs of ELIAS ROBY to PRYOR ROBY. S 17, T 3, R 3. Signed POLLY (x) ROBY; CHARLES (x) REED (& his wife) CLOY (x) REED; ISAAC ROBY (& his wife) SALLY ROBY (no signature); HENRY (x) BARBER (& his wife) CATY (x) BARBER. Witn: JAMES CLARK, GEORGE ROBY. rec 1815. JP's note: HENRY & CATY BARBER signed from Champaign Co. pp 126, 127

BUTLER COUNTY LAND RECORDS: BOOK E

Deed dated 1815. NICHOLAS DAVIS & NARIAH his wife to JAMES CLARK of Fairfield Twp. Hamilton lot 54. Signed NICHOLAS DAVIS, NARIAH (x) DAVIS. Witn: JAMES HEATON, E. McCONNEL. rec 1815. pp 187, 188

Deed dated 1815. JOHN NELSON & ELIZABETH his wife to MARGARET EWING. Rossville lot 83. Signed JOHN NELSON, ELIZBETH (x) NELSON. Witn: ROBT TAYLOR, SAMUEL McCLURE. rec 1815. p 189

Deed dated 1815. Admtr of RICHARD BIRCH the elder to SAMUEL MORRISON. S 1, T 1, R 3. Signed R. BIRCH, admtr. Witn: JAMES McBRIDE, JOSEPH HOUGH. rec 1815. pp 190, 191

Deed dated 1815. Admtr of RICHARD BIRCH the elder to SAMUEL MORRISON. S 1, T 1, R 3. Signed and witn as above. rec 1815. pp 191, 192, 193

Authorization dated 1814. Directed collection of copies of the original field notes of the surveyors of the Miami Purchase as previously ordered by the Ohio Assembly. Signed Commissioners WM. C. SCHENCK of Warren Co, JAMES HEATON of Butler Co, JOHN P. GASTON of Hamilton Co. Witn: JP ETHAN STONE. rec 1815. p 193

Deposition dated 1813. JOHN CLEVES SYMMES testified he purchased land from US govmnt and ordered survey of land between the Miamis. He retained surveyors' memoranda, delivered to THOMAS HENDERSON for examination. The notes were returned to Symmes but were destroyed when his house at North Bend, Hamilton Co, burned. Signed JOHN CLEVES SYMMES. Witn: ETH. A. BROWN, Ohio Supreme Ct. Justice. Post script: SIMON STOCKDALE and SINEUS PIERSON (since decd) transcribed original notes. JAMES HEATON and JOHN GASTON had the same liberty to do so. rec 1815. pp 193, 194, 195

Copies of field notes from original surveys dated 1788 & 1789. Base line from 1st meridian on south bend of Ohio River. Signed ISRAEL LUDLOW, surveyor, p 195. Survey notes of JOHN DUNLAP, pp 197, 198. Survey notes of JOHN LINN p 201. Survey notes of JOHN GANO p 202. Survey notes of ISRAEL LUDLOW p 204. Survey notes of JAMES HENRY p 206. Survey notes of WILL WELLS p 208. Survey notes of ABNER HUNT p 209. Survey notes of JAS. F. BAILEY p 209. Survey notes of HENRY HEATON p 210. Survey notes of JNO. R. MILLS p 212. Survey notes of WILL WELLS p 215. Survey notes of EVAN SHELBY p 216. Survey notes of

BUTLER COUNTY LAND RECORDS: BOOK E

ISAAC TAYLOR p 217. Survey notes of JAMES F. BAILEY p 218. Survey notes of EPHRAIM KIBBY p 219. Survey notes of JOHN TUTTLE p 219. rec 1815. pp 195 to 222

Statement dated 1814. THOMAS HENDERSON declared the foregoing an accurate copy of notes. rec 1815. p 223

Commissioners' statement of authenticity dated 1815. Signed JOHN R. GASTON, JAMES HEATON, W. C. SCHENCK. rec 1815. p 224

Additional field notes dated 1789. JOHN DUNLAP, surveyor: field party consisted of LUTHER KITCHEL, marker; JOHN VAN EATON, flagman and hunter; ISAAC FREEMAN, packman; JOSHUA P. FONDLER and SYLVESTER WHITE, chainmen. rec 1815. pp 224, 225, 226

Directions dated 1815. Recorders of the affected counties to enter copies of the field notes of the Miami Purchase into their deed records. Signed Commissioners SCHENCK, HEATON & GASTON. rec 1815. p 227

Deed dated 1815. FELIX ASHCRAFT & ELIZABETH his wife to JOHN HARDEN JR. S -, T 3, R 1. Signed FELIX (x) ASHCRAFT, ELIZABETH ASHCRAFT. Witn: STACY HEATON, BLEWITH GRISSOM. rec 1815. pp 227, 228

Deed dated 1815. ANNA MARTIN, widow, of Madison Twp to HENRY HOFFMAN of same. S 7, T 2, R 4; bound by lnad of SAMUEL DICKEY, decd and MOSES DENMAN. Signed ANNA (x) MARTIN. Witn: JAMES H. MARTIN, HENRY WEAVER. rec 1815. pp 228, 229, 230

Deed dated 1815. ADAM DEEM & JANE his wife to HENRY HOFFMAN. S 7, T 2, R 4. Signed ADAM DEEM, JANE DEEM. Witn as above. rec 1815. pp 230, 231, 232

Deed dated 1815. HENRY TAYLOR & ELIZABETH his wife to THOMAS SIMMONS. S 36, T 5, R 2 in Millford Twp. Signed HENRY TAYLOR, ELIZABETH (x) TAYLOR. Witn: JP ROBT. TAYLOR, LEWIS LAING. rec 1815. pp 232, 233

Deed dated 1815. HENRY TAYLOR & ELIZABETH his wife to ANDREW SMITH. S 36, T 3, R 2. Signed as above. Witn: ROBT. TAYLOR, THOMAS (x) SIMMONS. rec 1815. pp 233, 234

Deed dated 1815. Lt. JOHN SIMMONS & MARY his wife to Lt. GEORGE STALL, both men of US Army. Hamilton lot 195. Signed JOHN SIMMONS, MARY SIMMONS. Witn: WM. MURRAY, JOHN WRIGHT. rec 1815. pp 234, 235

BUTLER COUNTY LAND RECORDS: BOOK E

Deed dated 1815. ELLIS JOHN & MARGARET his wife to JONATHAN CONNERY. S 14, T 3, R 2; bound by land of MICHAEL HILDERBRAND, land formerly owned by ISAAC JOHN, to BENJAMIN DECKER. Signed ELLIS JOHN, MARGARET (x) JOHN. Witn: JOHN AYERS, JOHN JOHN. rec 1815. pp 235, 236, 237

Deed dated 1815. JOHN C. McMANUS & CATY his wife to THOMAS R. SMILEY. Hamilton lot 52. Signed J. CALL McMANUS, CATY McMANUS. Witn: JAMES HEATON, DEBORAH L. HENDRICK. rec 1815. pp 237, 238

Deed dated 1814. RUTH REED, admtr of DAVID REED, late of Lemon Twp, to SHOBAL VAIL. S 19, T 2, R 4; bound by land of JOSEPH HENDERSON, heirs of ROBT CARRICK decd, ARCHIBALD CAMPBELL, JOHN CARSON. Signed RUTH (x) REED. Witn: GEORGE SHELLHOUSE, HENRY WEAVER. rec 1815. pp 238, 239, 240

Deed date illeg. ELIAS BOUDINOT by agent JACOB BURNET to JOHN BRYSON. S 14, T 2, R 4. Signed ELIAS BOUDINOT by JAC. BURNET. Witn: ROBT. WALLACE JR, WILLIAM IRWIN JR. rec 1815. pp 240, 241

Deed dated 1815. HUGH VAIL & LYDIA his wife to JOHN P. FINKLE. Middletown lot 51. Signed HENRY VAIL, LYDIA VAIL. Witn: WM. HARVEY, HENRY WEAVER. rec 1815. pp 241, 242

Deed dated 1815. HUGH VAIL & LYDIA his wife to JOHN TULLIS. Middletown lot 50. Signed HENRY VAIL, LYDIA VAIL. Witn: JAMES GRIMES, HENRY WEAVER. rec 1815. pp 242, 243

Deed dated 1815. JOHN TULLIS & ELINOR his wife to JOHN P. FINKLE. Middletown lot 50. Signed JOHN TULLIS, ELINOR TULLIS. Witn: JOSEPH BUCHANON, HENRY WEAVER. rec 1815. pp 243, 244, 245

Deed dated 1815. TOBIAS BARCALOW & ELIZABETH his wife to NICHOLAS BARCALOW. S 11, T 2, R 4. Signed TOBIAS BARCALOW, ELIZABETH BARCALOW. Witn: ARTHUR POLHEMUS, HENRY WEAVER. rec 1815. pp 245, 246

Deed dated 1815. NICHOLAS BARCALOW & JANE his wife to TUNIS VOORHEES. S 2, T 2, R 4; bound by land of SAMUEL McCREA. Signed NICHOLAS BARCALOW, JANE BARCALOW. Witn: DANIEL BARCALOW, HENRY WEAVER. rec 1815. pp 246, 247, 248

Deed dated 1815. DANIEL BARCALOW & CATHERINE his

BUTLER COUNTY LAND RECORDS: BOOK E

wife to TUNIS VOORHEES. S 14, T 2, R 4. Signed DANIEL BARCALOW, CATHARINE BARCALOW. Witn: NICHOLAS BARCALOW, HENRY WEAVER. rec 1815. pp 248, 249

Deed dated 1815. JOHN MATHERS & JEAN his wife of Hamilton Co to ELLIS JOHN. S 8, T 3, R 2. Signed JOHN MATHERS, JEAN MATHERS. Witn: JOSEPH McKNIGHT, ISAAC HUNT. JP BENAJAH AYERS. rec 1815. pp 249, 250

Deed dated 1812. Exctr of STEPHEN VAIL to JACOB WEIDNER. Middletown lots 31 & 47; finalize 1804 sale. Signed AARON VAIL. Witn: WILLIAM PERRY. rec 1815. pp 250, 251, 252

Deed dated 1815. JOHN GREER & ELINOR his wife to PIERSON SAYRE. Hamilton lot 70. Signed JOHN GREER, ELINOR GREER. Witn: JAMES HEATON, JOS. H. BENHAM. rec 1815. pp 253, 254

Deed dated 1815. ROBERT ROSEBROUGH & MARY his wife to GEORGE ST. CLAIR. S 9, T -, R -; bound by land of W. NIXON. Signed ROBERT ROSEBROUGH, MARY (x) ROSE- BROUGH. Witn: DAVID MARTIN, JP JOHN RAINEY. rec 1815. pp 254, 255

Deed dated 1815. Admtrs of JOHN YOUNG, decd, to JAMES YOUNG. S 10, T 5, R 2. Signed SAMUEL McCLEARY ROBERT YOUNG. Witn: MATTH. RICHARDSON, MOSES CAMPBELL. rec 1815. pp 255, 256, 257

Deed dated 1810. USA to JOHN McKEAN. S 23, T 3, R 3. rec 1815. p 257

Deed dated 1815. JOHN P. FINKLE & CATHARINE his wife to JOSEPH GALBREATH. Middletown lot 39. Signed JOHN P. FINKLE, CATHARINE FINKLE (german script). Witn: WM HARVEY, EZEKIEL B. McCLURE. rec 1815. pp 258, 259

Deed dated 1815. JESSE KENWORTHY & RACHEL his wife of Preble Co to REBECCAH COMBER. S 6, T 3, R 3. Signed JESSE KENWORTHY, RACHEL KENWORTHY. Witn: WIL- LIAM KENWORTHY, JESSE HOLSON. rec 1815. pp 259, 260

Deed dated 1815. JAMES SCHENCK & ANN his wife of Warren Co to DANIEL BAKER. S 10,T 2, R 4. Signed JAMES SCHANCK, ANN SCHANCK. Witn: ANN DEARDORFF, JP JACOB DEARDORF. rec 1815. pp 260, 261

Deed dated 1815. ABRAHAM CHASE to ISAAC L. CHASE. S 6, T 4, R 1. Signed ABRAHAM CHASE. Witn: ABRAHAM C. ROLL, ETHAN STONE. rec 1815. pp 262, 263

BUTLER COUNTY LAND RECORDS: BOOK E

Deed dated 1815. MARTIN BAUM & ANN his wife of Cincinnati to CARLTON WALDO of Warren Co. S 27, T 4, R 1. Signed MARTIN BAUM, ANN BAUM. Witn: JOHN MAHARD D.C. WALLACE. rec 263, 264

Deed dated 1815. BENJAMIN HINDES & ELIZABETH his wife to SAMUEL DAVIS. S 19, T 3, R 3; bound by land of JOHN KIRKPATRICK, SILAS GARRISON. Signed BENJAMIN (x) HINDES, ELIZABETH (x) HINDES. Witn: CHARLES SWEARINGEN, ELIZABETH (x) HINDES. rec 1815. pp 264, 265

Deed dated 1815. SAMUEL I. BROWNE of Cincinnati and JAMES HINDS to LEWIS DAVIS. S 3, T 3, R 3; tract bought in 1812 by HINDS and JAMES BROWNE, assignee of ROBERT CARSON. Samuel the heir of JAMES BROWNE, now decd. Signed SAMUEL I. BROWNE, JAMES HINDS. Witn: JAMES SILVER, BETSEY SILVER. rec 1815. pp 266, 267

Deed dated 1815. JONATHAN PIERSON & MATILDA his wife to ABSALOM GOODENOUGH. Hamilton lot 54. Signed JONATHAN PIERSON, MATILDA PIERSON. Witn: JAMES HEATON, NICHOLAS DAVIS. rec 1815. pp 267, 268

Deed dated 1814. JOHN GARRISON & SUSANNA his wife of (illeg) Co, IN Ter'y to JOHN KIRKPATRICK. S 19, T 3, R 3; bound by land of BENJAMIN HINDS, MOSES CRUM. Signed JOHN GARRISON, SUSANNA (x) GARRISON. Witn: CHARLES SWEARINGEN, SAMUEL ROBBINS. rec 1815. pp 268, 269

pp 269, 270 bound out of order

Deed dated 1815. THOMAS HILL & SARAH his wife of Miami Co to JOHN NELSON. Rossville lot 80. Signed THOMAS HILL, SARAH HILL. Witn: JAMES (illeg), NATHAN HILL. rec 1815. pp 269, 270, 271

Deed dated 1815. JOHN SUTHERLAND & NANCY his wife to WM. DECHANT of PA. S 18, T 1, R 4; bound by land of JAMES REED, M. DOUGHTY, E. BOYLES. Signed JOHN SUTHERLAND, NANCY R. SUTHERLAND. Witn: DAVID VANCE, HENRY WEAVER. rec 1815. pp 271, 272

Deed dated 1815. FRAZEE BISHOP & ELIZABETH his wife to WILLIAM HARVEY. Middletown lot 52. Signed FRAZEE BISHOP, ELIZABETH BISHOP. Witn: BENJ. SMITH, HENRY WEAVER. rec 1815. pp 273, 274

Deed dated 1815. JOHN P. FINKLE & CATHERINE his wife to WILLIAM HARVEY. Middletown lot 50. Signed JOHN P. FINKLE, CATHERINE FINKLE (german script). Witn:

BUTLER COUNTY LAND RECORDS: BOOK E

WM. TANNEHILL, HENRY WEAVER. rec 1815. pp 274, 275

Deed dated 1815. JOHN FREEMAN JR & BETSEY his wife to JOHN P. FINKLE. S 26, T -, R 4; bound by land of JOSHUA BUTLER. Signed JOHN FREEMAN JR, BETSEY (x) FREEMAN. Witn: JOHN SHAFER, WM. HARVEY. rec 1815. pp 275, 276, 277

Deed dated 1815. WILLIAM HARVEY & ISABELLA his wife to JOHN P. FINKLE. Middletown lot 34. Signed WM. HARVEY, ISABELLA HARVEY. Witn: WILLIAM TANNEHILL, HENRY WEAVER. rec 1815. pp 277, 278

Mortgage dated 1815. JOHN WEIKEL of Lahi (Lehigh?) Co, PA to WILLIAM BALDWIN. S 6, T 2, R 4. Signed JOHN WEIKEL. Witn: SQUIER LITTELL, HENRY WEAVER. rec 1815. pp 278, 279

Deed dated 1815. WILLIAM RAINEY & ANNA his wife to WILLIAM DECAMP. Rossville lot 77. Signed WILLIAM RAINEY, ANNA RAINEY. Witn: JAMES HEATON, ENOCH SCUDDER. rec 1815. pp 279, 280

Deed dated 1814. WILLIAM SQUIER & SARAH his wife to JOHN SHROYER. S 33, T 2, R 4. Signed WM. SQUIER, SARAH (x) SQUIER. Witn: ELLIS SQUIER, HENRY WEAVER. rec 1815. pp 280, 281, 282

Plat of Templeton dated 1813. Templeton in S 12, T 2, R 4. MICHAEL TEMPLE & MICHAEL TEMPLE JR, proprietors. rec 1815. pp 282, 283

Deed dated 1815. CHARLES ATWELL & SUSANNA his wife, dau of JOHN CLAP decd, to WILLIAM HALL. S 27, T 2, R 2. Signed CHARLES ATWELL, SUSANNA (x) ATWELL. Witn: JOHN REILY, SAMUEL DAVIS JR. rec 1815. pp 283, 284

Power of Attorney dated 1815. JACOB LEWIS appted Dr. SAMUEL MILLIKIN to collect debts on his behalf. Signed JACOB LEWIS. Witn: DANL MILLIKIN, JAMES HEATON. rec 1815. pp 284, 285

Deed dated 1808. SETH GARD & MARY his wife of Springfield Twp, Hamilton Co, to DAVID SUTTON. S 2, T 4, R 2. Signed SETH GARD, MARY(x) GARD. Witn: PETER KEEN, MEES ARGO. rec 1815. pp 285, 286

Plat of Sunbury dated 1815. S 18, T 2, R 4 in Madison Twp. JACOB C. SNYDER, proprietor. rec 1815. pp 287, 288

BUTLER COUNTY LAND RECORDS: BOOK E

Deed dated 1814. REUBEN REEDER & REBECCA his wife to TILGHMAN SHORT. S 24, T 3, R 2. Signed REUBEN REEDER, REBECCAH REEDER. Witn: JP WILLIAM PERRY, JONATHAN REEDER. rec 1815. pp 288, 289

Deed dated 1814. FRAZER HARRISON & ELENOR his wife to TILGHMAN SHORT. No S-T-R; "lying on North side of land...bought of Reuben Reeder." Signed FRAZER HARRISON, ELENOR (x) HARRISON. Witn: J. W. PERRY, REUBEN REEDER. rec 1815. pp 289, 290

Deed dated 1815. ANNA MARTIN to THOMAS ISRAEL. S 7, T 2, R 4; "purchased of SAMUEL DICKEY, late of Madison Twp, decd" except land sold to HENRY HOOPMAN. Signed ANNA (x) MARTIN. Witn: WILLIAM BALDWIN, HENRY WEAVER. rec 1815. pp 291, 292

Mortgage dated 1815. THOMAS ISRAEL & CHRISTEEN his wife to ANNA MARTIN. S 7, T 2, R 4; paymt due 1821. Signed THOMAS (x) ISRAEL, CHRISTEEN (x) ISRAEL. Witn as above. rec 1815. pp 292, 293

Deeddated 1815. WILLIAM BALDWIN & MARY his wife to JOHN WEIKLE of Lahi Co, PA. S 6, T 2, R 4; bound by ALLEN SIMPSON's land. Signed WILLIAM BALDWIN, MARY BALDWIN. Witn: SQUIER LITTELL, HENRY WEAVER. rec 1815. pp 293, 294

Certificate dated 1815. JONATHAN DAYTON acknowledged he signed and delivered the "within deed". Signed D. D. CRANE (of NJ). Witn: S. WHITEHEAD. no "within" deed recorded. rec 1815. p 295

Deed dated 1815. JOSEPH HAYS & MARY his wife to JOSEPH BANKER. S 11 & 12, T 2, R 4. Signed JOSEPH HAYS, MARY (x) HAYS. Witn: JAMES HEATON, TIMOTHY L. GARRIGUS. rec 1815. pp 295, 296

Deed dated 1815. WILLIAM HARVEY & ISABELLA his wife to JAMES CLARK & WILLIAM McCLEAN. S 12, T 3, R 4; bound by land of JOHN LOWRY, JAMES STUART. Signed WM. HARVEY, ISABELLA HARVEY. Witn: JOHN P. FINKLE, HENRY WEAVER. rec 1815. pp 297, 298

Deed dated 1815. THOMAS FISH & MARTHA his wife to JAMES MATHERS. S 19, T -, R 4; "being lot 2...as laid off by heirs of JOHN REED, decd". Signed THOMAS FISH, MARTHA (x) FISH. Witn: JP JAMES CLARK, THOS. KING. rec 1815. pp 298, 299

Deed dated 1815. ABSALOM GOODENOUGH & SARAH his wife

BUTLER COUNTY LAND RECORDS: BOOK E

to NICHOLAS DAVIS. Hamilton lot 54. Signed ABSALOM GOODENOUGH, SARAH (x) GOODENOUGH. Witn: JAMES HEATON, Z. COLBY. rec 1815. pp 300, 301

Deed dated 1815. HUGH VAIL & LYDIA his wife to FRAZER BISHOP. Money paid by Bishop or, on his behalf, by JOHN TULLIS. Middletown lot 52. Signed HUGH VAIL, LYDIA VAIL. Witn: WM. HARVEY, HENRY WEAVER. rec 1815. pp 302, 303

Deed dated 1815. JOHN STOCKTON & DEBORAH his wife of Lemon Twp to PETER KNEASE of Madison Twp. S 8, T 2, R 4. Signed JOHN STOCKTON, DEBORAH (x) STOCKTON. Witn: HENRY HOFFMAN, HENRY WEAVER. rec 1815. pp 303, 304

Deed dated 1814. JOHN SUTHERLAND & NANCY his wife to DANIEL KEYT & DAVID R. KEYT. Hamilton lots 147 & 148. Signed JOHN SUTHERLAND, NANCY R. SUTHERLAND. Witn: JAMES HEATON, JOHN C. CRUME. rec 1815. pp 304, 305

Power of Attorney dated 1815. JOSEPH BLOOMFIELD of Burlington Co, NJ appted JOHN REILY as atty to convey title to S 19, T 2, R (not given) to Col. JOHN SEWARD of Sussex Co, NJ. Land rec Bk A, pp 245, 246 & 247. Signed JOSEPH BLOOMFIELD. Witn: THOS. ADAMS, STOGDALE STOKES. rec 1815. pp 305, 306

Mortgage dated 1815. JOHN SEWARD as above to JOSEPH BLOOMFIELD as above. S 19, T 2, R 3. Signed JOHN SEWARD. Witn: M. G. WALLACE, JAMES McBRIDE, DANL. MILLIKIN. rec 1815. pp 306, 307, 308

Deed dated 1815. LAURENCE CAVENAUGH & ANN his wife to JOHN REILY. Hamilton outlot 18. Signed LAURENCE CAVENAUGH, ANN CAVENAUGH. Witn: DANL. MILLIKIN, CHARLES K. SMITH. rec 1815. pp 308, 309

Deed dated 1815. JAMES PORT or POST & ELEANOR his wife to SAMUEL PORT or POST. S 17, T 4, R 1; reserved right to take stone in any quantity needed. Signed JAMES PORT or POST, ELEANOR (x) PORT or POST. Witn: JOHN BURK, BENJAMIN LAURENCE. rec 1815. pp 309, 310

Deed dated 1815. CHRISTOPHER HARVEY & ELIZABETH his wife of Crosby Twp, Hamilton Co to JOHN LITTLE of Ross Twp. S 28, T 3, R 2; bound by land of CHARLES COEN, JOAB COMSTOCK, JONATHAN TIMBERMAN. Signed CHRISTOPHER HARVEY, BETSEY HARVEY. Witn: JP WILLIAM D. JONES, THOMAS LONG. rec 1815. pp 311, 312

BUTLER COUNTY LAND RECORDS: BOOK E

Deed dated 1815. STEPHEN VAN SCOYOC & NANCY his wife to JOSEPH POTTER. S 15, T 2, R 2. Signed STEPHEN (x) VANSCOYOC, NANCY (x) VANSCOYOC. Witn: JOS. GASTON, JAMES MILEY, WILLIAM JOYCE. rec 1815. pp 312, 313

Deed dated 1815. ABRAHAM FREEMAN & EMMA his wife, late EMMA QUICK, to HENRY VAIL. S 20, T 2, R 4; formerly owned by JOHN QUICK, decd. Bound by land of HUGH VAIL, JOHN TAYLOR. Signed ABRM. FREEMAN, EMMA (x) FREEMAN. Witn: EZEKIEL BALL, JULYAN (x) KING. rec 1815. pp 313, 314, 315

Deed dated 1815. JOHN RICHARDSON & JANE his wife of Ross Twp to NICHOLAS DEMORET of Cincinnati Twp, Hamilton Co. S 20, T 3, R 2, except land previously sold to JOHN BROWN. Signed JOHN RICHARDSON, MARY RICHARDSON. Witn: WILLIAM D. JONES, SAMUEL DEMORET. rec 1815. pp 315, 316

Deed dated 1814. RICHARD WATTS to JOHN K. WATTS, IRENE WATTS & JOSEPH WATTS of Warren Co, minors & heirs of JAMES WATTS, decd, late of Butler Co. S 22, T 2, R 4; bound by land of THOMAS WADE, BENJAMIN BRIDGE, WIDOW QUICK, DAVID HEATON. Signed RICHARD (x) WATTS. Witn: NICHOLAS HOGAN, R. BIRCH. rec 1815. pp 316, 317, 318

Deed dated 1815. JOHN RICHMOND JR & MARY his wife of Ross Twp to HUGH MONTGOMERY of Morgan Twp. S 2, T 3, R 1. Signed JOHN RICHMOND JR, MARY (x) RICHMOND. Witn: none. rec 1815. pp 318, 319

Deed dated 1812. MICHAEL PEARCE & PHEBE his wife to WILLIAM SQUIER. S 4, T 1, R 4. Signed MICHAEL PEARCE, PHEBE PEARCE. Witn: HENRY WEAVER, PHEBE PEARCE. rec 1815. pp 319, 320, 321

Deed dated 1815. HENRY HOUSS & ANN his wife to WILLIAM SQUIER. Bridgetown lots 5 & 7. Signed HENRY HOUSS, ANN HOUSS. Witn: THOMAS CARLE, HENRY WEAVER. rec 1815. pp 321, 322

Deed dated 181. WILLIAM R. WRIGHT & SARAH his wife to JOHN SHUCKMAN. S 31, T 3, R 4. Signed WILLIAM R. WRIGHT, SARAH (x) WRIGHT. Witn: WM. SQUIER, HENRY WEAVER. rec 1815. pp 322, 323

Deed dated 1814. SHOBAL VAIL & MARY his wife to JONATHAN MARTIN. Middletown lot 8. Signed SHOBAL VAIL, MARY VAIL. Witn: JAMES HEATH, SAML POWELL.

BUTLER COUNTY LAND RECORDS: BOOK E

rec 1815.   pp 324, 325

Deed dated 1815.   JOHN SUTHERLAND & NANCY RAMSEY SUTHERLAND his wife to BENIJAH S. HATT.   Rossville lot 54.   Signed JOHN SUTHERLAND, NANCY R. SUTHERLAND. Witn: JP ROBT. TAYLOR, PETER FLEMING.   rec 1815.   pp 325, 326

Deed dated 1815.   MATTHEW NICHOL & ABIGAIL his wife to DANIEL McDONALD.   S 29, T 2, R 4; bound by land of ELIZABETH CANFIELD, sold by JAMES SUTTON JR.   Signed MATTHEW NICOL, ABIGAIL NICOL.   Witn: EZEKIEL BALL, JAMES McCLELLAN.   rec 1815.   pp 326, 327, 328

Deed dated 1815.   JAMES MILLS & SARAH his wife to JOHN SUTHERLAND.   Rossville outlot 26.   Signed JAMES MILLS, SARAH MILLS.   Witn: JOHN REILY, JAMES HEATON. rec 1815.   pp 328, 329

Deed dated 1812.   MATTHEW HUESTON & CATHERINE his wife to LAURENCE CAVENAUGH.   Hamilton lot 113. Signed M. HUESTON, CATHERINE HUESTON.   Witn: JAMES HEATON, WILLIAM MURRAY, DANL MILLIKIN.   rec 1815.   pp 329, 330

Deed dated 1815.   LAURENCE CAVENAUGH & ANN his wfie to JOSEPH HOUGH & SAMUEL MILLIKIN.   Hamilton lot 113. Signed LAURENCE CAVENAUGH, ANN CAVENAUGH.   Witn: JOHN REILY, ROBT. TAYLOR.   rec 1815.   pp 331, 332

Deed dated 1815.   UZAL EDWARDS & MARY his wife to JONAS MEKER ST.   A seventh part of S 19, T 3, R 3. Signed UZAL EDWARDS, MARY EDWARDS.   Witn: SAMUEL HARTER, DANIEL HARTER.   rec 1815.   pp 332, 333

Mortgage dated 1815.   NICHOLAS DEMORET of Cincinnati to JOHN RICHARDSON.   S 20 & 29, T 3, R 2 in Ross Twp, except land sold to JOHN BROWN.   Signed NICHOLAS DEMORET.   Witn: WILLIAM D. JONES, SAMUEL DEMORET. rec 1815.   pp 333, 334, 335

Assignment dated 1815.   JOHN RICHARDSON to SAMUEL KENNEDY.   All rights to the above mortgage.   Signed JOHN RICHARDSON.   Witn: JAMES HEATON, G. W. STALL. rec 1815.   pp 335, 336

Deed dated 1815.   ISAAC LINDLEY & ABIGAIL his wife to ALEXANDER ABEL.   S 12, T 4, R 1.   Signed ISAAC LINDLEY, ABIGAIL LINDLEY.   Witn: JP J.M. DORSEY, HIRAM LINDLEY.   rec 1815.   pp 336, 337

BUTLER COUNTY LAND RECORDS: BOOK E

Deed dated 1815. SARAH CASSIDY to THOMAS BLAIR. S 35, T 2, R 2. Signed SALLY CASSIDY. Witn: JAMES HEATON, MARY HEATON. rec 1815. pp 337, 338

Deed dated 1815. JOHN CALDWELL & ELIZABETH his wife to THOMAS MITCHEL of Lebanon Co, PA. S 27, T 2, R 3; bound by JOHN LINE's land. Signed JNO. CALDWELL, ELIZABETH CALDWELL. Witn: JAMES HEATON, JAMES McBRIDE. rec 1815. pp 339, 340

Deed dated 1814. JOHN CLEVES SYMMES of Cincinnati to WILLIAM HENRY HARRISON, Major General, US Army, and JOHN CLEVES SHORT of Cincinnati. Surplus land in unidentified sections of Miami Purchase. Signed JOHN CLEVES SYMMES. Witn: THOMAS HENDERSON, DANIEL SYMMES rec 1815. pp 340, 341

Notice dated 1815. Land to be sold for delinquent taxes. Hamilton lots: SAMUEL BEELER lot 83; JOHN GREER lots 111, 112, 162; heirs of JOHN MILLS lots 72 & 73. Rossville lots: JAMES MADILL lot 80; B.S. HATT lot 54; JAMES ROSS lot 90; JOHN WINGATE lot 7; JAMES GREER lot 19. Signed WILLIAM HARVEY, collector. Witn: JAMES HEATON. rec 1815. pp 342, 343

Deed dated 1815. JAMES STEWART & MARY his wife to JOSEPH STEWART. S 8, T 3, R 3. Signed JAMES STEWART, MARY H. STEWART. Witn: JAMES CLARK, WILLIAM H. CLARK. rec 1815. pp 344, 345

Deed dated 1815. MATTHEW HUESTON to EDWARD HARLAN. S 11, T 4, R 2. Signed M. HUESTON. Witn: WILLIAM KOX, JAMES HEATON. rec 1816. pp 345, 346

Deed dated 1814. THOMAS HUNTER, tax collector for Fairfield Twp, to NANCY McDONALD for use of LEVI McDONALD, assignee of ROSS GORDON. Hamilton lots 23 & 24 seized for taxes, sold to Gordon in 1813. Signed THOMAS HUNTER. Witn: JAMES McBRIDE, J. ANTHONY. rec 1816. pp 346, 347, 348

Deed dated 1816. LEVI McDONALD to WILLIAM C. REDDY. Hamilton lots 23 & 24. Signed LEVI (x) McDONALD. Witn: JAMES HEATON, SAML. KENNEDY. rec 1816. pp 348, 349

Deed dated 1813. SAMUEL DAVIS & SUSANNAH his wife to ELIZABETH, SAMUEL & JAMES DAVIS, sons & dau of DANIEL DAVIS, decd. S 14 & 15, T 1, R 2; purchased from Samuel and his brother JOHN DAVIS during the lifetime of both John and Daniel. Subject to dower rights of

BUTLER COUNTY LAND RECORDS: BOOK E

MARGARET DAVIS, widow of Daniel. Signed SAMUEL DAVIS, SUSAN DAVIS. Witn: PHILIP RAY, CHARLES SWEARINGEN. rec 1816. pp 349, 350, 351

Deed dated 1813. JOHN DAVIS & SAMUEL DAVIS to heirs of DANIEL DAVIS (see preceding deed). S 14 & 15, T 1, R 2 purchased in 1796 from John Cleves Symmes; rec Hamilton Co Bk B, pp 1, 2, 3. JD & SD sold one equal third part to brother DANIEL DAVIS in 1797. JOHN DAVIS died at Colerain Twp, Hamilton Co in 18--. SAMUEL to complete sale as directed by Butler Co Court in 1806. Signed SAML. DAVIS. Witn: JOHN REILY, DAVD. BEATY. rec 1816. pp 351, 352, 353, 354.

Deed dated 1816. JAMES T. MORTON & SALLY his wife to JONATHAN W. POWERS. Hamilton lot 64. Signed JAMES. T. MORTON, SALLY T. MORTON. Witn: JOHN FIELDS, JAMES HEATON. rec 1816. pp 354, 355

Deed dated 1815. JOHN SUTHERLAND & NANCY his wife to JOSEPH WATSON. Rossville lot 30. Signed JOHN SUTHERLAND, NANCY R. SUTHERLAND. Witn: DANL MILLIKIN, WM. W. PHARES. rec 1816. pp 355, 356

Deed dated 1815. MOSES MARSH & PHEBE his wife to JOHN PRYER. S 30, T 3, R 1. Signed MOSES MARSH, PHEBE MARSH. Witn: WILLIAM JINKINS, REBEKKAH DEARMOND. rec 1816. pp 357, 358

Deed dated 1815. JOHN SUTHERLAND & NANCY his wife to DAVID DICK. Rossville 30. Signed JOHN SUTHERLAND, NANCY R. SUTHERLAND. Witn: DANL MILLIKIN, WM. W. PHARES. rec 1816. pp 358, 359

Deed dated 1816. DAVID DICK to WILLIAM CROOKS. Rossville lot 30. Signed DAVID DICK. Witn: WM. TAYLOR. rec 1816. pp 359, 360

Deed dated 1816. ZACHARIAH PARRISH & PHEBE his wife to JOHN E. SCOTT. S 36, T 6, R 2. Signed ZACHARIAH PARRISH, PHEBE PARRISH. Witn: MATTHEW RICHARDSON, HENRY TAYLOR. rec 1816. pp 360, 361, 362

Deeed dated 1815. JOSEPH BLOOMFIELD of NJ to JOHN SEWARD, Sussex Co, NJ. S 19, T 2, R 3. Signed JOSEPH BLOOMFIELD by JOHN REILY, atty. Witn: M.G. WALLACE, JAMES McBRIDE, DANL MILLIKIN. rec 1816. pp 362, 363

Deed dated 1815. JOHN WILSON & NANCY his wife to MARGARET KYLE & ANN KYLE. S 6, T 1, R 3. Signed

BUTLER COUNTY LAND RECORDS: BOOK E

JOHN (x) WILSON, NANCY (x) WILSON. Witn: ROBT. TAYLOR, JOHN TRABER. rec 1816. pp 363, 364, 365

Deed dated 1815. DAVID FLENNARD & SUSAN his wife to JOHN ALLEN. S 10, T 2, R 3. Signed DAVID FLENOR, SUSAN (x) FLENOR. Witn: JOHN C. SMALLEY, HENRY WEAVER. rec 1816. pp 365, 366

Deed dated 1815. SHOBAL VAIL & MARY his wife to EPHRAIM WOODRUFF. Middletown lot 6. Signed SHOBAL VAIL, MARY VAIL. Witn: DANIEL VAIL, EZEKIEL BALL. rec 1816. pp 366, 367

Deed dated 1816. JOHN LOWRING & MARY his wife to ABNER ENOCH. S 17, T 2, R 4. Signed JOHN LOWRING, MARY (x) LOWRING. Witn: STEPHEN BALL, EZEKIEL BALL. rec 1816. pp 367, 368, 369

Deed dated 1815. EDWARD HARLAN to MATTHEW HUESTON. Hamilton lot 236. Signed EDWARD HARLAN. Witn: JAMES HEATON, MARY HEATON. rec 1816. pp 369, 370

Deed dated 1816. THOMAS COOCH & HANNAH his wife to JOHN WELCH of Philadelphia, PA. S 29, T 5, R 2. Signed THOS. COOCH, HANNAH COOCH. Witn: T.W. COOK, ELIZA DEVER, MATTH. RICHARDSON. rec 1816. pp 370, 371, 372

Deed dated 1813. JOHN FREEMAN & ELIZABETH his wife to JOSHUA BUTLER. S 26, T 2, R 4. Signed JOHN (x) FREEMAN, ELIZABETH (x) FREEMAN. Witn: HENRY WEAVER, ELISHA SUTTON. rec 1816. pp 372, 373

Deed dated 1815. JOSHUA BUTLER & DRADEN his wife of Franklin Co, IN Ter'y to JOHN SHAFER. S 26, T 2, R 4. Signed JOSHUA BUTLER, DRADEN BUTLER. Witn: JOHN WHITWORTH, RICHARD (x) FREEMAN. rec 1816. pp 373, 374

Deed dated 1815. JACOB BURNET & REBECCA his wife to WILLIAM HUNTER. S 33, T 2, R 2. Signed JAC. BURNET, REBECCA BURNET. Witn: EMILY BENJAMIN, ETHAN STONE. rec 1816. pp 374, 375, 376

Mortgage dated 1816. THOMAS REDDICK of Oxford Twp to LUTHER FREEMAN. Miami University lot 4, S 13, T 5, R 1. Signed THOMAS (x) REDDICK. Witn: ZACARIAH P. DEWITT, WILLIAM BRIDGEFORD. rec 1816. p 376

Deed dated 1815. MOSES BONNELL & MARY his wife of Cincinnati to ABNER HOWARD of same. S 22, T 3, R 3,

BUTLER COUNTY LAND RECORDS: BOOK E

purchased by Bonnell in 1813 from JOHN PEARSON & WILLIAM PIERSON. Signed MOSES BONNELL, MARY BONNELL. Witn: ETHAN STONE, JAMES BUXTEST. rec 1816. pp 377, 378

Deed dated 1815. DENNIS KELLY & POLLY his wife of Cincinnati to ABNER HOWARD of same. S 22, T 3, T 3. Signed DENNIS KELLY, POLLY KELLY. Witn: JOHN MAHARD ABNER T. WOOLEY. rec 1816. pp 378, 379

Deed datd 1816. LAURENCE CAVENAUGH & ANN his wife to ROBERT MARTIN. Rossville lot 59. Signed LAURENCE CAVENAUGH, ANN CAVENAUGH. Witn: MATTH. RICHARDSON, THOMAS MATTIER. rec 1816. pp 380, 381

Deed dated 1814. SAMUEL DICK & MARTHEW his wife to JOHN WILKINSON. Rossville lot 50. Signed SAMUEL DICK, MARTHEW DICK. Witn: JAMES SMITH, J. C. McMANUS rec 1816. pp 381, 382

Deed dated 1815. JOHN P. FINKLE & CATHARINE his wife to WILLIAM HARVEY. Middletown lot 34. Signed JOHN P. FINKLE, CATHARINE FINKLE (german script). Witn: JOHN HEATON, HENRY WEAVER. rec 1816. pp 382, 383

Deed dated 1801. JAMES SMITH, Sheriff of Hamilton Co, NW Ter'y to ADAM DICKEY. In 1800, JOSEPH HENRY obtained judgement against JOHN REED for slander. One-ninth part of tract inherited by Reed from his father seized, sold for debt; no S-T-R given. Signed JAMES SMITH. Witn: none. rec 1816. pp 383, 384, 385

Deed dated 1815. WILLIAM GARRETT to ROBERT GARRETT. Middletown lots 23 & 43. Signed WILLIAM (x) GARRETT. Witn: F. CLARK, JOHN GARRETT, JOHN AYERS. rec 1816. pp 386, 387

Deed dated 1815. LEVI JENNINGS & ELIZABETH his wife to heirs of ABRAHAM SIMPSON: widow JANE SIMPSON, SAMUEL SIMPSON, RACHEL CARLE and heirs of JONATHAN SIMPSON. S 32, T 2, R 4 purchased by Abraham, now decd. Signed LEVI JENNINGS, ELIZABETH (x) JENNINGS. Witn: ABRAM HUFF, HENRY WEAVER. rec 1816. pp 387, 388

Deed dated 1815. EDWARD BEBB & MARGARET his wife of Morgan Twp to JOHN BROWN JR of same. S 27, T 3, R 1. Signed EDWARD BEBB, MARGARET BEBB. Witn: JAMES SHIELDS, JOHN RICHARDSON. rec 1816. pp 389, 390

Deed dated 1815. JAMES MARTIN & ANN his wife to

BUTLER COUNTY LAND RECORDS: BOOK E

WILLIAM DOUGLASS. S 21, T 5, R 2. Signed JAMES MARTIN, ANN MARTIN. Witn: MATTH. RICHARDSON, ADAM RICHEY. rec 1816. pp 390, 391, 392

Plat of Jacksonburg dated 1816. Located on boundary of S 11 & 14, T 3, R 3; "road from ISAAC HOFF's toward WILLIAM PHARES crosses the road from Hamilton to NATHANIEL BELL's". Signed JOHN CRAIG, JOHN BAIRD, HENRY WEAVER, proprietors. rec 1816. pp 392, 393

Deed dated 1814. JOSEPH EVANS & ESTHER his wife of Montgomery Co to JAMES HINDS. S 17, T 3, R 3. Signed JOSEPH EVANS, ESTHER EVANS. Witn: ISAAC CONARROO, LEVI HAWKINS. rec 1816. pp 393, 394, 395

Deed dated 1815. JAMES MILLS & SARAH his wife to PHILIP GORDON. Rossville lots 8, 85, 87. Signed JAMES MILLS, SARAH MILLS. Witn: JAMES HEATON, WILLIAM SUTHERLAND. rec 1816. pp 395, 396

Deed dated 1812. Exctr of STEPHEN VAIL to ARCHIBALD CAMPBELL. Middletown lot 40; finalize 1806 sale. Signed AARON VAIL. Witn: JOHN HUSTON. rec 1816. pp 397, 398, 399

Deed dated 1816. JAMES ROBISON & JANE his wife to JOHN P. FINKLE. S 8, T 2, R 4; bound by land of ANTHONY BURDGE. Signed JAMES ROBISON, JANE (x) ROBISON. Witn: JP JAMES CLARK, BESY SMITH JR. rec 1816. pp 399, 400

Deed dated 1816. NATHANIEL FRENCH to CARLTON WALDO. Middletown lot 19. Signed NATHANIEL FRENCH. Witn: JEREMIAH FRENCH, WILLIAM ARMSTRONG. rec 1816. p 401

Deed dated 1815. ISAAC VANNICE & ELIZABETH his wife to CORNELIUS VANNICE. S 14, T 2, R 3. Signed ISAAC VAN NUYS, ELIZABETH (x) VAN NUYS. Witn: JOHN SUNDERLAND, HENRY WEAVER. rec 1816. pp 402, 403

Deed dated 1812. JOHN VANNICE & ELIZABETH his wife to ISAAC VANNICE. S 14, T 2, R 3; bound by land of STEPHEN SLIFER. Signed JOHN VANNICE, ELIZABETH (x) VANNICE. Witn: CALEB WILLIAMS, HENRY WEAVER. rec 1816. pp 403, 404

Plat of Bloomfield, undated. S 32, T 2, R 4. Signed MICHAEL PEARCE, DAVID ENYART, proprietors. rec 1816. pp 405, 406

Deed dated 1816. WILLIAM MURRAY & DEBORAH his wife

BUTLER COUNTY LAND RECORDS: BOOK E

to HENRY WATSON. S 26, T 4, R 2. Signed WILLIAM MURRAY, DEBBY MURRAY. Witn: WILLIAM C. KEEN, JAMES HEATON. rec 1816. pp 406, 407

Deed dated 1816. AARON SOUTHARD & NANCY his wife to JOHN P. FINKLE. S 30, T 2, R 4. Signed AARON SOUTHARD, ANN (x) SOUTHARD. Witn: SAMUEL MATIX, HENRY WEAVER. rec 1816. pp 407, 408, 409

Deed dated 1816. WILLIAM HARVEY & ISABELLA his wife to ADDISON SMITH. Middletown lot 52. Signed WILLIAM HARVEY, ISABELLA HARVEY. Witn: JOHN SHAFER, JAMES STEWART. rec 1816. p 409

Deed dated 1816. WILLIAM FRAZEE & MARY his wife to FREEMAN CONKLING. S 7, T 2, R 3. Signed WILLIAM FRAZEE, MARY FRAZEE. Witn: JAMES HEATON, JACOB L. CONKLING. rec 1816. pp 409, 410, 411

Mortgage dated 1816. FREEMAN CONKLIN to WILLIAM FRAZEE. Land as above; paymt due 1819. Signed FREEMAN CONKLING. Witn above. rec 1816. pp 411, 412

Deed dated 1816. PHILIP KEMP & CATHARINE his wife to heirs of JOHN BAKE JR, decd: JACOB, MARIAH, ELIZABETH, ELEANOR & CATHARINE BAKE. S 15, T 2, R 4; dower rights to HANNAH BAKE, widow of John. Signed PHILIP KEMP, CATHARINE (x) KEMP. Witn: DAVID CRANE, WILLIAM KEE. rec 1816. pp 412, 413, 414

Deed dated 1815. ROBERT JOHN & ASENATH his wife to WILLIAM HUFFMAN of Montgomery Co. Middletown lot 35. Signed ROBERT JOHN, ASENATH JOHN. Witn: JEREMIAH CRAIN, WILLIAM HARVEY. rec 1816. pp 414, 415

Deed dated 1815. -- WOOD & CATY his wife of Hamilton Co to heirs of JOHN CASSIDAY, decd: CATY, ABBY, EZRA, ELIZA, ALEXANDER, PATRICK & PHEBE CASSIDAY. S 10, T 1, R 2; previously divided among heirs of ISAAC FREEMAN. Signed STEPHEN WOOD, CATHARINE WOOD. Witn: JEREMIAH PRYOR, MARY ANN (x) PRYOR. rec 1816. pp 415, 416, 417

Power of Attorney dated 1815. SAMUEL McMANUS of New Orleans, LA appted JOHN C. McMANUS as Atty to conduct business, collect debts. Signed SAMUEL McMANUS. Witn: JOHN DICK, FIELDING L. FARMER. rc 1816. pp 417, 418

Deed dated 1816. ABSALOM GOODENOUGH & SARAH his wife to SAMUEL FIELDS. Hamilton lot 54. Signed ABSALOM GOODENOUGH, SARAH (x) GOODENOUGH. Witn: JAMES HEATON

BUTLER COUNTY LAND RECORDS: BOOK E

JAMES CLARK. rec 1816. pp 418, 419

Deed dated 1816. SAMUEL FIELD to AZUR R. MILLS. Hamilton lot 54. Signed SAMUEL FIELDS JR. Witn: JAMES HEATON, SAMUEL MILLER. rec 1816. pp 419, 420

Deed dated 1816. ROBERT BROWN & RACHEL his wife to JOHN P. FINKLE. S 29, T 2, R 4; bound by land of DAVID WOOLVERTON, ABNER ENOCH. Signed ROBERT BROWN, RACHEL BROWN. Witn: ADDISON SMITH, WILLIAM HARVEY. rec 1816. pp 420, 421, 422

Deed dated 1816. JOHN P. FINKLE & CATHARINE his wife to JAMES ROBINSON. S 29, T 2, R 4. Signed JOHN P. FINKLE, CATHARINE FINKLE (german script). Witn: JAMES CLARK, BENJAMIN SMITH. rec 1816. pp 422, 423

Power of Attorney dated 1815. JOSEPH POTTER appted Major THOMAS DUGAN of Cincinnati as atty to deliver deed to OLIVER M. SPENCER and/or DANIEL SYMMES. S 14, T 2, R 2; bought from JOHN DIXON. Signed JOSEPH POTTER. Witn: CYRUS B. GLOVER, JOHN ROUX. rec 1816. pp 423, 424

Deed dated 1816. JOSEPH POTTER by atty THOMAS DUGAN to OLIVER M. SPENCER and DANIEL SYMMES. S 20, T 2, R 2; formerly owned by JOHN DIXON. Signed JOSEPH POTTER by atty. Witn: ANDREW BURT, HUGH MOORE. JP's note: ELEANOR POTTER, wife of Joseph, relinquished right of dower. rec 1816. pp 424, 425, 426

Deed dated 1816. JOSEPH POTTER by atty above to DANIEL SYMMES. S 14, T 2, R 2; "where family of Joseph now resides". Bound by land of -- TALBOT, DR. CARMICHAEL, GENL. JAS. FINDLAY & -- STANLEY's heirs. Signed, witn and JP's note as above. rec 1816. pp 426, 427

Deed dated 1816. JOHN WILKINSON & MARY his wife to ELIZABETH ANDREW & ABRAHAM ANDREW. Rossville lot 52. Signed JOHN WILKINSON, MARY WILKINSON. Witn: JOHN HUNTER, J.C. McMANUS. rec 1816. pp 428, 429

Deed dated 1816. GABRIEL HENSLEY & ANN his wife to DAVID RISK of Hamilton Co. S 23, T 3, R 3; bound by DANIEL GOBLE's land. Signed GABRIEL (x) HENSLEY, ANN (x) HENSLEY. Witn: JP JAMES CLARK, WILLIAM H. CLARK. rec 1816. pp 429, 430

Deed dated 1816. JAMES MATHERS & ANNE his wife to PETER ZEIGLER. S 19, T -, R 4. Signed JAMES MATHERS

BUTLER COUNTY LAND RECORDS: BOOK E

ANNE MATHERS. Witn: JAMES CLARK, SAMUEL CLARK. rec 1816. pp 430, 431, 432

Deed datd 1816. PETER ZEIGLER & ANN his wife to JAMES MATHERS. S 14, T 2, R 4; "where I now live". Signed PETER ZEIGLER, ANN (x) ZEIGLER. Witn: as above. rec 1816. pp 432, 433

Deed dated 1816. JOHN VANNICE & BETSEY his wife to JOSHUA COX & his younger son, DAVID COX, heirs of DAVID COX the elder, decd. S 11, T 2, R 3. Purchased by David the elder; will gave Joshua use during lifetime, David the younger ownership after father's death. Signed JOHN VANNICE, BETSEY (x) VANNICE. Witn: JAMES SMITH, CORNELIUS VANNICE. rec 1816. pp 433, 434, 435

Deed dated 1815. WILLIAM PARKINSON of Morgan Twp to MAXWELL PARKINSON of Reily Twp. S 6, T 4, R 1. Signed WILLIAM PARKINSON. Witn: KING DEARMOND, HANNAH (x) DEARMOND. rec 1816. pp 435, 436

Deed dated 1815. JAMES MILLS JR to GEORGE H. ARNOLD. Rossville outlot 9. Signed JAMES MILLS JR. Witn: AZUR R. MILLS, JAMES MILLS. rec 1816. pp 436, 437

Deed dated 1815. ISRAEL WATTS & MARY his wife of Preble Co to JAMES DIXON of same. No S-T-R; bound by ADAM DICKEY's land. Signed ISRAEL WATTS, MARY (x) WATTS. Witn: none. rec 1816. pp 438, 439

Deed dated 1816. JAMES PIPER & ALICE his wife to JOHN P. FINKLE. Middletown lots 17 & 18. Signed JAMES PIPER, ALICE PIPER. Witn: ABNER ENOCH, ADDISON SMITH. rec 1816. pp 439, 440

Deed dated 1803. ISRAEL RUNYON & MARY his wife of Somerset Co, NJ to SAMUEL RANDOLPH of Middlesex Co, NJ. S 26, T 2, R 2 in Hamilton Co, NW Ter'y; bought by ELIAS RUNYON. Conveyed to his heirs: JOHN, ISRAEL, ELIAS, PETER & JEAN RUNYON. Signed ISRAEL RUNYON, MARY RUNYON. Witn: RICHARD RUNYON, JAMES AUTEN. rec 1816. pp 440, 441

Deed dated 1815. NIMROD RANDOLPH of Fairfield Twp to JACOB LEWIS of same. S 24, T 2, R 4; formerly owned by SAMUEL RANDOLPH (see above). Inherited by DRAKE RANDOLPH & sold to Nimrod. Signed NIMROD RANDOLPH. Witn: THOMAS LEWIS, JAMES LEWIS. rec 1816. pp 441, 442, 443

BUTLER COUNTY LAND RECORDS: BOOK E

Deed dated 1816. BRICE VIRGIN to JEREMIAH VIRGIN. S 2, T 2, R 3. Signed BRICE VIRGIN. Witn: JAMES HEATON, MARY HEATON. rec 181. pp 443, 444

Deed dated 1815. JOHN VANNICE & BETSEY his wife to JOHN COX & his younger son, DAVID COX, heirs of DAVID COX the elder, decd. S 11, T 2, R 3. Purchased by David the elder; will gave John use during lifetime, David the younger ownership after father's death. Signed JOHN VAN NICE, BETSEY (x) VAN NICE. Witn: JAMES SMITH, CORNELIUS VAN NICE. rec 1816. pp 444, 445, 446 (bound out of order)

Deed dated 1816. JOHN McCINSTRAY & CHARITY his wife to FRANCIS ST. CLAIR. S 4, T 4, R 2; bound by land of GEORGE BOYER. Signed JOHN (x) McCINSTRAY, CHARITY (x) McCINSTRAY. Witn: JAMES HEATON, DAVID LINE. rec 1816. pp 446, 447, 448

Deed dated 1815. DANIEL DOTY & BETSEY his wife to STEPHANUS CLARK. S 18, T 2, R 2; bound by land of JACOB ROUND. Signed DANIEL DOTY, BETSEY DOTY. Witn: MOSES BREES, EZEKIEL BALL. rec 1816. pp 448, 449

Deed dated 1816. GEORGE H. ARNOLD to WILLIAM WILSON. Rossville outlot 9. Signed GEORGE H. ARNOLD. Witn: SAMUEL McCLURE, ROBT. TAYLOR. rec 1816. pp 448, 449

Deed dated 1812. USA to ANDREW KARR, assignee of exctr of DAVID LOGAN. S 9, T 2, R 4. rec 1816 p 451

Deed dated 1815. Heirs of WILLIAM McCLURE to WILLIAM SHEAFOR. S 25, T 2, R 4; bound by land of heirs of JOHN SINKEY, decd. Signed JOHN McCLURE of Butler Co; ANTHONY LOGAN, JANE LOGAN, JAMES McCLURE, MARTHA McCLURE, all of Mongomery Co; DAVID McCLURE & RUTHY McCLURE of Jefferson Co, IN by attys JAMES STEELE & DAVID McCLURE. rec 1816. pp 451, 452, 453, 454

Deed dated 1815. ANDREW WAGGONER & MARY his wife of Madison Twp to THOMAS LINGLE of same. S 7, T 2, R 4. Signed ANDREW (x) WAGONER, MARY (x) WAGONER. Witn: LEONARD WEAVER, HENRY WEAVER. rec 1816. pp 454, 455

Deed dated 1816. ROBERT MARTIN to JAMES YOUNG. One seventh part of S 23, T 5, R (illeg). Signed ROBERT MARTIN. Witn: MATTH. RICHARDSON, MATTHEW J. RICHARDSON. rec 1816. pp 455, 456

p 455, 456 repeated

BUTLER COUNTY LAND RECORDS: BOOK E

Plat of Middletown addition dated 1816. Signed HUGH VAIL, SHOBAL VAIL, JOHN CUMMINGS, DANIEL DOTY, ABNER ENOCH, proprietors. rec 1816. pp 457, 458

Deed dated 1816. Admtrs of PATRICK CASSIDY, decd, to WILLIAM HALL. S 10, T 1, R 2; lot 3 as ordered by Butler Co Court in 1803. Signed JAMES HEATON, SALLY CASSIDY. Witn: JNO. CAMPBELL, G.W. STALL. rec 1816. pp 458, 459

Deed dated 1812. JOHN ENYART & NANCY his wife to WILLIAM ENYART. S 14, T 2, R 2. Signed JOHN ENYART, NANCY (x) ENYART. Witn: THOMAS SELFRIDGE, STEPHEN CRANE. rec 1816. pp 459, 460

Deed dated 1812. JOHN ENYART & NANCY his wife to WILLIAM ENYART. S 20, T 2, R 2. Signed and witn as above. rec 1816. pp 461, 462

Deed datd 1815. WILLIAM ROBERTSON & POLLY his wife to JONATHAN COOK. S 11, T 5, R 2. Signed WILLIAM ROBERTSON, POLLY ROBERTSON. Witn: JAMES PATTY, NATHAN STUBBS. rec 1816. pp 462, 463

Deed dated 1816. ELI COOK & MARTHA his wife of Preble Co to JONATHAN COOK. S 11, T 5, R 2. Signed ELI (x) COOK, MARTHA COOK. Witn: ELI COOK, NATHAN STUBBS. rec 1816. pp 463, 464

Deed dated 1815. ISAAC STANLEY to JAMES P. RAMSEY. Hamilton lots 111, 112. Signed ISAAC STANLEY. Witn: JOHN REILY, SAML. DAVIS JR. rec 1816. pp 464, 465

Deed dated 1814. JOHN SUTHERLAND & NANCY his wife to JAMES P. RAMSEY. Hamilton lots 121, 122. Signed JOHN SUTHERLAND, NANCY R. SUTHERLAND. Witn: JAMES HEATON, JOHN C. CRUME. rec 1816. pp 465, 466

Deed dated 1815. JAMES SHIELDS & CHRISTIAN his wife to JAMES COOK. S 34, T 3, R 2; bought from PATRICK SHIELDS. Signed JAMES SHIELDS, CHRISTIAN (x) SHIELDS Witn: MICHAEL AYERS. rec 1816. pp 466, 467, 468

Deed dated 1815. ABRAHAM F. FREEMAN & KATY his wife to THOMAS WARD. S 35, T 3, R 3, except land sold to MICHAEL HAGEMAN; bound by land of JOHN FITZ FREEMAN. Signed ABRAHAM F. FREEMAN, KATY (x) FREEMAN. Witn: JAMES HEATON, JOSEPH BROOKS. rec 1816. pp 468, 469

Deed dated 1815. JOSEPH HAYS & MARY his wife to MARK DIXON. S 22, T 2, R 4. Signed JOSEPH HAYS, MARY (x)

BUTLER COUNTY LAND RECORDS: BOOK E

HAYS. Witn: EZEKIEL BALL, BENJAMIN HAYS. rec 1816. pp 469, 470

Deed dated 1815. JOHN KENNEDY & PRISCILLA his wife to JOHN THOMPSON. S 17, T 5, R 2. Signed JOHN KENNEDY, PRISCILLA (x) KENNEDY. Witn: MATTH. RICHARDSON, MATTHEW J. RICHARDSON. rec 1816. pp 470, 471

Deed dated 1816. JOHN ELLIOTT to DANIEL RUMPLE, both of Ross Twp. S 11, T 3, R 2; bound by land of JAMES ELLIOTT, MATTHEW TIMBERMAN, WM. MORRIS, WM. BALDWIN, JAMES MOORE. Signed JOHN ELLIOTT. Witn: JOHN DUNN, JAS. DUNN. rec 1816. pp 471, 472, 473

Deed dated 1810. DAVID ENYART & SUSANNA his wife to BENJAMIN ENYART. S 9, T 2, R 3. Signed DAVID ENYART SUSANA (x) ENYART. Witn: JOHN AYERS, ZECHARIAH SUTTON. rec 1816. pp 473, 474

Deed dated 1816. BENJAMIN ENYART & MARY his wife of Warren Co to PETER RUNNION. S 9, T 2, R 3. Signed BENJAMIN (x) ENYART, MARY (x) ENYART. Witn: RICHD. PARSELL, JP ABRAHAM VAN VLEET. rec 1816. pp 473, 474

Deed dated 1814. DAVID ENYART & SUSANNAH his wife to VINCENT DAVIS. S 9, T 2, R 3. Signed DAVID ENYART, SUSANNAH (x) ENYART. Witn: JOHN AYERS, JOSEPH WORTH. rec 1816. pp 475, 476

Deed dated 1814. VINCENT DAVIS & ANNA his wife to DAVID CLARKSON. S 9, T 2, R 3. Signed VINCENT DAVIS, ANNA DAVIS. Witn: JOHN VINNAGE, RUNA CLAWSON. rec 1816. pp 476, 477, 478

Deed dated 1814. DAVID ENYART & SUSANNAH his wife to DAVID CLARKSON. S 9, T 2, R 3; bound by land of JAMES CUMMINGS & JOSEPH RANDOLPH. Signed DAVID ENYART, SUSANNA (x) ENYART. Witn: JOHN AYERS, JACOB LEWIS. rec 1816. pp 478, 479

Deed dated 1816. WILLIAM McMANUS & REBECAH his wife to ELI POTTER. S 7, T 4, R 2. Signed WILLIAM McMANUS REBECAH McMANUS. Witn: M. HUESTON, JOHN SIMMONS. rec 1816. pp 479, 480

Deed dated 1816. JACOB HAWN & PEGGY his wife of Warren Co to ISAAC SLOTE, SARAH BALL & JOANNA REEDER of same. S 12, T 2, R 4; bound by MOSES VAIL's land. Signed JACOB HAWN, PEGGY HAWN. Witn: W. C. SCHENCK, JAMES W. LANIER. rec 1816. pp 480, 481

BUTLER COUNTY LAND RECORDS: BOOK E

Deed dated 1816. WILLIAM McCLAIN & PEGGY his wife to JOHN SHAFOR. Middletown lot 14. Signed WILLIAM Mc-CLAIN, PEGGY McCLAIN. Witn: JOSEPH C. HARRIS, WM. HARVEY. rec 1816. pp 481, 482, 483

Deed dated 1815. EMANUEL BURGET & CATHARINE his wife late GARDNER, dau & heir of HENRY GARDNER, decd, to JOHN B. WILLIAMS. S 6, T 3, R 2. Signed EMANUEL BURGET, CATHRON (x) BURGET. Witn: JP WM. C. MITCHELL, THOMAS (x) FOSET. rec 1816. pp 483, 484

Lease sale dated 1816. ROBERT TAYLOR to LUTHER FREEMAN. 99 yr lease of Miami University lands; lot 1 in S 14. Entered 1810. Signed ROBERT TAYLOR. Witn: JAMES L. MAXWELL, #2 illeg. rec 1816. pp 484, 485

Deed dated 1816. ISAAC WILES & ELIZABETH his wife to SAMUEL EASTIN. Hamilton lot 75. Signed ISAAC WILES, ELIZABETH (x) WILES. Witn: JAMES HEATON, SAMUEL McCULLAGH. rec 1816. pp 485, 486

Bond, no date. GARRET LAREW to BENJAMIN STONE. Deed to S 23, T 3, R 2W in IN Ter'y to be delivered by 1821. Signed GARRET LAREW. Witn: ABIGAIL AYERS, MICHAEL AYERS. rec 1816. pp 486, 487

Deed dated 1816. THOMAS HUNTER, tax collector of Fairfield Twp to JAMES SMITH. In 1812, Hamilton lot 35 sold for taxes to Smith. Signed THOMAS HUNTER. Witn: SAML. DAVIS JR, JOHN McCLURE JR. rec 1816. pp 487, 488

Deed dated 1815. M.S. PETITT of Cincinnati to THOMAS RAWLINS of same. Hamilton lot -; deed given to Petitt by RICHARD DAVIS. Signed M.S. PETITT. Witn: THOMAS EWING, JAMES EWING. rec 1816. pp 488, 489

Deed dated 1815. ESTHER THOMAS to children of LEWIS THOMAS, decd: TABITHA CLARK late THOMAS, JAMES THOMAS & SARAH THOMAS, minors. S 11, T 3, R 3. Text confusing; may be that heirs were ch of Lewis as stated or possibly Tabitha was remarried widow of Lewis and James & Sarah her children. Signed ESTHER THOMAS. Witn: JAMES HEATON, CHRISTOPHER LINTNER. rec 1816. pp 489, 490, 491

Deed dated 1816. JOSEPH VAN HORNE & MARTHA his wife to WILLIAM HILL. Millville lot 21. Signed JOSEPH VAN HORNE, MARTHA VAN HORNE. Witn: JAMES BEATY, ELIAKIM ROSS. rec 1816. pp 491, 492

BUTLER COUNTY LAND RECORDS: BOOK E

Deed dated 1816. JOSEPH VAN HORNE & MARTHA his wife to ELIAKIM ROSS. Millville lot 12 in S 4, T 3, R 2. Signed JOSEPH VAN HORNE, MARTHA VAN HORNE. Witn: JAMES BEATY, WILLIAM HILL. rec 1816. pp 492, 493

Deed dated 1816. JAMES ROLLF & SIBEL his wife to HENRY SHIPLEY SR of Fayette Co, PA. S 6, T 3, R 5. Signed JAMES ROLLF, SIBEL ROLLF. Witn: CORNELIUS (illeg), WILLIAM JENKINS. rec 1816. pp 493, 494

Deed dated 1816. ELIAS BOUDINOT of NJ to ROBERT BROWN. S 14, T 2, R 4. Signed ELIAS BOUDINOT by JAC. BURNET, agent. Witn: WILLIAM RAMSAY, JOHN MAHARD. rec 1816. pp 495, 496

Bill of sale dated 1815. GEORGE HARLAN to WILLIAM MURRAY. Livestock, household goods. Signed GEORGE HARLAN. Witn: ZEBL. COLBY, G. McCORIND. rec 1816. pp 497, 498

Deed dated 1816. JOSEPH GAILBREATH & MARY his wife to HERMAN McCLURE of NY state. S 31, T 2, R 4, bound by ADAM DICKEY's land. Signed JOSEPH GAILBREATH, MARY GAILBREATH. Witn: JOHN P. FINKLE, EZEKIEL BALL. rec 1816. pp 498, 499

Deed dated 1815. ISAAC WILES & ELIZABETH his wife to CORNELIUS THOMAS. S 2, T 2, R 2 "whereon said Cornelius now lives". Signed ISAAC WILES, ELIZABETH (x) WILES. Witn: JAMES HEATON, JONATHAN LINE. rec 1816. pp 499, 500

Deed dated 1815. CORNELIUS THOMAS to BENJAMIN LAING of Essex Co, NJ. S 24, T 2, R 2. Signed CORNELIUS THOMAS. Witn: HUGH DRAKE, JOHN STILES. rec 1816. pp 500, 501

Deed dated 1816. WILLIAM COOLEY & NANCY his wife to BENJAMIN WOLDEN of Hamilton Co. S 33, T 5, R 2; bound by SIMON BROADBERRY's land. Signed WILLIAM COOLEY, NANCY (x) COOLEY. Witn: JAMES WOLDEN, J.M. DORSEY. rec 1816. pp 501, 502

Deed dated 1816. MICHAEL PEARCE & PHEBE his wife to ISAAC WISEMAN DENMAN. Bloomfield lot 6. Signed MICHAEL PEARCE, PHEBE PEARCE. Witn: GARRET SHURTE, HENRY WEAVER. rec 1816. pp 502, 503

Deed dated 1816. MICHAEL PEARCE & PHEBE his wife to JOHN DENMAN. Bloomfield lot 3. Signed MICHAEL PEARCE, PHEBE PEARCE. Witn: GARRET SHURTS. rec

BUTLER COUNTY LAND RECORDS: BOOK E

1816. pp 504, 505

Deed dated 1816. MICHAEL PEARCE & PHEBE his wife to JOHN DENMAN. S 4, T 1, R 4; bound by DAVIS BALL's land. Signed MICHAEL PEARCE, PHEBE PEARCE. Witn: #1 german script, HENRY WEAVER. rec 1816. pp 505, 506

Deed dated 1816. JAMES McBRIDE, Sheriff, to JACOB LEWIS. In 1815, Lewis obtained judgement against JAMES H. PARCELL, by reason of a mortgage. Sheriff seized Hamilton lot 185; sold at auction. Signed JAMES McBRIDE. Witn: JOS. BENHAM, JOS. HOUGH, WM. GREENLEE. rec 1816. pp 506, 507, 508

Deed dated 1816. CONRAD DARR & CATHARINE his wife to BENJAMIN PURSAIL. Darrtown lot 53. Signed CONRAD DARR, CATHARINE DARR. Witn: MATTH. RICHARDSON, WILLIAM BRYAN. rec 1816. pp 508, 509, 510

Deed dated 1814. DANIEL DOTY & BETSEY his wife to NICHOLAS BALEY. S 27, T 2, R 4; bound by land of CYRUS OSBURN. Signed DANIEL DOTY, BETSEY DOTY. Witn: HENRY VAIL, EZEKIEL BALL. rec 1816. pp 510, 511

Deed dated 1813. ISAAC PAXTON & MAGDALANE to JOHN SIMMONS. S 11, T 2, R 3. Signed ISAAC PAXTON, MAG-DALANE PAXTON. Witn: H.B. HAWTHORN, HENRY WEAVER. rec 1816. pp 511, 512

Deed dated 1816. STEPHEN LUDLOW & JANE his wife of Lawrenceburgh, Dearborn Co, IN Ter'y to DANIEL MILLIKIN. Hamilton lots 195, 204, 205. Signed STEPHEN LUDLOW, JANE P. LUDLOW. Witn: THOMAS PORTER, ALEXANDER PROUDFITS. rec 1816. pp 512, 513

Deed dated 1816. DANIEL MILLIKIN & JOAN his wife to SAMUEL GRAY. Hamilton lot 192. Signed DAN. MILLIKIN JOAN MILLIKIN. Witn: ALEXANDER PROUDFITS, SARAH GRAY. rec 1816. pp 515, 516

Deed dated 1816. JACOB HAWN & PEGGY his wife of Warren Co to DAVID FOX. S 12, T 2, R 4; sold to Hawn by JACOB KRAUTZ, bound by MOSES VAIL's land. Signed JACOB HAWN, PEGGY HAWN. Witn: JOSEPH TROXELL, J. W. LANIER. rec 1816. pp 516, 517

Deed dated 1816. ROBERT GARRETT to JOSEPH HAYS of Switzerland co, IN Ter'y. Middletown lots 23 & 43. Signed ROBERT GARRETT. Witn: WALTER HAYES, EZEKIEL BALL. rec 1816. pp 517, 518

BUTLER COUNTY LAND RECORDS: BOOK E

Deed dated 1816. NICHOLAS BALEY to JOSHUA HILL and ELENDER HILL. S 27, T 2, R 4. Signed NICHOLAS BAILEY. Witn: JOHN NICLE. rec 1816. pp 518, 519

Mortgage dated 1816. CORNELIUS RYERSON to ALEXANDER McCALL of Hamilton Co. S 10, T 2, R 2. Signed CORNELIUS J. RYERSON. Witn: ADAM HILL, JOHN MAHARD. rec 1816. pp 519, 520, 521

Deed dated 1816. CARLTON WALDO to NATHANIEL FRENCH. S 27, T 4, R 1. Signed CARLTON WALDO. Witn: JAMES HEATON, MARY HEATON. rec 1816. pp 521, 522

Deed dated 1815. JEREMIAH FRENCH to NATHANIEL FRENCH. Middletown lot 19. Signed JEREMIAH FRENCH. Witn: JOSEPH (illeg), JAS. HARDING SR. rec 1816. pp 522, 523

Deed dated 1816. JOHN SNABLEY & MARGARET his wife to DAVID WILLIAMSON, all of Madison Twp. S 9, T 2, R 4. Signed JOHN (x) SNABLEY, MARGARET (x) SNABLEY. Witn: JAMES JONES, JACOB WEIDNER. rec 1816. pp 523, 524

Deed dated 1816. JOHN P. FINKLE & CATHARINE his wife to ANTHONY BURDGE. Lot 8, S -, T 2, R 4. Signed JOHN P. FINKLE, CATHARINE FINKLE (german script). Witn: PETER (x) HERBACH, WM. HARVEY. rec 1816. pp 524, 525

Deed dated 1815. SAMUEL SMITH & MARTHA his wife of Union Co, IN Ter'y to CHARLES CONE of Crosby Twp, Hamilton Co. S 32, T 3, R 2. Signed SAMUEL SMITH, no wife's signature. Witn: JOAB COMSTOCK, SAMUEL SMITH JR. rec 1816. pp 525, 526

Deed dated 1814. DAVID BEATY & MARGARET his wife of Fairfield Twp to JAMES BEATY, his son. S 33, T 4, R 2; bound by NINIAN BEATY's land. Signed DAVID BEATY, MARGARET (x) BEATY. Witn: DAVID BRANT, JOSEPH VANNOSTRAN. rec 1816. pp 526, 527

Deed dated 1816. PHILIP WIGGINS & COMFORT his wife to ROSSWELL GROSVENOR. Lease of Miami University lot 1 in S 24, T 5, R 1 by JOSEPH HUNTER in 1811; assigned to JONATHAN WARD in 1814; assigned to Wiggins in 1815. Signed PHILIP WIGGINS, COMFORT WIGGINS Witn: LEVI LEE, JAMES J. BEELER. rec 1816. pp 527, 528, 529

Deed dated 1815. JONATHAN WARD & POLLY his wife of

BUTLER COUNTY LAND RECORDS: BOOK E

Oxford Twp to PHILIP WIGGINS of same. Lease of Miami University lot 1 as previous deed. Signed JONATHAN WARD, MARY WARD. Witn: GEORGE BARNARD, J. W. DORSEY rec 1816. pp 527, 528, 529

Mortgage dated 1816. ROSSWELL GROSVENOR to PHILIP WIGGINS. Miami University lot 1 as above. Signed ROSSWELL GROSVENOR. Witn: LEVI LEE, JAMES J. BEELER. rec 1816. pp 531, 532

Deed dated 1810. JEREMIAH BUTTERFIELD & POLLY his wife of Hamilton co to JOSEPH BOLTON. S 33, T 3, R 2; bound by land of heirs of FRANCIS WHITINGER decd. Signed JEREMIAH BUTTERFIELD, POLLY BUTTERFIELD. Witn: JAMES TEMPLETON, JAMES SHAW, JAMES COMSTOCK. rec 1816. pp 532, 533

Deed dated 1816. OBEDIAH WILLEVER & HANNAH his wife to JOSEPH WILLEVER, all of Reily Twp. S 23, T 4, R 1. Signed OBEDIAH WILLEVER, HANNAH (x) WILLEVER. Witn: JOHN BURK, DAVID DeCAMP. rec 1816. pp 534, 535

Deed dated 1814. JOHN ARMSTRONG of Columbia, Hamilton Co to WILLIAM G. ARMSTRONG, son of said John. Hamilton lot 115. Signed JOHN (x) ARMSTRONG. Witn: JAS. C. MORRIS, F. B. MILLER. rec 1816. pp 535, 536

Deed dated 1816. DAVID RICHEY & ANN his wife of Preble Co to SAMUEL JEFFREY. S 31, T 3, R 3. Signed DAVID RICHEY, ANN RICHEY. Witn: JOSEPH WASSON, ANNA WATT. rec 1816. pp 536, 537

Mortgage dated 1816. SAMUEL BROWN of Ross Twp to WILLIAM MITCHELL of Reily Twp, MAXWELL PARKISON of same and DAVID GIBSON of Crosby Twp, Hamilton Co, exctrs of estate of ISAAC GIBSON JR, late of Fairfield Twp. S 3, T 3, R 2 "where S. BROWN now lives"; bound by land of WILLIAM JONES. Signed SAMUEL BROWN. Witn: BENJ. CILLEY, JOHN DUNN. rec 1816. pp 537, 538, 539

Deed dated 1815. WILLIAM REED & REBECKA his wife to JOHN MULFORD. S 31, T 2, R 4. Signed WILLIAM REED, REBECKA (x) REED. Witn: JOB MULFORD, ANTHONY BURDGE. rec 1816. pp 539, 540

Quitclaim dated 1816. HANNAH MULFORD, widow of DAVID of Lemon Twp to JOHN MULFORD, admtr of estate of said DAVID MULFORD. Release of dower rights. Signed HANNAH (x) MULFORD. Witn: HENRY WEAVER, BENJAMIN SWEETS. rec 1816. pp 540, 541

BUTLER COUNTY LAND RECORDS: BOOK E

Quitclaim dated 1816. Heirs of DAVID MULFORD to JOHN MULFORD, heir and admtr as previous deed. David died leaving 2 sons, 1 dau. Quitclaim to all financial dealings of estate. Signed JOB MULFORD, EDMOND ALLDRIDG, JANE ALLDRIDG late MULFORD. Witn: BENJAMIN SWAT, JOHN TULLIS. rec 1816. p 541

Mortgage dated 1816. ALEXANDER SIMPSON of Ross Twp to exctrs of ISAAC GIBSON JR, decd. (see Bk E, pp 537 to 539.) S33, T 3, R 2 •where...SIMPSON now lives•. Signed ALEXANDER SIMPSON. witn: W. D. JONES, JAMES SHIELDS. rec 1816. pp 542, 543

Deed dated 1816. DAVID ENYART & SUSANNA his wife to SILAS POINER. Bloomfield lot 33. Signed DAVID ENYART SUSANNA ENYART. Witn: MOSES BREES, HENRY WEAVER. rec 1816. pp 543, 544

Deed dated 1816. DAVID ENYART & SUSANNA his wife to PETER POINER. Bloomfield lot 32. Signed and witn as above. rec 1816. pp 544, 545

Deed dated 1816. BENJAMIN BRIDGE & ELIZABETH his wife to DAVID HEATON. S 22, T 2, R 4; bound by land of heirs of JAMES WATTS. Signed BENJAMIN BRIDGE, ELIZABETH (x) BRIDGE. Witn: JAMES HEATON, BENJAMIN BRIDGE JR. rec 1816. pp 545, 546, 547

Deed dated 1816. THOMAS R. SMILEY & POLLY his wife to ABSALOM GOODENOUGH. Hamilton lot 52. Signed THOMAS R. SMILEY, POLLY SMILEY. Witn: JAMES HEATON, MARY HEATON. rec 1816. pp 547, 548

Deed dated 1816. ABSALOM GOODENOUGH & SALLY his wife to ABRAM HEATH of St. Clear Twp. Hamilton lot 52. Signed ABSALOM GOODENOUGH, SALLY (x) GOODENOUGH. Witn: M. HUESTON, THOMAS HUESTON. rec 1816. pp 548, 549

Deed dated 1816. HENRY ROW & SARAH his wife to JOHN DENMAN. Brownstown lot 4. Signed HENRY (x) ROW, SARAH ROW. Witn: THOS. (x) BERRY, HENRY WEAVER. rec 1816. pp 549, 550

Deed dated 1816. JAMES POCOCK & ANN his wife to SARAH CURRYER, their daughter and widow of WILLIAM CURRYER. S 26, T 3, R 3. Signed JAMES POCOCK, ANN (x) POCOCK. Witn: GEORGE P. WILLIAMSON, P. WILLIAMSON. rec 1816. pp 550, 551

Mortgage dated 1816. SARAH CURRYER to JAMES POCOCK.

BUTLER COUNTY LAND RECORDS: BOOK E

Payment due 1818 for land in previous deed. Signed SARAH CURRYER. Witn as previous deed. rec 1816. pp 552, 553, 554

Deed dated 1816. DANIEL WILSON & ELIZABETH his wife of Montgomery Co to JAMES HARPER. S 19, T 5, R 2. Signed DANIEL WILSON, ELIZABETH (x) WILSON. Witn: JOHN RUSSELL, JAMES RUSSELL. rec 1816. pp 554, 555

Deed dated 1816. JOHN KERR & REBECA his wife to WILLIAM HALL. S 20, T 2, R 2. Signed JOHN KERR, REBECA KERR. Witn: JOS. GASTON, JOHN THORNBARY. rec 1816. pp 555, 556

Deed dated 1799. JAMES TALMADGE of Dutchess Co, NY to STEPHEN GANO of Rhode Island. S 17, T 3, R 2. Signed JAMES TALMADGE. Witn: ANN TALMADGE JR, JAMES TALMADGE JR. rec 1816. pp 555, 556

Deed dated 1816. ROBERT BROWN & RACHEL his wife to DANIEL McDONALD. Middletown lot 13. Signed ROBERT BROWN, RACHEL BROWN. Witn: EZEKIEL BALL, JOHN MILLS. rec 1816. pp 557, 558

Deed dated 1815. JOHN S. POTTER & SUSANNA his wife to DANIEL SYMMES of Cincinnati. S 15 & 16, T 2, R 2; bound by land of WILLIAM ENYART. Signed JOHN S. (x) POTTER, SUSANNA (x) POTTER. Witn: JOS. GASTON, MARTHA GASTON. rec 1816. pp 558, 559, 560

Deed dated 1816. JAMES HAMILTON of Adams Co, Mississippi Ter'y, by his atty JESSE HUNT to JACOB HARTZEL of PA. S 4, T 2, R 3. Signed JAMES HAMILTON by JESSE HUNT. Witn: SAMUEL CUNNINGHAM, JOHN MAHARD. rec 1816. pp 560, 561

Power of Attorney dated 1816. JAMES HAMILTON as above named JESSE HUNT of Cincinnati as atty to convey land above per sale made by JOHN HAMILTON. Proceeds to be divided equally with said JOHN. Signed JAMES HAMILTON. Witn: SAMUEL SHORTSON, JOHN MAHARD. rec 1816. p 561

Deed dated 1816. WILLIAM PADDOCK & SARAH his wife to PHILIP LANDIS. S 1, T 2, R 3. Signed WILLIAM PADDOCK, SARAH (x) PADDOCK. Witn: JAMES LEE, HENRY WEAVER. rec 1816. pp 562, 563

Deed dated 1815. JOHN MILLER & PHEBE his wife of Franklin Co, IN Ter'y to AARON AUSTEN. S 14, T 5, R 1. Signed JOHN MILLER, PHEBE (x) MILLER. Witn:

BUTLER COUNTY LAND RECORDS: BOOK E

JAMES BECK, JAMES CARLISLE. rec 1816. pp 563, 564

Deed dated 1816. GEORGE ISEMINGER & MARY his wife of Morgan Twp to JOSHUA V. ROBINSON of same, HUGH SMITH and CYRUS N. SMITH of Cincinnati. S 34, T 3, R 1. Signed GEORGE ISEMINGER, MARY (x) ISEMINGER. Witn: PETER SHOAFF, KING DEARMOND. rec 1816. pp 564, 565

Deed dated 1816. GEORGE ISEMINGER & MARY his wife as above to heirs of JOHN COWGILL, decd. S 34, T 3, R 1; bound by land of MICHAEL SHOOK, WALTER ARMSTRONG. Signed as above. Witn: J. V. ROBINSON, CHARLES MILLS. rec 1816. pp 565, 566, 567

Bond dated 1815. SAMUEL MORRISON to RICHARD BIRCH. Deed to S 1, T 2, R 3 in Fairfield Twp to be delivered by 1817. Signed S. MORISON, R. BIRCH. Witn: JAMES McBRIDE, JOSEPH HOUGH. rec 1816. pp 567, 568

Deed dated 1816. ABEL STOUT & THEODOCIA his wife to GEORGE KRAMER of Green Co, PA. Tract 1: S 20, T 5, R 2; bound by land of WILLIAM SUTTON. Tract 2: S 21, T 5, R 2. Signed ABEL STOUT, THEODOCIA STOUT. Witn: JOHN REILY, CHARLES K. SMITH. rec 1816. pp 569, 570

Deed dated 1816. ELI POTTER to WILLIAM McMANUS. S 7, T 4, R 2. Signed ELI POTTER. Witn: none. rec 1816. pp 570, 571

Deed dated 1816. JAMES DUNN & NANCY his wife to JAMES ELLIOTT. S 14, T 3, R 2. Signed JAS. DUNN NANCY DUNN. Witn: JOHN DUNN, GEORGE DUNN. rec 1816. pp 571, 572

Deed dated 1816. ABNER HOWARD & SALLY his wife of Cincinnati to NATHANIEL EDSON of same. S 22, T 3, R 3. Signed ABNER HOWARD, SALLY HOWARD. Witn: E. STONE, SAMUEL BETTS. rec 1816. pp 572, 573, 574

Mortgage dated 1816. NATHANIEL EDSON to FRANCIS WEST, ELISHA STANLEY & ROSSWELL H. GRANT, Merchants. S 22, T 3, R 3. Signed NATH'L. EDSON. Witn: D. WADE, E. STONE. rec 1816. pp 574, 575

Deed dated 1816. HENRY HOUSS & ANN his wife to JONAS SMALLEY. Brownstown 31 in Madison Twp. Signed HENRY HOUSS, ANN HOUSS. Witn: HENRY (x) ROW, HENRY WEAVER. rec 1816. pp 575, 576

Deed dated 1816. HENRY HOUSS & ANN his wife to JOHN BEERS. Brownstown 30. Signed and witn as above.

BUTLER COUNTY LAND RECORDS: BOOK E

rec 1816. pp 577, 578

Deed dated 1816. HENRY BALSER & SARAH his wife to JOHN H. BALSER. S 21, T 2, R 3. Signed HENRY (x) BALSER, SARAH (x) BALSER. Witn: PETER CUMMINGS, HENRY WEAVER. rec 1816. pp 578, 579

Deed dated 1816. ROBERT BROWN & RACHEL his wife to JOHN P. FINKLE. S 29, T 2, R 4; bound by land of DAVID WOOLVERTON, JAMES ROBERSON. Signed ROBERT BROWN, RACHEL BROWN. Witn: JOHN BEERS, EZEKIEL BALL. rec 1816. pp 579, 580

Deed dated 1814. Exctrs of MATTHEW MARKLAND, decd, to BRICE VIRGIN. Princetown lot 25. Signed SAMUEL ENYART, JOHN AYERS. Witn: PLATT BOYLES, THOMAS DONALDS. rec 1816. pp 580, 581

Deed dated 1816. JACOB FETTER to JONAS SMALLEY. Brownstown lot 32 in Madison Twp. Signed JACOB FETTER. Witn: ROBERT BROWN, WILLIAM VIRGIN. rec 1816. pp 581, 582

Deed dated 1816. HENRY HOUSS & ANN his wife to JACOB FETTER. Brownstown lot 32. Signed HENRY HOUSS, ANN HOUSS. Witn: HENRY (x) ROW, HENRY WEAVER. rec 1816. pp 582, 583

Deed dated 1816. BENJAMIN CLARK to JUSTUS CARELY. S 33, T 3, R 2; bound by land of STEPHEN CAMPBELL. Signed BENJN. CLARK. Witn: LUTHER TILLOTSON, KING DEARMOND. rec 1816. pp 583, 584, 585

Deed dated 1816. JOHN FREEMAN of Lemon Twp to heirs of ARCHIBALD CAMPBELL, decd: son & daus JACOB CAMPBELL, ELIZABETH DENMAN late CAMPBELL, CATHARINE & CHARLOTTE CAMPBELL. S 26, T 2, R 4; dower rights to MERCY CAMPBELL, widow of Archibald. Signed JOHN (x) FREEMAN. Witn: SAMUEL DAVIS JR, JOHN McCLURE JR. rec 1816. pp 585, 586

Deed dated 1815. JOHN BAKE of Wayne Twp to HENRY BAKE, his son. S 23, T 3, R 3. Signed JOHN BAKE. Witn: WILLIAM SMITH, SAMUEL ROBBINS. rec 1816. pp 586, 587

Deed dated 1816. JUSTUS CARELY & ELIZABETH his wife to BENJAMIN CLARK. S 33, T 3, R 2; bound by land of FRANCIS KELSHAMMER, once owned by STEPHEN CAMPBELL. Signed JUSTUS CARELY, ELIZABETH (x) CARELY. Witn: LUTHER TILLOTSON, KING DEARMOND. rec 1816. pp 587, 588

BUTLER COUNTY LAND RECORDS: BOOK E

Deed dated 1816. JAMES RUSK & SALLY his wife to JAMES SCHENCK of Warren Co. S 11, T 2, R 4. Signed JAMES RUSK, SALLY (x) RUSK. Witn: EZEKIEL BALL, DAVID SCHENCK. rec 1816. pp 587, 588

Deed dated 1816. WILLIAM WILSON & MARY his wife to JAMES GALBREATH. S 33, T 2, R 2; adj JACOB POWERS' land. Signed WILLIAM WILSON, MARY WILSON. Witn: JOS. GASTON, JACOB POWERS. rec 1816. pp 590, 591

Deed dated 1816. FREEMAN CONKLIN & SARAH his wife to BENJAMIN FULKERSON. S 7, T 2, R 3, subject to mortgage held by WILLIAM FRAZEE. Signed FREEMAN CONKLIN, SARAH CONKLIN. Witn: JAMES HEATON, ISAAC COOK. rec 1816. pp 590, 591

Deed dated 1814. USA to JOHN PRYER of Hamilton Co. S 31, T 3, R 1. rec 1816. p 592

Deed dated 1816. MOSES BREES & ANN his wife to JOHN TAYLOR. S 34, T 2, R 4; adj by DAVID ENYART's land. Signed MOSES BREES, ANN (x) BREES. Witn: DAVID ENYART, HENRY WEAVER. rec 1816. pp 592, 593, 594

Deed dated 1815. JAMES MILLS JR to JOHN SUTHERLAND. S 17, T2, R 3. Signed JAMES MILLS JR. Witn: JOHN REILY, JAMES HEATON. rec 1816. pp 594, 595

Deed dated 1816. SHOBAL VAIL & MARY his wife to JOHN TULLIS. S 19, T 2, R 4; adj by land of heirs of ROBERT CARRICK decd, ARCHIBALD CAMPBELL, JOHN CARSON. Signed SHOBAL VAIL, MARY VAIL. Witn: HENRY WEAVER, EZEKIEL BALL. rec 1816. pp 595, 596

Mortgage dated 1816. THOMAS MURDOCK to ADAM RODEBAUGH of Montgomery Co. S 4, T 1, R 2. Signed THOMAS MURDOCK. Witn: BEN M. PIATT, M. HUESTON. rec 1816. pp 596, 597

Deed dated 1815. SAMUEL DICK & MARTHA his wife of Ross Twp and ANDREW LEWIS & MARTHA his wife of Hanover to JOHN SQUIER. S 11, T 2, R 4; once owned by JOHN WATSON. Signed SAMUEL DICK, MARTHA DICK, ANDREW LEWIS, MARTHA LEWIS. Witn: DAVID DICK, JOHN DUNN. rec 1816. pp 599, 600

Mortgage dated 1816. JOHN EMRICK & MARY his wife to GEORGE EMRICK and ANDREW EMRICK of Montgomery Co. S 1, T 2, R 4; adj by JOHN MILLS' land. Signed JOHN EMRICK (german script), MARY (x) EMRICK. Witn: HENRY WEAVER, WILLIAM KERR. rec 1816. pp 600, 601, 602

BUTLER COUNTY LAND RECORDS: BOOK E

Deed dated 1816. JACOB LEWIS to JONATHAN WATKINS of Summerset Co, NJ. Hamilton lot 185. Signed JACOB LEWIS. Witn: JOHN C. AYERS, JOHN AYERS. rec 1816. pp 602, 603 (see next three deeds)

Deed dated 1816. JACOB LEWIS to JONATHAN WATKINS. Rossville outlot 5. Signed and witn as above. rec 1816. pp 603, 604

Deed dated 1816. JACOB LEWIS to JONATHAN WATKINS of Barneds Twp, Summerset Co, NJ. S 24, T 2, R 2 in Fairfield Twp. Signed and witn as above. rec 1816. pp 604, 605

Deed dated 1816. JACOB LEWIS to JONATHAN WATKINS. S 24, T 2, R 2. Signed and witn as above. rec 1816. pp 605, 606

Deed dated 1816. GEORGE W. STALL & BARBARA his wife to JAMES HEATON. Hamilton lot 195. Signed G. W. STALL, BARBARA STALL. Witn: DANIEL MILLIKIN, ALFRED CALDWELL, DAVID LATHAM. rec 1816. pp 606, 607

Deed dated 1815. HEZEKIAH BROADBERRY & AGNESS his wife to SIMEON BROADBERRY. S 34, T 5, R 2. Signed HEZEKIAH BROADBERRY, AGNESS BROADBERRY. Witn: JAMES HEATON, GEORGE SNIDER. rec 1816. pp 608, 609

Deed dated 1815. HEZEKIAH BROADBERRY & AGNESS his wife to JAMES BROADBERRY. S 34, T 5, R 2. Signed and witn as above. rec 1816. pp 609, 610

Mortgage dated 1816. WILKINS BUTLER to heirs of REBECCA GIBSON, decd: WILLIAM BEATY, DAVID, MARGARET, ELIZABETH & ESTHER GIBSON. One fourth part of S 33, T 2, R 2. Names reversed in deed text: WILLIAM BUTLER, WILKINS BEATY. Signed WM. BUTLER. Witn: CHARLES K. SMITH, SAMUEL DAVIS JR. rec 1816. pp 610, 611, 612

Mortgage dated 1816. WILLIAM BUTLER to heirs of REBECCA GIBSON: DAVID, MARGARET, ELIZABETH & ESTHER GIBSON. (no Beaty named). S 33, T 2, R 2. Signed and witn as above. rec 1816. pp 612, 613

Mortgage dated 1815. ELIHU LINE to WILLIAM HUNTER. S 14, T 2, R 3. Signed ELIHU LINE. Witn: JAMES HEATON, JACOB GARRIGUS. rec 1816. pp 614, 615

Deed dated 1815. ELI JOHNSTON & RACHEL his wife in

BUTLER COUNTY LAND RECORDS: BOOK E

his own right, JAMES MILLS & SARAH his wife, MAXWELL PARKINSON & MAHALA his wife as assignees of JAMES MAHAN to JAMES MAHAN. S 2, T 3, R 2. Signed ELI (x) JOHNSTON, RACHEL (x) JOHNSTON, JAMES MILLS, SARAH MILLS, MAXWELL PARKISON, MAHALA PARKISON. Witn: JAMES SMITH, J. C. McMANUS. rec 1816. pp 615, 616

Power of attorney dated 1816. JACOB HARTSEL of Upper (illeg) Twp, Lehigh Co, PA appted JACOB WILLIAM DECHANT of the same place as atty. Granted right to sell tract of land purchased from JOHN HAMILTON; no S-T-R. Signed JACOB HARTSEL. Witn: DANIEL COOPER, JOHN ROMIS. rec 1816. pp 616, 617

Deed dated 1816. JACOB HARTSEL of Lehigh Co, PA to HENRY KERN. S 4, T 2, R 3. Signed JACOB HARTSEL by atty J. WM. DECHANT. Witn: JOHN GOOD, HENRY WEAVER. rec 1816. pp 617, 618, 619

Deed dated 1807. JOHN WATSON & ISABELLA his wife to DAVID GARRIGUS. S 15, T 1, R 2. Signed JOHN WATSON, ISABELLA (x) WATSON. Witn: WM. WALLACE, WM. McCLELLAN. rec 1816. pp 619, 620

End of Book E

APPENDIX

SYMMES' MIAMI PURCHASE...

At the end of the Revolutionary War, Congress needed settlement on the border country of the Northwest Territory to safeguard the colonies against British infiltration and Indian disruption. Cheap land was the easiest inducement to accomplish this end. The Congressional Act of 1787 allowed John Cleves Symmes to purchase a tract lying between the two Miami Rivers, from the Ohio River north approximately to the present Butler-Montgomery counties border. Symmes shouldered the administrative burdens of surveying and organizing the tract and recording land sales. Israel Ludlow surveyed much of Symmes' purchase and was paid in prime land, now in Hamilton, the county seat.

The Purchase was surveyed into townships six miles square, each composed of 36 sections. Several sections were set aside: section 16 for the benefit of schools and section 29 for the use of the clergy. Symmes sold land for 2/3 of a dollar per acre plus a penny farthing per acre for surveying and recording fees. A section, 1 mile square or 640 acres, cost $426.69 with expenses of $8.89.

Settlement was assured by Forfeiture, a strategy which limited speculation by wealthy Easterners in the Ohio Territory. Residence and improvements had to be made within two years, either by the buyer or his representative. The settler was required to live on the land for a period of seven years with specific duties of road building and defense. If these provisions were not met, one-sixth of the land was forfeited by the buyer with title reverting to the land registrar. This opened the door to the Volunteer Settler.

The Volunteer Settler applied for the vacated property. By fulfilling the duties and terms of settlement, he received free land. The original purchaser was supposed to be compensated by a higher value for his remaining property, due to the efforts of the volunteer.

This proved to be a successful scheme to expand the scope of the new country and achieve Congress' goals. Within twenty years, the Indians had been decimated and the survivors driven west. Farmland was cleared and towns established. Ohio proudly joined the Union as the seventeenth state in 1803.

INDEX: names in text may have variant spelling

ABEL, Alexr 214 228
ABELVIE, Ann 33
ABERCROMBIE, Hugh 101 131
..215   218   Rachl   218
..Rosana 218
ABRAHAM, Lot 68 210
ADAMS, Geo 41 James 66 69
..Polly 69 Sarah 41 Thos
..226
ADAMSON, Sarah 161
AGDON, Francis 33 Jonthn
..10   22   Stephen 11
AGNEW, Brant 103
ALBRED, Thos 173
AL(D)RIDGE, Edmund 82 218
..245 Edw 128 Jane 182
..218 245
ALEXANDER, Davd 203 Wm 203
..Saml 62 130
ALGER, Caty 126 Skillman
..74 126
ALLEN, E. 127 Elizb 87
..Gabrl 75 87 Henry 147
..James 95 John 131 231
..Phebe 87 Rachl 87 Richd
..87 Saml 87   Thos 132
ALLENDORF Fredrk 130 215
..Nancy 215
ALSTON, Thos 43 102 190
..202
ANDERS, Danl 180
ANDERSON, Euphemia 113
..Isaac 113   John   187
..Mariah 149 Robt 113 134
..Thos 190   W.C. 124
ANDRE, Malcolm 131 187
ANDREW(S),   Abrhm   235
..Elizb 235   James 207
..John 28 97
ANTHONY, Fanny 75 217 J.
..229   Wm 68 75 133 217
ARGO, Mees 224 Moses 199
ARMSTON   (see   Urmston)
..Davd 6 22 40 41 52
ARMSTRONG, Archbd 105 175
..Isabella 161 James 35
..67 161 John 23 25 26
..36 161   206 244   Rebca
..175   Ruth   139   144
..Stephn 139 144 Walter
..103   247   Wm 139 141
..142 145 147 149 155

ARMSTRONG, Wm (cont)159
..165 181 183 233 244
ARNET, Seth 138
ARNOLD, Geo 236 237 Jacb
..172
ASBORN, Elias 45
ASHCRAFT, Elizb 220 Felix
..220
ASHTON, Cathr 204 Joseph
..204 Martha 204 Mary 204
..Sarah 204
ASTON, Joseph 137 Saml 86
..89 129
ATHERTON, Aaron 196
ATWELL, Chas 224 Susana
..224
AULD,Michl 19 Sarah 19
AUSTIN, Aaron 162 194
..246
AUTEN, James 236
AUTOR, Thos 131
AVERY, Anna 29 Chas 12 15
..29 34 206   Danl 29 85
AWL, Michl 9
AYERS, Abigl 109 111 183
..240 240 Alexr 157 159
..184 Amsey 216 Anna 69
..134   136   Benajah   222
..Davd 36 Elizb/Betsey 35
..172   208   Isaac   218
..Jackson 11 34 35 59 72
..97 184 208 James 62 65
..67 113 152 166 167 215
..John 23 41 66 85 86 88
..100 102 104 111 112 120
..123 124 126 128 133 134
..136 137 147 151 154 159
..171   178   186   188 192
..196 199 208 210 212 221
..232 239 248 250 Julia
..215 Michl 11 76 97 109
..118 122 131 133 140 166
..169 172 178 183 201 218
..238 240 240   Saml 36 69
..134 215 216 218 Sarah
..178   Thos 197

BADGLEY, Moses 50 51
BAILY, Henrietta 208 Jas.
..219 220 Nichlas 242 243
..Robt 12
BAIRD, Jane 129/130   149

253

INDEX: names in text may have variant spelling

BAIRD, (cont) John 233
..Joseph 129 149
BAKE, Cathr 234 Elnr 234
..Elizb 234 Hannah 234
..Henry 248 Jacob 234
..John 234 248 Mariah
..234
BAKER,Aaron 19 73 206 Ba.
..64 Caleb 88 Danl 83
..99 222 Davd 162 Hannah
..73 206 John 26 55 56
..98 Lydia 101 107
..Melyn 5 95 172 Prudnce
..172 Sarah 88 99
..Thos 101 107
BALDWIN, Edw 79 Elizb 75
..99 Jesse 43 John 19 25
..29 75 99 Joseph 94 98
..104 109 Mary 57 90 225
..Sarah 109 Thos 99 100
..106 107 146 Wm 57 79
..86 90 107 108 120
..224 225 239
BALL, Abel 44 Davis 116
..126 127 204 211 242
..Dennis 33 63 139 147
..154 155 Elizb 77 139
..Ezekl 15 33 40 52 163
..167 172 176 183 185
..192 203 208 209 227
..228 231 237 239 241
..242 246 248 249 Hannah
..40 44 Isaiah 18 63
..139 154 155 Isrl 4
..Mary 204 211 Margt 154
..155 Phebe 154 155 176
..209 Polly 127 Sarah
..204 239 Stephn 231
..Zophar 19 22 63 139
BALLARD, John 33
BALSER, Henry 196 248 John
.. 248 Sarah 248
BANE(S), Evan 11 35 37
..Lina 35
BANKER, Joseph 200 225
BANTA,(see Bonta) Albert
..69 157 165 198 Nancy
..157 198
BARBEE, Benj 197
BARBER, Caty 218 Henry
..218
BARKALOW, Cathr 222 Danl

BARKALOW, Danl (cont) 127
..221 222 Derrk 211 Elizb
..127 181 221 Harmon 114
..148 James 120 Jane 221
..Mary 76 83 91 115 120
..Nichls 221 222 Tobias
..127 181 221 Wm 47 76 78
..83 91 115 120 Zebuln 50
..83 115
BARNARD, George 244
BARNET, Jacb 157 James 11
..46 163
BARRET, John 148
BARROW, Joseph 29
BARTON, John 71 89 99
..Martha 48
BATES, Seth 39 Usual 42
BAUM, Ann 63 223 Martin 63
..110 223 Jacb 94 97 100
..102
BAXTER,John 54 68 69 171
BAYLES, Saml 89
BAYLEY, Lewis 64 79
BAYMILLER, Jacb 168 179
BEACH, Moses 8 22 27 62
..Sarah 181 Solmn 102 181
..Uzal 8 120 Wm 34
BEALE, Jonthn 182
BEATS, Uzal 26
BEATY, Davd 17 19 25 31 39
..43 45 55 63 68 115 124
..185 189 196 212 230 243
..J.R. 99 James 5 199 240
..241 243 Jeremh 123
..John 5 17 19 28 36 42 121
..123 189 Margt 243
..Ninian 200 243 Wilkins
..250 Wm 250
BEAUCHAMP, Isaac 74
BECK, James 76 77 81 83 85
..112 114 153 164 247
BECKET, James 184 John 78
..85 178 215 Mary 178
BECKHAM, Geo 139
BEEB, Edw 68 210 232 Mary
..210 232
BEELER, Amelia 187 James
..93 112 116 195 243 244
..Margt 92 Mary 93 95 96
..Saml 30 92 93 95 96 187
..195 229
BEERS, John 247 248

INDEX: names in text may have variant spelling

BELCH, Wm 123
BELL, Jacb 11 116 126 189
..Mary 57 149 Nathl 57 88
..149   233   Sarah 189 Wm
..179
BELT, John 192
BENEFEIL, John 71
BENHAM, James 132 Jos. 201
..208 222 242 Richd 37
..Robt 111
BENJAMIN, Emily 231
BENNETT, Geo 203 Jacb 134
..195   James 40
BERRY, Thos 11 245
BERT, John 22
BETTS, Saml 247   Wm 34
BIGELOW, Aaron 154
BIGGS, Aaron 198
BIGHAM, Danl 176 Geo 176
..177   Wm 5 124 127 139
..147 197 199
BIRCH, R/Richd 132 143
..150 153 177 191 219 227
..247
BIRES, Phlp 30
BISHOP, Benj 9 Elizb 223
..Frazee 43 44 223 226
BLACK, Joseph 34
BLACKBURN, Bryson 63   210
..Davd 139 140 149 Esther
..210 Hamilton 210   James
..60 66 67 124 154 179 210
..Mary 210   Saml 207
BLACKFORD, Reuben 187
BLACKMAN, Truman 132
BLAIR, A. 134 Margt/Peggy
..72 90 93 94 116 134 142
..150 187 216 217 218 Thos
..69 71 72 76 84 90 93 94
..97 102 108 109 112 116
..119 134 142 143 144 150
..172 175 187 188 216 217
..218 229
BLOOMFIELD, Joseph 29 111
..226 230
BLUE, Fredk 43 44 130 John
..35 74 78 116 204 Mary
..204
BOLLEN, Henry 126
BOLTON, Joseph 30 92 244
BOMBERGER, Wm 74 75 76 77
..82 84 95 101 110 114 125

BOMBERGER,Wm 129 153 183
BONE, John 182 Mary 182
BONNEL, Elizb 58 Lewis 58
..Mary 232 Moses 153 208
..231 232   Paul 214 Saml
..58
BONTA, Albert 137   Nancy
..137
BORTH, Christn 162
BOUDINOT, Elias 13 17 33
..34 79 80 108 111 130 132
..142 167 181 200 207 211
..221 241
BOUM (see Bourn) Benj 164
..Saml 164
BOURN (see Boum) Benj 158
..Saml 158
BOWLING, Henry 169
BOWMAN, Aaron 61 Charltt
..151 172 Richd 172 Saml
..122 151 172
BOYD, Anna 23 Danl 23 John
..197
BOYER, Geo 199 237
BOYLES, E. 142 155 223
..Platt 248   Saml 218
BRADBERRY, Davd 194
BRADFORD, Belinda 41 John
..144
BRADY, James 27   John 27
BRANNON, Andw 199
BRANT, Davd 39 45 55 68
..243
BRASHER, John 16 17 39
BRECKENRIDGE, Robt 81
BRECOUNT, John 75
BREES, Anna 178 249 Azria
..88 91 Hannah 88 91 John
..53 88 91 162 Moses 172
..178   193 237 245 249
..Susana 88 91
BRELSFORD, Benj 129 John
..129 130 Pierson 130
BRIDEFORD, Wm 231
BRIDGE, Benj 126 163 227
.. 245 Elizb 245
BRIGGS, Wm 33
BROADBERRY, Agnes 55 250
..Henry 196 Hzkiah 55 130
..132 190   203 250 James
..130 250 Simeon 131 163
..241 250

INDEX: names in text may have variant spelling

BROADWELL, Davd 10 13
..Simeon 11 97 134 Wm 10
..34
BRODERICK, Wm 80 98 100
..103 186 Robt 137
BROKAW, Danl 195
..Ferdinand 26 30 144
..Patton 166 Tiney 26
BROOKS, Joseph 135 238
BROUSIS, Danl 57 60 209
..Elizb 209 Margt 209
..Sarah 209
BROWN(E) Abigl 11 Andw
..129 150 Ann 131
..Cathr/Kitty 126 155 187
..Charltt 18 Ethan 59
..64 219 Henry 6 24 30
..43 51 53 68 70 74 75
..76 77 79 81 82 83 84
..92 95 101 105 110 112
..113 114 125 126 129
..153 155 157 164 169
..174 183 187 Ignatius 11
..James 223 Jane 29 John
..7 11 18 34 59 66 74
..75 90 110 131 227 228
..232 Joseph 167 199
..Margt 7 Mary 11 179
..Rachl 110 204 208 235
..246 248 Robt 77 161
..174 175 189 208 217
..235 241 246 248
..Richd 86 Saml 86 131
..161 167 172 179 199 203
..223 244 Stephn 64 70
..Thos 29 Wm 55 165 181
BROWNSON, Josiah 88
BRUCE, Chas 4 41 42 50
..137 139 217
BRUN/BRUYN, Chas 31 James
..130
BRUSH, Adelaide Elijah
..105 141 163
BRUTH, A. 83
BRYAN, James 93 Wm 242
BRYSON, John 221
BUCHANAN, Armstong 110
..John 6 7 16 24 38 Joseph
..221 Rebcca 6 38
BUCKHANNON, Wm 215
BUCKLES, Mary 182 Wm 182
BUFFINGTON, Jonah 29

BURCH, Henry 135 Mary
..135
BUR(D)GE, Anthny 233 243
..244 Joseph 62
BURGET, Cathr 240 Emanl
..240
BURGIN, John 125
BURK(E), Alexis 176 Elizb
..150 176 Hannah 119 173
..John 139 146 158 176
..182 189 208 217 226
..244 Rebcca 208 Thos
..150 186 208
BURKET, Geo 211
BURNET, Davd 37 62 68
..Isaac 80 179 Jack 6 Jacb
..20 29 63 78 80 82 85 96
..104 111 116 119 124 130
..132 141 142 157 162 167
..177 178 181 207 211 221
..231 241 Joe 27 Phebe 68
..Rebca 63 78 85 116 119
..124 178 231 Wm 33
BURNS, Anthony 71 Archbld
..108 Guilford 64 John
..61
BURR, Wm 103
BURT, Andrw 206 235
BURTON, Davd 187 Wm 187
BUSENBARK, John 106 Robt
..106
BUTLER, Draden 231 Joshua
..197 218 224 231
..Mahitable 212 Wilkins
..250 Wm 82 212 250
BUTTERFIELD, Jermah 12 30
..49 244 Polly 30 244
BUXTEST, James 232
BUXTON, Brook 83
BUYERS, Geo 31 Nancy 31
BYRES, Geo 30 60

CADWELL, Aaron 46
CAIN, John 22 Richd 22
..93
CALDWELL, Abrhm 118 209
..Alfred 250 Ann 118 209
..Danl 83 118 209 Elizb
..117 118 169 200 214 229
..James 117 118 214
..John 85 137 141 178 187
..200 218 229 Mary 118

256

INDEX: names in text may have variant spelling

CALDWELL, Robt 118 206
..Saml 169 Thos 117
CAMP, James 202
CAMPBELL, see Kempbell.
..Archbld 211 221 233 248
..249 Cathr 248 Charltt
..248 Elias 17 108 Elizb
..248 Enos 131 Jacb 197
..248 John 33 40 65 108
..158 238 Mercy 248 Moses
..222 Nancy 33 Rachl 102
..156   Robt 102 Richd 156
..Saml 165 198 Stephn 40
..47 160 178 248 Tms 58
CANFIELD, Abm. 34 Elizb
..176 228
CANTERFIELD, Abm 34
CAR, see KERR
CARELY, Elizb 248 Justus
..248
CARLE, Rachl 232 Thos 201
..227
CARLISLE, Harriet 156 196
..James 135 136 196   247
..Zachrh 158
CARMICHAEL, Dr. 235
CARNEY, Davd 134
CARNS, Alexr 194
CARPENTER, Geo 41 J. 77
..Joseph 60
CARRICK, Robt 125 156 167
..221 249   Ruth 125 167
CARSON, Alexr 211 John 25
..46 190 206 211 216 221
..249 Leah 211 Mary 46
..Robt 58 223
CARTER, Cathr 41 64 71
..Mordich 191 Reuben 41 71
..134   Robt 151   Wm 194
CARY, Abel 48 55 Eunice
..55
CASE, Dorcas 109 113
..Joseph 109 113 Lewis
..139
CASSIDY, Abby 234 Alexr
..234 Caty 234 Eliza 234
..Ezra 234 John 57 60 88
..143 159 190 234 Patrk 57
..234 238   Phebe   234
..Sarah/Sally 85 190 229
..238
CATROW, Cathr 83 Chas 83

CATROW, (cont) Chrsta 79
..Joseph 32 33 Peter 79
..Polly 32 33
CATTERLIN, Ephrm 26 43
..116 205   Sally 43
CAVENAUGH, Ann 75 107 152
..205 226 228 232 L/Lawr
..30 49 67 68 75 78 106 107
..116 118 120 145 146 152
..205 226 228 232
CHADBOURN, Ivory 107
CHAMBERLAIN, John 32 51 91
..127 169 Mary 32 51 Nancy
..91
CHAMBERS, Alexr 65 90 Mary
..65 90 Saml 90
CHANDLER, Rachl 160 Sarah
..160 Swithin 159 160
CHAPMAN, John 53 Rachel
..53
CHARLES, Nehemiah 46
CHARLTON, James 128
CHASE, Abrhm 99 146 222
..Elizb 99 129 Isaac 222
..Valntne 99 129
CHENOWETH, Anw 36
CHESTERTON, Charity 144
..202   Geo 144 202
CHETWOOD, John 33
CHEW, Andw 11 132
CHRISTY, Andr 6 8 15 21 22
..36 37 64 101 134 Elizb 6
..15 21 37 101 134 Saml
..191
CHURCHILL, Lemuel 88 91
..Patience 88 91
CILLY, Benj 91 244 Dorcas
..48   Jonthn 43 48 91
..Joseph 44 190 Thos 168
CLAP, Charltt 92 John 7 45
..92 124 224
CLARK, Abigl 104 Abrhm 188
..Aletha 134   135   199
..Betsey   194 Chas 104
..Danl 94 96 Eliza 215
..Eunice 96 F. 232 Jacb
..120 162 James 10 34 55
..61 72 97 99 104 119 122
..134 135 136 150 163 167
..168 171 182 189 190 194
..195 196 199 204 206 208
..213 215 218 <u>219</u> <u>225</u> 229

INDEX: names in text may have variant spelling

CLARK, James (cont) 233
..235 236 Janey 194 John 8
..97 175 180 201 Jonthn
..127 156 Martha 179 Robt
..109 215 Saml 60 102 179
..194 235 Sarah/Sally 162
..175 Stephns 19 60 193
..194 237 Tabitha 240
..Tompson 7 35 Wm 37 103
..171 204 214 229 235
CLARKSON, Davd 188 239
..James 124 Runey 195
CLAWSON, Andw 42 117 Runa
..239
CLEM, Henry 200 John 143
..Susanh 143
CLIZBE, Ira 113 114 Joseph
..113
COCHRAN, Henry 22 Thos
..66
COEN, Chas 226 Edw 54 57 61
..140 167 180 199 203
..Hugh 140 James 57 61 140
..Jane 61 Margt 57 61 140
..199 Nancy 167 Thos 140
..167 180
COGY, James 145
COHOON, Thos 27 110 111
COL(E)BY, Isaac 208
..Joseph 78 207 208
..Margery 208 Z. 226
..Zebl 241 Zerobabel 196
COLLARD, Timthy 208
COLLETT, Joshua 123
COLLINS, Henry 81 Joel 92
..96 125 141 150
COLLVER, Daniel 90 135
COLWELL, Abram 92 98 139
..174 214 Abrhm 112 118
..James 58 John 29
COMBER, Rebca 222
COMSTOCK, Eunice 28 68
..James 92 133 244 Joab 28
..40 45 61 68 75 125 133
..178 226 243 Ruth 28
..Thankful 68
CONDIT, Elizb 202 Silas
..151 202
CONE, Chas 28 40 45 47 50
..243 Grace 45 50 Jane 28
..40 45 50 Rufus 50
CONGER, David 20 25 138

CONILL, Abrhm 175
CONKLIN(G), Davd 200 208
..Else 74 Henry 206
..Freeman 234 249 J 188
..Jacb 158 162 234 Josiah
..65 74 Mr 64 Sarah 249
CONN, Jos. 20 21 24 25 27
..28 37 99 121
CONNER, Danl 7 12 29 Davd
..69 180 207 Mary 215
..Moses 215 Nancy 207
..Susan 12
CONNERY, Jonthn 201 221
CONOROE, Isaac 142 233
..John 142
CONWAY, John 29
COOCH, Eliza 137 143 Hanna
..96 137 141 143 231 Thos
..45 96 127 137 141 143
..231
COOD, G. 48
COOK, Conrad 194 Eli 238
..Isaac 249 Jonthn 238
..Martha 238 T. 231
COOLEY, Nancy 54 131 179
..241 Wm 22 54 131 179
..249
COON, Isaac 36 Israel 36
..John 95 Sarah 36
COOPER, Danl 6 17 251
..Jonthn 158 164 Lenrd 213
..Wm 158
COOPSTICK, Thos 181
CORBLY, Stephn 128
CORNELIUSON, Andw 169 209
..Mash 169
CORNELL, Rebca 172 Wm
..173
CORNTHWAITE, Edw 119 165
..181
CORRY, Elnr 120 145 Wm 14
..18 19 20 22 24 25 26 27
..30 31 32 38 39 41 45 50
..63 75 77 101 120 145 157
..168 173 200 204
CORTMEL, --152
CORWIN, Davd 217 Matths 9
..204
COSC, John 91
COUNCELL, Saml 76
COWGILL, John 247
COX, Ann 11 79 Davd 11 236

INDEX: names in text may have variant spelling

COX, Davd (cont) 237 John
..11 76 111 125 237 Joseph
..56 Joshua 237 Nancy 11
..Richd 29 Rub. 37 Wm
..229
CRAIG, Hugh 18 John 233
..Robt 108
CRANDLE, Elihu 194
CRANE/CRAIN, D. 225 Davd
..149 184 195 234 Elias 33
..45 54 Elizb 149 195 Geo
..159 Jeremh 234 Jonthn 57
..Joseph 5 Mary/Polly 84
..150 197 202 Moses 41 45
..Phebe 45 54 202 Richd
..149   151 203 Robt 159
..181 Stephn 45 59 84 92
..114 117 150 168 173 197
..202 238
CRAVEN, James 20
CRAWFORD, John 97 Martha
..214 Wm 214
CRISSEY, Wm 71 82
CRIST, John 120
CROCKET, James 185
CROOKS, Amey 108 Anny 189
..James 18 129 Saml 129 Wm
..106   107 108 120 189
..230
CRUME, Danl 74 97 Isaac
..114   John 195 226 238
..Moses 10 96 102 148 161
..164   223 Sarah 161 164
CRUSE, Henry 62 159 Sarah
..159
CULBERTSON, Saml 24 121
CULLORN, Wm 41
CULLUM, Allen 11 26 34 72
..80 171 201   Edw 65 Geo 38
..42 62 65 Margt 65 Polly
..34 72 Wm 42
CULVER, Danl 148
CUMMIN(G)S, David 6 46 63
..93 J.N. 19 James 62 72 75
..137 152 170 178 196 199
..209 239 John 22 26 37 64
..96   160 167 170 180 238
..Julia 62 Peter 248 Sarah
..62 72
CUNNINGHAM, Rd 86 Saml 246
..Wm 156
CURD, Davd 131

CURRY, Wm 143
CURRYER, Wm 159 161 245
..Sarah 245 246
CURTIS, Nicholas 83 145
CUSTLETON, Jonthn 130
CUTLER, Enos 22

--- D ---

DAILY, Wm 109
DALAROCK, see Delaroch
DALRYMPLE, James 103 111
..166
DALTON, Susan 29
DANFORD, Benj 93
DANNIST, John 189
DARBY, Ezra 98
DARCOS, Saml 139
DAREIS, Saml 167
DAREY, Owen 129
DARKIES, Saml 46 47 49
..92 112
DARNELL, I. 46
DARR, Cathr 208 242
..Conrad 107 163 166 208
..242
DAVID, Wm 59 94 151
DAVIS, Agness 47 130 162
..Amos 116 138 Anna 239
..Benj 7 13 15 21 49 61
..84 87 99 102 141 171
..179 214   Danl 229 230
..Davd 117 121 204 Elizb
..229   James 229 Jane
..198 214 Jemima 44 John
..47 65 87 131 133 162
..170 180 197 198 214 229
..230 Jonthn 44 Joshua 43
..44 54 55 56 72 Lewis 223
..Lucy 7 20 Margt 230
..Mariah 219 Martha 10 195
..Nancy 7 8 13 14 125 133
..Neriah 131 Nichls 131
..153 192 208 219 223
..226 Richd 205 240 S.
..94 Saml 71 105 118 148
..162 167 188 195 206 216
..223 224 229 230 238 240
..248   250   Sarah   214
..Susan/a 71 195 230 Thos
..34 Vincnt 44 239
DAVS, Nicholas 49

INDEX: names in text may have variant spelling

DAY, Elizb 88 91 Ezkl 88
..91 Lot 88 91 Mary 88
..Phebe 88 91 Sarah/Sally
..88 91 202 Sephronia 88
..91 Stephen 147 202
DAYTON, Aaron 38 Elias 33
..37 43 86 98 106 126 180
..Jonthn 4 7 10 18 30 33
..34 37 38 43 44 83 98 105
..106 126 141 152 180 225
..Susan 33 98 152
DEARDORF, Ann 222 Jacb 149
..222
DEARMOND, Hannah 90 236
..King 90 140 184 236247
..248   Rebca 230
DEARSOT, Simon 26
DEATH, John 47
DEBOLT, John 93 Rachl 93
DECAMP, Davd 244 Job 175
..Mary 175   Wm 224
DECHANT, Jacb 213 251 Wm
..223
DECKER, Benj 41 201 221
DEEM, Adam 77 86 220 Gency
..86 Jane 220
DEEN, Eliza 175
DEL(A)PLANE,   James   26
..Jane 39 Joseph 12 18 39
..51   Joshua 17 26 47
DELAROCH, Alexr 179 180
..Michl 82 110 112 134 179
..202
DEMORET, Nichls 227 228
..Saml 227 228
DeMOSS, Peter 14
DEMOTT, Abrm 77   79   86
..Hannah 77 79 86
DEMPSTER,Hugh 16 Lety 16
DENMAN, Elizb 116 138 152
..248 Isaac 241 John 241
..242 245   Mary 148 201
..Moses 116 138 148 152
..201 220   Wm 116 201
DENNISTON, Wm 116
DENNY, James 201
DEVER, Eliza 231
DEWITT, Zachr 231
DEYBREAD, Geo 63 77 Joseph
..63 68   Susana 63 77
DICK, Davd 230 249 G.84
..115 John 234 Martha 172

DICK, Martha (cOnt) 184
..199 232 249   Saml 24 30
..50 115 153 159 172 184
..199 207 210 232 249
DICKEY, Adam 27 62   164
..177 232 236 241 Cathr 49
..John 46 48   Saml 27 49
..220   225
DICKSON, Platt   151   156
..163
DILL, Eliza 8
DILLON, Polly 119 Thos 38
..96 119   Saml 51 56 159
..200 201 Wm 47 71 87 91
..97 112 142
DILLY, Solmn 128
DINE, John 146 151
DIXON, Christr 9 James 236
..John 5 235   Mark 238
DOMIAH, Mr 50
DONALD(S), Elizb 172 199
..James 199 Thos 172   186
..199 248
DORSEY, J.214 228 241
DOTY, Betsy 185 191 194
..237 242 Bina 63 Cornls
..53 Danl 19 60 185 187
..191 194 204 215 237 238
..242 Janey 194 John 19 60
..194 215 Reuben 61 Sarah
..194 Wm 215 Zina 19 194
..215
DOUGHERTY, Cath 54 Jno
..54
DOUGHTY, John 34 161 M.
..142 155 223
DOUGLAS, Jane 135 John 105
..Robt 135 Wm 163 233
DOWING, John 99
DOWTY, Reuben 5
DRAKE, Elizb 101 102 Hugh
..241   James   151 204
..John 98 Moses 101 102
..107 133
DRESKELL, Besey 166
DROLLINGER, Hannah   73
..Philp 14 22 38 63 73 122
DRUMMOND, Geo 19 25 29 39
..44 45 Rosanna 39 44 45
DUBOIS, Benj 47 115 168
..169   Danl 47 53 169
DUCHMAN, Jacb 184

INDEX: names in text may have variant spelling

DUFF, Alex 15   Davd 79 84
..Wm 15
DUFFIELD, Davd 71 90 105
..118 143 Rebca 90 105
..143
DUFFLES, D. 94
DUGAN, Danl 16 Thos 235
DUNGAN, Joseph 127
DUNLAP, John 219 220
DUNLAVY, Francis 4 36
DUNN, Geo 247 Isaac 91
..James 10 12 19 38 42 65
..66 67 70 99 100 106 107
..120 146 149 180 239 247
..John 10 42 108 134 146
..151 188 189 217 239 244
..247 249 Lydia 42 Nancy
..99 100 106 107 120 146
..247   Robt 42
DUNWOODY, Robt 74
DURRAS, John 199
DUVALL, Elnr 69 Jeremh 55
..Polly 24 26   Nelly 55
DYER, Edw 125 171 Jane
..171
EAGLESFIELD, Phebe 149
..209 Theophls 147 149 209
EARHART, Geo 123 161 164
..Martin 154   Mary   161
..Michl 123 161 164
EARLY, Wm 138
EASTON, Elizb 19 Moses 19
..Saml 240
EDGAR, Davd 42 Mary 42
EDSON, Nathl 247
EDWARDS, Davd 88 89 91
..John   88   Joseph   103
..Lering 88 Mary 111 228
..Rachl 88   Uzal 54 111
..202 228
ELDER, Ely 145
ELLIOT, Arthur 25 50 51
..145 196 204 Elizb 157
..James 42 100 107 146 156
..239 247 John 106 107 146
..239 Joshua 83 95 123 145
..157 Margt 156   Micajah
..128 Polly 145 Robt 171
..Wm 83 86   100 128 171
..186
ELY, Cathr 42 51 71   73
120 122 Joseph 42 51 71 73

ELY, Joseph (cont) 120 122
EMMERSON, Edw 101 James
..101 158 164
EMRICK, Andrw 249 Geo 249
..Jacb 140 John 150 154
..249 Mary 150 249
ENOCH, Abner 174 176 203
..231 235 236 238 Davd 11
..24 77 130 Elizb 174 176
..203   Isaac 24 James 11
..Nancy 130
ENOS, Elihee 22
ENYART, Anna 14 22 75 137
..158 162 164 186 194 210
..Benj 6 9 18 24 33 40 41
..52 53 82 83 85 102 179
..194 239 Davd 6 52 53 82
..85 102 188 204 211 233
..239 245 249 Elizb   37
..Joanna 9 24 41 John 81 98
..238 Jonah 22 37 68 69
..Lewis 168 194 Mary 82 83
..85   102 239 Nancy 238
..Rufus 40 41 52 158 161
..Saml 14 15 21 22 35 40 52
..53   75   89 123 130 137
..147 158 171 186 189 194
..201 210 248 Sarah 158
..162 164 245 Susana 239
..Wm 81 98 114 151 238
..246
ERNST, Matt 15
ERWIN, see Irwin
ESPY, Elizb 60 Thos 60
ESTE, Chas 134 135 David
..87 105 110 112 117 132
..135 139 144 146 147 163
..168   173 176 177 182
..Louisa 112
EVANS, Esther 142 190 233
..Joseph 71   77 142 143
..190 233 Moses 190 Wm 91
..183
EVERINGER, Nath'l 51
EVERINGHAM, Enoch 81
EWING, James 11 20 21 24 27
..28 33 37. 38 39 48 51 64
..78 85 121 240 Margt 66
..212 219 Robt 216 Saml
..66 212 Thos 240
FAIRE, Joseph 213
FALCONER, see Faulkner

INDEX: names in text may have variant spelling

FARES, see Ferres
FARMER, Fielding 234
FAULKNER, Isaac 180
FEATHERLAND, Fredrk 179
FETTER, Jacb 248
FERGUSON, - 152 Alijah 89
..Athel 78 Elizb 73 78
..James 72 89 153 Jane 89
..153 Saml 73 74 78
..Thos 73
FERRES, Robt 108 136 183
FIELDS, Foster 154 John
..230 Lovis 154 Saml 154
..234 235 Sarah 154
FINCH,James 88 Zopher 88
FINDAL, Wm 40
FINDLAY, James 20 21 27 28
..31 35 37 39 40 45 46 48
..51 95 113 121 127 155
..160 163 177 191 205 235
..Jane 95 113 119 141 142
..145 191 John 24 80
..N.C. 31 35 39 40 45 51 80
..127
FINKLE, Cathr 215 222 223
..232 235 243 John 168
..195 203 213 215 216 218
..221 222 223 224 232 233
..234 235 236 241 243
..248
FINNEY, Elizb 36 James 83
..89 John 36 Sarah 89
FISH, Martha 225 Thos
..225
FISHER, Frdrk 8 15 16 17
..47 James 16 John 16
FISLER, Elizb 170 John
..170
FITHIAN, Geo 61
FITZ FREEMAN, Abraham 59
..Ezra 63 98 108 154
..Henry 59 John 59 60
..213 238
FITZRANDOLPH (also see
..Randolph) Benj 7 14 21
..Esther 14 Joseph 14 18
..Rebca 35 175 Saml 7
..Sarah 7 14
FLEENOR, Danl 93 96 97 100
..102 128 142 195 Davd
..94 96 97 100 102 231
..Elizb 93 Geo 93 96 97

FLEENOR, Geo (cont) 100
..102 128 142 Margt 100
..Mary 94 96 99 100 102
..Susna 96 97 231 Rudolph
..93 97 100 102
FLEMING, - 33 Alexr 9
..Bartho. 64 Elnr 117
..Elizb 147 149 164 Peter
..228 Robt 72 75 88 98
..117 130 138 146 147 168
..186 Thos 35 78 98
FLOO, Thos 155 160
FLOREN/FLORER, Wm 64, 70
FLOWERS, James 184
FOLKERTH, John 126 148
..206 215 216
FONDLER, Joshua 220
FORD, Mahlon 4 22 23 26
..35 36 38 54 Sophia 54
FORNEY, Moses 103
FORSETH, Wm 24
FOSET, Thos 240
FOSTER, Danl 154 Dorcas
..154 Freeborn 154 James
..154 John 154 Lovia 154
..Luke 5 48 Phebe 48
..Rachl 154 Stephn 154
..Thos 154 Zebulon 38
FOUTS, Joseph 39
FOWLER, Alexr 73 James 39
..Robt 48
FOX, Davd 242 Thos 159
FRANCIS, Davd 54 129 140
..180 200 John 47 76
..Wm 47 76
FRAREY, Saml 184 189
FRAZEE, Mary 234 Wm 234
..249
FRAZER, Davd 173 Sarah 173
..Wm 53 151
FRAZY, Saml 145 157
FREEL, Benony 64 Chas 64
..Esther 64 James 64
FREEMAN, Abigl 57 190
..Abrhm 17 27 59 60 66
..67 106 110 124 159 165
..190 197 227 238 Caty 165
..238 Clarkson 17 59 60
..61 99 108 110 114 163 173
..182 184 197 Eliza 126
..Elizb/Betsy 33 197 224
..231 Emma 227 Ezra 10

262

INDEX: names in text may have variant spelling

FREEMAN, Ezra (cont) 11
..57 60 66 67 85 88 98
..108 124 154 175 Harriet
..213 Henry 59 61 Isaac
..17 59 110 190 220 234
..John 70 123 124 126 136
..138 190 197 208 213 218
..224 231 248 Jude 154
..Luther 231 240 Richd
..231 Thos 204 218 Wm 61
..90 York 85 154 165
FREEN, Joseph 195
FRELAND, Peter 182
FRENCH, Jemima 214 Jeremh
..233 243 Nathl 214 233
..243
FRIERSON, Wm 139
FRUIT, Geo 12 24 25
FRYE, Nathl 23
FUDGE, Davd 92
FULKERSON, Benj 188 210
..249
FULLER, Jeremh 113
FULLERTON, Isabelah 143
GABLE, Danl 14
GAINS, Richd 192
GALBREATH, James 241 John
..222 Joseph 216 241
..Mary 241
GANO, John 22 33 219 Mary
..33 Stephn 172 <u>246</u>
GARD, Aaron 206 Ginne 206
..John 138 Mary 199 224
..Rachl 86 146 218 Seth
..199 224 Stephen 86 146
..217 218
GARDNER, Cathr 240 Henry
..240
GAREL, Stephen 99
GARRET, Elizb 197 John 197
..232 Robt 232 242 Wm
..186 197 232
GARRIGUS, Abigl 53 59 61
..86 94 96 102 151 Davd 34
..35 52 53 59 61 70 72
..86 94 96 102 151 156
..181 251 Jacob 86 250
..Jeptha 102 Mary 86
..Timthy 225
GARRISON, Aaron 94 Abrhm
..4 5 32. 40 43 45 Anne
..148 Davd 34 John 94 96

GARRISON, John (cont) 118
..223 Mary 4 5 Rachel 5
..32 43 45 Saml 94 Silas
..94 118 148 167 223
..Susanh 94 96 118 223
GARVER, Saml 131
GASTON, James 179 John 13
..14 16 124 202 219 220
..Joseph 90 114 179 181
..185 194 208 212 227 246
..249 Martha 114 185 194
..246 Mary 14 16
GATES, James 79
GEBHART, John 103
GEE, Benj 152 Edw 57 58
..Job 58
GIBSON, Agness 47 David 47
..162 244 250 Elizb 250
..Esther 250 Isaac 188
..250 James 160 John 211
..Margrt 250 Rebca 250
..Theo 11 48 Tho 11
GILDERSLEEVE, Asa 88 91
..Isaac 16 89 John 16 88
..89 91 Silas 88 91
GILKIE, Robt 69
GILL, Jane 85 183 Stephen
..72 85
GILLESPIE, Geo 108 John
..157 Neil 109 Thos 58
GLASSCOCK, Hezkh 111
GLINES, John 129
GLOVER, Cyrus 235 Elias
..59
GLOVINGER, Philp 184
GOBLE, Abner 154 168
..Benony 98 103 154 167
..Danl 29 56 70 122 235
..Jacob 109 113 Jonthn 109
..Sarah 154
GOFORTH, Aaron 25 174
GOLDSMITH, Mary 59
..Zacheus 59 92
GOLDTRAP, John 28
GOOD, John 251 Peter 184
GOODENOUGH, Abslm 156 159
..173 176 192 195 208 223
..225 234 245 Isaiah 192
..Sarah/Sally 173 192 208
..225 234 245
GOODWIN, H. 173 Thos 11
GORDON, Elnr 132 John 6 7

INDEX: names in text may have variant spelling

GORDON, John (cont) 24 87
..Lewis 104 132 Nancy 100
..Philp 8 69 100 105 125
..233 Ross 229
GORE, Levi 46 49 Rebcca
..49
GOUDY, Wm 150 171
GOULEY, Wm 19
GRAFT, Abrhm 107 209
GRAHAM, Aaron 65 Joseph 41
..Patrk 42 Sarah 42 65
GRANT, John 36 Rosswell
..247 Wm 52
GRAY, John 213 Joseph 163
..Mary 151 Robt 92 Saml
..115 126 151 165 242
..Sarah 242 Thos 11 17
..Wm 48 120 192
GREEN(E), Henry 109 Jesse
194 Joseph 109 Peter 195
213 214 Polly 214 Timothy
24 54 82
GREENLEE, Wm 150 177 242
GREER, Arabel 131 Elnr 155
..156 166 168 170 187 208
..222 Isabella 168 James
..164 229 John 5 7 10 13
..14 28 38 93 155 156 166
..168 170 187 196 208 222
..229
GREGG, Amos 25
GREGORY, Davd 59 99 110
..152 Saml 59 118 Wm 99
..110
GRIFFE, Davd 65
GRIFFIN(G), Aaron 98 Danl
..11 29 Phebe 23 24 Wm
..194
GRIFFIS, Danl 12 Davd 43
..60 133 136 170 Polly
..43 136
GRIFFITH(S), Danl 65 87
..141 Davd 141 James 44
..Kathr 131 Nathan 33 131
..200
GRIMES, James 221
GRIPE, Joseph 80
GRISSOM, Blewith 220
GRISWOLD, James 181 211
GROSVENOR, Rosswell 243
..244
GROVES, John 55

GRUMMON, Davd 30 144 John
..144
GUNN, John 15 17 26
GUNKLE, John 152 166
GUTHRIE, Robt 144 202
HAGEMAN, Adrian 149 Isaac
..159 Margt 106 Micha 149
..Michl 85 104 106 165 178
..238 Simon 150
HAHN/HAUN/HAWN, Dorcas
..154 Elizb/Betsy 14 23
..128 Jacb 115 239 242
..John 14 23 128 Joseph 14
..23 65 111 Michl 14 23
..40 128 Peggy 239 242
..Polly 14 23 Salome 14
..Saml 14 23 Sara 14
HAINS, Joseph 163
HALDERMAN, John 142
HALL, Abrhm 184 195 Anna
..56 Cornls 39 41 42 56
..181 Henry 200 Hugh 144
..181 John 49 53 56 68 70
..75 78 86 87 89 94 98
..112 128 131 141 142 146
..148 155 181 Joseph 11 34
..Mary 200 Nancy 144
..Richd 170 Wm 38 56 224
..238 246
HALSEY, Ichabod 9
HALSTEAD, John 90
HAMAN, Uol 217
HAMILTON, Alexr 71 82 204
..Andw 86 135 148 James
..13 17 21 26 51 52 246
..251 John 8 25 41 50 52
..174 196 Mary 82 Wm 153
..156
HAMMER, Elihu 188 Elizb
..188 John 170
HAMMES, A. 173
HANCOCK, Joel 87 John 88
..195 Nancy 195
HAND, Enoch 121 148 John
..39
HARDEN, Catrin 27 28 58
..143 John 27 28 38 56
..58 95 143 220
HARDING, Jacb 28 Jas 243
HARLAN(D), Edw 9 80 83
..229 231 Geo 9 41 42 43
..44 48 70 73 74 80 81

INDEX: names in text may have variant spelling

HARLAN(D) Geo (cont) 106
..113   127   138   142   241
..Hannah 87 175 Sarah 83
..Wm 69 87 106 107 116 117
..159   175
HARPER,   James   198   246
..John 62 79   Saml 14 197
..Wm 49   173   184
HARRIS, Joseph 240 Joshua
..217 Mark 57 214 Wm 139
HARRISON, Anna 34 Bazel
..128 181 189 192 Elnr 225
..Frazer   109 225 Martha
..189 192   Wm   14   34   40
..185   190   193   229
HART, Isaac 109 John   98
..Sarah 109
HARTER,   Danl   228   Saml
..228
HARTZEL, Abrhm 98 132 133
..169   201   Eve 132   133
..201   Jacb   213   246   251
HARVEY, Asa 28   40 43 44
..45   49   50 133   Christr
..28 40 43 50 226 Elizb
..4   41   62 139   154 226
..Henderson   44   Isabella
..26 195 213 224 225 234
..James   13   John 4 14 22
..41   53   62   86   Wm   4   23
..26   62 162 163 164   190
..195   197   201   203   211
..213 215 216 221 223 224
..225   229   232   234   235
..240   243
HASLET, Elizb 191 James 19
..192   Joseph   191   192
HATCH, W.S. 55 95 Wm 213
HATFIELD, Geo 169 Owen 171
..Whitefield   171
HATHAWAY, E. 56 95 Ebnzr
..70
HATT, B. 229 Benijah 228
HAWKINS,   Benj   194   198
..James   198   Levi   233
..Olive 194 198
HAWLEY, Isaac 178 185 187
..188   196   206   216   218
HAWN, see Hahn
HAWTHORN, Hugh B.   66   69
..72   73 74 84 90 92 113
..115   165   168   170   178

HAWTHORN, Hugh (cont) 179
.. 190   242
HAYS, Benj 239 James 37 45
..Jane 41   Joseph 121 183
..207   225   238 242 Mary
..225   238   Wm   26   36   37
..41   45   59   64   67   72   91
..127   194   242
HEATH,   Abrhm   245   James
..133   148   183   186   216
..227
HEATON, Ann 203 Davd 155
..163   Danl   85   93   107
..Davd   227 245 Ebnzr   93
..107   133   203   Henry 219
..James   4   5   8   24   29   37
..41   46 47   48   49   52   53
..56   59 62   67 78   81   85
..91 102 107 112 117 119
..120 130 134 135 138 149
..154   159   163   171   174
..175   177   178   181   192
..203   206   210   216   219
..220 229 231 237 240 243
..245   250   John   55   67
..232   Mary 9 24 52 102
..107 120   148 177 178 192
..203 206 229 231 237 243
..245   Stacy   220
HEAVILAN,   Joseph   133
..Lydia 133
HEDDEN, Isrl 19
HEGEMAN,   see   Hageman
..Adrian 15 29   Elizb 29
HEIGHWAY, Saml 41
HELSHAMMER, Frances 160
HEMINGER, see Iseminger
..Geo   67 68   71 Mary 68
..71
HENDERSON,   Isaac   46
..Joseph 130 193 207 221
..Thos   172   190   219   220
..229
HENDRICKS, Davd 8 9 Debrh
..221   Rosannah 8 9
HENRY, Eliza 120 James 56
..69   219   John 15 Joseph
..9   19   136   232   Olivr
..143   147   150   176
HENSLEY,   Ann 235   Gabrl
..56   235
HERBACH, Peter 243

INDEX: names in text may have variant spelling

HERBERT, Celicia 192 217
..Elnr 109 153 159 161
..Wm 7 17 35 54 83 109
..116 153 159 161 177
HERMAN, Danl 97
HERRON, John 184
HERSHMAN, Danl 217
HERVY, see Harvey
HESLEY, Henry 53 109 138
HESS, Danl 189
HICKMAN, John 96
HIDAY, Jacob 12 30 80 91
..115
HIGGINS, Cornls 195 John
..82 Jonthn 139 140 149
..Margt 139 140 149 Thos
..58 82 111 149 170
HILANDS, Andrw 5 Mary 5
HILDERBRAND, Davd 103
..Michl 15 103 201 221
HILE, Philip 202
HILL, Adam 243 Danl 41
..Elndr 243 Jesse 62
..Joshua 243 Nathn 223
..Robt 62 Sarah 51 223
..Thos 36 42 50 51 75 223
..Wm 240 241
HINCLE, Anthony 192
HIND(E)S, Benj 167 223
..Elizb 223 James 121
..223 233
HINDSEY, Cornls 143
HINGERFORD, John 12
HITE, Henry 30 43
HOAG, Elezr 95 131 200
HODGE, John 139
HOFF, Cathr 146 151 166
..Isaac 107 116 146 150
..151 163 166 198 233
HOFFMAN, Abrhm 129 Elizb
..129 161 164 217 Geo 129
..217 Henry 220 Isaac 129
..Jacb 129 161 164 John
..105 129
HOGAN, Hugh 9 Nicholas 155
..193 227
HOHN see HAHN
HOLDEN, John 27
HOLDERMAN, John 190
HOLE, Danl 9 Mary 9
HOLLINGSWORTH, Joseph 198
..Wm 194

HOLLOWAY, Joseph 17
HOLMES, John 132 215
HOLSON, Jesse 222
HOO, Thos 154
HOOD, Elnr 13 14 Hatham?
..13 14 48
HOOP, Thos 113
HOOPMAN, Henry 225
HOOVER, Cathr 142 Davd
..142
HOPE, D. 198
HOPKINS, Frncs 216
HORLAND, John 16
HORMEL, Elnr 94 101 147
..John 93 94 101 147
HORNER, Elijah 167 217
..Nathn 66 Nichls 171
HOUGH, Jane 112 113 116
..138 165 176 186 216 218
..Joseph 44 46 69 76 90 93
..94 98 109 112 113 116
..117 134 138 144 153
..165 176 186 193 202
..205 207 216 218 219
..228 242 247
HOUGHHAM, Aaron 87 88 135
..Elizb 135
HOUGHLAND, John 178
HOUSE/HOUSS, Ann 72 175
..201 227 247 248 Henry
..6 34 72 175 185 189
..201 227 247 248 Jacb 92
..John 185
HOUSTON, Jane 5
HOWARD, Abner 231 232 247
..Geo 96 128 Sally 247
HOWELL, Lewis 43 55 Silas
..26
HOWRY, Saml 120
HOYLE, Mary 40 Philip 40
HUBBARD, Mary 79 R. 183
HUESTON, Cathr. 8 35 66
..130 171 228 John 133
..161 162 M./Matthew 8
..24 35 66 73 78 81 92
..104 114 125 130 134
..136 138 142 171 185 189
..195 202 206 228 229 231
..239 245 249 Thos 245
HUFF, Abrhm 18 166 177
..178 201 232 Isaac 116
..Magdln 166 177 178 201

INDEX: names in text may have variant spelling

HUFFAM, see Hussam,
..Jarvis 57 190 Wm 234
HUFFMAN, Jacb 161 Joseph
..126
HUMES, John 111 Mariah
..111
HUMPHREYS, Isaac 29
HUND, Saml 198
HUNGERFORD, Warren 163
HUNT, - 59 92 Abijah 17 33
..80 90 111 114 124 207
..Abnr 219 Anna 95 Danl 80
..Davd 17 Edw 132 142
..Elezr 25 Elizb 90 124
..Ira 7 25 123 138 178 198
..Isaac 57 222 Jesse 33 90
..108 124 246 Margt 199
..Mary 9 Ralph 5 9 12 19
..34 71 218 Saml 142 149
..167 169 170 194 217
..Sarah 95 Thos 7 25 28
..45 56 62 68 69 73 87 95
..Trec 25 Wm 86 172 178
..199
HUNTER, Andw 143 Hannah 64
..John 235 Joseph 32 54
..64 117 243 Thos 26 35
..68 125 135 157 168 190
..229 240 243 Wm 231 250
HURIN, Enos 37 45 62 137
..Silas 37 56 95
HURST, Elizb 123 John 107
..123
HURT, Edw 133
HUSSAM see Huffam, Jacb
..141
HUSTON, Elizb 28 40 50
..John 6 138 152 233
..Margt 6 Matthw 17 19
..Paul 48 Saml 28 40 50
HUTCHENSON, Jonthn 15
HUTCHIN, Wm 201
HUTSON, John 164 177 178
..Ruth 178
HYNDMAN, Saml 52 145
IMMICK, John 115 117
INGRAM, John 29
INYARD, see Enyart
IRVIN, Robt 163
IRWIN, Alexr 173 Jacb 165
..James 15 33 John 87 96
..Jos. 27 Mary 116 119

IRWIN, Mary (cont) 178
..189 196 Morton 96
..Richd 174 Robt 5 74
..85 116 175 178 183 185
..189 196 Wm 130 142 181
..200 211 221
ISEMINGER, Geo 247 Mary
..247
ISRAEL, Chrstn 225 John
..150 Thos 225
JACQUES, Richd 135 Sally
..135
JACKSON, Mary 176
JAMES, James 31
JAMESON, John 25 151
JANE(S). Saml 9 60
JAY, Jonas 110
JEFFREY, Saml 244
JENKINS, John 139 141
..Wm 210 230 241
JENKINSON, John 64 Joseph
..44 64 73 Sarah 64
..Susana 135 Wm 135
JENNINGS, Elizb 97 116
..126 232 Levi 97 116
..126 232
JINKINS, see Jenkins
JOHN(S) Asenath 234 Ellis
..14 15 41 103 172 201
..221 222 Enoch 192 215
..Ethan 83 Ezkl 192 Isaac
..103 111 221 John 201
..221 Margt 15 41 103 221
..Rhoda 103 Robt 195 234
..Thos 72 83 172
JOHNSON, Abigl 45 Elizb
..164 Ezekl 129 James
..85 99 157 164 183 194
..206 John 45 85 108 149
..152 164 Joseph 64
..Martha 85 Moses 35 Saml
..61 85 140 183 Sarah 206
..Thos 72 85 183 Uzal 45
..Wm 197 209 210
JOHNSTON, - 209 210 Davd
..182 Eli 250 251 Elizb
..182 James 12 131 162
..182 187 Rachel 251
..Sarah 157 162 182 187
..Sterling 96
JOHNSTONE, John 140 Saml
..140

267

INDEX: names in text may have variant spelling

JONES - 37 Abrhm 108 129
..Danl 99 Evan 163 185
..199 James 243 John 50
..Jonthn 77 Justus 23 26
..108 Lydia 78 207
..Maurice 90 140 167 Mary
..170 Michl 34 Nancy 90
..Nichls 78 207 Saml 170
..Sara 26 108 199 Stephn
..195 Wm 140 167 180
..185 191 192 199 204
..207 226 228 244 245
JOYCE, James 91 109 Wm
..227
KARR, Andw 237
KAUTZ, see Krautz Hannah
..115 Jacob 27 115
KEDEY, Moses 16
KEE, Wm 234
KEEN(E), Jacb 192 Jemima
..150 Nancy 25 Peter
..150 199 234 Rachl 196
..Richd 25 Wm 185 188
..196 214 216 234
KELLY, Dennis 156 232
..Elizb 167 Geo 88 167
..Jane 112 John 170
..Joseph 88 217 Kezia 217
..Martha 170 Mary 112
..Moses 16 Olvr 56 112
..126 182 Polly 232 Wm
..16
KELSHEIMER, Frances 160
..Francis 178 248 Margt
..178
KELSEY, Thos 154 160 168
..176 205
KEMP, Cathr 109 234 Elizb
..203 Jacob 57 103 110
..117 John 203 Mary 103
..110 117 Philp 109 110
..234
KEMPBELL, Cathr 209 Geo
..209
KENDELSPERYER, Jacb 211
..Sarah 211
KENNARD, Geo 172
KENNEDY, James 5 179 Jane
..51 Joel 199 John 239
..Joseph 46 47 49 148
..Prsclla 239 Saml 18 19
..22 51 63 139 154 228

KENNEDY, Saml (cont) 229
KENWORTHY, Jesse 222
..Rachl 222 Wm 222
KERCHEVAL, James 190
KERGAN, Elizb 214 Michl
..214
KERN, Henry 251
KERR, Jane 176 John
..114/115 169 176 246
..Rebca 246 Wm 206 249
KERSHNER, Geo 94 96 97
..100 102 Margt 94 96
..97 100 102
KESLING, Geo 92
KEYT, Danl 177 226 Davd
..226
KIBBEY, Ephrm 20 35 220
..Phebe 35
KILLGORE, C. 8 Chas 34,
..64
KING, Aaron 32 Cathr 182
..Frdrk 64 Isaac 156 John
..216 Julyn 227 Margt 132
..Thos 40 156 202 225
KINGERY, John 113
KINMAN, Levi 109 113 114
..143 Mary 113 114
KINNAN, Cathr 9
KINNEY, Abrm 33 Hannah
..33
KINSEY, Cornls 175 Eliza
..175 176 Sarah 175 176
..Wm 175 176
KIRBY, Justus 163
KIRKPATRICK, Alexr 80 184
..Geo 85 151 Jacb 191
..John 167 223 Saml 71
KITCHEL, Ashbel 108 John
..108 Joseph 81 162
..Luther 220 Polly 108
..Moses 25 Rachl 162
KITTY, W. 23
KNEASE, Peter 226
KNIPE, John 167 Sophia
..167
KOX, Wm 229
KRAMER, Geo 247
KRAUTZ, see Kautz Jacb
..242
KUN(S), Geo 80 Jacob 80
..Peter 138
KYLE, Ann 182 230 James

268

INDEX: names in text may have variant spelling

KYLE, James (cont) 158
..182 John 182 Joseph
..182 Margt 182 230
..Saml 158 166 Sarah
..158 166 Thos 158 166
.. Wm 182

LABASHE, Chas 34
LAFERTY, Michl 22 42 45
..46 52 55
LAING, Benj 241 Lewis 144
..169 220
LAMME, Wm 8
LANDIS, Philip 246
LANE, Elkanah 108
..Hendrick 47
LANG, Chas 166
LANGDON, Solmn 212
LANGSTON, Lazarus 93
LANIER, Ellis 175 Helena
..169 J/James 27 108
..127 152 165 169 180
..198 239 242
LAREW, Abrhm 103 131 Benj
..131 215 218 Garret
..240
LARKIN, Edw 25
LARIMORE, John 167
LARISON, Geo 61 Thos 50
LARSH, P 187
LATHAM, Davd 161 250
LAU, John 180
LAURENCE, Benj 226
LAYMAN, Davd 166
LEDYARD, D. 110
LEE, Adam 89 Cathr 89 Davd
..96 Geo 59 65 87 133 141
..James 60 200 214 246
..Levi 140 243 244 Lewis
..100
LEESON, James 73
LEGG, Arthr 65 87 133 141
..Casndr 6 20 195 Owen 97
..Susana 36 210 Wm 4 6
..9 14 20 22 36 65 84
..87 112 123 133 141 177
..195 210
LEGISON, Robt 171
LEIGH, Isaac 113 114
LEMMON, Davd 166 Lemuel
..143
LEMOND, Wm 54 62

LESTER, Thos 59 92
LEWIS, Andw 144 249 Debra
..10 21 111 J. 17 183
..Jacb 4 6 8 9 10 14 15
..16 17 20 21 24 26 29 32
..40 45 60 70 111 115 175
..224 236 242 250 James
..236 Jonthn 151 Martha
..249 Thos 236
LIANAN, John 83
LIBLEY, Solmn 24
LILLY, John 211
LIMPUS, Jonthn 164
LIND(E)LY, Abigl 214 228
..Hiram 214 228 Isaac 114
..214 228
LINE, Benj 4 33 Davd 104
..237 Elihu 104 122 157
..250 Henry 33 Jacb 38
..104 138 171 176
..Joanna 122 173 178 John
..6 33 40 52 104 105
..122 157 158 173 229
..Jonthn 33 104 122 157
..173 178 210 241 Nancy
..157 Rebca 4 33 Ruth 171
..176 Salome 33 104 105
..Sarah 33 52 Solmn 15
..18 33 69 104 105
LINGLE, Jacob 62 67 153
..159 Mary 159 Thos
..237
LINKEY, John 211
LINN, Adam 71 89 99 106
..John 24 71 89 99 106
..219
LINPRY, James 111
LINTNER, Christr 240 Mary
..72 Peter 21 72
LISTON, Edmnd 74 78 90 99
..Elizb 74 78 90 99
LITTELL, Mary 146 Squier
..62 118 146 210 217 218
..224 225
LITTLE, John 226
LITTON, John 81
LIVINGSTON, B. 215 John
..130
LIVISTON, James 217 Nancy
..217
LLOYD, J.W. 16 Joseph 41
..50

269

INDEX: names in text may have variant spelling

LODER, Isabella 177 John
..4 6 62 64 69 177 189
LOGAN, Anthony 171 216 217
..237 Alexr 217 Davd 176
..237 Henry 149 Jane 171
..217 237 Patrk 71 Thos
..22
LONG, Benj 70 86 181 Davd
..159 184 186 188
..Gideon 186 Henry 176 196
..Noah 134 145 147 148 159
..Robt 43 Sarah 145 159
..184 186 188 Thos 226
LONGFELLOW, Elijah 135
..Eluah 22
LONGWORTH, Nichls 63 101
..141
LOPER, Jacb 145
LORIMORE, Joseph 168
LOVE, Peter 162
LOWES, James 12
LOWRING, John 231 Mary
..231
LOWRY, Abrhm 195 203 Cathr
..123 Catrin 41 Fielding
..86 181 James 126 John
..39 123 225 Rachl 195
..Rosanh 126 Widow 171
..Wm 123 126
LOY, Geo 32 51 73 168 Jacb
..32 33 John 83 Nancy
..169
LUCAS, Jemima 60 81 200
..214 John 60 81 200 214
..Susannah 60
LUDLOW, Charltt 8 11 20
..21 23 24 27 28 31 32 35
37 39 40 45 46 48 51 80 121
127 Elizb 39 Isrl 4 5 7 8
10 11 15 16 17 21 23 24 28
31 32 35 38 39 40 45 46 48
51 52 80 141 142 143 145
146 121 127 154 155 160
163 177 205 <u>219</u> Jane 242
John 5 15 20 21 24 28 31 32
35 <u>37</u> 39 40 46 48 51 80 104
125 127 141 142 143 145
146 154 160 163 <u>176</u> 177
205 Mary 37 Max 5 Stephan
15 39 60 242 Susan 5 37
176 Wm 39 81 202
LULLEN, Jacob 69

LUMMIS, Ephr 40 Joseph 19
..136
LUSK, Davd 135
LYON(S), James 14 15 19
..38 63 68 72 73 122
..139 172 176 John 14 145
..Jonthn 100 Mrgt 39
..Nancy 73 Sally 37 39
..Saml 12 35 37 39 Solmn
..15
LYTLE, Andrew 35 Hannah
..182 Margt 182 215
..R./Robt 56 105 119 134
..141 182 215
MACFARLAND, Stephn 139
..200
MACK, Betty 28 40 50
..Richd 28 40 50
MACKLIN, Thos 163
MADILL, James 229
MAGILL, James 30 144
MAGOFFIN, Beriah 16 115
..116 117
MAGOON, Josiah 48
MAHAN. Archbd 48 Elizb 48
..John 251 Patrk 149
MAHARD, Ann 16 54 67 157
..John 16 18 19 22 25 31
..32 35 39 40 43 48 51 54
..57 60 61 63 67 80 85 89
..91 125 132 153 157 177
..184 223 243
MAHONY, John 12 13 17 54
MAKEN, Geo 62
MALLORY, John 156 167
MALOLLY, (see MULLALOY),
..Joseph 28 58
MALOY, Patrk 212
MALSON, Nicholas 75
MAN, John 58 90
MANAGHAN, James 177
MANSFIELD, John 45
MANSON, Elizb 198 John
..198
MAPES, James 29 56 70
..122 139 145 Nelley
..56
MARKLAND, Bryson 98
..Matthew 133 136 147
..186 248
MARKS, John 161 164 Rebca
..161 164 Wm 10 164

INDEX: names in text may have variant spelling

MARSH, Danl 81 John 53 71
..106 Learing 53 Mary 53
..Moses 230 Phebe 230
..Simeon 152 Timothy 53
MARSHALL, Benj 189 Fanny
..28 149 Gilbert 93
..James 28 40 90 108 149
MARTIN, Ann/a 49 56 145
..205 220 225 233 Cathr
..9 Davd 188 222 Danl 80
..Ephrm 9 Giles 203 Hiram
..165 Isaac 86 148 195
..217 James 9 10 56 92
..145 146 157 205 220
..232 233 John 157 Jonah
..165 Jonthn 148 217 227
..Mary 148 149 195 Nathl
..161 Robt 232 Wm 119
..125 148 156 205
MARTS, Abrhm 203
MASHBURN, Matthew 57
MASHWEGAT, C 180
MASK, Danl 212
MASON, John 125
MASTERS, Moses 71
MASTERSON, Chas 18
MASTON, John 202
MATSON, Elizb 79 Enoch 79
..84 Isaac 14 26 27 29 70
..79 84 James 79 Joanna
..14 29 70 79 84 John
..54 79 163 Lavina 79
..Mary 54 79 163 Thos 79
MATHERS, Anne 236 James
..225 235 236 Jean 222
..John 222
MATTHEWS, Thos 77
MATTIER, Thos 232
MATTIX, Elnr 94 203 John
..90 101 102 107 133
..Saml 93 94 203 234
MAUGH, John 191
MAXWELL, James 209 240
..John 17 61 86 102 185
..Robt 12 Thompson 105
MAYER, John 110
MAYS, Danl 151
McADAMS, Thos 30 200
McAULEY, Ezkl 170
McBRIDE, James 49 53 54
..55 60 61 63 68 70 71 77
..80 81 87 100 117 119

McBRIDE, James (cont) 125
..127 139 153 163 174
..177 180 184 190 196
..202 204 219 226 229
..242 247
McCAINE(S), Davd 71 James
..118 John 20 Richd 119
..130 Wm 86
McCALL, Alexr 212 243
..John 41
McCAN, John 117
McCANCE, David 58 77
McCAREN, Barnbs 50 81 82
..Mary 82
McCARNROCK, James 173
McCARTER, John 34
McCASHEN, James 108
McCINISTRY, Cathr/Caty 21
..171 Charity 237 John
..171 214 237 Wm 21 171
McCLAIN/McCLANE, Allen 15
..Isabell 89 John 15 99
..Margt/Peggy 192 240 Wm
..88 89 183 192 240
McCLAMROE, James 81 108
..112 139
McCLARY, Mary 92 Saml 92
McCLEAN, Isabell 89 125
..John 33 150 171 Wm
..89 125 136 225
McCLELLAN(D), Benj 46
..Betsy 126 Danl 46 126
..James 21 46 54 65 73
..87 141 147 151 228
..Mary 30 68 78 153 155
..172 Robt 96 Wm 4 6
..10 13 24 29 30 39 42 43
..45 50 51 52 61 68 77 78
..87 94 100 101 116 123
..125 127 134 142 145 147
..149 153 172 174 189
..209 251
McCLEAREY, Saml 124 222
McCLEAVE, Benj 135 Wm
..135
McCLOSKY, Elizb 209 John
..199 209
McCLURE, Davd 71 216 217
..237 Ezkl 161 184 192
..215 216 222 Herman 240
..James 171 216 217 237
..John 171 216 217 237

INDEX: names in text may have variant spelling

McCLURE, John (cont) 240
..248 Martha 24 171 216
..217 237 Patsy 23 Mary
..192 Robt 14 40 Ruthy
..171 216 237 Saml 161
..219 237 W. 19 24 27 192
..Wm 4 9 33 108 111 216
..217 237
McCLUNG, Joseph 207
McCLUTCHE, John 73
McCONNELL, E. 202 208 219
..Ezekl 114 Saml 37 38
..92
McCORIND, G. 241
McCORMACK, Cathr 9 Da. 71
..Geo 29 John 9 191
McCOWEN, John 33
McCOY, Quinn 115
McCRACKEN, John 23 24 176
..Martha 24
McCRANE, Richd 46
McCRAY/McCREA, Elizb 81
..Phineas 81 133 140
..150 154 189 Margt 193
..Martin 91 Saml 181 221
..Sarah 133 154 189
..Susanh 140 Wm 133 140
..150
McCREARY, Wm 214
McCULLOUGH, Elizb 30 82
..138 147 149 164 180
..Robt 125 Saml 37 119
..240 Thos 12 17 20 30
..38 41 55 66 67 73 82
..87 88 100 139 147 170
..178 180 189
McDANIEL, Danl 176
McDONALD, Danl 203 208
..228 246 James 45 John
..64 66 188 212 Levi 175
..197 229 Margt 157 Nancy
..229 Rebca 66 212
McDOUGALL, Geo. 105 198
..Joseph 198
McDOWELL, Joshua 206
..Matthew 14 25
McEWEN, Hugh 88 115 James
..104 110 Jane 121 John
..5 27 47 117 121 Thos
..151
McFARLAND, Abel 11 Cathr
..45 200

McFEE, S 132
McGARA, John 52
McGARVEY, Andw 87 183
..Nancy 183
McGARY, John 145
McGEE, Benj 152
McGILL, James 66
McGILLIARD, John 144 202
..208
McGILVRY, Alexr 111
McGINNIS, James 162
McGITH, James 212
McGOMERY, Wm 207
McGONIGLE, Cathr 59 199
..John 55 166 Philp 52 53
..55 59 197 199
McGRAW, Thos 38
McGREW, John 12
McGRIFFIN, John 74
McGUFFIN, John 97
McINTIRE, James 28 29 126
..Margt 29 Robt 28 84
..Thos 28 29
McKANE, see McCaine
McKEAN, John 50 71 73 120
..122 222 Wm 25
McKIM, Wm 120 138
McKINISTRY, see McCinistry
McKNIGHT, Joseph 222
McLARN, Thos 168
McLEAN, John 68
McMAHON, Elizb 192 John
..205 Joseph 37 158 166
..192
McMAKEN, Andw 192 Elizb
..158 192 Geo 72 Jane 182
..John 158 Joseph 26 158
..182 192
McMANAMAN, James 212
McMANAMY, James 212
McMANUS, A. 159 Caty 221
..Chas 184 189 J./John
..102 153 180 181 192 206
..221 232 234 235 251
..Rebca 180 239 Saml 234
..Wm 140 180 239 247
McMECHAN, Davd 119
McMILLAN, Constance 20 25
..63 Francis 37 Wm 12
..15 20 25 63
McMURRAY, Joseph 95

INDEX: names in text may have variant spelling

McNABB, John 121 Wm 121
McNAMIE, Michl 16 20 27
McNUTT, James 179
McPIATT, Benj 12
McWHORTER, Alexr 33
MEEKER, Sam. 19 W.P. 19
MEEKS, Dorothea 14 15 22
..25 83 122 172 Edw 5
..14 15 22 25 83 122
..172 184
MEGIE, Benj 152
MEKER, Jonas 228
MELOAN, John 96
MERCER, John 8
MERRILL, Anna 213 Jacob
..213 214 John 73 137 147
..189 Sarah 137
METZGER, Barbara 195 213
..Peter 195 213 214
MICHAEL, Paul 31
MILES, John 90
MILEY, Abrhm 101 103 145
..194 Cathr 194 James 227
..John 194 Susanna 194
MILLER, Dickinson 191 Eve
..166 F. 244 Henry 85
..165 166 Ichabod 15
..Ira 200 Isaac 142 Jacb
..57 79 86 192 193 John
..140 191 246 Phebe 140
..246 Saml 6 235
MILLIKIN, Danl 52 55 72
..80 91 106 130 132 135
..136 149 153 154 171
..176 182 193 200 205
..209 217 242 250 Joan
...242 Robt 136 200 208
..224 228 230 Saml 130
..176 224 228
MILLS, Azur 77 161 173
..191 193 235 236 Chas
..247 Isaac 4 James 57
..66 68 69 70 73 74 76
..77 80 82 83 88 89 91 94
..98 105 134 135 136 147
..151 156 161 166 172 173
..178 180 187 191 196 210
..213 228 233 236 249
..251 John 29 200 219 229
..246 249 Sarah 89 94
..135 172 173 193 200
..210 228 233 251 Wm

MILLS, Wm (cont) 174
MINGS, Wm 25
MINOR, Eli 196 Wm 106
..107
MIRANDA, James 79
MITCHELL, Esther 56 Thos
..229 Wm 5 18 34 38 56
..57 66 79 212 240 244
MONTANYE, Abrhm 156
MONTFORT, Lawrence 86
MONTGOMERY, Hugh 227
MOORE, Alexr 103 Anny 85
..Elenr 31 170 Elias 193
..Elizb 193 Gersham 82 85
..Hugh 42 46 52 55 59
..197 235 James 40 107
..146 239 Levi 18 158
..Lewis 82 83 84 85 Mary
..55 Patrk 5 14 19 27
..34 41 52 63 73 139 147
..154 Robt 53 Solmn 152
..Thos 170
MOORHEAD, John 209 Robt
..209 Thos 209
MORDOCK, Ashbel 152
MOREHOUSE, James 214 Mary
..214
MORES, Jacob 64
MORFIT, Wm 212
MORGAN, Ephr 141 Pallas
..163 Thos 109
MORNINGSTAR, Michl 113
MORREL, Calvin 27
MORRIS, Abigl 142 Elizb 55
..Jacb 94 101 Jas. 244
..John 22 55 142 Robt 142
..Thos 26 Wm 108 189
..218 239
MORRISON, Aschey 197 Benj
..197 James 121 142 180
..Saml 142 143 188 210
..219 247 Sarah 197
MORROW, John 28 121 145
..157
MORSE, Benj 212 Isaac 78
MORTON, Abigl 122 James
..122 145 179 185 196
..206 230 Sally 230
MOSS, Isaac 75 87 131
..141 143 173 216
MOTT, James 101 136
MOUDY, Alec 207 Petr 207

INDEX: names in text may have variant spelling

MUIR, Wm 46
MULFORD, Affe 218 Davd
..86 98 106 114 118
..120 126 127 133 134
..164 180 185 218 244
..245 Euphefinia 182
..Hannah 106 118 126
..127 218 244 Jane 245
..Job 120 152 182 218
..244 245 John 120 182
..185 218 244 245
..Mary 182 185 218
MULLEN, Thos 58
MULLALOY, Elizb 80
..Joseph 58 79 80
MUMMY, Joshua 192
MUNN, Aaron 202
MURDOCK, Asahel 88 Thos
..85 88 249
MURPHY, Elnr 81 88
..Eunice 188 189 James
..137 162 188 189 192
..John 22 69 81 88 123
..188 Petr 4 14 22 81
..86 88 188 Susanna
..188
MURRAY, Debra 119 132
..180 234 Delly 78
..James 43 112 Michl
..137 Pamela 112 Wm 16
..30 41 42 43 68 76 78
..87 96 100 112 119 132
..137 138 149 150 154
..155 158 161 164 170
..174 179 180 201 209
..220 228 233 234
..241
MUSSELMAN, Christn 184
MUTCHENER, Mary 159
..Philp 89 159 161
MYERS, Petr 197

NEIL, Patrk 74
NELSON, Barbara 146 Adam
..127 Danl 36 42 212 Elizb
..219 Esthr 212 John 6
..159 161 219 223 Joseph
..45 Mary 45 Nancy 127 Wm
..127 146
NEWHOUSE, John 186 210
NICHOLS/NICKELS, Abigail
..228 Humphrey 32 41 58 81

NICHOLS/NICKELS, Hmpry
..(cont) 88 89 159 James
..58 John 243 Isabella 58
..89 Matth 77 191 209
..228 Sally 58 Wm 58
..113 123 165 180 198
NIMMO, Matthew 10
NIXON, Allen 8 36 122 212
..Geo 36 212 Margt 122
..212 Mary 36 Moses 36
..Phanny 8 W. 222 Wm 8
..36 122 157
NOBLE, Wm 16
NORRIS, Gersham 215
NUTT, Aaron 85

OEOLL, Urighan 22
OGDEN, (see Agdon) Chas
..69 Jonthn 64 88
OGG, Isaac 80 Polly 80
OGLE, Eliza 163 Elizb 107
..180 Robt 61 70 163
..180 Wm 107 163 180
OLIPHANT, A. 156
OLIVER, Davd 134 184 Wm
..60
O'NEIL, Patrk 74
ORBISON, Jane 211 John 38
..54 Matth 211
ORCUTT, D.C. 8 93 Darius
..15 27 38 40
ORMSBY, Olivr 141
ORNDORF, Jane 109
..Peregrine 93 109
ORR, Arthur 121 123 149
..Keziah 159
OSBORN (see Asborn) Cyrus
..242 Danl 191 Esther
..198 Joseph 198 Lydia
..198 Rebca 191 Wm 59
..92
OSMON, Chas 141
OVERMAN, Jesse 169
OVERPECK, Jacb 167

PACK, John 81 98
PADDOCK, Ebnzr 77 78 151
..152 204 Kezia 77 78
..151 204 Nancy 152
..Sarah 246 Wm 78 204
..246
PAGE, Danl 57 88 167

INDEX: names in text may have variant spelling

PAGE, (cont) John 70
..Nathan 121 123 193
..Rebca 121 193
PAINE, Mary 70 Saml 70
PANTIER, James 86
PANTON, John 7
PARADISE, John 23
PARCE, Phebe 146
PARCEL, James 115 181 242
..Polly 115
PARKER, John 101 Jonthn
..59
PARKI(N)SON, James 67 90
..John 67   M.   40   90
..Mahala 57 61 62 67 140
..251 Maxwell 57 58 61
..62 67 75 140 236 244
..251 Wm 140 236
PARK(S),   Culbertson   91
..Jane 40 Joseph 40 173
PARRISH, Gard 206 Phebe
..230 Zachrh 130 206 230
PARSEL, Cathr 23 John 17
..Nichls 23 62 Richd 239
PARSONS, Danl 68 75 99
..202
PATTERSON, Constant 187
..Flora 209 Francis 155
..John 9 46 77 93 137
..138 156 187 Joseph 73
..100 206 216 Mary 100
..P. 155 R/Robt 5 209
PATTON, David 11 29 101
..111 Elizb 190 Isaac 190
..211 James 29 Jane 37 75
..197 Thos 29 102 Wm 4
..11 30 35 37 62 68 69 72
..75 121 139 154 158 197
..199   201
PATTY, James 238
PAUGH,   Danl   166   Mikel
..136
PAXTON, Isaac 11 16 68
..80   85   89 101 112 161
..177 242 Laney 89 Magdln
..80   101   177   242
PEACOCK,Robt 23
PEAK, Asa 48 Jacb 14
..Joseph 4 6 22 86 100
..137 159 Ruth 86 Sarah
..48
PEARCE/PIERCE, Benj 210

PEARCE/PIERCE   (cont)
..Elisha 210 Eliza 210
..Elizb 210 James 105 210
..Joseph 210 John 156
..210 Michl 77 86 118
..121 156 204 211 227
..233 241 242 Peggy 210
..Phebe 86 118 121 156
..227   241   242
PEARSON, see Pierson
PEAUGH, Joseph 12, 13,
..17
PECK, Danl 147 Davd 147
PERCIVAL, Jabez 114
PERINE, Danl 122 152 201
..Wm 152
PERRY, Danl 78 101 158 164
..J. 225 Rhoda 78 101
..158   Saml 63 Wm 64 67
..70   79 83 127 222 225
PERSAIL(S), Benj 134 135
..157 210 242 Elizb 157
..James 111
PETERS, Philp 215 Richd
..174   Wm 42
PETERSON, Saml 91
PETITT, M. 205 240
PETRO, Paul 40
PHARES, Wm 74 75 76 77 82
..84 95 101   110 113 114
..125 153 158 160 171 174
..175 183 186 187 230
..233
PHELPS, John 7 25 69 95
PHILLIPS, Elizb 5 John 5
..218   Jonathan 5 L. 120
..Mary 218   Ralph 12 19
..23 34 104 120 134 135
..138 Ruth 120 Wm 24
PHRANER, Gasper 202 Ruth
..202 Zebedee 202
PIATT, Abrm 78 Benj 69 249
..Jacb 131   John 60 69
..193   216
PICKENS, Wm 50
PIERSON, Abel 190 Danl 39
..41 55 152 Davd 45 Elnr
..44 53 67 94 119 Elizb
..153 156 Huldah 153 156
..John 11 89 153 156 232
..Jonthn 82 89 92 94 119
..153 179 189 195 208 223

INDEX: names in text may have variant spelling

PIERSON, (cont) Ludlow 39
..44 49 53 67 82 89 94
..98 119 121 Malinda 119
..Matilda 94 153 179 189
..195 223 Pine 120 Sineus
..11 20 21 23 24 28 31
..32 35 39 40 46 48 51 80
..105 127 219 Wm 89 153
..156 232
PIKE, Zebulon 43
PINE, Benj 199
PIPER, Alice 236 James 138
..183 236
PITMAN, Jonathn 211
PLASKET, Robt 170 Saml 170
..Wm 170
PLATT, Saml 198
POARCES, John 127
POAST, Peter 191
POCOCK, Ann 245 Danl 212
..James 212 245 Salem 87
..122 159 161 212
POINDEXTER, John 174
POINER, Petr 245 Silas
...245
POLHEMUS, Arthur 181 203
..221
POLLY, James 61
POOL, W.H. 97
POPEJOY, Mary 152 Nathan
..152
PORT, Elnr 226 James 226
..Saml 226
PORTER, Thos 242
POST, Elnr 226 James 226
..Saml 226
POTTER, Eli 239 247 Elnr
..14 235 Hiram 133
..Ichabod 29 John 246
..Joseph 4 6 13 14 22
..36 58 62 198 227 235
..Levi 121 Russel 86 148
..Saml 4 121 Susanh 246
POTTINGER, Saml 137 139
..152 167 187 Sarah 167
..Thos 104
POTTS, John 157 Stacy 18
POUND, Sarah 109 Thos 109
..113
POWELL, Saml 133 162 186
..217 227
POWERS, Aaron 92 139 145

POWERS (cont)Abigl 194
..Danl 185 194 Davd 9 39
..57 125 Elias 117
..Elizb 125 Jacb 9 24 71
..83 89 99 106 116 125
..144 249 Jonthn 230
..Joseph 19 23 29 39 41
..202 Martha 139 Mary 9
..44 147 148 Nancy 83
..99 106 144 Salome 23 41
..202 Thos 18 44 147 148
..150 163
PRAUGH, Joseph 54
PRICE, Ann 141 Benj 39
..Hannah 202 John 125 Rees
..86 Sarah 86 Selah 84
..Thos 84 Wm 96 141 202
PRINCE, Joseph 7 Sarah 30
..144
PRINE, Danl 166
PRINTARD, A. 207
PRITCHARD, James 79 John
..101 102 107 133 Rhonda
..102 107 133
PROUDFITS, Alexr 242
PRYOR, Jeremh 234 John 230
..249 Mary Ann 234
PUGH, Davd 204
PURSAIL, see Persails

QUICK, Cornls 12 19 20
..Emma 151 163 227 Hannah
..19 20 John 53 227
QUINN, John 79

RAINEY, Anna 224 John 125
..131 144 164 209 222
..Saml 131 144 164 Wm
..216 224
RALSTON, Davd 100
RAMAGE, Jean 117 Thos
..117
RAMSEY, James 155 164 171
..185 187 199 238 John
..28 40 50 Lucy 28 40 50
..Wm 241
RANDLE, Alla 57 136 Benj
..46 49 55 57 120 136
..Margt 146
RANDOLPH, (see FitzRan-
..dolph), Benj 7 15 96
..Drake 14 168 236 Joseph

INDEX: names in text may have variant spelling

RANDOLPH Joseph (cont) 21
..37   42   44   50   96   134
..136   140   157   161   173
..196   216   239   Nimrod
..168   208   209   216   236
..S.F.   23   Saml   7   10   23
..168   236   Sarah   7   168
..Thos 91
RAWLINS, Ann 205 Thos 205
..240
RAY, Philp 230
READING, Samuel 82 131
REDDICK, Thos 231
REDER, Rebca 109 Reubn
..109
REDEY, Wm 229
REED/REID, Chas 182
..Chrstr/Stophl   90   203
..Cloey   182   Davd   125   156
..167   221   James   37   44
..49   55   87   101   142   146
..155   213   223   John   197   225
..232   Nathl   153   Isaac   11
..Rebca 164 244 Ruth 125
..156   221   Wm 164   244
REEDER, Aaron 42 Danl 89
..Geo   49   Jacb   22   47   76
..Jesse   198   Joana   239
..Jonthn   225   L.   121   Nathl
..89   Rebca   229   Reuben   49
..229   Stephen   14
REES, Jacb 139
REEVE, Eber 103 Joab 103
..John   37   103   184   Mary
..103
REILY, John 6 8 9 10 13 14
..17   18   21   25   27   29   30   31
..32   34   35   37   38   40   41   42
..43   45   47   49   50   51   52   55
..57   63   65   68   75   76   77   82
..96   106   118   120   127   136
..141   145   153   155   160   170
..177   188   189   190   205   215
..226   228   238   247   249
..Nancy   77   120   155   171
..185   188
REVES, Isaac 34
REYNOLDS, Alfred 193
RHEA, Henry 63 121
RHODES, Saml 120
RICE, Benj 37
RICHARDS, Jabez 185

RICHARDSON, Aaron 29 73
..92   206   216   Ann   56   105
..119   120   Edmund   12   35
..51   Jane   51   74   110   227
..John   12   35   74   75   81   110
..227   228   232   Mary   227
..Mathw   9   10 56   84   92   93
..95   96   105   119   130   139
..146   161   163   179   195   198
..205   211   215   222   230   233
..237   239   242   Rebca   130
..179   211
RICHEY, see Ritchey
RICHMOND, John 61 107 184
..190   227   Mary   227
RICKART, Delilah 166 Jacb
..92   105   119   166
RICKEY, Adam 63
RIDDELS/RIDDLES, Wm 38 98
..132   187
RISK, Charltt 142 143 145
..146   154   160   177   205
..Danl   122   Davd   199   235
RITCHEL, John 11 Luther
..4
RITCHEY, Adam 233 Ann 244
..Davd   244   John   182
..Martha 202 Robt 189 202
..217   Thos 202
ROBERTS, Ann 142 Thos
..142
ROBERSON, James 248
ROBERTSON, Polly 238 Wm
..238
ROBESON, James 168 215
..233   Jane   168   233   Mary
..215   Wm   84   165   179   193
..207   215
ROBINS, Isaac 46 Jane 161
..164   Jonthn   169   Saml   142
..161   164   186   223   248
ROBINSON, see Robeson,
..James 235 Jane 179 John
..5   121   179   Joshua   247
..Wm   5   62   63   121
ROBY, Chas 218 Cloy 218
..Elias   92   182   218   Geo
..68   73   206   218   Isaac
..152   182   218   Naomi 206
..Polly   218   Pryor   218
..Sarah/Sally   45   218
..Wm   36   45

INDEX: names in text may have variant spelling

RODEBAUGH, Adam 249
ROE, Danl 27
ROISAL, James 209
ROLL, Abrhm 222 Joseph 162
..Matthias   132 134 141
..162   185   187 Mary 162
..185   187
ROLLF, James 241   Sibel
..241
ROLLINS, Seneca 112
ROMIS, John 251
ROOD, Hulda 56 159 Reuben
..56   65   75   159
ROSEBROUGH, Mary 38 157
..222 Robt 14 38 157 222
ROSENCRANS, Jacob 126
ROSS, Eliakim 240   241
..Ignatus 15 James 79 94
..113   207   210   229
..Phineas 188 W. 110 197
ROUND, Andrw 110 Davd 110
..Jacb 110 237 Philp 26
ROUX, John 235
ROW, Henry 245 247 248
..Sarah 245
ROWAN, Jacob 194
ROWLAND,   Jonthn   121
..Joshua 39 44 68
ROYSDON, J. 96 107 180
RUE, Lewis 37
RUFFIN, Wm 6 7 87 184
RUGLASS, Elizb 169 James
..169   176
RUMPLE, Danl 239
RUNYON, Anna 10 Anne 23
..Danl 10   Elias 10 115
..175   236   H. 106 Henry
..167   Isrl   10 236 Jane
..10   175   Jean   239 John
..10 26   108 239 Margt 10
..Mary 236   Petr 10   239
..Richd 10 239 Reune   23
..66
RUSH, Jacb 72 James 108
..Jemima 101   Lenrd 101
..Thos 101
RUSK,   James 249   Sally
..249
RUSSELL, Chas 11 Ester 172
..Geo   136   136 James 40
..171   172   246 John 150
..246   Mary 172 Moses 114

RUSSELL, (cont) Robt 125
..Sylvstr 10 13
RUTEY, John 187
RYCRAFT, Joseph 217
RYERSON, Cornls 243
RYNEARSON, Reynard 54
RYNO, Ephr 101

SACKETT, Aaron 216 Alexr
..124   135   173
SALADAY, Jacob 49
SALER, Joseph 196
SALLE, Danl 147   148 209
SAMPLE, Any 213   John 18
..213
SANDERS, Paul 179
SANKEY, Hanna 143   Thos
..96
SAUNDERS, Paul 82
SAUSBERRY, R. 218
SAYRE, Ann 206   Calvn 35
..Cathr 103   206   216
..Elias   72   Pierson 72
..103   134   206 216 222
SCHANK,   Ann   222   James
..214 222
SCHENCK, Abigl 57   190
..212   Chrenynce   167
..Davd   249   James   249
..John 42   77   90 99 127
..130   138   140   148 167
..169   Mary 99   Obadh 57
..59   62   159   190 212 P.
..42   84   96   104 Petr
..174   Saml 99 135   Wm
..22   47   57   60 64 91
..96   121   180   212   219
..220   239
SCHNIBLY, John 191
SCOTT, Davd 84   James 51
..56   84   133   215 Jane
..84   John 84   166 186
..187   205 216   230 Mary
..84   Moses 207 Richd 84
..Robt 84   Saml 95 126
..158   180 186   199 Thos
..212   Wm 6   86   174
SCUDDER, Aaron 61   Benj
..172   Elizb 197 Enoch
..224   Ephr 162   Stephn
..53   119 151   197
SEAL, Joseph 14

INDEX: names in text may have variant spelling

SEAMAN, Jonas 36
SEDAM, Cornl 12 13 17 33
..41 54 80 111 132 143
..150 189 200 207 Eliza
..12 13 17 41 54
SEELY, Jonathan 12 15
..Saml 88
SELFRIDGE, Thos 238
SELLERS, Isaac 144
SELLMAN, J/I 125
SEMOND, Wm 12 17
SERING, Saml 100
SEWARD, Anny 133 196 Byrum
..133 151 196 210 Caleb
..65 Danl 113 124 168
..173 Isaac 70 124 126
..186 196 James 41 65
..John 226 230 Mary 33
..Phebe 151 Saml 41 70 124
..126 133 136 147 151
..196 208 210 215
SEXTON, Zadock 77 132 144
SHAFER, Betsy 158 Geo 143
..158 John 152 224 231
..234 240 Petr 18 22 127
..Philp 164 Wm 18 237
SHAFF, Frdrk 103 183
..Sarah 183
SHALEE, Michl 159
SHANE, John 122
SHANKE, John 81
SHANNON, Saml 10
SHARP, H. 62 Horatio 56 95
..John 122
SHAW, Albin 12 25 45 49 56
..91 159 163 Eunice 12 45
..159 163 James 244 John
..24 49 56 159 Knoles
..24 39 45 49 50 56 80
..Robt 76 91 Salla 24 56
..Sarah 24 Sophia 39 50
SHEAFOR, see Shafer
SHELBY, Evan 219
SHELLHOUSE, Geo 211 221
SHERARD, James 169 Saml
..132
SHERMAN, S. 10
SHIELDS, Chrstn 238 Danl
..62 Isaac 23 James 57
..58 135 140 179 192
..199 232 238 245 Jane
..179 Patrk 62 218 238

SHINER, John 167
SHIPLEY, Henry 241
SHOAFF, Peter 247
SHOOK, Geo 71 103 Michl 68
..247 Mary 103
SHORT, Chas 112 J.C. 157
..160 185 190 193 229
..Peyton 31 Tilghman 225
SHORTSON, Saml 246
SHRADER, Aaron 196
SHREDER, John 138
SHREVE, Caleb 23
SHROYER, John 224
SHUCK, Geo 102 Mary 102
SHUCKMAN, John 227
SHURT, Garret 241
SIGERSON, Robt 27 143
..201
SILL, Thos 60 65 71 78
..84 85 87
SILVER, Betty 21 223 James
..21 22 79 84 100 104
..141 163 223
SIMCOCK, James 99
SIMMONS, John 162 220
..239 242 Mary 220 Thos
..68 220
SIMONTON, John 214 Wm 147
..161 168 183 191
SIMONS, Solmn 187
SIM(P)SON, Abrhm 116 232
..Alan 49 86 225 Alexr
..91 245 Ann 56 148
..Betsy 84 92 96 198 Ephr
..42 James 9 10 56 Jane
..232 Jesse 9 10 56 163
..Jonthn 232 Lydia 175
..Moses 206 Saml 232
SINCLER, Richd 44
SINKEY, John 211 237
SINNARD, Abrhm 144 John 58
..97 144 Peggy 97 Thos
..144 Wm 58 144
SKINNER, Danl 15 103 169
..Isabel 169
SLAUGHTER, James 28
SLAYBACK, Abel 188 217 <u>218</u>
..Amelia 218 Wm 144
SLECK, Cathr 29
SLIFER, Elizb 93 97 100
..102 Jacb 93 97 100
..102 195 213 Stephn 93

INDEX: names in text may have variant spelling

SLIFER, Stephn (cont) 97
..100   102   112   121   233
..Susanh   94   97   100   102
..213
SLOAN, Davd 8 43 48 59 64
..92   117   168   173 Michl
..16   Rachel 64   117
SLOO?,   Thos 141   142   143
..145
SLOTE, Isaac 239
SLOVER, Abm 117
SMALLEY, John 17 18 22 51
..231   Jonas 144 247 248
..Jonthn 17   Lewis 115
SMILIE, James 100 John 75
..Polly 216   245   Ross 174
..Thos 215   216   221   245
SMITH, A. 65 181 Addison
..234 235 236 Andw 93 211
..220   Benj 106   110   223
..235   Besy 233   Chas 226
..247   250   Christr   132
..Constance 137 Cyrus 247
..Davd 43   106   143   158
..Elijah 36   Elnr   211
..Eliza 96   Elizb 38   59
..60   61   71   84   87   97
..142   147   181   Ephr   70
..Harriet 176   Hezkh   122
..Hugh 247   Isaac 109
..James 6   8   12 15   20 <u>24</u>
..25   30   31   60   63   66   <u>67</u>
..74   78   89   94 98 100 115
..131 135   136 143 149   163
..168   173   190   195 202
..206   209 217 232 236   240
..251   Jeremh   218   John
..12   17   54   59   60   61   65
..71   73   84   87   96   97 125
..146   181   199   213 Joseph
..35   142 Lewis 61 Martha
..48   61   125   243   Olivr
..105   Peter 122   Phebe 89
..Robt 57   73   91   147   S.
..61   Saml   48   50   91 125
..131   163   174   243 Susan
..122   207   Willard 143
..144   154   160   168   176
..200   212   213   Wm 10 35
..38   73   107   154   160   190
..248
SMOCK,   Geo   60   191

SMOCK,   (cont) John 18   22
..Margt 191
SNABLEY   see   Schnibly
..John 243   Margt 243
SNAPP, Cathr 153   159
SNIDER/SNYDER,   Geo   9 27
..30   60   80   121 250 Jacb
..65   90   224 Susanh 30
..121
SNODGRASS, Davd 149
SOUDER, Geo 80
SOUTHARD,   Aaron   94   147
..149   234   Abrhm 11 157
..Ann   234   Geo   11   12
SPADER, Peter 111
SPEER, Thunes 148
SPENCER, A.M. 26 36 Andrsn
..67   74   90   92   108   112
..141   143   144   161 175
..186   187   188   Ann 35 37
..46   64   67   69 Dianna 106
..110   Ezra 45 Joseph 106
..110   O.M.   23   35   111
..Mary/Polly 92   108   141
..144   175   188 Mercy 175
..Oliver   5   22   23   26 35
..36   37 46   64 67   69   79
..95   235   Col. 4
SPINNING,   Elizb   112
..Hannah   183   Ichd   196
..Jonthn   55   57   69   112
..Wm   132   183   192   215
SPROUL, Robt 174
SQUIER,   Ellis   180   224
..John 249   Meeker   173
..Sarah   175   180   185   192
..217 224   Wm   52   118
..136   175   180   183 185
..192   201 217 224   227
STACKHOUSE,   Clinton   110
..138
STACY,Jerusha 120   Warham
..64   67   79   120
STALL,   Barbara   179   250
..Geo 162   172   173   179
..220   238   250   Mariah
..179
STANBERRY, Wm 158
STANLEY, - 55 235 Diantha
..213 Elisha 247   Frdrk
..214   Isaac 6   7   8   13 27
..29   30 <u>31</u> 35   36   38 41 42

280

INDEX: names in text may have variant spelling

STANLEY, Isaac (cont) 43
..44 46 48 49 50 52 53 54
..55 57 61 62 68 69 70
..71 72 73 75 78 80 83 87
..91 93 94 97 101 116 117
..127 131 135 143 149 156
..159 166 170 175 182 186
..187 196 205 207 James
..213 Nakey 55 Salley 43
..Wm 17 27 42 43 80 95
..101 213 238
STARK, Archd 10 14 22 52
..58 134 158 182
..Elnr/Nelly 58 158 182
..Isaac 158
STARKEY, James 143
STAUFFER, Chris. 197
ST.CLAIR, A. 15 Arthur 38
..47 196 Frances 196
..Francis 237 Geo 222
STEEL(E) Agnes 205 Arch 9
..James 40 76 77 79 81
..83 85 112 114 153 164
..216 217 237 Joseph 205
..Robt 63 Sally 23 Thos
..139
STEIN, Edw 136
STEVENS, Obadh 61 Olvr
..75
STEVENSON, Cornls 131
..Phebe 131 Shores 124
..136
STEWART/STUART, -- 39
..Andw 185 188 196 206
..216 Benj 184 Chas 17
..80 139 144 Davd 80
..Isabella 196 James 18
..19 24 169 171 199 204
..206 208 225 229 234 John
..80 Joseph 18 208 229
..Mary 229 Pallas 53 Saml
..9 83 Wm 134 158 164
..185 214
STILES, Elizabeth 77
STITES, Benj 141 196
..Martha 17 39 150 Saml
..4 17 39 150 171
STOCKDALE, Simon 156 219
STOCKTON, Cathr 34 Debrh
..226 John 226 Philip 34
..160
STOKES, Stogdale 226

STONE, Abigl 132 Benj 131
..240 E/Ethn 20 89 116
..124 126 132 153 165
..188 193 196 200 201
..211 219 222 231 232
..247 Thos 168
STONEBREAKER, Boston 143
..Geo 196 John 131 200
..Rebca 200 Sabaston 200
..Susanah 143
STOUT, Abel 6 127 247
..Theodocia 6 127 247
STRATTON, John 60
STREET, Abram 71 Wm 120
STRICKLAND, Danl 108 112
..148 152 177 183
STUBBS, Nathan 49 57 70
..86 88 93 109 161 164
..169 170 217 238
STUMP, Geo 83 Wm 79
SUNDERLAND, John 89 233
..Sarah 89
SURFACE, Andw 92
SUTHERLAND, John 6 7 8
..24 28 30 43 51 53 54 60
..64 68 69 70 74 76 77
..79 81 82 83 84 92 95
..100 101 105 110 112
..113 114 125 126 135 143
..144 148 153 154 157 158
..160 164 166 170 172 174
..176 177 182 185 186 187
..191 193 199 201 204 207
..223 225 228 230 238
..249 Nancy 126 135 144
..148 149 158 160 166
..170 171 176 177 185
..187 191 193 199 201
..205 223 225 228 230 238
..Wm 189 216 233
SUTTON, Danl 11 141 Davd
..36 107 206 224 Elisha
..197 231 Geo 36 199 206
..Hannah 206 James 9 11
..46 174 176 208 209
..217 228 Jermh 36 John
..36 Jonah 186 Joseph 75
..Mary 36 Nancy 176 209
..217 Rosana 36 Rebeckah
..36 Wm 127 247 Zachr
..85 239
SWAN, Caleb 23

281

INDEX: names in text may have variant spelling

SWAT, Benj 245
SWEARINGEN, Barbara 23 25
..49 76 149 Caty 46 98
..109 Chas 37 46 63 68
..71 75 80 88 93 103 104
..142 152 167 181 187
..223 230 Isaac 4 7 22
..23 24 28 29 38 42 43 45
..46 49 50 51 55 56 58 62
..63 65 68 69 71 72 73 75
..76 82 95 99 122 126 131
..149 183 John 76 93 98
..114 154
SWEETS, Benj 244
..Trephenice 213
SWIFT, Rebca 87 204 Thos
..74 86 87 88 90 204
SWINDLES, Elisha 194
SYMMES, Celadon 8 16 20
..23 24 26 30 32 35 43
..46 56 59 63 64 65 66
..67 69 84 92 104 120 134
..136 140 157 173 Danl
..59 63 97 134 173 184 229
..235 246 Elizb 84 Esther
..84 John 4 7 9 26 30
..34 38 39 40 60 62 76
..87 91 98 99 100 112 115
..127 130 140 144 151
..157 160 172 173 184
..190 197 212 219 229
..Peyton 90 97 184 Phebe
..23 24 26 43 64 84 136
..140 Rebca 38 52 59 63
..64 134 175 Susan 4 9 87
..Timt'y 84 Wm 4 14 21
..22 23 26 36 38 45 48
..52 59 63 73 84 134
..136 157 173
TALBOT, - 235 Archbd 61
..205 John 13 Polly 205
..Tobias 13
TALMADGE, Ann 246 James
..246
TANNEHILL, James 156 167
..Wm 218 224
TAPPEN, Saml 39 57
TAPSCOTT, James 51 76 91
..115 127 169
TAYLOR, Caty 164 Charltt
..29 Danl 204 Elizb 79
..84 130 220 Esther 84

TAYLOR Esther (cont)213
..Henry 130 220 230
..John 84 114 183 188 193
..204 213 227 249 Jonah
..169 Jonthn 42 Polly
..213 Robt 68 80 114 135
..164 171 178 189 213
..219 220 228 231 237
..240 Wm 184 189 213
..230
TEAGARDEN, Moses 137
TEITSORT, Abram 146 147
..152 184 187 198 Esther
..198 John 151 Margt 184
..Petr 147 198 Wm 146
..151
TEMPLE, John 214 Michael
..79 200 224
TEMPLETON, James 244
TENNERY, Geo 11
TERRIEL, Abel 71
TERRY, Enos 25 Joh. 99
THOMAS, Abrhm 189 Arthur
..203 Cornls 124 210
..241 Esther 206 240
..Frances 90 James 185
..196 240 Lewis 240
..Margt 74 78 106 Richd
..37 90 111 Sarah 240
..Tabitha 240 Waltr 162
..Wm 74 77 78 99 106
..185 196
THOM(P)SON, Ann 58 Benj
..183 Danl 158 161 Davd
..183 Elizb/Betsy 62 183
..Henry 14 169 170 182
..Isaac 198 James 58 111
..166 John 119 169 239
..Jonthn 143 Joseph 97
..162 209 Mary 169 Nancy
..169 Peggy 183 Smith
..209 Wm 98
THORN, Azarias 16 53 75
..120 121 175 Nancy 121
..Theodocia 53
THORNBERRY, John 202 246
THROCKMORTON, James 62
..185
TIBLELS, John 173
TIEGLER, Peter 181
TILLSON, Luther 78
TILLOTSON, Luther 248

282

INDEX: names in text may have variant spelling

TIMBERMAN, Matth 239
TINDLE Wm 114
TOLBERT, Keziah 159
..Thos 159
TOLER, John 48 Wm 101
TORRENCE, Amma 66 74 77
..177 189 Geo 113 118
..119 153 189 191 John
..5 8 22 27 31 42 43
..50 51 52 54 74 76
..77 98 113 124 134 145
..174 177 189 Mary 118
..119 189
TRABER, Henry 113 134
..John 113 134 231
TRAVIS, Amos 23
TREEN, Joseph 147 151
..170 195
TRIM, John 185 194
TROXELL, Geo 183
TUCKER, John 151 Nancy
..25 R. 13 Walter 25
TULLIS, Davd 202 Elnr
..221 John 221 226
..245 249
TURNER, Isaac 67 79
..Jedidiah 110 111
TUSK, Davd 135
TUTTLE, Jabes 126 John
..220

URMSTON/see Armston, Davd
..36 37 44
VAGNER, Andw 148 Christr
..148 Elizb 148 Mary
..148
VAIL, Aaron 42 103 117
..132 133 136 138 144
..147 152 161 162 164
..222 233 Danl 231
..Elizb 48 Henry 18 42
..242 Hugh 117 136 164
..168 204 221 226 227
..238 Lydia 221 226
..Mariah 117 Mary/Polly
..23 104 110 152 162
..165 167 168 186 217
..227 231 249 Moses 10
..23 42 99 104 110 115
..120 152 165 239
..Randal 42 117 166 167
..Shobal 136 152 163 166

VAIL, Shobal (cont) 167
..168 186 217 221 227
..231 238 249 Stephn 42
..48 124 132 133 134 136
..138 144 147 152 161
..162 164 222 233
VALLENTINE, Amos 10 18 22
..42 45 55 62 63 70 86
..105 106 118 Hannah 45
..Levi 45 Rhoda 22 23
..42 45 55
VAN ARSDALEN, Cornl 28
..Garret 91
VAN ARSDOLE, Wm 30
VAN CAMP, Aaron 105
VANCE, Davd 172 190 John
..23 26 97 122 223
..Margt 173 Mary 92 112
..114 173 Saml 24 92
..105 112 114 173
VANCLEEVE, Jos. 218
VANCLEIF, Benj 130 149
VANDEGRIFFE, Susanh 103
VANDERVEER, Allchey 47 76
..Artr 47 76 Margt 47
..Tunis 47
VANDIKE, Henry 5 7 26 75
..John 134 Polly 7
VANDINE/VANDUYN, Isaac 26
..33 186 208 209 210
..Lydia 186 208 209
..Matthew 23 33 Martin 34
..138 178
VAN EATON, John 220
VANGORDEN, Benj 210
VANHISE, Wm 215
VAN HORNE, Clarissa 123
..Joseph 111 160 209 240
..241 Martha 240 241
VANIE, Saml 39
VANNERT, Garret 26
VANNEST, Garret 132 165
..Geo 151 154 Jane 165
..John 150 154 Lenchy
..154
VANNICE/VAN NUYS, Cornl
..16 28 233 236 237
..Elizb/Betsy 76 80 98
..101 112 123 161 186 187
..233 236 237 John 11
..36 68 76 80 85 89 91
..98 101 103 112 123 130

283

INDEX: names in text may have variant spelling

VANNICE, John (cont) 161
..177 186 187 233 236
..237 Isaac 16 28 89
..233
VANNOSTRAN, Joseph 243
VAN S--, Danl 75
VANSANT, James 136
VAN SCOYOC, John 218 Nancy
..227 Stephen 48 227
VANSICKLE, Abrhm 93 147
..John 117 136 147 148 150
..164
VANTREES, Emanul 58 71
..103 Hartman 12 25
VANTUYL, Michl 191 203
VAN VALKINBURGH, Goikum
..179 184
VAN VLEET, Abrhm 239
VAUGHN, James 201 John 58
..Ruth 58
VESBRYCK, Richd 204
VINNEDGE, John 4 37 41 43
..53 54 82 83 89 117
..121 136 155 157 164
..165 172 178 185 188 195
..239 Polly 177 Rosannah
..164 165 195
VIRGIN, Brice 47 64 123
..126 237 248 Jeremh 237
..Rezin 62 Sarah 123
..Thos 9 112 Wm 6 248
VORHEES, Lamme 36 Peter 5
..7 36 95 Tunis 221
..222
WACHOP, Thompson 34
WADE, D. 168 173 247
..Davd 12 54 80 96 109
..126 134 159 Elisha
..164 207 Nancy 207
..Noah 69 71 72 74 75
..76 77 87 88 91 96 98
..105 113 116 144 145
..Thos 46 60 227
WAGONER, Andw 237 Christr
..138 148 201 Mary 237
WAGNER, Andw 49 Godfrey
..28 45 54 Martin 23
..Sarah 23
WALDEN, Jesse 192
WALDO, Carlton 148 243
WALDRON, Davd 208 Francis
..166

WALKER, Caleb 207 Davd 93
..Ezkl 16 208 Geo 162
..James 23 31 207 208
..John 62 85 Joseph 62
..190 212 Sarah 23 Thos
..55 Wm 83
WALLACE, D. 223 Debrh 203
..Henry 89 177 John 5
..Mathw 39 40 45 84 124
..180 203 207 208 230
..251 Nath. 48 Robt 116
..130 142 203 221 Wm
..22 52 83 91 125 168
..173 178 251
WALLEN, Ashbel 137 Elias
..14 Nathan 151
WALLER, Ashbel 20 36 82
..Levi 71 80 162 Solmn
..80
WALLS, Richd 156
WALTER, Isaac 112
WALTZ, Isaac 133
WARD, Benj 62 64 James 168
..John 26 92 Jonthn 243
..244 Mary/Polly 244
..Thos 238
WARDELL, Solmn 96
WARE/WEAR, Alexr 121 127
WARNER, Jabez 28 40 50
..Sarah 28 40 50
WARNOCK, Margt 125
WARWICK, Robt 48 140 145
..Sarah 145
WASSON, Henry 91 100
..Joseph 244 Sarah 91
WATKINS, Jonthn 250
WATSON, Abrm 30 Agnes 183
..Henry 234 Isaac 105
..Isabella 251 John 8
..144 183 249 251
..Joseph 230 Saml 126
WATTS, Alice 151 155 163
..188 193 204 Anna 244
..Cathr 16 26 Henry 16
..26 27 92 93 Irene 227
..Isrl 151 152 156 163
..164 236 James 227 245
..John 227 Joseph 227
..Mary 152 236 Richd 151
..155 157 163 187 188
..193 204 227
WAUGH, Alexr 180

INDEX: names in text may have variant spelling

WAYT, Andrew 58
WEAVER, Ann 145 186 188
..Henry 10 12 15 18 30
..32 33 42 49 50 51 53
..58 65 66 70 71 73 75
..76 78 83 87 90 91 116
..121 123 137 145 <u>147</u> 149
..<u>150</u> <u>163</u> 175 180 <u>184</u> 185
..186 188 189 195 203 204
..221 <u>233</u> 241 242 244
..248 251 Lenrd 49 65
..121 123 149 175 185
..189 185 203 209 237
..Richd 36 Susan 51 137
..147 150 163
WEBB, Joseph 93 149
..Josiah 177
WEBSTER, Wm 55 57 108
..150
WEIDNER, Jacb 109 152 207
..222 243
WEIKEL, John 224 225
WEIR, Alexr 60
WELCH, John 18 60 231
WELLS Francis 16 Wm 59
..92 165 219
WELSH, John 144
WEST, Chas 7 25 56 62
..95 Elezr 68 73 86 87
..Francis 247 Henry 68
..Molly 95 Polly 79 Thos
..64 67 79
WHALEN, James 202 Thos
..103 111 202
WHIPPLE, Elizb 133
WHISTLER, W. 87
WHITE, Abrhm 159 181
..Amos 159 181 Chas 117
..Edw 38 J. 30 120 127
..145 146 Jacb 209
..James 57 69 82 Mary 181
..Sylvstr 220 Thos 186
..Wm 70 107 120 181
WHITEHEAD, Jemima 202 S
..225
WHITEHILL, Robt 33
WHITEMAN, Lewis 189
WHITINER, Debore 207
WHITINGER, Elizb 106
..Francis 39 45 58 244
..Henry 58 Jacb 106 110
..167 Nicholas 118 167

WHITINGER, (cont) Sarah
..167
WHITMORE, Miles 24
WHITSON, Willis 90 105
WHITTLESEY, Duran 25 56
..69 95 100 111 123
..Ruth 95 123
WHITWORTH, John 87 92
..112 114 117 120 136
..140 145 147 152 155
..157 163 181 205 231
WICKART, Barthlmw 180
WIGGINS, Comfort 243
..Philip 243 244
WILCOCKS, - 106 Peter 39
..45 55 68 99 120
WILCOX, Celicia 217
WILES, Elizb 36 55 86
..105 132 194 240 241
..Isaac <u>6</u> <u>7</u> <u>13</u> 16 26 <u>31</u> <u>36</u>
..<u>37</u> 42 <u>46</u> <u>50</u> 52 <u>55</u> <u>70</u> <u>86</u>
..<u>87</u> <u>91</u> 102 105 110 132
..137 145 174 194 207
..210 240 241
WILHELM, John 17
WILHOLMS, John 108
WILKINS, James 96 172
..174 Lydia 96 Michl
..217
WILKINSON, Elijah 201 202
..Elizb 201 202 James 31
..John 202 232 235 Mary
..235 Saml 201
WILLEY, Isrl 33 50 Judah
..12 25 30 33 39 40 45
..48 50 56 68 80 159
..160 163 Noah 49 185
WILLIAMS, Alexr 53 Caleb
..89 233 Davd 78 Enos
..35 65 70 86 93 94
..100 101 147 161 196 207
..Hatfield 145 Joel 5 34
..57 60 66 80 91 109
..111 115 125 130 156 160
..165 184 209 John 135
..240 Joseph 86 M. 61
..Marsh 48 70 71 78 101
..127 135 155 158 159
..164 170 173 181 214
..Nancy 71 Phebe 5 57 60
..111 115 125 130 156
..160 165 209 Wm 34

INDEX: names in text may have variant spelling

WILLIAMSON, Davd 5 36 84
..123 124 131 149 243
..Geo 42 55 124 245
..Hannah 106 119 Hezkh
..131 Joseph 148 167
..Mary 148 149 167
..P./Peter 22 42 55 62 83
..84 89 95 99 106 118
..119 122 124 131 134
..145 150 158 166 179
..197 202 245 Wm 158
WILLIS, Hannah 11 39
..Wm 201
WILLIVER, Hannah 244
..Joseph 244 Obedh 150
..208 244
WILSON, Alexr 16 70 73
..74 93 108 112 148 149
..Andw 131 Ann 61 Arthur
..140 Brown 61 167 Danl
..84 246 Ebnzr 70 121
..Elizb 121 246 Hugh 73
..143 193 James 105 108
..113 122 150 153 174
..175 186 188 193 207
..216 Jane 174 186 John
..70 73 148 149 156 191
..230 231 Joseph 207 216
..Josiah 70 86 Margt/
..Peggy 136 Mary 70 86
..249 Nancy 230 231
..Peter 14 40 Ruth 191
..Sally/Sarah 131 143
..Wm 12 63 81 120 122
..124 136 191 237 249
WINANS, Eliza 196 207 John
..68 80 85 123 196 207
WINGATE, Amma 71 74 76 77
..91 98 113 124 137 139
..145 174 177 193 John 9
..13 16 18 19 31 38 48
..68 69 71 72 73 74 76 77
..80 91 96 97 98 100
..113 116 117 124 137 139
..142 144 145 166 174 177
..189 193 206 Mary 38
WINTON, Elizb 63 88 93
..97 98 105 125 165 181
..John 63 105 195 207
..Matth. 10 52 63 88 93 97
..98 105 125 137 165 181
..196 Robt 105 165 181

WITHROW, Anna 107 James 27
..74 93 97 98 103 104
..134 186 190 Jane 108
..John 107 161 Sarah 74
..93 98 103 104
WITSON, Jas. 169
WOLDEN, Benj 241 James
...241
WOLF, Ann 194 Fredrk 152
..Michl 194
WOLLARS, Wm 189
WOOD, Cathr 234 Elihu 47
..48 Isaac 70 119 Jane
..119 Kitty 66 Stephen
..14 64 66 100 104 173
..234 Wm 29 200
WOODMANSEE, Danl 67 166
..Saml 172
WOODMAYER, Danl 168
WOODRUFF, - 64 Danl 54 62
..65 87 96 133 157 212
..Edw 65 Elihu 46 47 48
..49 55 119 130 148
..178 194 Ephrm 231
..Isaac 186 Isrl 94 96
..121 Joel 61 64 65 123
..Margt 48 55 148 178
..Nathan 43 Nathl 48 Phebe
..48 84 Polly 65 Timty
..22 30 48 62 63 68 73
..75 84 107 139 186
WOODWARD, Reuben 50 122
..Wm 50 73 122
WOOLEY, Abner 232
WOOLVERTON, Davd 148 176
..203 217 235 248
..Thos 37
WORTH, Joseph 43 44 120
..239
WYNN, Thos 8
WRAILKEL, Moses 63
WRIGHT, Jemima 214 John
..220 Sarah 227 Wm
..204 227

YEAGER, Nicholas 134
YEATMAN, Griffin 42 90 95
..125 126 131 132 140
..141 143 145 151 154
..155 160 172 190 216
YEATS, Joseph 210
YEAZLE, Abrm 85

INDEX: names in text may have variant spelling

YOUNG(S), Abijh 137 Alexr
..61 70 114 205 Andw
..114 205 Benj 137
..Elizb 137 James 84 92
..205 222 237 Jane 84
..John 53 61 70 114 222
..Philp 137 Robt 61 70
..222 Saml 163 Serah
..114

ZEIGLER, Ann 236 Peter 235
..236
ZIMMERMAN, John 198

www.ingramcontent.com/pod-product-compliance
Lightning Source LLC
Chambersburg PA
CBHW071422150426
43191CB00008B/1012